BEYOND SHAREHOLDER PRIMACY

BEYOND SHAREHOLDER PRIMACY

Remaking Capitalism for a Sustainable Future

STUART L. HART

With a foreword by
Brian Griffith

STANFORD BUSINESS BOOKS
AN IMPRINT OF STANFORD UNIVERSITY PRESS · STANFORD, CALIFORNIA

Stanford University Press
Stanford, California

Special discounts for bulk quantities of Stanford Business Books are available to corporations, professional associations, and other organizations. For details and discount information, contact the special sales department of Stanford University Press by emailing sales@ www.sup.org.

Printed in the United States of America on acid-free, archival-quality paper

Library of Congress Cataloging-in-Publication Data available on request.

Library of Congress Control Number: 2023952332
ISBN 9781503636217 (cloth)
ISBN 9781503638747 (ebook)

Cover design: Will Brown
Cover photograph: Sua Truong/Unsplash

CONTENTS

PART III

Institutional Redesign:
Business's Indispensable Role in System Change

ACKNOWLEDGMENTS

This book builds on my prior volume, *Capitalism at the Crossroads*, so I once again owe a continuing debt of gratitude to everyone I thanked in the acknowledgments for that book, first published in 2005. Over the past decade plus, however, as my experience and thinking have evolved, I have developed a whole new set of colleagues and companies that I'd like to recognize, along with a few old friends who continue to be amazing sources of counsel, feedback, and insight.

Let me start with the inspiration for the book. As I delved deeply into the history of capitalism—the work that forms the intellectual foundation for this manuscript—one book was particularly influential—Jed Emerson's *The Purpose of Capital*. Jed's book not only provided the metaphor of "capitalist reformation" used in this book (see the bottom of his page 57) but also ignited my personal motivation for writing the book. As I note in the Prologue, the horrors of the coronavirus pandemic created an inadvertent window of opportunity—two years of mostly working from home—for me to truly immerse myself in reading and writing. At first, I felt that my continuing work activities—both at the university and with client companies I was advising—were a bit of a distraction from this intellectual journey. Jed helped me realize, however, how important it is to blend both; he drew the important distinction between taking a "sabbatical" to read and engaging in what he called a "reading life":

> In the sabbatical, one's time is spent away from work and usually focused upon a given end or product—to study a particular period of time, to produce a book or article—whereas in the reading life, one looks to integrate reflection, the groomed and tailored thoughts of others and the wisdom of the ages, into and within your life.[1]

What Jed called his "year of thinking dangerously," when he combined reading with continuing client advisory work as he wrote his own book, became the model for my approach in writing this book: the new thoughts and perspectives I uncovered through reading deeply in domains outside my traditional area of expertise were commingled with my ongoing, work-related experiences with companies, university colleagues, and students. The result, I hope, is a creative synthesis, a version of what Don Schön once described as "reflection in action."[2]

I thus owe a huge debt of gratitude not only to Jed, but also to the representatives of companies and organizations that figure prominently in this book. These include Brian Griffith, executive chairman of Griffith Foods, along with CEO TC Chatterjee, Chief Strategy Officer Jim Thorne, and CFO Matt West; Steve Fisher, CEO of Novelis, along with former CSOs John Gardner and Jessica Sanderson; Steve Goldstein, chief communications officer at the Long-Term Stock Exchange, along with former ESG Analyst Evan Sanfield; Sanjay Sharma, dean of the Grossman School of Business at the University of Vermont, and all my colleagues at the Sustainable Innovation MBA Program. I owe an additional special thanks to Brian Griffith for penning the foreword to this book. His message, along with my experience in working with him these past several years to embed sustainability into every fiber of his company, has contributed immeasurably to the pages of this work.

Several people deserve a special shout-out. My long-time colleague, Professor Jac Geurts, who traveled all the way from the Netherlands to teach in our SI-MBA program, was especially impactful. His thoughtful and constructive comments helped me completely rethink and reshape several of the chapters in the book, particularly Chapters 1–4. Ken Mirvis, who works with our SI-MBA students to sharpen their messaging and communications, has also been extremely helpful on my behalf. He has literally read every word of this manuscript more than once, providing not only constructive editorial feedback but also thoughtful conceptual comments and suggestions. Joe Fusco, an executive at Casella who has been closely involved with our SI-MBA program, also provided invaluable feedback on the entire book manuscript. He was particularly helpful in restraining my tendency to become overly antagonistic, given my strong views. Fred Keller, founder of B-Corp Cascade Engineering, has also provided invaluable comments, particularly about Chapters 4 and 7.

Professor Chuck Schnitzlein, who is the faculty director of SI-MBA at the University of Vermont and teaches all the finance in the program, was especially generous with his time in giving me thoughtful feedback on Chapter 8, "Redefining the Meaning of Value." His combination of academic finance knowledge combined with his practical experience in asset management proved invaluable. Tom Haslett, Cofounder and partner at Tilt Investment Management also provided important feedback on Chapter 8. Professor Dita Sharma also provided extremely useful feedback on Chapters 1 and 2 and was instrumental in helping me see the importance of summary slides given the dense nature of those chapters. Thanks also to SI-MBA graduate Dana Gulley for providing challenging suggestions from the perspective of someone dedicated to being a changemaker in a world characterized more by jobseekers.

Paul Polman and Andrew Winston not only helped shape my thinking about the importance of system change for sustainability through their outstanding book *Net Positive*, but also provided important feedback, especially on Chapter 7, "Reinventing Business Education." University of Michigan professor Andy Hoffman also helped me deepen and improve my argument, especially with regard to the first part of the book focused on history. Andy invited me to teach a session in his new course titled "Reexamining the Form and Function of Modern Capitalism," where I was able to use Chapters 1 and 2 as the reading, helping me sharpen both the message and the delivery. My long-time colleague Professor Ted London, also at Michigan, provided extremely useful comments and constructive suggestions about the entire manuscript, but was especially insightful when it came to the connections across the chapters. Vipul Arora, whom I first met as a recent college graduate in the late 1990s and has gone on to become a remarkable sustainable entrepreneur, also provided thoughtful feedback on virtually the entire manuscript.

I'd also like to recognize and thank my Enterprise for a Sustainable World colleagues Kate Napolitan and Priya Dasgupta. They were instrumental in working with me on the Transformation Sustainability Benchmarking work referred to in the book. The concepts of both Aspirations and Quests (Chapter 5) and the New Corporate Architecture (Chapter 6) resulted from the benchmarking work and are central to the message for each of these chapters. Kate also provided helpful comments and suggestions for both of these chapters.

Of course, I'd be remiss if I did not recognize the crucial contribution made by my editors—Steve Catalano and Richard Narramore at Stanford Business Books, and Kate Wahl, Editor-in-Chief at Stanford University Press. From the very first conversation with Steve about the book, he, and later Richard and Kate, provided nothing but positive support and encouragement. The book also benefitted tremendously from the thoughtful feedback of three anonymous reviewers for the press who devoted significant time and attention to the task.

Closer to home, I'd like to thank my brother Paul and old college friend

Jonathan Richman for taking the time to read the manuscript and offer their thoughts, comments, and feedback. I'd also like to thank my son-in-law (and Michigan MBA) Bill Crane, who read the entire manuscript, starting with the earliest drafts in 2020. His interest, positive feedback, and helpful comments helped motivate me to persevere during the darkest depths of Covid during the spring and summer of 2020. He was also of great assistance when it came to effectively positioning the Denouement and the Sustainable Capitalism Framework. I also have fond memories of sitting outside that year in the depths of winter with Bill, my older daughter, Jaren, and older granddaughter, Mallison, often with pages of the manuscript flying around in the cold wind. Occasionally, younger daughter Jane and other son-in-law Onir would also join in the festivities from New York via Zoom.

Finally, I'd like to thank my wife, Patricia, who not only read and edited the entire manuscript, but more important, created the environment that enabled me to disappear upstairs to my third-floor office for extended periods over the better part of three years to write this book. Such a contribution could only be made out of love, and for that, I am truly blessed.

Stuart L. Hart
Ann Arbor, Michigan
August 2023

FOREWORD

This remarkable book is many things.

It is a survey, well-researched and thoughtfully reasoned, of the history and possible future of capitalism and human civilization more broadly.

It is also a call to consciousness for individuals, organizations, communities, and nations, asking us to think through how the ways we live and do business impact our neighbors near and far and the planet we all share.

And it is an invitation to participate in the next reformation of commerce, rethinking and reshaping the business and public policy landscape to change the course of human events, rebalance the destructive anomaly of shareholder primacy, and achieve truly sustainable capitalism.

Even more fundamentally, this is a book about hope. Hope for change. Hope for humanity. Hope for the planet. Hope for the future.

Today, with all the vast and grave struggles of our time, all the cynicism, doubt, and fear that threatens to drive us to despair and paralysis, we all need more hope.

And not mere wishful thinking but real and true hope, based on historical precedent, informed by current realities and grounded in a clear-sighted vision of the challenges we face and the solutions available to us, now and in the years to come.

To be sure, hope is not a strategy. But hope is often a prerequisite for action to create and drive change. And there is hope here and much more. There is also a roadmap of priorities—along with strategies, tactics, and examples—to serve as a guide and playbook to the emerging capitalist reformation.

With all the suffering, injustice, and systemic challenges in the world today, it isn't very difficult to look at the state of modern life and begin to become pessimistic, even despondent. Indeed, the difficulties we face are serious and, in some cases, seemingly intractable.

Climate change, biodiversity loss, inequality, political extremism, war, gun violence, unlawful and unjust incarceration, nativism, racism, sexism, antisemitism, and other forms of discrimination—there's a lot to be troubled about. And the dominant economic force in the world—shareholder capitalism—grinds on, contributing to global dysfunction with an endless push for greater efficiency and higher short-term profits and leaving in its wake an ever-widening swath of destruction.

Look a little deeper and a little wider at the history of the past half-century, however, and there are reasons for optimism. People and our institutions have made a difference. Positive changes have happened. Progress has been made.

On a global basis, extreme poverty is down sharply, along with famines and widespread malnutrition. Many diseases have been cured—or become far more treatable. Life expectancy is up, infant mortality down. Democracy has expanded while totalitarianism has declined. Education and job opportunities for women and some long-marginalized populations have increased. Affordable access to information and communication has expanded exponentially.

Of course, there is much more to do. In fact, that's why we're all here, reading this book. But these and other positive historical developments give me hope. Humanity can move forward. We can begin to fix the messes we've made—and those we've inherited. And we can change the world for the better.

Most of us recognize the depth of change required to address the issues we face. As Einstein said, "We cannot solve our problems with the same level of thinking that created them."

Given this, business—collectively—should be committed to driving transformation that transcends sustainable, "do no harm" thinking and embraces a regenerative mindset. We can enable our social and environmental systems to heal and thrive, in part by advancing the circular economic innovations increasingly needed by the world and valued by the market.

In fact, as an unapologetic conscious capitalist, I believe nothing accelerates and scales valued solutions faster than capitalism. Business has a unique opportunity to define problems differently and address unmet needs proactively through innovative and profitable goods and services.

All of which is why I find this book so incredibly exciting. This story of hope on the march—carefully crafted, nuanced and compelling—draws our eyes inescapably to the horizon and to all that's possible and to a meaningful, history-making movement we can all be part of.

On a personal note, I'm also thrilled that this volume will bring the work, wit, and wisdom of author Stu Hart to a much larger audience, a great and growing community of individuals, companies, nonprofits, NGOs, and other organizations. And not only now, at the time of publication, but for years to come.

Over the past several years, our company, Griffith Foods, has been on a journey to remake our enterprise as a sustainable and eventually regenerative business dedicated to serving our stakeholders, communities, and neighbors as we pursue our corporate purpose: "We blend care and creativity to nourish the world."

You'll hear more about this journey in Chapter 5, but I want you to know that my friend and fellow changemaker Stu Hart has been an invaluable partner in helping us evolve and transform Griffith Foods into a company organized around the defining notion that business can and must be a force for good in the world, helping lead the way to a sustainable, regenerative future.

Of course, we're only one company, with a century of history as a new product and recipe development partner. We connect farmers with food companies, including some of the world's largest. And we're making a difference, enabling more nutritious, planet-friendly diets through sustainably and equitably sourced ingredients. Yet there's only so much that one company—or even one industry—can do.

Today, we're inspired by all those around the world on a similar journey, walking alongside us and striving to serve and create value for our people, partners, customers, communities, shareholders, ecosystems, other living organisms, and humanity at large.

Tomorrow, with the help of this book and others like it, we expect to have many more alongside us, joining a great and growing movement on a joyful journey to transcend shareholder primacy and remake capitalism for a sustainable future.

I look forward to seeing you on the rising road ahead!

Brian Griffith
Executive Chairman, Griffith Foods

The Sustainable Business Movement Is Broken

Over the past three decades, I've worked with scores of companies as a "sustainability" consultant and advisor, and there has been real progress—my clients, and corporations in general, have evolved from an early focus on pollution prevention and eco-efficiency to broader goals for product and business sustainability. Unfortunately, one refrain from executives and business leaders has remained tragically consistent: "If sustainability initiatives prevent me from 'making the numbers,' then they will probably not happen." Indeed, since the onset of the shareholder primacy era in the 1980s, business leaders have consistently bemoaned the fact that they have become slaves to quarterly earnings and short-term performance.

Business leaders and boards requiring proof of the "business case" for sustainability has been a subtle way of saying that any initiatives focused on broader stakeholders' needs must not impede hitting the earnings growth targets needed to maximize shareholder value in the short term. Consequently, companies—particularly public corporations—are systematically disabled from realizing the transformational changes needed, so long as shareholder primacy dominates our collective business and investing culture. The good news is most business leaders I know recognize that we have reached the point of no return when it comes to this logic. They realize increasingly that until we free ourselves from the tyranny of shareholder primacy—by transforming the institutions and systems that define the priorities and rules of the game for capitalism—the state of the world will continue its precipitous march to oblivion.

Defining these new priorities—the new prime directive or *objective function*—and setting the new rules of the game—the "operating system" for a truly sustainable form of capitalism—are the primary objectives for this book. It is informed by the recognition that capitalism has run out of control before—at least twice in the last four centuries—and been pulled back from the brink. It is heartening to understand that the past four decades of what I call "shareholder capitalism" are not the norm at all: capitalism has been run with very different operating systems and objective functions before. Shareholder primacy is not preordained. We can learn from these two previous capitalist "reformations" when it comes to the corporate transformations and institutional redesigns needed to remake capitalism once again, in a way that reverses the extractive and inequitable nature of our current reality.

The Radicalization of a Business School Professor

Since the early 1990s, I've taught scores of courses on sustainable business and thousands of MBA students, some of whom have gone on to leadership roles in major corporations, ventures, investment firms, and NGOs. I've purposefully combined peer-reviewed research with a practitioner's bent, publishing highly cited articles in both leading academic *and* business journals.[1] I've also written books on the topic, perhaps the best-known being *Capitalism at the Crossroads*.[2] I've built my own nonprofit consulting firm, Enterprise for a Sustainable World, and cofounded the Base of the Pyramid Global Network, dedicated to harnessing the power of business to serve the poor and underserved.[3]

I've also been an "academic entrepreneur," having founded or cofounded several new academic programs focused on sustainable business at four different universities.[4] Yet, as I take stock of all this work, I can only conclude that it has been almost entirely inadequate: my research and writing, which constituted some of the earliest work seeking to reconcile sustainability, strategy, and financial performance, has done little more than help rearrange the proverbial deck chairs on the *Titanic*, providing cover for accelerating climate change, species loss, and rising economic inequality.

The business-school-based programs and centers I have started, while important, have influenced only a small proportion of the enrolled students each year, with most business school graduates still believing in the gospel of shareholder primacy and market fundamentalism.[5] As my colleague Sanjay Sharma and I have observed, most business school sustainability initiatives, like those of their corporate counterparts, can best be described as "saddlebags" in that they hang off the side of the existing organizational edifice and do not actually change the core—the "horse"—in any meaningful way.[6]

The prevailing "win-win" strategies—eco-efficiency, sustainable sourcing, circularity, green growth, sustainable innovation, and even business initiatives to serve the poor at the "base of the pyramid"—have done little more than build incremental awareness, slow the rate of damage, and spawn some new ventures and business models. The recent surge of "clean tech" and "impact investing" are indeed some of the more hopeful developments in recent years. Yet even the current boom in sustainable investing and "ESG" reporting have not changed the fundamental calculus for business in our current age of capitalism— shareholder primacy and market fundamentalism continue to reign supreme. Without more fundamental change to the institutions that define, support, and enable capitalism, the actions of individual companies and entrepreneurs will continue to fall short.

From Sustainable Business to Sustainable Capitalism

If earnings, share price, and financial markets incorporated the full costs of business and economic activity—including their unintended environmental and societal side effects—then shareholder-driven capitalism might indeed steer us toward a sustainable world. However, the positive effects of win-win "greening" strategies—the focus of most work in sustainable business over the past thirty years—have been swamped by the massive and unsustainable economic growth driven by what investment analyst Duncan Austin calls "externality-denying capitalism."[7]

The World Bank, for example, reports that less than *4 percent* of global carbon emissions are currently priced at levels consistent with the Paris Agreement's temperature goals, providing clear evidence that few of today's market transactions are fully costed.[8] More broadly, the Force for Good Initiative concludes that at the midpoint of implementing the Sustainable Development Goals (2022), the world has little hope of achieving them by 2030, with a whopping *$102–135 trillion* gap in the investment required.[9] As long as the measurement of growth and financial success is externality-denying, notes Austin, "then the growth that is meant to solve problems may simply create more of those problems along the way . . . [it constitutes] not the solution but the *driver* of social and environmental harms."[10]

If I am honest with myself, most of the work I have done over the past thirty-plus years has resulted less in systemic transformation than in incremental improvement or, at best, a few new sustainable business experiments. For most existing companies, there remains a fundamental disconnect between sustainability and core strategy, let alone corporate purpose.[11] Sustainability continues to be framed as a set of initiatives separate from the core business, requiring a "business case" before they can be pursued. The can has been kicked down the road such that we have now arrived at the point of no return—we must either transform rapidly or face unthinkable environmental and social consequences in the decades ahead. You will see this disconnect—and the need for a fundamental change in course—addressed directly both in Part II of this book, "Corporate Transformation," and Part III, "Institutional Redesign."

I also found myself driven to understand more deeply how and why we had come to this point of world crisis driven in large measure by shareholder primacy. I was curious to see if "capitalism" had ever faced similar circumstances before and was reassured when I uncovered many lessons from history useful in dealing with our present predicament. As noted above, capitalism had indeed run amok before—at least twice. Yet today's challenges are also unprecedented in many ways: never before, for example, had capitalism threatened the basic life support system of the planet. Part I of this book, "The Past Is Prologue," explores the relevant historical lessons and "rhymes" from the past as well as the unique challenges we face looking forward.

Reading widely and deeply these past few years about business and economic history has enabled me to blend lessons from history with my ongoing work with companies seeking to embed sustainability into core strategy and purpose, as well as with initiatives to redesign key systems and institutions to transform the operating system for capitalism itself. This book is the product of that intellectual journey; it combines the theoretical with practical frameworks and tools, and the historical with leading-edge, "next practice" examples. It focuses on the role that business and business leaders can (and must) play in driving this transformation—the third capitalist reformation—but should also be of interest to those in civil society, government, and education with a commitment to creating a truly sustainable economy and world. I hope you find the book informative and thought-provoking. But most important, I hope you find it useful for moving beyond a continuous improvement mentality to the transformational mindset we so desperately need.

BEYOND SHAREHOLDER PRIMACY

PROLOGUE

Better Angels Versus Animal Spirits

"In the philosophy of Heraclitus, enantiodromia is used to designate the play of opposites in the course of events—the view that everything that exists turns into its opposite...."

CARL JUNG (1949)

In the year 1665, England was ravaged by yet another devastating wave of bubonic plague. Businesses and organizations were forced to shut down to blunt the spread of the dread disease. Among those institutions temporarily closed: Cambridge University, where a twenty-three-year-old Isaac Newton was finishing his undergraduate degree at Trinity College. The quarantine forced the young Newton to retreat to his family's estate at Woolsthorpe Manor, located a safe distance away from the epidemic that killed over a hundred thousand—a quarter of the population—in London.[1]

For the next year or so, Newton sheltered in place, giving him the solitude and intellectual freedom to explore, uninterrupted, the farthest reaches of his imagination. It was during this period of quarantine that Newton stretched the boundaries of optics, set forth the basic contours of what would come to be known as calculus, and formulated the theory of gravity: "Whilst he was pensively meandering in a garden, it came into his thought that the power of gravity (which brought an apple from a tree to the ground) was not limited to a certain distance from Earth, but that this power must extend much further than usually thought. 'Why not as high as the Moon, said he to himself, and if so, it must influence her motion and perhaps retain her orbit.' Whereupon he fell to calculating what would be the effect of that supposition."[2]

1

Newton's year in quarantine came to be known as an *Annus Mirabilis*—a remarkable or notable year in history; a year of wonders and miracles, with profound implications for the future. Out of death and misery came Enlightenment.

Fast forward to 2020. As I sat in my home office beginning to write this book, we all seemed to be living through a similarly epic time in history: I was self-quarantined at home (no manor, unfortunately) as the coronavirus pandemic raged on, having already killed hundreds of thousands of Americans.[3] Simultaneously, we were in the throes of a precipitous economic meltdown not seen since the Great Depression as well as an unprecedented social uprising over systemic racism and social injustice ignited by the murder of George Floyd—an unarmed Black man killed ruthlessly by the police in the city of Minneapolis in 2020. And looming over all of this were the existential threats of runaway climate change, mass extinction, and toxic inequality which (ironically) constituted the root causes of the immediate crises.

By 2021, as my writing continued, the stock market had roared back, making the wealthiest 10 percent who owned most of the stocks even richer than before the pandemic, perpetuating and even exacerbating class divisions and perceived elite privilege. I then witnessed something I thought I would never see in my lifetime: an actual attack on the US Capitol by an angry segment of American citizens that had lost faith in the ability of the country, and the capitalist system that underpinned it, to deliver what Harry Truman called a "Fair Deal" for people.

Then, in February 2022 the unthinkable happened: Vladimir Putin's Russia invaded the sovereign nation of Ukraine, igniting a brutal military struggle, humanitarian disaster, and refugee crisis not seen since the Second World War. The combination of the Ukrainian war, supply disruptions in China, and rebounding demand from two years of Covid restrictions precipitated a spiral of inflation not seen since the 1970s, and the prospect of a global recession. Controversial rulings by the US Supreme Court on gun and abortion rights in June 2022 then sparked another round of social unrest and discontent, threatening to tear the country apart. And in the summer of 2023, something never seen before in US history happened—the criminal indictment of a former president—multiple times.

It is entirely possible that this combination of once-in-a century crises and disruptions precipitates a further spiral into social division, authoritarianism, and xenophobia. The storming of the Capitol in Washington on January 6, 2021, served to heat up what was already a cold civil war in the US—and inflame an antidemocratic trend that has infected the entire world in recent years. Witness the ominous "echo-insurrection" that occurred in Brazil in January 2023 after the defeat of Jair Bolsanaro in the presidential election.

But it is also possible that we are in the midst of another *Annus Mirabilis*—a time that will come to be seen as a turning point, when, as Willis Harmon quipped, there came a "global mind change" and society changed course in a fundamentally positive way.[4] Deep change tends to occur in historical moments— punctuation points—when public consciousness cracks open and new ideas can rush in.[5] Kurt Lewin famously noted that before transformational change can happen, organizations and societies must first "unfreeze" the conventions, norms, and standard operating procedures that had previously been taken for granted. The cascading crises of the Covid years seem more than qualified to meet this requirement. Could it be that we stand at the threshold of a new age in human—and business—history?

What Goes Around Comes Around

The Swiss psychiatrist Carl Jung drew heavily upon the ancient Greek philosophers in formulating his groundbreaking theories in analytical psychology. Among his most important insights was the karmic tendency of human emotions to metamorphose into their opposites—what he called "Enantiodromia." In his *Collected Works*, Jung described his use of the term as "the emergence of the unconscious opposite in the course of time." Jung observed that the emergence of new unconscious ideas occurs when an extreme one-sided tendency dominates conscious life; eventually an equally strong countervailing tendency builds: euphoria becomes melancholy; valued becomes worthless; and good becomes bad.[6]

Perhaps Enantiodromia can help us better understand the implications of the trajectory of the world today: Brexit in Europe, rising nationalism, and the resurgence of strongmen around the world. Failing states, epidemic disease, mass migration, climate change, and fear of terrorism have been driving a worldwide shift toward isolationism replete with border walls and travel bans. Globalization, financialization, and automation have widened the gap between the haves and have nots, resulting in a swell of dislocated communities, people left behind, and a shrinking middle class in the so-called industrialized world. A resurgence of bigotry and white supremacy in America has fanned the flames of domestic terrorism. A nostalgic desire to return to the high-paying factory jobs and mass consumption of old is fueling a rejection of science and denial of global climate change. Many now legitimately fear that these accelerating global trends will inevitably lead to rising ethnic, religious, and racial intolerance; nativism; authoritarianism; military conflict; climate crisis; and environmental meltdown.

But what if all these disturbing trends are actually a blessing in disguise? What if they represent the last gasp of a dying system? What if the coronavirus pandemic forced us out of our complacency . . . and complicity? What if the storming of the US Capitol on January 6, 2021, represented an inflection point in history? What if Putin's brazen attack of Ukraine ends up uniting the world against authoritarianism, bringing with it a rebirth of democratic values? What if we are on the verge of a major shift in worldview that will catapult us toward a truly sustainable future? Remember that the principle of Enantiodromia teaches us that extreme one-sidedness builds up a tension, and the more extreme the position, the more easily it can shift to its opposite.

A Hillary Clinton presidency would probably not have created such an extreme. On the contrary, it would likely have resulted only in incremental improvement to the faltering neoliberal order insufficient to rise to the challenges—rather than deep change. What if our current conundrum is the start of a giant pendulum swing in the opposite direction? What if the rise of Gen Z signals a sea change in our attitudes about climate, racism, social issues, and guns? What if we are witnessing the demise of shareholder primacy and market fundamentalism as the organizing principles of capitalism? What if we are on the cusp of a new age of business and society characterized by tolerance, social inclusion, racial justice, regeneration, and environmental sustainability? Remember: it's always darkest just before the dawn.

From Luther to Fink

In 1517, Martin Luther posted his "95 Theses" on the door of the church in Wittenberg, Germany, challenging the orthodoxy of the Catholic Church and unleashing a wave of religious, political, and intellectual upheaval. The Protestant Reformation was fundamentally a challenge to papal authority—it held that the Bible, not Church tradition, should be the sole source of spiritual authority. In other words, it was time for Christian practice to be driven by *parishioners* rather than the needs of the high priests and religious elites.

Fast forward to 2018. When Larry Fink, CEO of BlackRock, issued his first letter to CEOs imploring that companies focus on societal purpose (not just maximizing shareholder returns), it was not unlike Martin Luther's "95 Theses."

He amplified a wave that had been building for more than three decades—a "capitalist reformation."[7] Indeed, since Fink's initial letter, the Business Round-table and the World Economic Forum have both issued formal statements re-defining the purpose of business as one that makes a positive contribution to society, not simply maximizing returns to shareholders.[8] Certainly, proclama-tions are not the same thing as real action: recent admonitions about the insin-cerity of "woke" capitalism—that stated concerns for societal issues by some financiers and corporate leaders are little more than cover for gaining more market power—should not be ignored.[9] But perhaps the time *had* finally come for business to be driven once again by the needs of all stakeholders, not just those of the high priests of Wall Street, CEOs, and the financial elite.

The problem is that business—and business education—tend to be patho-logically *ahistorical*. Most people in companies think useful business knowl-edge has a "half-life" and that anything older than a few years has passed its expiration date. This attitude is reinforced by business schools where MBA students demand "new" cases and readings, and faculty tend to oblige to keep their teaching ratings high. The result is a profoundly unreflective culture, in which "new" wins out over experience or historical perspective. The truth is that the current state of the shareholder-driven capitalist endeavor has existed for only a relatively short period of time. Knowledge of history, therefore, can be empowering, offering lessons that the deepest understanding of current re-ality can never provide.

The current movement to remake capitalism is not the first time the economic system has undergone significant transformation. In fact, between the time of Luther and Fink, capitalism has undergone *three* major cycles of reformation—beginning with the fall of feudalism and the rise of mercantilism in the seven-teenth century (Exhibit P.1). Each cycle has been initiated by a movement that propels capitalism to a new stage of development, animated by what John May-nard Keynes described as our "animal spirits."[10] These more primal forces—greed, extraction, lust for power—lead to an extreme, one-sided tendency toward exploitation, concentration of wealth, and degradation of the social fabric and environment. Such excesses then produce a countermovement animated by what Abraham Lincoln described as our "better angels."[11] These more compas-sionate forces—empathy, mutuality, concern for the common good—then lead to new "reformed" versions of capitalism. Think of it as three Enantiodromia cycles of capitalist reformation, with the third unfolding as we speak.

What becomes clear is that capitalism's *operating system* (the "code" that de-fines how to play the game) and *objective function* (the narrative myth that sets

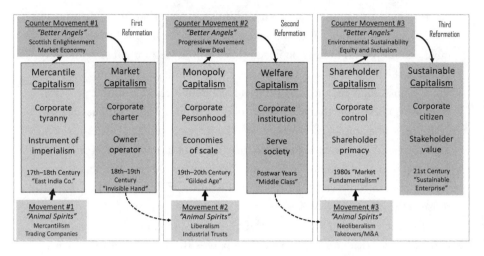

Exhibit P.1. **Preview: Three Capitalist Reformations**

forth the prime directive—what the system seeks to prioritize and promote) all but determine societal outcomes. Today's shareholder capitalism, for example, seeks to maximize the returns to a single stakeholder—investors—by maximizing the quarterly earnings growth of companies. As executive turned author Ed Chambliss notes, focusing on returns to a single constituency group while downplaying or disinvesting in others (such as employees, suppliers, customers, and communities) is like trying to balance on a "one-legged stool."[12]

But like past cycles of capitalist reformations, tomorrow's sustainable capitalism aims to expand this logic by defining societal contribution—serving all stakeholders—as the objective function with profitability representing only one of the many necessary prerequisites to achieving this larger end. As Darden School professor Ed Freeman explains, this version of capitalism taps the "power of AND" rather than seeing the various stakeholders' interests as inherently in conflict—a zero sum game.[13]

The use of the term "reformation" here also seems apt, given the religiosity and ideological fervor of the crusaders for the various forms of capitalism throughout history. As we will see, this has included passionate belief in such things as Deism, Social Darwinism, and market fundamentalism. Indeed, there is a mythical quality to the rhetoric used by advocates for the various incarnations of capitalism. Witness the use of terms such as *invisible hand, general equilibrium, magic of the market, trickle down, economic liberty,* and most recently, *sustainability* and *regeneration.*

Reader's Roadmap

Through it all, there is a certain sense of déjà vu—that which goes around comes around again. Indeed, the first section of the book will make it apparent that many of the challenges capitalism faces today—concentration of wealth at the top, monopoly power, environmental degradation, and toxic levels of inequality—have been confronted before. And while the scale and scope of the challenges we face today may be unprecedented, we can learn from history so, as the saying goes, we are not doomed to repeat it.

Chapter 1, "Capitalism's Heritage: Extraction Is Not Preordained," takes a deep dive into the roots of our current predicament. It begins with an effort to understand the origins of the capitalist "mindset," given that the modern orientation toward progress, prosperity, and science dates back only to the Renaissance and ensuing Age of Exploration. For the first two reformations, I try to identify and distill those *elements, events, patterns,* and *practices* most important to the evolution of the capitalist idea. Conclusion? There is nothing preordained about today's obsession with quarterly earnings and shareholder primacy. Chapter 2, "The Next Capitalist Reformation: Sustainable Capitalism," then explores the rise of neoliberalism and shareholder capitalism in the 1980s and the countervailing forces that now drive the transformation to what I refer to as "sustainable capitalism." In essence, the first two chapters provide the detailed narrative to accompany Exhibit P.1. The story is told from an American perspective since, for at least the last century, the US has had an outsized impact on the evolution of capitalism around the world. Indeed, the still dominant model—shareholder capitalism—is largely an American creation.

Chapter 3, "History Rhymes: Enduring Lessons for Today," then distills the learnings from these past cycles of capitalist reformation and explores their implications for the third reformation—the one that is unfolding now before our eyes. I focus on four enduring lessons from this historical journey: (1) Self-interest is not the same thing as selfishness—by returning to the roots of classical economic thinking, we can develop a more expansive view of what it means to be "self-interested" in business (spoiler alert: self-interest has historically been rooted in the idea of serving others); (2) Managerial stewardship trumps the "principal-agent" problem—by looking at past capitalist cycles, we can identify models for managerial behavior and governance that differ markedly from the caricature of the selfish, shirking opportunist needing control assumed by modern financial economic theory; (3) Monopolies are not markets—even though monopolists still use the language of the price system, it is clear from history that the societal benefits of "market" economies are largely nullified when capitalists are allowed to concentrate industries and wealth; and (4) Reinvestment must take precedence over extraction—by examining the long debate about reinvestment of profits versus extraction of wealth, it becomes clear why the former is essential if the promise of capitalism and the profit motive are to deliver positive societal benefits.

History teaches us that capitalism has been run using very different *operating systems* in the past, and that such systems are little more than *social constructions*, premised upon narratives, stories, and myths about the way the world—and the economy—should work. Some operating systems bring out the "animal spirits" on the part of capitalists prompting the need for reformations that better harness and encourage their "better angels." The chapter concludes that while there are indeed enduring lessons that can and must be carried forward into our own time, the scale and scope of the third capitalist reformation is like nothing that has come before: never before has the capitalist system actually threatened the very environment and climate system that underpins its existence.

The second section of the book then applies these learnings to the corporate transformations—innovations in strategy, organization, and governance— that will be needed to realize the next capitalist reformation. In Chapter 4, "The Great Race," I expound upon the unique and daunting challenges we now face in redressing the ravages of our current reality: shareholder capitalism. While we have made incremental progress over the past forty years with so-called "win-win" strategies, the challenges we now face—the climate crisis, environmental degradation, toxic inequality, structural racism—present existential threats: we have run out of "on-ramp" and there is no time to waste. I argue that in essence, we are in a race against time. Will a new sustainable and inclusive form of capitalism overtake and make obsolete the extractive and inequitable shareholder capitalism that has ruled the world for the past forty years? The next decade will decide the question. The fate of humanity—and other vulnerable forms of life on Earth—hang in the balance. Drawing upon the Sustainable Development Goals, I coalesce the myriad issues we face into three overarching *grand challenges* for the world in the decades ahead.

First, we must alleviate extreme poverty in the developing world, by enabling a truly sustainable and regenerative form of rural and agricultural development, one that simultaneously raises incomes, slows urban migration, and averts environmental meltdown; second, we must reverse rising inequality and discontent among those left behind by deindustrialization in the *developed* world by vanquishing racism and creating a truly inclusive economy, one based on next-generation, inherently clean and regenerative technology. Addressing these first two challenges is prerequisite to successfully confronting the third: an exploding urban population fueled by rural people migrating to megacities around the world in search of a better life and livelihood—a population that could exceed five billion by 2030. These three sustainability challenges provide companies with potential "North Stars" to help focus their quests for purpose and provide fertile ground for prioritizing strategy and investment in the years ahead.

Chapter 5, "Re-Embedding Purpose," focuses on the importance of making societal purpose core to the DNA of business. It is high time that we move beyond the tendency for companies to "purpose wash" by claiming lofty societal aspirations and sustainability goals while failing to integrate them into core strategy and operations. Given the scale and scope of the challenges we face in the decade ahead, nothing less than transformative change by companies will suffice. Drawing from several company examples based upon my own research, I develop a framework that distinguishes among what I call Foundational (sustainability) Goals, Business Aspirations, and Corporate Quests. On the basis of my personal experience in working with Griffith Foods to embed purpose, I propose a practical approach for developing an integrated set of Foundational Goals, Aspirations, and Quests that truly bring purpose to life; this approach provides the much needed *"connective tissue"* between lofty purpose and operating reality to translate Purpose into business strategy, operating plans, and metrics.

Chapter 6, "Redesigning the Corporate Architecture" then sketches the new corporate organization that will be required if we are to successfully embed purpose and effectively confront the social and environmental challenges of the twenty-first century. We examine the elements of this architecture—captured by the metaphor of a "House"—by exploring the "next practice" innovations of several leading-edge companies pushing the envelope in this regard. What these innovators reveal is just how important it is to engage the entire organization in the transformation process, integrating the new purpose and strategies into the systems and culture of the organization. I then tell the story of one company's transformation from a conventional primary aluminum producer to a mission-driven company focused on circularity and sustainability—the transformation from Alcan to Novelis. This story is based on my experience serving as a member of the company's corporate sustainability advisory council (SAC) during the transformation process.

As important as corporate transformation will be for the third capitalist reformation, it will still prove woefully inadequate so long as the larger systems supporting and defining capitalism—policy regimes, market infrastructure, educational institutions—are badly misaligned. We are now past the point where we can meet the moment through the actions of individual companies alone—even if they are transformational in nature. While the sustainable business movement of the past thirty years, including new corporate forms such as B Corps, have been valiant and important, they are destined to fail by themselves: it's a bit like arming soldiers with innovative new clubs but still asking them to attack a machine gun nest. They learn quickly to hunker down—or get mowed down. The time has come for business leaders to step up to the role of *catalyst* for system and institutional redesign. Indeed, a recent Harvard Business School study on the state of capitalism makes clear that government alone cannot solve these problems; business must step up to the plate.[14]

Companies have indeed become increasingly engaged with societal issues (for example, deforestation, inequality) and policies (such as carbon pricing, reform of subsidy regimes). I argue, however, that the *root causes* (and real leverage points) for dealing with our predicament reside at the institutional level—those systems which underpin, define, and enable the capitalist endeavor itself. History teaches us that *institutional* change will be crucial if companies—and capitalism—are to realize their full potential as agents of positive change in the future.[15] Institutions designed on principles of selfishness and greed favor winner-take-all economies and companies motivated by short-term financial gain. We thus face a structural crisis of the financialized form of capitalism that has dominated for the past forty years. We will need to overhaul virtually every institution from education to finance—B-Schools to Bourses—if we are to realize the deep change that is required—a new operating system and objective function for capitalism and redefinition of the very meaning of value itself. The third section of this book therefore addresses these two key institutional redesigns and the role that business must play if we are to fully realize the next capitalist reformation (Exhibit P.2).

Chapter 7, "Reinventing Business Education," focuses on the imperative of transforming business education if we are to effectively confront the challenges we face in the twenty-first century. For the past four decades, business schools have been churning out millions of graduates who go on to leadership roles in big banks, investment firms, hedge funds, corporations, and consulting firms— the actors that have perpetrated shareholder capitalism on the world and subjugated the world's companies with short-termism and shareholder primacy. If

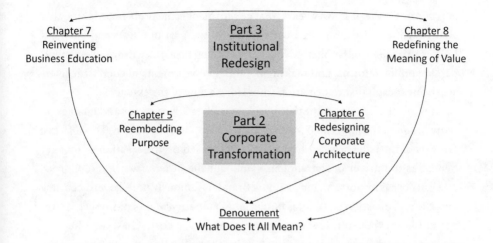

Exhibit P.2. Transformations and Redesigns for a Sustainable World

we are to realize the next capitalist reformation, we must address this key root cause of our current crisis.

We must return business education to its roots: an institution dedicated to developing leaders with a set of professional ethics and a commitment to the common good, with business as the instrument. We must exorcise the demons of shareholder primacy and market fundamentalism from our business schools if we are to develop a new generation of business leaders with a different perspective about the role of business in the world. After providing a sense of the historical evolution of business education over the past century plus, I suggest how companies and business leaders can and must become champions of business education reinvention. I recount my experience in helping to build a completely new business program at the University of Vermont—the Sustainable Innovation MBA program (SI-MBA). At Vermont, we had the rare opportunity to start with a "clean sheet" and develop a new program from scratch with different DNA, which we believe provides a model for what business education needs to become in the years ahead.

In Chapter 8, "Redefining the Meaning of Value," I argue that the time has come for business to fundamentally change the narrative regarding the roles of government and finance. Historically, government has played a central role in propelling countries—particularly the US—to new levels of technological progress and prosperity. The time is now to reverse the neoliberal myth that has plagued us for the past forty years: that government is the problem. Making this change will require a renewed willingness on the part of CEOs and business leaders to become outspoken advocates for paying taxes, elevating government, passing policy reforms, and making the public investments needed to accelerate the next capitalist reformation since time is now of the essence.

It is especially important that business leaders advocate for and enable the reinvention of the *financial infrastructure* that supports capitalism. The *objective function* of the enterprise system must be refocused on the creation of societal benefit as the driver of shareholder value, not the other way around. Corporate purpose is important, but as Louis Brandeis famously noted over a century ago, the real question is, *What is the purpose of the economy?* Is it simply growth, shareholder value, and low consumer prices at any cost? Or should healthy market economies be designed to maximize the well-being of everyone and the sustainability of the underlying environment upon which all economic activity depends? The time has come to put the horse back in front of the cart. The creation of long-term, societal value should drive stock price, not short-term profits. Ending the age of shareholder primacy is the audacious goal of the recently launched Long-Term Stock Exchange (LTSE). Much like the SI-MBA, I tell the story of how the LTSE seeks to disrupt and creatively destroy the current public equity market system and replace it with one more in line with a truly sustainable world.

Finally, in the Denouement, I attempt to bring all the strands and elements of the preceding chapters together. I observe that we are at a critical juncture in human history, one where "market fundamentalism" achieved near religious status but left a hole in peoples' hearts—and pocketbooks. Humans need myth and meaning in their lives, but modern capitalist society has marginalized everything that was once sacred. I argue that sustainability and the emergence of sustainable capitalism might just represent the new story—the myth—that people so desperately need. To make this new story take root, however we also need a new *operating system* for business and capitalism itself. The final section of the Denouement puts forward the elements of such a new operating system: a set of principles and an integrative framework—"The Sustainable Capitalism Framework"—that pull together all the learnings and lessons from this book.

PART I

The Past Is Prologue

CAPITALISM HAS BEEN REMADE TWICE BEFORE

ONE

Capitalism's Heritage

EXTRACTION IS NOT PREORDAINED

Capitalism is today under siege—from Bernie Sanders's democratic socialist indictment that unfettered capitalism is to blame for our unprecedented levels of inequality and climate crisis, to entrepreneur Vivek Ramaswamy's free-market admonition that stakeholder or "woke" capitalism is little more than a corporate game of pretending to care about something other than profit and power, precisely to gain more of both.[1]

Regardless of economic ideology or political persuasion, however, there can be no doubt that the last four decades have witnessed environmental impacts and social disparities that were unimaginable even during my childhood years in the 1950s and 1960s. While capitalism has indeed produced some of the most amazing advancements in all of human history, the business mindset of shareholder primacy has pitted financial returns against human needs and environmental integrity. What economists have traditionally referred to as "negative externalities"—those damages imposed on society by economic exchanges for which no market price is paid—are no longer peripheral issues. In a very real sense, negative environmental and social externalities have now become the main event.[2]

As a consequence, recent years have witnessed a growing chorus of scholars, pundits, and practitioners calling for a fundamental reinvention of capitalism.[3] As unique and unprecedented as our current conundrum feels, however, it is important to realize that the current groundswell to "reimagine" capitalism is not the first time that the venerable economic system has undergone significant transformation. "Animal spirits" have gotten out of control in the past—only to be tamed by our "better angels." Indeed, capitalism has experienced structural crisis—and been "remade"—at least two times before. Numerous authors have traced various aspects of the trials and tribulations of the capitalist endeavor over the past five centuries.

In this chapter, I summarize and describe in depth the emergence of capitalism and its first two cycles of reformation, as displayed in Exhibit 1.1, beginning with the European "Age of Exploration" in the fifteenth and sixteenth centuries. There are important lessons to be learned from this history that are relevant for our time—the third reformation—which will be considered in depth in the next chapter. Let the exhibit serve as your guide for the first part of the book as we explore the roots of our current predicament. Before starting this journey, however, allow me to briefly reflect on the roots of the capitalist idea itself. Where did it come from and how did capitalism first emerge in the world?

Capitalism's Origin Story

Markets and trade are as old as human civilization. As John McMillan points out in *Reinventing the Bazaar*, the urge to engage in "business" seems to be part of the human experience, at least since the time of the Agricultural Revolution. Throughout recorded history, humans have traded with each other and engaged

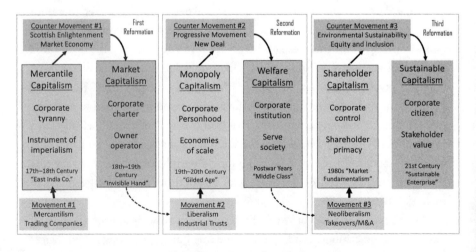

Exhibit 1.1. The Three Capitalist Reformations

in exchange relationships for mutual benefit. Adam Smith noted "man's propensity to barter, truck, and exchange with one another." Markets and bazaars have flourished for thousands of years. Mesopotamians charged interest on loans before they discovered how to put wheels on carts. The invention of money only accelerated this phenomenon by making it easier to exchange value.[4]

Yet for most of Western history, until about the sixteenth century, economic stagnation—a true "steady-state"—was the natural order of things: per capita income barely grew for well over a millennium, from the fall of the Roman Empire until the fall of feudalism—the so-called "Middle" and "Dark" Ages.[5] The ideas of progress and social mobility were nonexistent. Aside from kings and nobles, most people spent their entire lives within a few miles of where they were born, laboring as serfs or slaves. Life truly was, as Thomas Hobbes quipped, "nasty, brutish and short." As Daron Acemoglu and James Robinson so astutely observed in *Why Nations Fail*,

> The fear of creative destruction is the main reason why there was no sustained increase in living standards between the Neolithic and Industrial Revolution. Technological innovation makes human societies prosperous, but also involves the replacement of the old with the new, and the destruction of economic privileges and political power of certain people. . . . Prior to seventeenth-century England, extractive institutions were the norm throughout history . . . [they] did not permit creative destruction.[6]

Historians have nonetheless recognized the existence of long-distance trading as a commercial activity, dating back to the days of the Silk Road and great East-West trading routes through the Indian Ocean. The Chinese engaged in long-distance trade carried out by independent merchants all the way back to the time of the Han dynasty (206 BC–220 AD) as did the Arabian Empire between the seventh and mid-thirteenth centuries, encompassing western Asia, North Africa, and the Iberian Peninsula.[7]

Europe, however, was a relative latecomer to trade and remained "backward" for a long time as feudalism gripped the continent following the fall of the Roman Empire. India, China, and the Islamic world were far more developed by comparison. Only in the twelfth century did the northern Italian cities (such as Venice, Florence, Genoa) become actively engaged in long-distance trade, with large fortunes accumulated by the financiers and merchants involved. Yet even as long-distance trade in Europe lagged that of the East, it would eventually emerge as the most dynamic.[8]

Early long-distance trade could best be described as "precapitalist" in that its impact on society was quite limited, described by historian Jürgen Kocka as "little capitalist islands in a sea of non-capitalist, subsistence conditions."[9] The dawning of the European Age of Exploration, however, set the stage for the emergence of capitalism as a societal order. It all started in the fifteenth century, with the commercial exploitation of the west coast of Africa for its gold, ivory, and slaves. These profit-seeking sea voyages captained by "explorers" such as Christopher Columbus, Amerigo Vespucci, and Vasco da Gama were financed by the Portuguese and Spanish crowns in combination with wealthy Italian merchant-financiers. In fact, the African trade is where Christopher Columbus (Cristoforo Colombo in his native Genoa) began his seafaring, raiding, and slaving career.[10]

At the time, Europe was mired in a prolonged "bullion famine." The exhaustion of European gold and silver mines combined with a high trade deficit with the more prosperous East had created a drastic shortfall in precious metals. Put simply, Europe's exports—mainly woolens and cloth—were less valuable than its imports. *Bullion* (gold and silver) was the only thing that could purchase the spices, silks, and other luxuries that European aristocrats craved, which explains in part the mercantilist obsession with bullion as the ultimate measure of national wealth. While short on bullion, Europe did however have a well-developed system for financing long-distance sea voyages, built on the extensive experience of the Italian merchants and financiers.[11]

As historian Patrick Wyman importantly points out in *The Verge*, the Portuguese and the Spanish added critical new dimensions to the Italian commercial model that would become core to the system of mercantile capitalism that was to take over the world in the sixteenth century:

> One thing stands out about this milieu: a distinct orientation toward profit-seeking, combined with a willingness to inflict violence. Strong religious sentiments, namely the concept of crusading, and the ideals of knightly chivalry wove themselves into a tapestry of lucrative bloodshed. Early Atlantic adventurers . . . were hardly bold, altruistic explorers seeking out new knowledge in distant and uncharted waters. They were operating within a world of violent commercial enterprise where religious war and profit hunting went hand in hand.[12]

The African commercial model was then spread to the East and to the New World at a time when Martin Luther's Protestant Reformation was simultaneously fomenting religious upheaval across Christian Europe. Vasco da Gama's

1497 voyage around the Cape of Good Hope opened the ocean route around Africa to India and Asia—the richest trading system in the world. The Portuguese aimed to dominate the trade in spices from the Indies, reaping huge profits from importing cloves, cinnamon, ginger, pepper, gold, pearls, and silk, along with exporting healthy doses of piracy, holy war, and barbarism. Bullion filled the royal coffers, and merchant investors grew immensely wealthy.[13]

Columbus's "discovery" of the Americas in 1492 would prove ultimately to be the most transformational event of the Age of Exploration. Initially, however, he was convinced he had found the way around the rim of the Indian Ocean to the East. Money poured in for follow-up expeditions, but it soon became apparent that what Columbus had found was not an easy passage to the East but rather an entirely new continent—one without much in the way of gold (at least initially) and bereft of developed markets for luxury goods back home. It was after this realization that Columbus first floated the idea of enslaving people on a massive scale as a way of making the expeditions pay off, just as they had done in West Africa. The brutal tactics Columbus employed, including the mass exploitation of the native population, and slaving as a business model, set the tone for the Conquistadors to follow—Cortés in Mexico and Pizarro in Central and South America.[14]

The empires of the Aztec and the Inca fell within a generation of Columbus's initial voyage. Enslavement and religious conversion went hand in hand, justifying not only the genocidal conquests of natives but also their enslavement to produce gold and silver. The early sixteenth century also witnessed the beginning of the transatlantic trade of permanently enslaved Africans: to build the highly profitable plantation economies that came to define the New World—sugar, tobacco, rice, and later, cotton—an estimated twelve million African people would be enslaved and sold to fledgling "capitalists" whose corporations were the instruments of New World settlement.[15]

The first enslaved Africans were shipped to the Americas in 1518, one year after Martin Luther nailed his 95 Theses to the church door in Germany. It was their uncompensated labor that helped fuel the economic growth of the New World and the rise of Europe as the dominant force in the world. Could the practices from the Spanish and Portuguese exploitation of West Africa be the source of capitalism's view of labor as a "factor of production"—a cost to be minimized? Could the centrality of the profit motive—largely unconstrained by rules and justified by religion—also have its origin in the early days of the Age of Exploration? Was it here where the primordial DNA for what was to become the first age of capitalism—mercantilism—in the seventeenth century was first established?[16]

Genesis of the Capitalist Mentality

While the term "capitalism" rose to prominence only in the mid-nineteenth century, as the first Industrial Revolution reached its zenith, it is clear from the previous section that the core ideas and practices have much older roots.[17] As we saw, use of the term "capitalist" can be traced all the way back to the fifteenth century, when it was used to describe the very "capital-rich men"—the Italian merchants and financiers who "brokered or dealt" in capital—who lent the money for all those long-distance voyages of exploration and exploitation.[18]

It was England and Holland, however, that began to develop a new kind of commercial infrastructure that extended beyond the finance of long-distance seafaring, penetrating into the world of *production*, with the advent of commercial farming and, later, cottage industry.[19] In fact, it was the emergence of English *agrarian* capitalism—with its enclosure of common lands, tenant farmers, and large landholdings—that appears to have created the preconditions for a truly capitalist *society* to emerge: commercial farming first established the ethic of competition, productivity growth, and "improvement," resulting in the waves of landless peasants (failed tenant farmers and those forced off the enclosed commons) who later became the wage laborers in the textile mills and factories of the first Industrial Revolution.[20]

It was in this context that the capitalist mentality first emerged as part of a larger societal transformation—what Adam Smith later described as the creation of a "commercial society," in which most goods and services are produced by companies for profitable exchange, and people—no longer self-sufficient—become participants in and *dependent* upon markets. It turns out that, beginning in the seventeenth century, English and Dutch "trading companies" played a crucial role in helping bring about this capitalist transformation, and much of this change related directly to the emergence of cotton and textiles as a global industry.[21]

The Age of Exploration also ushered in the Enlightenment, and along with it, a fundamental change in worldview by the masses. The world was no longer seen as flat, but rather as a round globe, revealing an entire "New World" unbeknownst to most Europeans before.[22] The earth was also no longer the center of the universe, but simply one of myriad planets rotating around countless stars like the sun. Starting in the sixteenth century, the Scientific Revolution introduced a whole new way of making sense of the world—through reason and the evidence of the senses, making it possible to discover and harness the laws of nature for the presumed betterment of humanity.[23] It was at this point that the Europeans began their steady ascent to economic, scientific, and military dominance in the world, finally surpassing the Middle East, India, and China in the nineteenth century.

At its core then, capitalism is really a *mindset*—a way of looking at the world—and the new "capitalist" way of thinking was forged in the crucible of the Age of Exploration. The *Oxford English Dictionary* gives a succinct definition of the term "capital": "accumulated wealth, reproductively employed."[24] As Thomas McCraw notes in his classic *Creating Modern Capitalism*, history is replete with empires and rulers that accumulated massive wealth—witness the pyramids in Egypt, the Forbidden City in China, or the cathedrals of Europe—but the accumulated wealth put to these uses was not "reproductively employed."[25]

Queen Elizabeth first legalized lending at interest in 1571, distinguishing commercial pursuits from the long-reviled "usury" charged by traditional moneylenders. With the ensuing rise of mercantilism and the Industrial Revolution, the world witnessed for the first time the *investment* of wealth for future gain. Innovation and progress became the watchwords, with old technologies and organizational forms swept out by the new. As Edward Chancellor insightfully noted, "Without interest, there could be no capital; without capital, no capitalism."[26]

With international trade, finance, and commerce on the rise, burghers (town dwellers), gentry (commercial farmers), manufacturers, and merchants began to overcome the hold of the monarchy and the feudal lords on the social and economic order. Increasingly, people came to see that they had agency to change their lot in life; they were not subject only to royal authority and outside forces beyond their control. *Progress* was now possible, whereby one's life might materially improve compared to that of one's parents or grandparents.[27]

And thus, the "capitalist mentality" was born. Capitalist thinking is all about making bets on the *future*—a psychological orientation toward the pursuit of prosperity. It's all about aspiration and striving, as measured by gains or losses in wealth and well-being. Capitalism rests on the assumption that economic growth is not only possible, but desirable, for individuals, families, communities, businesses, and countries.[28] As economist Joseph Schumpeter noted, [T]he atmosphere of industrial revolutions—of "progress"—is the only one in which capitalism can survive . . . stabilized capitalism is a contradiction in terms."[29] Such growth and innovation are best achieved, according to the capitalist logic, through access to credit, private ownership, rule of law, individual incentives, and exchange through markets, rather than central planning or authoritarian control (Exhibit 1.2).

The European Age of Exploration unleashed an economic boom unlike any other in human history. At the time, nature was seemingly limitless while capital was scarce, so it made sense to reward capital above all else.[30] The European colonization of the Americas produced a fledgling new civilization premised on land expropriation, slave labor, resource exploitation, and the "settling of the frontier."[31] In the process, this expansion all but extinguished the native population that had inhabited the continent for thousands of years. By some estimates, the death toll among indigenous peoples in the Americas after first contact with the Europeans, through either war or disease, was somewhere between fifty and eighty million people—a civilizational collapse so massive that it may have contributed to the so-called Little Ice Age: as native lands reverted to nature, they drew so much carbon out of the atmosphere that it may have actually *lowered* the global temperature.[32]

Starting in the seventeenth century, this capitalist mentality spread like a global pandemic such that it *became* the social and economic order in the West by the early nineteenth century, and established England and Europe as the dominant economic and military forces in the world.[33] The vehicle most responsible for fomenting this new mentality and dominance was the government-chartered corporation known as the "trading company." It was an entirely new breed of organization, fundamentally different from traditional royally chartered corporations, which focused on delivering local public goods like roads and bridges or the administration of municipalities or universities.

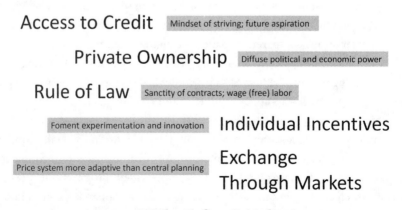

Access to Credit   Mindset of striving; future aspiration

Private Ownership   Diffuse political and economic power

Rule of Law   Sanctity of contracts; wage (free) labor

Foment experimentation and innovation   Individual Incentives

Price system more adaptive than central planning   Exchange Through Markets

Exhibit 1.2. What Defines Capitalism?

It would not be an overstatement to say that the Age of Exploration would not have been possible were it not for this new corporate form, financed through an innovation known as "adventure capital."[34] As we saw with Christopher Columbus, a ship or an entire fleet sailing off into the Atlantic required large up-front investments in vessels, supplies, and sailors to crew them. Beginning in the early 1500s, groups of wealthy merchants and nobles banded together to form investment partnerships enabling individual members to participate in commercial expeditions of their choosing. The Fellowship of Merchant Adventurers in England, for example, dates to 1505. As the century progressed, however, it became increasingly apparent that a more flexible organizational form was needed to spread the risk for investors, since the probability of any single overseas venture succeeding was low.

What emerged was the invention of the "joint-stock" company, which enabled wealthy individuals to buy transferable shares in an actual corporation. This corporation would then invest in a portfolio of expeditions, increasing the likelihood that at least one of them would hit pay dirt in the form of gold, silver, ivory, spices, furs, rubber, saltpeter, timber, or slaves, and later, indigo, tobacco, rice, sugar, and cotton grown on slave plantations. This corporate form, which spread risk by diversified investments for individual investors, anticipated the modern notion of private equity and venture capital.[35]

Joint-stock trading companies were run by and for the shareholders—the ancient roots of shareholder primacy. Power was controlled by a narrow group of wealthy merchants—the mercantile aristocracy—on the Court of Directors. All shareholders met quarterly to hear the directors' report and vote on corporate strategy and policy, with particular attention paid to sustaining high rates of dividend payments. The directors also oversaw the operations, with weekly board meetings to determine policy and strategy. Precise orders would then be sent to the overseas subsidiaries, implemented through a system of subsidiary presidents or "governors." Given the distance and time delay in communications, directors gave considerable discretion to local management to determine how best to carry out directives and achieve specific goals.[36]

The crown government took additional steps to sweeten the pot by limiting the potential loss of any individual investor, shielding them from liabilities beyond their initial investment, should the expeditions incur additional problems and costs (which they typically did) or failed outright. Thus, the idea of *limited liability*, which is a key feature of the modern corporation, was advanced in the Age of Exploration to further encourage private capital to invest in risky overseas ventures by limiting the downside risk. Indeed, while the Portuguese and Spanish were the "first to market" when it came to sea routes to the East and exploration of the New World, the Dutch and the English were the organizational innovators, first enabling such voyages to be financed entirely by private capital in the form of joint-stock, limited-liability corporations.

Thus the goal or *objective function* of this new mercantilist form of capitalism was not particularly new. Indeed, the use of power to accumulate riches dated back to the dawn of human civilization. What was revolutionary was the *operating system* and *narrative myth* enabling and justifying the endeavor: it was the first time a merchant-financier class (in collaboration with the crown) invested for financial gain at scale using new organizational instruments designed specifically for the purpose—adventure capital and the joint-stock, limited-liability corporation. The narrative myth used discovery and religious crusading to justify the wholesale subjugation of native populations and enslavement as a business model. Resource extraction, the quest for profits, unconstrained by rules or limitations, and the primacy of shareholders formed the cornerstones for the new system.

And so were established the core features of capitalism for the next four hundred years, characterized by repeated cycles of excess and exploitation followed by reform and reinvention in reaction to its most devastating and pernicious consequences.

Mercantile Capitalists: Fomenting the First Backlash

The British East India Company (EIC), founded in 1600, was one of several privately financed trading companies granted a royal charter by Britain to take advantage of the opportunities presented by the Age of Exploration. Some of these trading companies focused eastward, such as the Muscovy (1555) and Levant (1581) Companies, aimed at exploiting the newly discovered sea route from Europe to the East around the Cape of Good Hope. Others, such as the Royal African Company (1672) were created to exploit the African slave trade. Still others were oriented toward settlement and commercial development in the New World, notably the Virginia Company (1606), the Hudson Bay Company (1670), and the East India Company itself.[37]

Dutch merchants were also very entrepreneurial in using the joint-stock corporation vehicle to invest their way to empire, turning Amsterdam into a world financial center in the seventeenth century. The most famous Dutch trading company, the Vereenigde Oostindische Compagnie, was chartered in

1602 and became the instrument through which the Dutch colonized Indonesia, overtook the Portuguese, and came to dominate the spice trade, ruling the archipelago of Indonesia for nearly two hundred years. At the same time, the Dutch West Indies Company took early control of trade on the Hudson River in the New World, establishing the settlement of New Amsterdam, which ultimately became New York once the British seized control in 1664.[38]

What truly set these trading companies apart from modern corporations, however, was the granting of *monopoly* franchise over trade in their designated territories or domains. Modern-day "natural" monopoly corporations such as utilities are tightly regulated by government. The trading companies, however, while dependent upon government to renew their charters every twenty years, had nearly total freedom to exploit their monopolies in any way they saw fit—and did so with impunity. Such chartered monopolies enabled kings to reward those nobles, merchants, and financiers most loyal to them with permanent monopoly control over trade in specific geographies or with particular commodities. In exchange for granting legally enforceable monopolies, monarchs and nobles reaped profits far exceeding any cash or land investment they could have made at home, as feudalism waned.[39]

What made the EIC unique even among trading companies, however, was its fusion of joint stock, private financing, limited liability, and monopoly control with a truly global geographic scope. At its height, the EIC's empire—based largely upon the globalization of the cotton industry—stretched from Britain across the Atlantic to the Americas and around the Cape of Good Hope to the Gulf and on to India and China.[40] In many respects, the EIC was the precursor of the modern multinational corporation. Indeed, as Nick Robbins points out in his classic work *The Corporation That Changed the World*, the EIC "confronted and overcame many of the timeless questions facing business enterprise: how to keep employees motivated, customers satisfied, shareholders happy and society content."[41]

Initially, the EIC was just one of many companies competing for the spice trade in the East Indies, which had been opened first by the Portuguese and the Dutch in the sixteenth century. Only in the 1620s, when it became clear that the English could not win the spice race in the East Indies did the EIC shift its focus to India. Hoping to distinguish itself from the Dutch and the Portuguese, known for their strategies of conquest and subjugation, the EIC sought to focus strictly on trade, avoiding military entanglements—exporting Indian-made cotton textiles back to England, which were widely seen as the finest in the world. It is important to remember that Europe at the time still lived in the shadow of Asia, with India and China dwarfing the Europeans in terms of population as well as economic output and standard of living.[42]

By the 1680s, cotton textiles from India made up the majority of the EIC's imports to Britain. This influx of affordable, comfortable, and easy-to-wash clothing created a fashion and lifestyle revolution back home. The late seventeenth century constituted the peak of the boom, with the company's share price more than quadrupling.[43] For India, there was also a steady growth in income, output, and employment. Indeed, during this period, the EIC produced what we might think of today as "shared value" or "value for all its stakeholders." It sourced raw materials such as cotton, silk, tea, pepper, and saltpeter, but also continued to increase the export of Indian-made finished garments back to Britain. This produced steady profits for its shareholders, appealing imports for its customers, good prices for its Indian textile and material suppliers, and substantial customs revenues for the Crown.[44]

But things began to change dramatically as the EIC approached its second century. After the Glorious Revolution in 1688, the monopoly of the East India Company was challenged. British woolen producers were able to induce Parliament to ban the import of calicos, the EIC's most profitable item of trade. The EIC's directors were persuaded to make a fundamental shift in strategy, engineered by one of the most influential shareholders in the company's history—Sir Josiah Child.[45] Child believed that monopoly corporations like the EIC should be an essential component of England's commercial armory: he advocated that "profit and power must go together." He wanted the company to become a sovereign power in India and convinced the EIC's directors to give their blessing to an expeditionary force of ten ships and six companies of infantry—a private army—to force concessions from the Mughals (rulers) in Bengal, the EIC's stronghold in India.[46]

For the first half of the eighteenth century, the Indian subcontinent remained the "workshop of the world," accounting for nearly a quarter of global manufacturing output in 1750, compared with just 1.9 percent in Britain.[47] Indian textiles—hand-woven goods from cotton and silk produced in the villages—could still be sold at a profit in Britain at half the price of those made domestically. Bengal was the center of this industrial ecosystem, with as many as twenty-five thousand weavers producing clothing from thread spun by nearly a hundred thousand women, including many of today's household brand names: calico, dungaree, gingham, seersucker, and muslins.

Access to this market was regulated by Mughal trade policy that dictated what could be traded and by whom. The EIC did, however, enjoy an exemption from duties back home, giving it an advantage over the competition.[48] Yet the company also depended upon local traders—*banias*—who had the relationships with the farmers, spinners, and weavers in the villages. The weavers owned their own tools, controlled the rhythm of their work, and retained the right to sell their products to whomever they pleased. So, as European demand grew, local producers were able to both increase production and raise prices.[49]

By mid-century, despite exemption from duties back home, competition from other European traders for the lucrative Indian textile market began to cut into the EIC's profits. The company also had to pay taxes and duties on what was exported from Bengal to India, further eroding its returns, and leading to disagreements with the Nawab (Mughal ruler) in Bengal. Tensions grew between the EIC and the Mughals. Ultimately, under the direction of new governor Robert Clive, the EIC used its private army to literally *take over* Bengal to improve its commercial position. On June 23, 1757, the company's troops defeated a larger, but ill-prepared force of Bengali soldiers at Plassey, and then proceeded to install a puppet ruler to do the company's bidding. Bribes were used to divide the military commanders and cause key players to defect at crucial times. From that moment forward, the EIC essentially became an agent of the British State, administering Indian territories in return for a secure profit for its shareholders. A new form of commercial imperialism had been born.[50]

To procure the growing quantities of cotton and cotton textiles from India at more favorable prices, the EIC began to insert itself into the production process within India. They replaced the local *banias* (middlemen) with agents employed directly by the company. These agents aimed to force weavers into exclusive supply arrangements, thereby eroding their pricing power and, in the process, driving down their incomes. Increasingly, the EIC behaved not as a commercial trader, but rather as a ruler.[51]

On the one hand, the EIC's conquest of Bengal (and ultimately much of the rest of India) can be viewed as an extreme case of commercial enterprise "going rogue" and becoming an occupying force—a classic case of too much separation of ownership (investors) from control (governors). But on the other hand, as Nick Robbins points out, it can also be framed as nothing more than an aggressive business move engineered by local management—an extreme form of corporate takeover. Using this framing, Clive had made an amazing "acquisition" that put the company and its shareholders on a dramatic new path to profitability.[52]

Clive also exploited the opportunity to profit personally from the conquest of Bengal. Such behavior was encouraged since the EIC's overseas staff received minimal salary in exchange for the right to conduct private business on their own account within Asia. Within a few short years, Robert Clive had (corruptly) become one of the richest men in England.[53] And so we see, on full display, the potential perils of the separation of ownership from control. Robert Clive was a living case of what would come to be known as the "principal-agent" problem—a recurring issue for capitalism over the centuries.[54] As Nick Robbins so eloquently elaborated,

> A new catchphrase entered the language—a lass and a lakh a day [a lakh being 100,000 Rupees]—to describe the lifestyle of the Company's executives in Bengal enjoying the voluptuous mistresses (bibis) and their generous presents from state officials and Asian merchants.[55]

With the regulatory capacity of the Bengali state now under company control, the EIC was able to systematically eliminate any further competitive threats—from either Europeans or local merchants. The final step was the actual absorption of Bengal's treasury into the company's accounts: in 1765, the company was "granted" the *diwani* (tax revenue) rights for Bengal in exchange for a fixed annual payment back to the Nawab. Keep in mind that Bengal alone had a population of forty million people at the time—four times the entire population of Great Britain. The tax revenue of Bengal amounted to some £33 million per year—tens of billions in today's terms.[56]

Unsurprisingly, in the decade after Plassey, Bengal lost two-thirds of its revenues, and the decline of its global manufacturing eminence had begun. As more raw cotton was grown for export, the price of grain was driven higher, with a catastrophic famine the result.[57] What had started as a "mutual value" proposition gradually became a one-sided exercise in exploitation. Suppliers were increasingly squeezed as the company exerted its growing market power. It would be Bengal's weavers, however, who felt the full force of the EIC's new mercantilist strategy: from a position of relative economic independence, Bengal's weavers were forced into a position of near slavery. It is thus understandable why a Hindustani word became an everyday part of the English language during this period: "loot."[58] At the same time, EIC shares were the focus of an international speculative frenzy, driven ever higher by reports of further acquisitions in the East.[59]

Grameen Phone founder (and Bengali native) Iqbal Quadir provides a telling parable to illustrate this new form of economic imperialism and the impoverishing impact it had on what would eventually become Bangladesh. Said Quadir, "Imagine that a lioness kills a deer outside her den and then shares her kill with her cubs inside the den; she maintains separate, simultaneous, and symbiotic codes of conduct that are differentially applied 'inside' and 'outside.' The gentler inside rules are buttressed by the resources taken by force outside."[60] Historian Sven Beckert called this commercial capacity to divide the world into an inside (home country) and an outside (colonies) "War Capitalism."[61] As Beckert explained,

> We usually think of capitalism, at least the globalized, mass-produced type we recognize today, as emerging around 1780 with the Industrial Revolution. But war capitalism, which began to develop in the sixteenth century, came long before machines and factories. War capitalism flourished not in the factory, but in the field; it was not mechanized but land- and labor-intensive, resting on the violent expropriation of land and labor. . . . War capitalism, then, was the foundation from which evolved the more familiar industrial capitalism.[62]

Such "war capitalism"—also known as mercantilism—would become the economic organizing principle for postfeudal Europe, realized through trading company monopolists designed to foster growth and profits—and the accumulation of gold and silver bullion by monarchs—through conquest and subjugation. These corporations extracted valuable raw materials and goods from their colonies and territories and sold finished manufactured goods back to them, all while gradually eroding or discouraging the capability of the colonies or territories to produce finished goods for themselves. Indeed, as the first Industrial Revolution gained momentum, it became increasingly possible for English manufacturers to make cotton textiles and other products more cheaply—using cotton grown with slave labor in America and tariff protection—than the Indian artisans they supplanted, with devastating consequences: by the time of its demise in the mid-nineteenth century, the EIC and other trading companies had catalyzed a virtual reversal of fortunes, with England and Europe now the dominant manufacturers and exporters and India and China the commercial supplicants.[63]

Market Capitalism: The First Reformation

Across the Atlantic, in Britain's American colonies, patriots decried the same treatment as received by their Asian counterparts. For nearly two centuries, the colonies had been allowed to operate semiautonomously, but on the heels of the Seven Years War (called the French and Indian War in America), the British sought to recover some of their substantial debt from the war effort by raising duties and taxes on the colonies. The famine in Bengal had also caused EIC shares to lose value, and the company nearly went bankrupt. The British looked to the American colonies as a source of cash to cover these accumulating financial shortfalls. Accordingly, the Stamp Act of 1765 placed a duty or tax on any activity that required a government-stamped contract, document, publication, or filing. For many merchants and businesses in the American colonies—especially those in the "Yankee" North—the Stamp Act was a bridge too far.[64]

Tobacco plantation owners in Virginia and the Tidewater region—while more loyal to the king—were also adversely affected: they were large net exporters to Britain but depended on English financiers (known as "Factors") to arrange credit and sell their product. Such credit—along with slave labor—enabled men like George Washington, Thomas Jefferson, and James Madison to live the life of landed gentry. However, the planters feared becoming further indebted to the British and were especially concerned when the English governor of the Virginia Company, Lord Dunmore, threatened to *liberate* Virginia's slaves if the stamp duties were not paid.[65] The significance of this threat by Lord Dunmore should not be underestimated. Heather McGhee, in her book *The Sum of Us*, reminds us that the entire early American experiment depended on slave labor. Indeed, without the aid of the French, paid for by tobacco grown by African slaves, the colonies would have never won the War of Independence.[66]

In the northern colonies, merchants seized on the tea sold by the East India Company as a symbol of this oppression. On the night of December 16, 1773, protesters dressed as "Indians" dumped the company's tea into the Boston Harbor. That moment marks the unofficial start of the American Revolution. While popular lore has it that the tea revolt was in protest against "taxation without representation," the truth is that the EIC was actually "dumping" tea in the colonies at a *lower* price than the competition and was planning to sell it through exclusive distribution channels. The Boston Tea Party was thus an anticorporate protest led by the very merchants who would be disintermediated by the cutthroat move.[67]

It was during this period of turbulence that Adam Smith, a professor of moral philosophy at the University of Glasgow, was working on his theory concerning the natural laws of wealth creation, work which would ultimately become *The Wealth of Nations*. Contrary to the popular view, this icon of the Scottish Enlightenment had little use for monopolistic corporations in his vision of economic liberty and market economy. In fact, writing in the wake of the conquest of Bengal, Smith was horrified at the way the EIC "oppresses and domineers" the East Indies.

He warned of the proclivity of monopolistic corporations to engage in a "conspiracy against the public," using their economic muscle to erode the capacity of the state to regulate and tax for the common good.[68] And while he viewed profit as a necessary part of productive economic activity, he argued that it would be "highest in the countries which are going to ruin"—a direct contradiction to those who assert that the purpose of business is to maximize profits. In fact, he argued that the joint-stock structure should be strictly limited to utilities, water, canals, and financial services.[69]

Adam Smith's thinking about the superiority of a market-based economy was thus a direct response to the prevailing monopoly power wielded by the state-chartered "corporations" of the day. The title of his book represented a not-so-subtle swipe at the mercantilist preoccupation with accumulating precious metals as the strategy for building national wealth. Smith's vision of national wealth-building had more to do with the generation of livelihoods for the common people than the accumulation of wealth by the monarchy. In a very real sense, he was one of the world's first anticorporate activists: free enterprise— the pursuit of self-interest, division of labor, and freedom to trade—was utterly subversive to the mercantilist and aristocratic ways of eighteenth-century British commerce.

Smith's work was also a reflection of a larger *religious* transformation that was happening in Protestant Europe at the time. As Benjamin Friedman explains in his pathbreaking work *Religion and the Rise of Capitalism*, the orthodox Calvinist doctrines of human depravity and predestination (the idea that only a select few were preselected for salvation while the rest of humanity was doomed to eternal damnation) that had dominated both English and Scottish religious life since the Reformation were losing their grip. The Enlightenment brought a new and more expansive view of the potential for human agency, emphasizing the primacy of human reason in understanding the natural laws created by God—the so-called "natural theology" movement. Deism—the belief that a benevolent God created the universe but then played no ongoing role in it— was also widespread, both in Britain and America, by the latter half of the eighteenth century. For Deists, reason, moral behavior, and the practice of virtue, rather than adherence to doctrine, were what mattered.[70]

Remember that Adam Smith was a professor of *moral philosophy*, not economics (it took a century for the latter to emerge as a separate discipline). Religion then played a more central and integrated role in society than anything comparable in the Western world today. His conceptualization of a free-market economy was thus premised not only on competition among many specialized producers, but also on the pursuit of individual self-interest governed by strong moral values and ethics held by market participants. Indeed, Smith's most substantial work was not his *Wealth of Nations* but rather the earlier *Theory of Moral Sentiments*, which emphasized that *self-interest* is not the same thing as *selfishness*—that reciprocal exchange is the essence of life, both in personal relationships and business, and that such exchanges must be governed by moral behavior and virtue.

America's revolutionaries—many of whom were Deists—drew their inspiration from Adam Smith, John Locke, Baruch Spinoza, and other Enlightenment thinkers who were prominent at the time of the country's founding. They were also heavily influenced by the classical work of Greek and Roman philosophers, particularly Cicero and Epicurus. These philosophers also emphasized the importance of *virtue*, which in its time meant a concern for *others* and the *common good*, rather than simply high personal moral standards. The Declaration of Independence and the original Articles of Confederation were reflections of the Founders' unbending belief in virtue and patriotism when it came to the governance of the new republic.[71]

Smith used the metaphor of the "invisible hand" first and often in *Theory of Moral Sentiments* but mentioned it only once in *Wealth of Nations*. In both books, however, he emphasized that self-interest should lead to benefits for others—virtue in both the religious and classical sense. Indeed, his thinking about a functioning market economy was premised on the reinvestment of profits back into businesses—to grow and hire more employees—thereby creating an increase in collective wealth and prosperity. Smith abhorred the extraction of profits by business owners for nonproductive uses and frivolous consumption.[72]

It was actually Thomas Hobbes (not Adam Smith) who argued that humans are driven primarily by "appetites" (such as material consumption) and "aversions" (for example, fear of others). Hobbesian logic led to belief in a world without moral purpose, in which material gratification was life's only source of pleasure and selfish impulses must be restrained by authoritarian rulers. Thus neoclassical theories of economics (rational materialism, utility maximization) have more in common with Hobbes than they do with Adam Smith.[73]

Since the American colonies were originally settled by mercantilist trading companies—the Massachusetts Bay Company and the Virginia Company, for example—the Founding Fathers sought not only to liberate the fledgling colonies from the tyranny of the king, but also the yoke of monopoly and economic exploitation implicit in the imperialist corporations that dominated the world at the time.[74] Just like Smith, Locke, and Spinoza, many of the Founders hated big government and big corporations alike. Indeed, Thomas Jefferson argued (unsuccessfully) for the Bill of Rights to include "freedom from monopolies in commerce."[75]

At the dawn of the nineteenth century, only 335 profit-seeking corporations had been formed in the US, and nearly all of these were "utilities" focused on turnpikes, bridges, canals, and so on. Only *six* of these corporations were manufacturing companies.[76] For the first half century of the new American Republic, Adam Smith's market economy composed of small, specialized producers in competitive markets reigned supreme, at least in the North. The early stages of the first Industrial Revolution were thus characterized by market capitalism—large numbers of relatively small, independent producers, partnerships, and sole proprietorships, rather than large, concentrated corporations.

In fact, Americans in the early nineteenth century—at least white ones—enjoyed competitive free markets not just in commerce, but also in politics and religion. With separation of church and state, religious sects proliferated, creating a competition among the many different (mostly Christian) denominations. Much like Martin Luther's and John Calvin's Protestant Reformation, such competition afforded "direct access to divine grace and revelation subordinating clerical learning to every person's reborn heart." In this sense, evangelicalism and commercialism went hand in hand.[77] Cults and movements also proliferated in nineteenth-century America—Shaker communities, Mormonism, utopian socialism, temperance, and, significantly for the future, abolitionism. By the 1830s, America had emerged as the most egalitarian (save for African slaves), materialistic, individualistic—and most evangelical Christian—society in Western history.[78]

Corporations remained few and were chartered at the state (not national) level for defined periods of time and were required to demonstrate a clear public purpose. Given their experience with the British trading companies, the Founders explicitly sought to limit the scale of corporations and regulate their purpose to ensure they served the common good. During the 1830s, President Andrew Jackson and his fellow populists sought to further ensure that the growing industrial elite not accrue unwarranted privileges before average citizens could gain ground. In fact, prior to the Civil War, state legislatures explicitly rejected limited liability for corporations. Most states adopted "double liability," which made shareholders liable for *twice* the value of their investment in the company.[79]

It took time for the first Industrial Revolution brewing in England to spread to America. Water-powered textile mills fed by slave-grown Caribbean cotton and staffed by wage laborers began to proliferate in Manchester, England's, river valleys starting in the 1780s. The invention of the spinning jenny and the power loom then enabled British manufacturers to increase productivity by nearly *four hundredfold* by the early nineteenth century. Observers from the still pastoral America were terrified by what Sven Beckert called this "new Old World."[80]

The first large manufacturing corporation in the US—the Boston Manufacturing Company—was established only in 1813 and served as a prototype for the textile industry that would eventually arise in New England. Yet, over the next four decades, only a dozen or so large, publicly held textile firms were formed. By virtue of their size and stock ownership, these companies were literally known as "The Corporations," in contrast to the larger number of small, privately held textile firms. These few textile corporations stood alone in the industrial field prior to the Civil War.[81] The largest manufacturing corporations in the US in the 1830s typically employed fewer than a thousand people each.[82]

With the advent of the so-called "Second Industrial Revolution" in the 1840s, however, corporations began to grow much larger. Most significant for later industrial development was the introduction of the corporate model in the emerging railroad industry. Since railroad construction involved massive public land grants and heavy capital investment, it almost required recourse to the joint-stock corporate form. Once the first short railroad lines had been built, corporations enabled the consolidation and expansion of these into larger systems. The first major such corporation was the New York Central Railroad, incorporated in 1853. After the Civil War, however, the corporation came to dominate the railroad industry almost completely, with railroad companies employing tens of thousands of people each.[83]

In the South, however, the economy continued to be dominated by slave-based plantation agriculture. Whereas tobacco, rice, and indigo were the major crops in the early colonial years in Virginia and the Carolinas, Eli Whitney's invention of the cotton gin in the aftermath of the American Revolution made the previously labor-intensive processing of cotton suddenly practical—so long as it was *grown and harvested* using slave labor. In fact, Whitney's machine increased ginning productivity by a factor of *fifty*, making cotton agriculture spectacularly profitable and leading to a veritable "cotton rush" in the Deep South, where chattel slavery and an oligarchy of powerful plantation owners had been imported from the British slave colony of Barbados.[84] With the Louisiana Purchase in 1803 (which *doubled* the size of the fledgling United States), these gang slavery-based cotton plantations spread westward, from South Carolina and Georgia to Alabama, the Mississippi Delta, and beyond to Texas and Arkansas.[85]

The cotton rush greatly accelerated and transformed the slave trade. More than a million slaves were trafficked from the Tidewater and the upper South, where tobacco and indigo productivity had stagnated, to the Deep South and west, where cotton plantation agriculture was exploding. Tragically, nearly half of these trafficked slaves were separated from their children, spouses, parents, or siblings, inflicting previously unknown levels of human misery. The forced removal of the Native Americans from these lands—the so-called "Indian Removal" of the 1820s–30s—was also done primarily to facilitate the rapid expansion of slave-based cotton agriculture. Cotton raised with slave labor would quickly come to account for most of US exports and help compensate for the country's otherwise yawning trade deficit. Ultimately, American cotton production would come to supply 80 percent of the *world's* raw cotton, just prior to the Civil War.[86]

In many ways, the American Revolution was a blessing in disguise for the British: armed English capitalists from the East India Company had successfully reorganized the world's cotton industry by exploiting plantation-grown cotton in America as the primary source of raw material for the textile mills in England—and increasingly, the US North—to the detriment of raw cotton producers in India and Asia. By the 1830s, labor costs in England were much lower than those in India, enabling the British to increasingly dominate the global cotton market and "pretty much eliminate all rivals from the non-European world" in the global trade of cotton yarn and cloth. Finished cotton goods from India, now purchased directly from increasingly impoverished weavers, were shipped to *Africa* to pay for the slaves brought to America to work the plantations that supplied the raw cotton for the British mills.[87]

By the 1850s, the nearly four million slaves in the American Deep South, involved mainly with cotton agriculture, carried a market value of an estimated $3 billion. To put this in perspective, the value of all the assets associated with the other leading industry of the day—the railroads—was only about $1 billion, and the federal budget at the time was a mere $70 million. The highest concentration of steam power in the US was to be found in the Deep South (cotton gins), rather than in "industrializing" New England. Half of all the millionaires in the country at the time lived in the State of Mississippi. The US Deep South had become the nineteenth-century version of what Saudi Arabia would become with respect to oil in the twentieth—a place that became vastly wealthy as the largest producer of the commodity most in demand by the world's wealthy nations.[88]

It must also be remembered that slavery was legal in all the original thirteen colonies and persisted in the North until the 1840s. Black slave hands filled the New England textile mills with cotton and capitalized the Wall Street banks. Nearly half of the cotton woolens manufactured in New England mills during the 1840s were sold back to the plantations. New England's "industrial revolution" was thus intimately connected with the slave plantations of the Deep South.[89] Slaves were the most valuable asset class through the mid-nineteenth century and they were mortgaged, collateralized, and insured just like any other valuable asset would be today. Given the scale of investment involved, and the level of indebtedness, the idea of "freeing the slaves" seemed almost incomprehensible to plantation owners and financiers alike, making the Civil War almost inevitable.[90]

The trajectory of the American—and world—economy, however, was to be drastically transformed by wider industrialization, as advocated by Founding Father Alexander Hamilton. Hamilton saw Jefferson's vision of a country of small yeoman farmers and sole proprietors as somewhat disingenuous (remember that Jefferson owned a slave plantation at Monticello), but more important, a prescription for continued dependence on the British for manufactured finished goods. Indeed, even the westward expansion of pioneer farmers after the Civil War required infrastructure—railroads and canals—to get their crops to market.

Hamilton's aim was to use the power of government to build a much-needed national transportation system and catalyze the development of a domestic manufacturing capacity. Ultimately, Hamilton's strategy of protective tariffs for what he called "infant industries," infrastructure investment, and economic development won out. Western farmers and New England merchants alike saw that it was good for them to impose high tariffs on British imports bought primarily by wealthy Southern slave-owning cotton planters.

A series of tariff acts was passed beginning in 1789, but it was not until 1829 that protectionism became explicit US policy, led by Hamilton's successor to the cause, statesman Henry Clay. For most of the nineteenth century, tariffs on foreign goods constituted the main source of revenue for the federal treasury and set the stage for the rise, in the ensuing decades, of America as a leading industrial power through the creation of the "American System" of production, featuring the innovation of interchangeable parts in manufacturing.[91]

As an aside, Hamilton and Clay's strategy would today be labeled "import substitution" and vilified as a violation of free trade. In fact, few remember that America was a protectionist nation until after the Second World War, when free trade became US policy. As with the British in the nineteenth century, free trade made sense for the US only after the war, since by then it had become the world's undisputed leader in manufacturing.

With the outbreak of the Civil War, the Union no longer needed to mollify the Southern plantation owners, enabling the Hamiltonian view to vanquish Jeffersonianism once and for all. The mobilization of the railroad and telegraph industries helped provide the logistical advantage needed for the North to ultimately win the war. A naval blockade of Southern ports also dramatically reduced cotton exports to Britain—the lifeblood of the South's economy—and put an end to slavery. It was also during the Civil War that a piece of landmark legislation was passed that accelerated the Hamiltonian vision: The Pacific Railway Act, providing loan guarantees and massive land grants to railroad entrepreneurs to build the transcontinental railroad, creating the transportation infrastructure that would eventually connect the Pacific Coast to the East.[92] The Civil War thus enabled the Union to thwart the "plutocracy of the planters" and opened the door to a new form of plutocracy—industrial corporations—starting with the railroads.

Indeed, as journalist Henry George presciently noted, the "public domain" in the West was more than six times the size of the original thirteen states, the size of all of Europe at the time. With the passage of the railway act, fully two hundred million acres had already been granted to the railroads and other corporations by the 1870s, a privatization of public land unprecedented in the history of civilization. England had privatized the commons during the shift from feudalism to capitalism through a process known as "enclosure," but as economist Jon Erickson points out in *The Progress Illusion*, "that was kid's stuff compared to the closing of the western frontier."[93]

In 1879, George published a widely popular book, *Progress and Poverty*, that sold millions of copies and spawned a form of economic populism known as Georgism, which focused on the puzzle of increasing poverty and income inequality in the face of the technological advances of the Second Industrial Revolution.[94] George foretold the rise of a new American capitalist empire, born of massive land grants to industrialists, starting with the railroad tycoons including Leland Stanford and Cornelius Vanderbilt and continuing with industrialists such as Andrew Carnegie and John D. Rockefeller, who were able to privatize access to such subsurface resources as iron ore, coal, and oil.[95]

Georgism became synonymous with the movement for a single land tax: to remedy the ills of rising poverty and inequality, George believed that taxing income from labor or capital would discourage work, investment, and entrepreneurship. A single tax on land was instead a charge to use a resource that we once held in common. Shifting the tax base from labor to landownership would, in George's view, steer economic growth toward progress for all rather than poverty for many. The ideas of Henry George reached deep into society and would provide the intellectual foundation for what would later become the Progressive movement in America.[96]

As the Industrial Revolution gathered momentum, mechanization displaced skilled labor and the ranks of the urban underclass swelled. Steam engines powered by coal offered higher efficiency and greater control over the production process by capitalists—witness the impact of the cotton gin and power looms in the textile industry.[97] It was the era of Dickens and Scrooge, when laborers toiled in what William Blake famously called those "dark satanic mills," and discontent among the growing working class festered. As Karl Marx

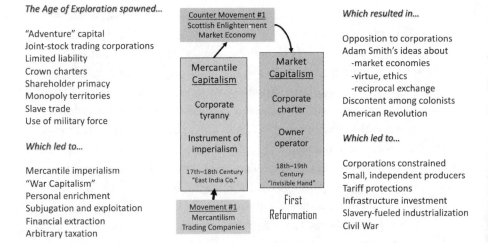

Exhibit 1.3. The First Capitalist Reformation

observed in *Das Kapital*, "the alienation of man thus appears as the fundamental evil of capitalist society." Indeed, it was from this cauldron of social and economic transformation that arose a new philosophy of political economy—communism—and growing anarchist and union movements. It was also at this time that the age of fossil fuels was born, along with the onset of climate change.[98]

Neither Adam Smith nor Alexander Hamilton could have foreseen, however, what industrialization would eventually bring: mass production powered by fossil energy, scale economies and mass distribution, and the rise of the modern industrial corporation. Despite Abraham Lincoln's best efforts to democratize land ownership (the Homestead Act) and education (the Morrill Land Grant Act) in the wake of the Civil War, corporations reached unprecedented levels of scale and monopoly power once again in the latter part of the nineteenth century in America.[99] The next age of rapacious capitalism had begun.

Corporations Unshackled: The Age of Monopoly Capitalism

The nation was still divided in the wake of the Civil War, during the era of Reconstruction, under President Ulysses Grant. Millions were rendered jobless in the subsequent depression and corruption was rampant. In 1873, Mark Twain and Charles Warner published *The Gilded Age: A Tale of Today*, satirizing the greed, graft, and political corruption that characterized the time.[100] The metaphor of "gilding," which involves applying a thin layer of gold over a baser metal, came to signify the period in US history from 1870 until the end of the century. Indeed, in his classic *The Robber Barons*, Matthew Josephson wrote that during the Gilded Age, "the halls of legislation were transformed into a mart where the price of votes was haggled over, and laws, made to order, were bought and sold."[101]

Few had more influence over the guiding philosophy of the era than Herbert Spencer, the father of "Social Darwinism." It was not Darwin who coined the phrase "survival of the fittest," but rather Spencer. His "laissez-faire" ideas shaped the thinking of political and business elites throughout the latter half of the nineteenth century, consistent with the prevailing British world order of "liberalism." Spencer believed that measures aimed at assisting the weak and vulnerable were actually cruel because they ran counter to nature's fundamental order. In his best-selling book *Social Statics*, he wrote, "The average vigour of any race would be diminished did the diseased and feeble habitually survive and propagate."[102] Social Darwinism was thus used as a cover for the trashing of social programs and labor rights, while providing a fig leaf for the unrestrained pursuit of monopoly control by the industrialists of the time.[103]

As noted earlier, by the 1870s, the railroad corporations had become increasingly powerful and Tom Scott—Civil War hero and head of the Pennsylvania Railroad—emerged as a key power broker during the disputed presidential election of 1876. Although Samuel Tilden, the Democratic candidate, won the popular vote by a narrow margin over the Republican, Rutherford B. Hayes, the situation set off a frenzy of horse-trading when it came to the electoral college votes (sound familiar?). For months after the election, political and corporate leaders led by Scott convened secret meetings and negotiations seeking to resolve the dispute, resulting in what came to be known as the Compromise of 1877. On March 2, 1877, a "commission" of five Supreme Court justices and ten congressmen announced that Hayes would be president.[104]

The most fateful provision of the Compromise was the promise that, in return for receiving the votes of the Southern electors, the Hayes administration would withdraw all federal troops from the South. That agreement effectively ended Reconstruction and enabled the old Southern establishment to reassert control, ushering in the era of "Jim Crow"—sharecropping, racial segregation, terror lynchings, Black disenfranchisement—that would last into the 1960s.[105] In return, Tom Scott's Pennsylvania Railroad received millions of acres of public lands and large federal subsidies to connect the lines of the Southern Railway Security Company to the West Coast. Hayes allegedly later complained, "This is government of the people, by the people and for the people no longer. It is now government of corporations, by corporations, and for corporations."[106]

In retrospect, 1877 proved to be a watershed year. The populist ideology of "free labor" that had held freed slaves and workers to the Republican Party during Reconstruction effectively fell apart. It was the year that the Republicans became the party of the industrial tycoons while the Democrats, having been the party of the Confederacy, were transforming into the party focused on *checking* the excesses of industrialization, standing increasingly with labor and farmers. During the 1880s, the factory system of production became truly widespread, bringing with it an unprecedented level of mechanization. Immigrants came to fill the millions of deskilled, monotonous, and low-paying jobs that the rapidly expanding industrial economy was creating. Labor unrest, which was on the rise, was increasingly put down with force, beginning with the Great Railway Strike of 1877.[107]

The Knights of Labor, founded in 1869 as a secret society, began organizing openly in 1878, advocating among other things the establishment of factory cooperatives, abolishment of wage labor, and government ownership of railroads. After successful strikes in 1883 and 1885, workers flocked to join the Knights, reaching 729,000 members by 1886. Increasingly, the labor movement came to be associated with the Paris Commune of 1871, and its "communists," "socialists," and "reds" agitating the so-called "dangerous classes" into acts of violence and anarchy.[108]

Nearly two hundred thousand workers struck across the country on May 1, 1886, with the "May Day" demonstrations in Chicago ending tragically in violence. The Chicago protests merged with a multiweek strike of the McCormick Reaper Company. On May 3, participants in both strikes gathered in front of the McCormick plant, where Chicago police and Pinkertons beat up workers and fired into the crowd, killing three. A mass meeting to protest the police brutality was then called for the next day in Haymarket Square. Toward the end of that protest on May 4, 1886, a bomb exploded among the police, killing eight police officers and injuring dozens of others; the police then proceeded to fire into the crowd, killing several protesters. With the blast, any trace of sympathy for labor among the middle class, media, law enforcement, and government evaporated. The anarchists—and organized labor—were deemed terrorists.[109]

From that point forward, the labor movement in America increasingly sought to distance itself from the anarchists and socialists. Labor's gains in the era of industrial capitalism would have to "come from negotiation and regulation, not ideology or revolution."[110] The Knights of Labor's loss was the American Federation of Labor's gain. The AFL accepted the existence of two conflicting classes (workers and employers) and saw the strike as the worker's most compelling tool. Strikes would continue into the 1890s and beyond, focused on the eight-hour day, wages, and working conditions. And with the rise of William Jennings Bryan in the 1890s, the Democrats finally had a presidential candidate who openly embraced farmers and organized labor.[111]

The Republicans nevertheless remained politically dominant during the latter part of the nineteenth century. Indeed, Grover Cleveland was the only Democrat elected president between the Civil War and 1912, when Woodrow Wilson took office.[112] It should come as little surprise then that during this period, most of the legal restrictions placed on corporations by the Founding Fathers were scaled back or eliminated. A lenient attitude toward bankruptcy also shifted the burden of risk with new ventures, allowing capitalists to pursue ever-riskier investments.[113]

The so-called "Robber Barons"—Scott, Vanderbilt, Stanford, Rockefeller, Carnegie, J. P. Morgan—encouraged and exploited these legal reforms and court rulings to amass huge personal fortunes while building empires in railroads, oil, steel, and electricity. For example, when the State of Ohio threatened the Standard Oil Trust with the corporate "death penalty"—charter revocation—John D. Rockefeller and his fellow industrialists called for states to change their corporate governance laws. New Jersey was the first to oblige by abolishing size limits for corporations and later, in 1888, eliminating the prohibition of corporations to hold stock in other companies, making it possible for the new Standard Oil of New Jersey to now centralize its entire empire under a single corporate charter.

Prior to the Sherman Antitrust Act of 1890, competitors within the same industry coordinated their business interests to limit price competition using "trusts." After 1890, trusts became illegal, but not outright consolidation. The result was a massive merger wave, particularly between 1898 and 1902, orchestrated by Wall Street firms such as J. P. Morgan. The pinnacle of this consolidation wave was the 1901 merger of Carnegie Steel and many of its competitors to form US Steel, America's first billion-dollar corporation. From the public's perspective, many of these new giants were little more than cartels created and controlled by Wall Street bankers.[114]

The continued use of the term "trust" to describe these large industrial combines was thus a throwback to a time before corporation law was revised to enable a company in one state to own shares in one from another. Ultimately, New Jersey and Delaware threw out all the old restrictions on corporations, enabling them to live forever, have interlocking boards, and define themselves for any "legal purpose." The large, monopolistic corporation was back, reminiscent of the trading companies of old, but now they were focused on cornering the market in the emerging industries of the Second Industrial Revolution rather than monopolizing foreign trade.[115]

Perhaps most significant, however, was the establishment of corporations as "legal persons" by the Supreme Court in 1886. For decades, the railroad corporations sought to be recognized as legal "persons" so they could be entitled to all the rights real people got in the Constitution and the Bill of Rights. The passage of the Fourteenth Amendment, however, written after the Civil War to guarantee the rights of citizenship to former slaves, gave the corporate lawyers a new angle with which to make their case. Indeed, despite being scolded by justices for attempting to exploit a law written on behalf of emancipated slaves, the corporate lawyers persisted.[116]

Finally, in 1886, a Supreme Court clerk injected his personal view while summarizing an opinion in the headnotes of the decision on the *Santa Clara*

County v. Southern Pacific Railroad Company case. The clerk wrote, "The defendant corporations are persons within the intent of the clause in Section 1 of the Fourteenth Amendment to the Constitution . . . which forbids a State to deny to any person within its jurisdiction the equal protection of the laws." From then on, corporate lawyers claimed personhood and more legal precedents were established in the ensuing years. By 1910, 307 Fourteenth Amendment cases had been brought before the Supreme Court, with 288 of these brought by corporations—only a handful were brought on behalf of freed slaves.[117]

The result? A dramatic wave of consolidation resulting in a concentration of economic power unlike anything seen before: at its peak in the late 1800s, for example, Rockefeller's Standard Oil Trust exceeded by far the size of the entire federal government. By 1904, around three hundred large firms controlled nearly 40 percent of the nation's manufacturing assets.[118] Had Adam Smith lived another century, he would almost certainly have been appalled by the excessive industry concentration, prominence of the financial sector, and cutthroat tactics used to drive smaller competitors from the market that came to define the industrial capitalism of the late nineteenth and early twentieth centuries. It would have reminded him of the British East India Company.

Welfare Capitalism: The Second Reformation

The second capitalist reformation began unexpectedly at the turn of the nineteenth century with the ascent of Vice President Teddy Roosevelt to the American presidency, in the wake of the assassination of Republican stalwart William McKinley. Roosevelt recognized the growing power imbalance between the industrial trusts on the one hand and the ability of the federal government to regulate them on the other. Much to the chagrin of the Republican establishment, he sought to bring them to heel, such that government could ensure that they were regulated and operated in the public interest; he believed that the power to control the economy should be in the hands of elected representatives of the people, not industrial oligarchs.[119]

In the words of Roosevelt: "It is no limitation upon property rights or freedom to contract to require that when men receive from government the privilege of doing business under the corporate form, which frees them from individual responsibility, and enables them to call into their enterprises the capital of the public," they do so "upon absolutely truthful representations. . . . Great corporations exist only because they are created and safeguarded by our institutions; and it is therefore our right and duty to see that they work in harmony with these institutions. . . . The government should have the right to inspect and examine the workings of the great corporations" because "the first requisite" to remedy the problem of the trusts "is knowledge, full and complete."[120]

Roosevelt also presided over what is now euphemistically called "the closing of the American frontier"—the end of the "cut and run" era of westward expansion in the country.[121] He was heavily influenced by none other than Henry George when the two ran against each other for mayor of New York City in 1886. Both lost to a Tammany Hall Democrat, but George finished well ahead of the future president. Among other things, Roosevelt learned the importance of populism and paying attention to the needs and wants of the electorate, not just the tycoons and monied interests.[122]

To avoid resource shortages and economic dislocation, it had become necessary for the federal government to step in to manage federal lands and resources. For the first time, Americans realized that resources were not limitless, and *conservation* would be essential to the survival and continued development of the nation. New institutions such as the US Forest Service, the National Park Service, and the Bureau of Land Management were created to usher in this new era of more activist government. Gifford Pinchot, the first chief of the US Forest Service, and founder of the Yale School of Forestry (now the School of the Environment), chronicled this "awakening" in his classic book *Breaking New Ground*. And so, the "Progressive Era" was born.

Progressivism meant *growing* the scale, scope, and capacity of the federal government to take on these new roles and responsibilities. Karl Polanyi referred to this counterbalancing of corporate power by government and civil society as the "double movement" while John Kenneth Galbraith later famously described it as the exercise of "countervailing power."[123] For most of the nineteenth century, revenues to support the federal government came from tariffs on imported goods, designed to protect domestic industries, along with "sin" taxes on alcohol and tobacco. Roosevelt realized that additional revenues would be needed to fund the growth in governmental capacity and advocated for a federal income tax to support it.[124]

Roosevelt came to be known as the "trustbuster," and by the end of his second term, he had filed forty-five cases under the Sherman Antitrust Act and achieved numerous breakups, none more dramatic than the initiation of the antitrust case against Standard Oil, the first and largest of all the industrial trusts. The trust-busting campaign continued under his successor, William Howard Taft, who pursued a whopping seventy-five cases. By the end of the 1910s, just about every major trust had either been broken up or had some encounter with antitrust law.[125]

The presidential election of 1912 proved to be another crossroads for the evolution of capitalism in America: Roosevelt ran again, this time as the head of his own progressive "Bull Moose" party, against both the Republican incumbent (Taft) and the newcomer Democrat Woodrow Wilson. Roosevelt campaigned on a platform he called "New Nationalism"; he now promised not to break up, but rather to *nationalize* and *supervise* the remaining trust monopolies—a "corporatist" approach that would become the model in both Germany and Italy during the 1920s and 1930s, leading ultimately to fascism. Wilson, in contrast, promised to restore a *competitive* economy by fighting the trusts with both antitrust law and regulation. Roosevelt and Wilson thus offered two different visions to the voters regarding the nature of capitalism in America.[126]

Woodrow Wilson won the election—the first Democratic president since Grover Cleveland. His "New Freedom" program built upon the breakup of Standard Oil in 1911 and established the federal infrastructure—including the Federal Reserve, the Federal Trade Commission, and the Clayton Antitrust Act—needed to protect labor and stop future trust-building. With the counsel of future Supreme Court justice Louis Brandeis, Wilson aggressively sought to *break up* the monopolies and regulate competition such that excessive concentration could never happen again in the future.[127]

Brandeis called his approach to economic policy "regulated competition." He was drawn into politics by his outrage over the rampant concentration that was happening in the country. He led the campaign to break up the corrupt New Haven Railroad monopoly and came to advocate against what he called the "curse of bigness."[128] Brandeis also thought deeply about what constituted a good society. For him, a worthy nation and economy were ones that "provided everybody sufficient liberties and adequate support to live meaningful, fulfilling lives." He, like the Founders, believed liberty was key to happiness—especially freedom from industrial domination. He also believed that business could be a higher calling, creating the conditions for human thriving. Brandeis would later say that in 1912, the nation picked decentralization over concentration and competition over monopoly—a trajectory that continued for much of the rest of the century, with some important detours.[129]

Unfortunately, the outbreak of World War I in August 1914 brought this "progressive awakening" to a temporary end. It also marked the end of the British Empire's era of liberalism and free trade that had characterized most of the late nineteenth century. To gear up for the war effort, Wilson recentralized power, and the monopolies were once again unleashed, with war-time profits driving industrial concentration to new heights. Following the war, Wilson's preoccupation with his vision for the League of Nations, along with an episode of significant inflation, resulted in political and economic chaos. Wilson—a Virginian—also had a blind spot when it came to race: with the airing of the racist film *Birth of a Nation* at the White House, Ku Klux Klan membership soared, replete with public parades in the streets of Washington. The influenza epidemic of 1918 subsequently decimated the country and the economy. Strikes and race riots ran rampant, spiking unemployment to more than 12 percent.[130]

As a result, the Republicans once again seized the presidency in 1920. With a campaign promise of "return to normalcy," Warren G. Harding proceeded to restore the old Republican policies of the late-nineteenth-century Gilded Age. Banker and tycoon Andrew Mellon was appointed treasury secretary and served in that capacity the entire decade of the 1920s. The policy agenda was focused on reducing taxes, abolishing regulations, and raising tariffs to protect the domestic industrial monopolies. The economy and the stock market soared, even as inequality reached record levels, and certain geographies—the South and the West in particular—were increasingly left behind.[131]

During the war, retail brokerages began offering war bonds to the public, opening the door to selling corporate shares directly to the public after the war. As a result, stock ownership in the industrial corporations became much more widely distributed during the "Roaring Twenties." At the turn of the century, for example, shareholders of a typical large, public corporation numbered in the tens of thousands, with the tycoons still retaining controlling interests. During the 1920s, however, that number increased to *hundreds* of thousands, with one to two million people, many of more moderate means, owning stocks for the first time. Whereas the tycoons of the nineteenth century generally secured capital from bankers, took personal risks, and amassed fortunes, these new, widely dispersed individual shareholders enjoyed protection from liability yet played little meaningful role in the management function.[132]

In their classic book *The Modern Corporation and Private Property*, Adolph Berle and Gardiner Means recognized that ownership of industrial corporations had once again become separated from functional control during the 1920s—a rhyme with the age of mercantile capitalism, when the trading companies also faced this challenge.[133] Such separation was unique, in many ways, to American capitalism: most other countries did not have well-developed stock markets, and even for those that did, families, banks, or governments typically held controlling stakes in most enterprises. By the 1920s, however, *two-thirds* of America's industrial wealth had been transferred from individual ownership (the tycoons) to distributed ownership by a multitude of small stockholders in publicly held corporations. Tragically, it was rampant speculation by these new, inexperienced investors during the Roaring Twenties that helped create the bubble that led to the Wall Street Crash of 1929.[134]

The 1920s was also the decade when the economy became fully dependent on fossil fuels. Garages and gas stations became ubiquitous as the automobile came to dominate the American lifestyle after World War I. Agriculture became mechanized for the first time, leading to rapidly falling prices for agricultural commodities in the years before the stock market crash. Consequently, farm income fell more than 70 percent in the late 1920s and early 1930s, driving many smaller farmers off the land. The farmers' suffering was then quickly felt in the cities since they could no longer afford to buy manufactured goods such as cars. The economy was caught in a vicious downward spiral—a depression from which it would fully emerge only with the mobilization for World War II.[135]

The Great Depression was a time of serious reflection—and recalibration. Some staunch capitalists even concluded that laissez-faire, with its associated belief in the self-regulating market, was to blame for the calamity. It was a time when the importance of competent, professional corporate management was recognized and promoted: rather than being viewed as self-interested "agents" needing control, professional managers were seen as a stabilizing force, blunting the cutthroat tactics and profiteering that had dominated the Gilded Age. Widely distributed ownership of large corporations made skilled and principled managers indispensable.

Berle and Means's book, published in the early 1930s, was the product of a five-year investigation into these emerging challenges in American corporate governance and control. Their work spanned the tumultuous end of the Roaring Twenties, the 1929 Crash, and the early years of the Great Depression. They found that the best solution to the challenge of distributed stock ownership was for big corporations to "develop into purely neutral technocracies, balancing a variety of claims by various groups in the community and assigning each a portion of the income stream on the basis of public policy rather than private cupidity."[136] They called this new operating model "managerial capitalism," foreshadowing what would come to be known as "stakeholder capitalism" in the

1980s. Since distributed shareholders in their words "manage not, invest not, nor do they accept liability," Berle and Means concluded that

> the property owner who invests in a modern corporation so far surrenders his wealth to those in control of the corporation. . . . He has become merely recipient of the *wages of capital*. [Such owners] have surrendered the right that the corporation should be operated in their sole interest. . . .[137]

The book and its message had tremendous impact, described as "epoch-making," and compared in significance to Adam Smith's *Wealth of Nations*. Not surprisingly, the book landed on the desk of presidential candidate Franklin Delano Roosevelt, and once elected, FDR invited both Berle and Means to join his administration.[138] Thus the principle of "managerial primacy"—the consignment of shareholders to receiving the "wages of capital" rather than the lion's share of the returns—provided the foundation for the full realization of the second capitalist reformation and the emergence of welfare capitalism during the 1930s.

Roosevelt's "New Deal" also reasserted the role of government in solving society's problems, with John Maynard Keynes as its primary intellectual force. FDR not only harnessed the institutions established under Woodrow Wilson but also launched a series of important new initiatives designed to break the downward spiral of the Depression and protect the most vulnerable, including the Works Progress Administration, the Social Security Act, and the National Labor Relations Act. Given the influence of Berle and Means, corporate executives came to accept ever more government involvement in their activities and ever more social responsibility—especially after the nation entered World War II.[139]

It was also in the depths of the Great Depression that the most consequential modern indicator of economic growth came into being—gross domestic product (GDP). As the Roosevelt administration grappled with how to end the Depression, it became clear that they lacked a quantitative sense of how bad things really were or whether their policy initiatives were having their intended effects. Enter Simon Kuznets. An expert in statistics and economics, Kuznets had developed a rough way of measuring the total output of an economy—the production of all goods and services. This metric was anxiously adopted by policymakers and, over the course of the 1930s, became *the* main tool for tracking economic improvement.[140]

However, Kuznets never intended GDP to be a measure of overall economic welfare—he intended it only as a rough indicator of growth or contraction in production and consumption. It was a "war time" tool that made no pretense to measure economic health or quality of life. Despite his warnings, however, GDP eventually became the de facto standard for measuring economic progress around the world, with policymakers and central bankers focusing their attention on GDP growth as the singular objective to this day, with tragic consequences for the environment and social equity.[141]

It was mobilization for World War II, however, that ultimately provided the boost needed to revive the country's ailing economy and launched the US on a truly remarkable period of growth and development. To prevent the profiteering and industrial concentration that resulted from the mobilization for World War I, FDR managed the mobilization and production for World War II through a government-run entity—the Defense Plant Corporation (DPC), a subsidiary of the Reconstruction Finance Corporation. The DPC ensured that the government owned the assets it financed, and it hired business leaders and engineers to run them. After the war, the government then used the sale of these industrial assets to create less concentrated automobile, construction, steel, and aluminum industries, to name just a few. The New Dealers made sure the experience of World War I would not be repeated. This time around, the mobilization for war made industries *more* competitive and set the stage for a vastly enlarged middle class and postwar shared prosperity—Brandeisian policy was back.[142]

After the Second World War, the US championed a series of steps aimed at building a new world order including the reorganizing of the world trading system. After more than a century of protectionism and tariffs on imports, Americans now led a coordinated effort to slash tariffs and liberalize national economies throughout the world. Policymakers promoted new international institutions such as the General Agreement on Tariffs and Trade, the World Bank, the International Monetary Fund, and the United Nations. Much like that of the British in the late nineteenth century, Washington's drive to open world markets made sense at this point, since the US had emerged from the war as the world's dominant industrial power.[143]

The US also proceeded to build a truly *inclusive* domestic economy: from the late 1940s until well into the 1970s, corporate America—while blind to such emerging societal challenges as civil rights, environmentalism, and the women's movement—was nonetheless committed to the provision of secure and well-paid employment, and acting as a good citizen in the communities where companies operated, consistent with the principles of managerial primacy.[144] Indeed, Gerald Swope, CEO of General Electric, proudly declared that his company practiced "welfare capitalism." The fear of communism no doubt influenced the country's political and business leaders when it came to accommodating the working class.

Nonetheless, it was during these postwar, Cold War years that America built a thriving middle class and lifted the Greatest Generation up by the bootstraps. While the corporate structures themselves were little more than upgraded versions of the industrial corporations of the Gilded Age, they were guided by leaders with a common bond forged during the Great Depression and World War II, and a concern about the spread of communism.[145] Together, corporations and government delivered shared prosperity: GDP soared while inequality plummeted. A progressive income tax system enabled sustained investment in infrastructure, home ownership, education, and technology.[146]

Yet structural racism persisted, embedded in many of the "progressive" policies noted above. For example, federal housing programs systematically excluded communities of color through a practice known as "redlining," under which minority neighborhoods were designated as off limits for loans. The federal highway program was also guilty of routing new freeways directly through minority communities as they connected cities to the interstate highway system. And while the GI Bill's language did not explicitly exclude African American veterans from its benefits, Southern Democrats drew on tactics they had previously used to ensure that the New Deal helped as few Black people as possible, insisting that the program be administered by the individual states, for example.[147]

Because American corporations were unrivaled in the world in the wake of the Second World War, they could afford to behave with a form of *noblesse oblige*.[148] Freed from direct shareholder oversight, corporate leaders could focus their attention on the greater good—employment, rising wages, and being good corporate citizens. As Charles Wilson, former CEO of GM said, "What's good for our country is good for General Motors and vice versa."[149] Indeed, General Motors became known facetiously as *Generous* Motors. In 1949, in what came to known as the "Treaty of Detroit," General Motors agreed, under pressure from the United Auto Workers, to provide health care and pensions for its workers. This agreement would become the norm across the entire auto industry and, eventually, most other unionized industries in the US.[150]

This agreement would also prove to be one that American corporations— including GM—would come to regret in later years as Japan, Germany, and other European countries recovered from the war's damage, building their own versions of capitalism—versions that included universal health care and pen-

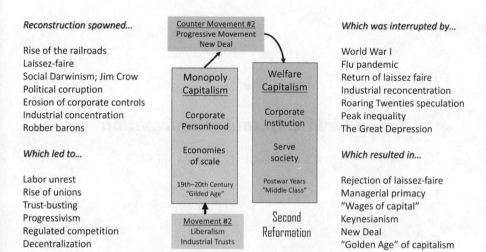

Exhibit 1.4. The Second Capitalist Reformation

sions provided directly by the government. Welfare capitalism underpinned the "golden age" of American corporate dominance from 1945 through 1975. In fact, in 1970, the year I graduated from high school, inequality reached its lowest level in American history. But as the 1970s wore on, the American welfare capitalism model came under increasing pressure, both from within and without. What emerged—the "Neoliberal Era" and shareholder capitalism—would literally flip the script and redefine the *objective function* for capitalism as narrow profit-seeking once again—the third time—with now existential consequences for the world. It is to this era—and the emerging countermovement for a sustainable capitalism—that we turn our attention in the next chapter.

TWO

The Next Capitalist Reformation

SUSTAINABLE CAPITALISM

The Great Recession of 2007–9 turned out to be far more than just a garden-variety financial crisis: it signaled the beginning of the end of an era. As we entered the second decade of the twenty-first century, the neoliberal order, which had dominated world economic affairs since the time of Reagan and Thatcher, began to unravel. The combination of free trade, free markets, tax cuts, and regulatory roll-back had failed to deliver on its promise. Rather than "lifting all boats," neoliberalism and its corporate analogue, shareholder primacy, had instead produced rising inequality, accelerating environmental degradation, mounting debt, and declining real incomes for the middle class, especially in the United States and the UK.

A deregulated financial sector had created a series of speculative bubbles in the stock and real estate markets, leading to the near collapse of the global financial system in 2008.[1] Government rushed in to bail out the big banks and financial institutions to the tune of nearly $1 trillion, while millions of ordinary people simply lost their jobs and homes. The bankers, financiers, and capitalists responsible were never held accountable. People began to lose faith in government's ability to serve the public interest. The US economy seemed to be deteriorating into a pro-big-business system run by corrupt politicians and financiers, rather than the pro-market system driven by competition that had been the cornerstone of the country.[2]

The fracturing of the neoliberal order opened politics to new, more extreme voices on both the right and the left. Brexit sent a shock wave throughout Europe. Donald Trump, a billionaire from the "1 percent," stunned the political establishment with his brash style and ethnonationalist rhetoric that struck at the heart of neoliberal ideology—walls needed to be built, immigrants expelled, and tariffs raised. The rise of Bernie Sanders, a democratic socialist against the "1 percent," was also a direct affront to neoliberalist logic, but from the other end of the political spectrum. This surge in populism and the vilification of the once-celebrated "global elites" led to a growing realization that not only neoliberalism, but democracy itself, was in crisis.[3]

The coronavirus pandemic delivered the coup de grâce; it laid bare the structural flaws in neoliberalism for everyone to see. When Covid-19 struck in 2020, it became immediately evident that neoliberalism was not up to the task. Massive state intervention was required to deploy vaccines, address mounting unemployment and homelessness, prevent mass business failure, provide stimulus, invest in infrastructure, and begin to address the looming climate crisis. The interventionist state—the bugbear of neoliberalism—was back.[4] While neoliberal advocates attempted to adapt to the new reality by propping up Wall Street and large corporations, there was no denying that "neostatism" had now become the new normal, for actors both on the left and on the right. Liz Truss's attempt at a Thatcher reboot in the UK in 2022 went over like a lead balloon. Apparently, the solution to neoliberalism's failings was not more neoliberalism. The question was, which vision for *capitalism's* future would ultimately prevail?

The World Economic Forum opined that we have arrived at the time of the "Great Reset," as if the pandemic offered capitalism an opportunity to start anew.[5] As was clear from the previous chapter, however, each new era in economic history responds to the contradictions and problems created by the previous one—there are no "do-overs." Economic eras are composed of coherent sets of political *and* economic institutions. During periods of structural crisis, progress cannot resume without major institutional change on both fronts. Until that occurs, stagnation and instability tend to persist.[6]

So long as shareholder primacy constitutes the objective function for capitalism, therefore, it is unlikely that we will be able to fully make the transition to a new era where economic as well as political institutions are in full alignment—to be fully remade. It is for this reason that I focus attention in this chapter—and the rest of the book—on the *next* capitalist reformation, the one that will define our time—the rise of sustainable capitalism. Let us first, however, examine how neoliberalism and its alter ego, shareholder capitalism, came

to dominate the world order beginning in the 1980s, with devastating consequences.

Parallel Universes: Alternative Variants of Capitalism

In the wake of the Second World War, several variants of capitalism emerged
in the world, each with its distinctive approach to taming the "animal spirits"
of monopoly capitalism. Two former European great powers—Britain and
France—receded to the background, with their empires lost and the world
grappling with how to deal with their former colonies, now the "Third World."
In contrast, the two industrial powers most devastated by the Second World
War—Germany and Japan—came storming back, in large measure because
the US did not allow the same mistake to be made again as in the aftermath
of the First World War: rather than punishing the vanquished with reparation
payments and other forms of retribution, the US-led Marshall Plan invested in
the countries destroyed by the war.[7]

The result was that both Germany and Japan developed unique variants of
capitalism in the postwar years that have been highly influential on other countries in Europe and Asia, respectively. Like the US with its welfare capitalism
model, both devised ways to temper the worst aspects of free-market capitalism
by ensuring a social safety net and promoting social cohesion through more
inclusive governance structures. Unlike America, however, where the postwar
welfare model of capitalism eventually gave way to a harsher neoliberalist approach beginning in the 1970s, the German and Japanese strains persist to this
day.[8]

Germany's "Rhine" model of capitalism was built on a strong craft tradition,
excellence in technical or vocational education, and commitment to small and
medium-sized business ("Mittelstand"). Unlike in America, where the labor
movement focused mainly on wages and working hours, German labor pushed
for greater economic democracy. The result has been the development of both
an advanced system of social welfare by the government—health insurance,
pension, and worker compensation—and a unique approach to labor relations
based upon "codetermination"—equal representation of labor and industry on
the supervisory boards of corporations.[9]

The Rhine model has proven to be a remarkably resilient strain of capitalism
that has avoided many of the problems of inequality and short-termism that
have plagued American capitalism over the past several decades. Similar strains
of capitalism have also evolved in the Netherlands and Switzerland as well as

the Nordic countries, where unique blends of entrepreneurship, free markets, and social welfare make up what is often referred to as the "Nordic" or "Viking" model of capitalism.[10]

Japan built on its strong historical tradition of competent bureaucratic government, in which civil servants are chosen on the basis of educational merit and achievement—the "best and the brightest." In this spirit, the Ministry of International Trade and Industry crafted long-range industrial policies to promote strategic or "sunrise" industries key to the country's future—for example, steel, heavy machinery, automobiles, and electronics. "Enterprise Unions" also enabled the large industrial companies to offer employment security to workers and managers alike.

The priorities of Japanese firms differed from those of their Western counterparts: Japanese business tended to downplay the importance of shareholders as the owners and instead considered the *employees* as the true core of the firm—employee primacy, if you will. The result was an operating system focused on new product development and growth, rather than return on investment and short-term profitability, which preoccupied their Western, particularly American counterparts.[11] As we will see, the Japanese model also influenced the so-called "Asian Tigers"—Singapore, South Korea, Hong Kong, Taiwan—which emerged in the second half of the twentieth century.

Both Russia and China descended into destructive experiments in totalitarianism, pitting the US against these two powers in a "Cold War" that continued into the latter part of the twentieth century. For the US, the Cold War simply redoubled the commitment of the "Greatest Generation" that won World War II and served to unite the country against a common enemy. For the Russians, the failed attempt at building a communist empire ended badly with the eventual fall of the Soviet Union in the early 1990s and the descent of Russia once again into autocracy and kleptocracy.

The Chinese, however, began a process of "opening up" their economy beginning in the late 1970s—a process that resulted in unprecedented growth and enabled China to become the number 2 economy in the world by 2010. Opening up also facilitated the development of a unique form of state capitalism—"Socialist Market Economy with Chinese Characteristics," as the Chinese called it. This model of capitalism incorporated elements of neoliberalism—liberalization, privatization, and a focus on export-oriented manufacturing industries, for example—but also carefully maintained control over state-owned enterprises and industries considered strategic to the country's future.[12]

These different varieties of capitalism were obscured by the Cold War, which pitted "capitalism" against "communism" at the world level. All capitalist systems do share some important things in common: a commitment to private actors owning and controlling property in accord with their interests, and demand and supply being set by prices in markets. However, with the fall of communism in the late 1980s, the variants became more clearly differentiated, with the US (and UK) staking out the extreme on the right.[13]

In fact, of all the varieties of capitalism that have evolved over the past half-century, it has been the American version that has proven to be the *most* extreme. In many ways, the current financialized version of American capitalism has turned out to be a "mutant strain," to borrow a term from the coronavirus era: like a highly infectious virus, it often seriously debilitates or even kills its host. America was its most equitable and prosperous in 1970, at the peak of welfare capitalism. After that, as market fundamentalism and shareholder primacy tightened their grip, the country became steadily more unequal—and unsustainable. So much so that by 2020, the US had reached peak *inequality* once again—a level not reached since 1929.[14]

Furthermore, when the neoliberal "Washington consensus" became the model for international development starting in the 1980s, it served mostly to *impoverish* the developing countries that followed it. The "shock therapy" of fiscal austerity, privatization, deregulation, and trade liberalization as enforced by the International Monetary Fund (IMF) worked in a few specific Latin American cases but was not an effective one-size-fits-all prescription for the rest of the world.[15] It is for good reason that the Washington consensus regime came to be known as the "Golden Straitjacket" by those who submitted to it: the IMF prescriptions required countries to pay back their foreign creditors and encouraged capital to flow freely in and out (so-called "hot money"). But the net result for the recipient countries was typically deep recession or even depression, provoking riots, social upheaval, or even the capture of the countries' assets by corrupt leaders and oligarchs—witness, for example, the plights of Russia, Indonesia, Thailand, Brazil, Mexico, Kenya, and Ethiopia during the 1990s.[16]

The few developing countries that have prospered over the past forty years—the Asian Tigers, for example—shunned this neoliberal development model. Instead, they followed the Japanese model, which is more akin to the *Hamiltonian* strategy from nineteenth-century America: tariffs to protect infant industries; an emphasis on education, social welfare, and infrastructure development; and export promotion. Lesson: trade liberalization is an *outcome* not a cause of economic development. A level playing field leads to *unfair* competition when the players are unequal, something both the British and Americans understood well in their early years of economic development.[17]

Thus, while the current American model of capitalism is only one strain—one "operating system," if you will—it has effectively infected the world, with a differential level of lethality depending on the "immune system" of the host country and commercial culture. What differentiates the American variant of capitalism over the past forty years from the other strains? The answer is an almost religious belief in the infallibility of unregulated markets and a laser focus on shareholder value as the only metric for success that really counts. Let's take a closer look at how this came to be.

The Rise of Neoliberalism

Corporations' role as societal institutions during the era of welfare capitalism in the US came to an end during the 1970s when Milton Friedman, an economics professor at the University of Chicago, assumed the leadership of the Mont Pèlerin Society and published a piece in the *New York Times Magazine* titled "The Social Responsibility of Business Is to Increase Profits."[18] The Mont Pèlerin Society had been founded by Friedrich von Hayek and his neoliberal colleagues in 1947 as the world was emerging from the ashes of the Second World War. They feared that, with the ascendancy of communism (as in China and the Soviet Union) and Keynesianism (such as the Marshall Plan in Europe and Japan and the New Deal in the US), the importance of free markets and free enterprise might get lost in the shuffle. Having just lived through the horrors of fascism in Germany, Italy, and Japan, they believed such concerns were not without merit.[19]

In many ways, the situation in the late 1940s was the exact opposite of what came to be over the past forty years: over the first four decades of the twentieth century, free-market thinking was marginalized in favor of government intervention and the importance of the state. For the past four, until the global pandemic struck in 2020, unfettered free-market thinking reigned supreme (at least in the US and UK) and the role of governmental intervention, the object of scorn. Milton Friedman and his colleagues at the University of Chicago had a lot to do with this transformation.[20]

While there had been back-channel attempts to undermine the New Deal by corporate interests and wealthy individuals dating back to the 1930s, they had failed to gain widespread traction before Friedman.[21] Even so-called "modern" Republicans like Dwight Eisenhower supported "big government" programs such as the Interstate Highway System and federal R&D spending. Lyndon Johnson then unleashed the economic libertarian's nightmare—the Great Society. Finally, adding insult to injury, Richard Nixon presided over the *expansion* of the regulatory state, with the creation of the Environmental Protection Agency, the Occupational Safety and Health Administration, and the Equal Employment Opportunity Commission.

The age of welfare capitalism was thus part of a larger political order—a coherent set of economic and political institutions—that transcended party politics. As historian Gary Gerstle observes in *The Rise and Fall of the Neoliberal Order*:

> The phrase "political order" is meant to connote a constellation of ideologies, policies and constituencies that shape American politics in ways that endure beyond the two-, four-, and six-year election cycles. . . . A key attribute of a political order is the ability of its ideologically dominant party to bend the opposition party to its will. . . . Thus, the Republican Party of Dwight D. Eisenhower acquiesced to the core principles of the New Deal order in the 1950s, and the Democratic Party of Bill Clinton accepted the central principles of the neoliberal order in the 1990s.[22]

The postwar years presented both a challenge and an opportunity for the advocates of neoliberalism and free-market capitalism. As the Baby Boom generation came of age, young people became increasingly disenchanted with the conformity that seemed to pervade this era of big government and unprecedented economic growth: the heroes who won the Second World War a decade prior now became bland "organization men," working for faceless corporations, cogs in bureaucracies, focused on climbing the ladder.[23] As the rising middle class decamped to the (largely white) suburbs in record numbers, the younger generation increasingly saw these communities as little more than a collection of "little boxes" on the hillside, all made of "ticky tacky," as the famous 1960s song lamented.[24]

There was also the growing realization that we might all wake up one day to what Rachel Carson called a "silent spring," given the mounting pollution burden being generated.[25] People in my parents' generation often referred to this pollution as "the smell of money," making my generation (the Baby Boomers) even more resistant and rebellious. It was the era of sex, drugs, and rock and roll. Civil rights, women's rights, and the environmental movement also exploded onto the scene. And underneath it all—a growing protest against the Vietnam War.

By 1970, the economic right had become extremely concerned about this so-called "counterculture" movement, which was openly contemptuous of both large corporations *and* government, a "rhyme" of Adam Smith and the American Founders in the late eighteenth century. I personally remember the vitriol that was directed at corporations during the 1960s, especially the makers of chemical defoliants like Agent Orange. Corporations were seen as "capitalist pigs"—nothing short of the "enemy." The War on Drugs and FBI overreach also promoted a growing mistrust of and disdain for government by young people, captured by the slogan, "stick it to the Man." Conservatives were so concerned about these developments that future Supreme Court justice Lewis Powell was commissioned by the US Chamber of Commerce to write a now-infamous memo in 1971 issuing a call to arms and long-term strategy for reversing this perceived "Attack on the American Free Enterprise System."[26]

Ironically, neoliberalism gained significant momentum during the 1970s, on the heels of Friedman's landmark publication. While Friedman was reacting *against* the 1960s antibusiness counterculture, he did so in a way that inadvertently tapped into the spirit of the times. As Kurt Anderson perceptively observes, in his soon-to-be classic *Evil Geniuses*, the 1960s were all about freedom and individualism—"do your own thing"; "if it feels good, do it"—in the parlance of the times. The economic libertarians tapped into this spirit by asserting their belief that business should also be allowed to do as it pleases. As Anderson noted,

> Milton Friedman's 1970 manifesto on behalf of shameless greed amounted to a preliminary offer by the philosopher-king of the economic right to forge a grand bargain with the cultural left. Both sides could find common ground concerning ultra-individualism and mistrust of government.[27]

Meanwhile, blocked by New Deal–era antitrust policies that limited horizontal integration, US corporations had been busily diversifying into unrelated industries as a means of maintaining employment growth and job security—key elements of welfare capitalism. ITT, for example, became one of the largest corporations in the world by buying insurance companies, bakeries, auto suppliers, hotel chains, trade schools, copper mines, and hundreds of other businesses. Unfortunately, the pursuit of sales and employment growth via diversification often came at the expense of profits: by the mid-1970s such "conglomerates"—

companies including ITT, United Technologies, Westinghouse, Textron, and even GE—had become chronically undervalued, resulting in prolonged stock market underperformance.[28] Business school academics showed empirically that such unrelated diversification strategies led to sub-par financial performance compared to more focused strategies. Bottom line: conglomerates were usually worth less than the sum of their parts.[29] Welfare capitalism had gone off the rails.

The Arab oil embargo in 1973 created a further opening for neoliberalism by causing oil prices to skyrocket while simultaneously plunging the country into an extended recession, all while the very countries the US helped resurrect from the ashes of World War II—Japan and Germany—presented a growing competitive challenge. The combination of high oil prices, inflation, economic slowdown, and poor stock market performance—a toxic mix called "stagflation"—called the very competence of *government* into serious question for the first time since the 1930s. This perfect storm provided just the opening the neoliberals needed. So, what began as a fringe view among a small group of economists at the University of Chicago grew rapidly starting in the 1970s into an economic ideology that would come to dominate the next four decades: unfettered free markets and shareholder primacy.

With the election of Ronald Reagan in 1980, economic libertarians also had their advocate in the White House. Trust in government had plummeted during the 1970s, fueled by the Vietnam War, Nixon's Watergate scandal, and the inability to tame "stagflation." Reagan was the ideal figure to make neoliberalist, antigovernment rhetoric the policy of the land. He was a charismatic, cowboy-like figure known from his days in television. His friendly way of expressing his disdain for government played right in to the zeitgeist of the times. Indeed, as Reagan famously quipped, "The government is not the solution to our problem, government *is* the problem."

Ayn Rand emerged as the avatar of the neoliberal movement, with her classic novels *The Fountainhead* and *Atlas Shrugged* finally gaining notoriety during the 1980s. Born Alisa Rosenbaum in turn-of-the-century Russia, she witnessed the seizing of her father's successful business by the Bolsheviks "in the name of the people." This experience made an impression that lasted a lifetime—when government invokes lofty ideals about helping others, it is really only a pretext for the use of force to steal hard-earned personal wealth. After her family fled Russia, she eventually came to America on a short-term visa—but knew she was never returning. Adopting the pen name Ayn Rand, she poured her childhood experiences into the melodramatic novels that would ultimately make her famous. The message: individual achievement is everything. Altruism is a dirty word—it is a "weapon of exploitation." Productive individuals—"makers"—lead moral lives because they do not extract resources from others, but instead depend on their own talents to advance. Those on the bottom—"takers"—contribute little but expect to be taken care of in the name of altruism and equity. This message became the anthem of the economic right.[30]

Rand's emotional message jibed perfectly with the apparent analytical rigor of yet another Chicago economist—Arthur Laffer. The so-called "Laffer Curve" was crafted to show how slashing taxes on corporations and the rich would cause them to invest more, thereby accelerating economic growth, and—*voilà*—raise the amount of tax revenue collected by government—a win-win of epic proportion. Laffer's work was parlayed into an entire economic philosophy called "supply-side economics," which formed the foundation for Reagan's economic policy. Critics labeled this approach "trickle-down economics," since the tax and regulation cuts would have had to make business boom and rich people profit so spectacularly that some of that money would actually trickle down to produce jobs and better paychecks for the "little" people. Fueled by a blizzard of supply-side-inspired tax and regulation cuts during Reagan's first term, the neoliberal agenda effectively became national policy.[31]

The Federal Reserve, under the leadership of new chairman Paul Volcker also rolled out a new weapon against inflation: high interest rates. The so-called "Volcker Shock"—double-digit interest rates followed by a sharp double-dip recession—finally mastered the inflation, but also helped ushered in a new era of capitalism. High US interest rates brought a flood of capital into the country, along with a worldwide economic recession. With the Volcker Shock, the US, rather than continuing to be a net exporter of capital and goods, became a net *importer* of capital and the consumer market of first resort for export-led economies such as Japan, Germany, and eventually China.[32]

Given ready availability of capital and credit, there was a speculative investment boom during the 1980s. Unlike previous capitalist reformations, however, under which investment was focused on new technology and productive activity, financiers instead "blew up the post-war industrial corporation and dethroned the managerial class."[33] Indeed, welfare capitalism would undergo a hostile takeover of sorts during the 1980s, and the favored strategy, as it turns out, also happened to be the *hostile takeover*. 1982 proved to be a pivotal year in this regard, with a landmark Supreme Court case, *Edgar v. MITE*, effectively eliminating state laws limiting hostile takeovers. The same year, the SEC reversed its long-standing ban on stock buybacks, allowing corporations to purchase their own stock once again to drive up the stock price.[34]

The proliferation of conglomerates had the unintended consequence of creating the perception that large corporations existed merely to make money, since there was no underlying *business* logic to justify their existence. As a result, conglomerates now faced an existential threat: the so-called "market for corporate control" was increasingly being used to break up these underperforming combines, which represented nearly two-thirds of the Fortune 500 by the late 1970s. Corporate raiders proliferated, in search of undervalued assets. The explosion of "junk" bonds, popularized by Michael Milken, provided a new and trendy way to finance the hostile takeover craze. A whole new financialized lexicon entered common parlance: leveraged buyouts, tender offers, white knights, greenmail, and poison pills.

Shareholder Primacy and "Welchism"

By the early 1980s, significant momentum had been built for the new shareholder-first business philosophy, propelled by, among others, celebrity authors, high-level political support, and financiers thirsty for more raw meat. Yet as *New York Times* columnist David Gelles astutely observes in *The Man Who Broke Capitalism*, no *corporate leader* had yet truly embraced this philosophy. Enter Jack Welch, who took the reins at GE in 1981. With stagflation still rampant and international competition on the rise, Welch decided to take GE— the epitome of the benevolent, postwar industrial employer—in a radical new direction. Through a sustained campaign of cost-cutting (through downsizing, outsourcing, and offshoring) and later, acquisitions, takeovers, and financialization (to drive *earnings growth*), Welch transformed GE into the greatest short-term-profit generator in history—with a singular focus on becoming the world's most valuable company. He pushed the stock price ever higher, at the expense of workers, communities, customers, and innovation, using stock buybacks and "creative" accounting practices as his sword and shield.[35]

Welch became the alpha male for the new shareholder primacy ideology— demonstrating the almost magical ability to consistently hit the numbers, quarter after quarter. He became the first celebrity CEO, spawning dozens of acolytes who went on to perpetrate "Welchism" on such other companies as Boeing, 3M, IBM, Chrysler, Allied Signal, Home Depot, Stanley, Goodyear, Kraft Heinz, and more. Welch became known as "Neutron Jack" for his propensity to "kill" the people in the company but leave the buildings intact. Many of his protégés also went on to earn similar nicknames—"Chainsaw Al" Dunlap at Scott, Larry "The Knife" Bossidy at Allied Signal, and John "The Cutter"

Trani at Stanley, just to name a few.[36] Welchism thus *redefined* how corporations measured success, prioritizing profits for shareholders above all else. Prior to the 1980s, for example, less than *half* of corporate profits went back to investors. By the 2010s, however, that figure ballooned to more than *ninety percent*.[37]

The spirit of late-twentieth-century capitalism was best captured by the signature line of Michael Douglas's character Gordon Gecko in the 1987 movie *Wall Street*: "Greed, for lack of a better word, is good."[38] Over the course of the 1980s, one-third of the largest industrial corporations disappeared through takeovers or mergers. Unlike in prior acquisition waves, however, the 1980s takeovers left the average corporation *smaller* and more focused, with their unrelated parts spun off. The size that mattered now was not revenue or employment, but market capitalization. The age of shareholder capitalism had begun.[39]

Michael Porter's book *Competitive Strategy* became the bible for MBA education across the country, and around the world. Analysis of his famed "five forces"—supplier power, buyer power, threat of entry, threat of substitution, and level of rivalry among firms in an industry—became the path to the "Holy Grail" of building protective "moats" (as Warren Buffett called them) around firms to maximize returns. Porter's techniques for analyzing industries and competitors effectively flipped the work of antitrust lawyers and economists on its proverbial head—the latter to indicate when an industry was becoming too concentrated (requiring antitrust action), and the former to craft strategies for *increasing* market power in the quest for "sustained competitive advantage."[40]

Financial deregulation provided additional jet fuel for the rise of shareholder primacy. The process began in the late 1970s, as the memory of the 1929 Crash and ensuing Great Depression waned in the minds of a new generation of leaders. The creation of 401(k) individual retirement accounts (which enabled company-funded pensions to be slashed) and the dramatic cutting of the capital gains tax early in Reagan's first term were key factors. These two policy shifts created a massive new revenue stream for Wall Street in the form of mutual funds and asset management. With the demise of defined-benefit pensions, Americans became increasingly invested in the stock market through their 401(k)s, with nearly *half* of American households owning stock by the end of the twentieth century. Suddenly, a significant proportion of the general population had become acutely aware of shareholder value—and clamored to maximize it.[41]

Asset appreciation depended on what Reagan called the "magic of the marketplace." Speculation on financial assets depended on transactional liquidity—that there would always be a buyer in a run-up. The guarantor of liquidity was now the Federal Reserve. Under the leadership of new Fed chair Alan Greenspan, the Fed aimed to maintain confidence in the belief that asset values would continue to appreciate, as if "by magical thinking." Because wages were stagnant, debt replaced income growth, with real estate speculation and mortgage refinance increasingly providing the discretionary cash yearned for by working-class households.[42]

The collapse of the Soviet Union in 1991 served only to turbocharge the neoliberal wave, even as a Democrat—Bill Clinton—was elected to presidential office. As Joe Stiglitz noted, the capitalist countries of the West simply could not risk imposing the full force of the neoliberal agenda on the rest of the world during the Cold War because developing countries were being wooed by both the West and the East. With the fall of communism, however, developing countries had nowhere to go so the "Washington consensus" could be imposed on them with impunity. Russia itself fell victim to such "shock therapy" in the 1990s, leading ultimately to the impoverishment of the country and the rise of Putin and the oligarchs.[43]

Eventually, even the venerable Glass-Steagall Act, which was passed in the depths of the Great Depression in 1933 to separate commercial and investment banking, was repealed in the waning days of the Clinton administration. The repeal of Glass-Steagall unleashed a flood of speculation and risk-taking by big banks—subprime mortgages, securitization, derivatives—that culminated in the 2008 financial crisis. The chipping away of New Deal–era regulations on the financial industry was, in many ways, an echo of the tycoons gradually removing the restrictions on corporations during the Gilded Age.[44]

Given its conceptual elegance and swashbuckling allure, the American model of shareholder capitalism rapidly became a global phenomenon. As Steven Pearlstein, in his book *Can American Capitalism Survive?*, makes clear, this brand of capitalism was premised on three axioms, or, perhaps more realistically, assertions: (1) *Government is the problem, not the solution*—only by cutting taxes and eliminating regulations can private investment and risk-taking be unleashed to work their magic; (2) *The purpose and responsibility of business is to maximize profits*—only by focusing on financial returns can management ensure success in an increasingly competitive global marketplace; and (3) *Concerns about environmental impact and inequality can be ignored*—the discipline of the unfettered free market inevitably yields the most efficient and cost-effective strategies, resulting in the greatest good for the greatest number.[45]

Providing the intellectual underpinnings for these axioms or assertions were two prominent theories advanced by economists, starting in the 1960s and gaining prominence during the 1970s and 1980s: the *efficient market hypothesis* and *agency theory*. The first is a theory from the field of financial economics, associated most strongly with Eugene Fama at the University of Chicago, which stated that asset (stock) prices fully incorporate all public and private information, making it virtually impossible to "beat the market."[46] It stemmed from the underlying assumption, accepted by virtually every Chicago-trained economist at the time, that absent interference from the government, the market pretty much gets things right. A corollary to this hypothesis is therefore that stock prices are a valid gauge of a company's true "intrinsic" economic value.[47] In short, a high stock price means that the company is creating high *societal* value, since stock prices include all known information: no need for pesky concerns about environmental impacts or social injustice—they are already incorporated into the stock price.

This "hypothesis" also helped fuel activist investors operating on the assumption that stock price is the best metric around which to measure company success. By implication, the best defense for executives against negative Wall Street feedback (or worse, a hostile takeover), is a high stock price. And the best strategy to drive up stock price is a set of short-term, zero-sum moves such as buying back existing shares, curtailing future research and development spending, reducing capital investments, and cutting or minimizing operating costs (including employee pay). All of these short-term actions paradoxically also serve to diminish the long-term position and sustainability of the firm— literally cutting off the corporate nose to spite its face.

The second theory supporting the rise of shareholder capitalism was agency theory (and its companion, transaction cost economics). This theory constituted a virtual reversal of the 1930s logic of "managerial primacy" articulated by Berle and Means in which principals (owners) *depend* on agents (executives and employees) to serve their interests as a result of distributed stock ownership.[48] Rather than being a positive and stabilizing force, agency theory asserted that "agents" (that is, executives and managers) are selfishly predisposed to feathering their own nests; wasting money on pet projects; and paying too much attention to the needs of employees, customers, and communities rather than to the narrow financial interests of the owners (in this case, presumed to be the shareholders in publicly held companies).

In one of the most highly cited academic business articles of all time, Professors Michael Jensen and William Meckling (both trained at the University of Chicago) reprised the Berle and Means argument regarding separation of ownership and control.[49] They applied the logic of the efficient market: companies whose executives failed to act in shareholders' interests would be punished with lower stock prices, so the job of monitoring executives' behavior could be left to Wall Street.[50] Furthermore, they asserted, the best way to align the interests of executives and shareholders was simply to tie executive compensation to share price. In the ensuing decades, stock-based executive compensation took off to the point at which the average chief executive in the US came to earn more than 350 times the pay of the average worker by 2020, compared to a ratio of only 25:1 in the mid-1960s. Tragically, the ensuing "Covid years" seem to have only exacerbated this problem: CEO pay increased by more than 10 percent from 2021 to 2022, more than double the pace of workers' wage increases.[51]

Beginning in the 1980s, the efficient-market-based approach to business education that originated at Chicago spread to other schools. Welchism and shareholder primacy, as taught at Crotonville—GE's "university"—also increasingly became the norm. US business schools embraced this ideology, with financial economics emerging as the dominant discipline in business education, a unified theory of economic performance: all-knowing financial markets guide investment decisions toward their optimum, and with the proper set of incentives, executives and managers follow this guidance without hesitation.[52] Flush with newly financialized MBAs, Wall Street developed the support infrastructure to aid and abet shareholder capitalism, with legions of analysts, asset managers, investment bankers, and hedge fund managers making predictions and pronouncements about how well companies' management were delivering the expected shareholder returns.

Earnings per share (EPS) and earnings growth became the gold standard. Quarterly earnings reporting to Wall Street became *de rigueur*. Earnings forecasts by analysts were consolidated into "consensus" estimates, known as "the number." Executives and managers knew exactly what performance target to hit. GE, for example, met or exceeded analysts' expectations for earnings growth every quarter for an entire *decade* during the 1990s—delivering outsized shareholder returns in the process. Rather than managing businesses, shareholder capitalism now dictated that executives focus their attention on managing *earnings* instead. Stock buybacks became the favorite management tool for driving up the stock price when needed. What had been banned prior to 1982 now accounted for the vast majority of corporate profits. GE set the all-time record with $50 *billion* in share buybacks in a single year. CEOs who failed to elevate the stock price in accordance with Wall Street's expectations were relegated to the dustbin of senior leadership history.[53]

Shareholder capitalism, powered by neoliberal Reaganomics, appeared to be delivering what Friedman and his followers had promised—a roaring bull market for the better part of twenty years at the close of the twentieth century. It wasn't long, however, before such market fundamentalism led to market extremism: the belief that (1) *All regulation is bad*—the goal is to eliminate (not reform) agencies with oversight responsibility, even if the result is a decline in public trust; (2) *Tax is a dirty word*—the best way to grow financial returns is to cut taxes to the maximum extent possible, especially for the wealthy, since they are believed to be the people who create jobs and employment in the first place, even if the result is growing income and wealth inequality; and (3) *Business exists to maximize shareholder value*—management should do whatever it takes to maximize returns to the preferred class (shareholders), including cutting wages, reducing R&D, squeezing suppliers, outsourcing production, and sometimes (even) screwing customers.[54]

To keep growing returns, companies had to keep getting *bigger*, and acquisitions were the fastest route to the promised land. Beginning in the 1990s, for example, Jack Welch unleashed an M&A boom at GE that would spread across the corporate world and lead industries to become progressively more concentrated and less competitive in the twenty-first century. As David Gelles noted, GE made nearly a *thousand* acquisitions during Welch's tenure as CEO, spending some $130 billion, and divested over four hundred businesses as well. Welch's motto of "fix it, close it, or sell it" meant GE retained only those businesses that were the most profitable in the moment, enabling the company to deliver on its shareholder-first obsession.[55]

Once again, the University of Chicago also had an out-sized influence by effectively changing the course of US antitrust law. While Robert Bork is perhaps best known as the Reagan Supreme Court nominee who was voted down by the Senate in 1987, his real impact was not his jurisprudence but rather the transformational impact he had on industry concentration in America. Bork was a left-wing zealot in his youth, but his time as a student at the University of Chicago during the 1950s resulted in what he described as "a religious conversion."[56] As a graduate student, he worked with Milton Friedman's brother-in-law, Aaron Director, as part of Chicago's Free Market Study. It turns out that this fateful encounter had major implications for the future of capitalism in the decades to follow.

The progenitors of neoliberalism—Hayek, Mises, and even Friedman in the early years—were staunchly *anti*monopolist, since big business held just as much potential to quash individual liberty as big government (as the Founders believed). But the financier of free markets work—the Volker Fund—was unabashedly probusiness, big or otherwise. They convinced Director to shift his view by offering generous financing for a new study focused on antitrust. Eventually the stance of the entire Chicago Economics Department shifted from antimonopolist to antiregulation, marking a sea change in neoliberal thinking.[57]

Since the Gilded Age and the 1890 Sherman Act, America had embraced antitrust as anticoncentration: when corporations became too large, most agreed, they tended to wield too much market power and political influence, crushing smaller players and eliminating competition. Bork and the Chicago economists, however, grew increasingly concerned that antitrust was too "leftish"— too anti-big-business. Rather than launching a direct attack, their genius was to offer a new interpretation of the meaning of antitrust. Bork argued, in one of the most influential articles of the century, that the role of government relative to monopoly wasn't to prevent any single company from getting too large, or even to ensure competitive markets. Instead, it was really about *consumer welfare*— the price the consumer paid. As long as the price was low, there was no need for antitrust enforcement.[58]

The antitrust argument regarding consumer welfare seemed in sync with the emerging consumer movement in the 1960s, driven by Ralph Nader and other consumer advocates. But rather than challenging the behavior of big corporations, Bork flipped the script: Who really cares how corporations behave or how big they get so long as they sell their products cheaply?[59] This Borkian interpretation of antitrust law spawned a whole new field—*law and economics*, led by Chicago-Schooler Henry Manne. With massive funding from the Olin Foundation, centers focused on law and economics were established at prestigious law schools during the 1980s—Harvard, Yale, Stanford, and Virginia. By the end of the 1980s there were more than seventy universities with law and economics programs.[60]

Corporate takeovers and industry concentration were suddenly legitimized—so long as they purported to maximize "economic efficiency" by keeping prices low. As a result, American industries have become steadily more concentrated over the past thirty years: 90 percent of American beer is now brewed by two companies; air travel is controlled by four companies; three companies control the agricultural inputs and seeds market; four megabanks now rule the massive financial services sector; and cable and internet access has become a virtual monopoly, with only one "choice" in most markets.[61] Indeed, as comedian John Oliver noted, even the "sweet escape of death" offers no solace: the coffin industry is now dominated by just two players—Matthews International and Hillenbrand.[62]

Recently, however, a new twist has been added to the monopoly and industry concentration debate: the largest corporations can now be found in the "tech" sector, where platform-based, network effects enable marketplaces connecting buyers and sellers online (for example, Amazon). Platform economics is part of a larger trend of business light-weighting, enabled by widespread availability of cloud services that dramatically reduce investment and transaction costs and barriers to entry. Indeed, information and communication technologies have fundamentally altered the markets for supply chains, labor, and distribution, making it possible to achieve outsized global market reach with very few assets or full-time employees. Zoom, for example, now hosts more than three hundred million videoconferences each day around the world but does so with fewer than five thousand full-time employees and rented server space.[63]

At their peak in 2021, the five tech giants—Apple, Amazon, Alphabet (Google), Microsoft, and Facebook (now Meta)—made up a full 20 *percent* of the total value of the stock market, dominating American business in a way unseen since the days of the railroads and industrial trusts. Despite the post-Covid layoffs that started in 2022, each Big Tech platform still controls different aspects of the economy; they all share one quality—each is a "gatekeeper" over a key digital channel of distribution. Apple monopolizes the mobile app store market; Google owns online search and search advertising; Amazon controls the online retailing market; Microsoft monopolizes the computer operating system market; and Meta is the dominant gateway to social media.[64]

It is déjà vu all over again—the return of the East India Company, the Robber Barons, and the Roaring Twenties, but this time wrapped in mortgage-backed securities, high-priced drugs, cable bills the size of rent payments, clicks, likes, and online followers. The Great Recession in 2008, however, marked a turning point. The $1 trillion bank bailout (Troubled Asset Relief Program) that followed the meltdown showed the awesome power of the finance industry: even though the bankers caused the crisis, the government provided massive largesse to defend the existing institutional structure, and the bankers themselves escaped without any real accountability for the crisis they had created.[65]

For the past decade plus, it has become increasingly clear that neoliberalism has failed to produce a sustainable and inclusive society. Despite the best efforts of incumbent leaders to prop up the current institutions, populism and ethnonationalism have overwhelmed the neoliberal political order. The global pandemic has ushered in a new age of the interventionist state. For capitalism, the implications are also clear: nearly four decades of shareholder capitalism has served mainly to enrich a few, create toxic levels of inequality, disenfranchise deindustrialized communities, create further racial divide, and bring the planet to the brink of environmental and climate meltdown.[66] The end of shareholder primacy is nigh. The question is, what will take its place?

Sustainable Capitalism: Toward a New Operating System

Many have pointed out that the very idea that shareholder capitalism is the dominant form of economic organizing is a figment of our imagination, since the vast majority of business activity still takes place through noncorporate means—sole proprietorships, partnerships, family firms, credit unions, and cooperatives, many focused squarely on community and societal needs. Cooperatives, for example, claim over one billion members globally. Market fundamentalism and shareholder primacy rule only the large, publicly traded corporations of the S&P 500—a small fraction of the millions of commercial entities comprised within the overall economy.[67]

Furthermore, the large public corporation itself is on the decline, with alternative forms of organizing—limited liability companies, for example—becoming more prevalent. While the two hundred largest public corporations reached revenues of over $20 trillion by 2015—nearly one-third of global GDP—the US had less than *half* as many public companies as it did twenty years earlier.[68] The merger and acquisitions boom over the past thirty years has resulted in the evaporation of some four thousand public companies and has made a few companies much bigger and many industries more concentrated.[69]

The *nature* of the public corporation itself is also changing. As Jerry Davis points out in *The Vanishing American Corporation*, the asset and employment intensity of corporations has fallen dramatically over the past two decades. For example, the combined global workforces of Zynga, Zillow, LinkedIn, Uber, Square, and Google—around eighty thousand—are still fewer than Blockbuster Video had in 2005. As Davis wistfully observes, "Corporations used to be social institutions; today they are more like webpages."[70]

Shareholder capitalism has been challenged ever since it gained prominence among large public corporations in the 1980s. As early as 1983, for example, Ed Freeman, in his classic *Strategic Management: A Stakeholder View*, made the case for why effective strategy-making must take account of *all* stakeholders, including employees, customers, suppliers, communities, and the environment—a "rhyme" of Berle and Means's notion of "managerial capitalism" from the 1930s. Klaus Schwab, founder of the World Economic Forum, also argued in the 1980s that companies should not put shareholders first, but instead needed to account for their impact on workers, the environment, and society at large. The stakeholder view of the firm has steadily grown ever since, providing an increasingly powerful counternarrative to the gospel of shareholder primacy.[71]

Even during the "Roaring 1990s"—the peak of market fundamentalism—cracks in the facade were clearly evident: the 1992 Rio Earth Summit unveiled a new strategy for decoupling negative environmental impact from economic and business growth—eco-efficiency.[72] Shortly thereafter, Paul Hawken published his pioneering book *The Ecology of Commerce*; John Elkington unveiled the concept of the "triple bottom line"; and my article on "beyond greening" first appeared in *Harvard Business Review*.[73] Strategies for waste and emission reduction, pollution prevention, product stewardship, and clean technology effectively shattered the perceived trade-off between financial and environmental performance. No longer would the shopworn logic of "externalities" rule the day, since it was now demonstrably clear that in many cases eco-efficiency actually *saved* money and reduced risks, rather than driving up costs.[74]

What's more, the emerging field of *behavioral economics* has all but destroyed the idea of efficient markets, beginning with the groundbreaking work on "prospect theory" by psychologists Daniel Kahneman and Amos Tversky, demonstrating that human decision making falls far short of rational optimizing.[75] Yale economist Robert Shiller further demonstrated the many ways in which financial markets are influenced by irrational behavior and a "herd mentality" on the part of investors.[76] George Soros made his fortune betting *against* efficient markets. Indeed, Soros's thesis of "reflexivity" stated that financial markets cannot be perfectly efficient because prices are reflections of the ignorance and biases of millions of investors.[77]

Richard Thaler largely confirmed Soros's assertions by finding that "noise" introduced by uninformed traders keeps stock prices away from their "intrinsic" values, making investment returns possible.[78] George Akerlof and Rachel Kranton have even shown the ways in which identity and social norms guide economic behavior, affecting how hard people work and what they aspire to.[79] Even Michael Jensen has had a change of heart when it comes to agency theory. By the early 2000s, he acknowledged that stock incentives for executives were not enough by themselves: if executives and managers failed to behave with *integrity*, markets could not work efficiently—a rhyme with none other than Adam Smith![80]

Justin Fox put all these matters in perspective in *The Myth of the Rational Market*; he observed that the efficient market hypothesis and agency theory arose toward the end of a long era of relative market stability—what I have called the age of welfare capitalism—characterized by tight government regulation and enduring memories of the Great Depression. Ironically, it may have been this relative calm, an artifact of a regulated financial era, that paved the way for the deregulation and wild exuberance of the past four decades. In the spirit of Jungian Enantiodromia, perhaps extreme market fundamentalism has now sown the seeds of its own demise.[81]

The 2008 financial crisis only served to deepen the concerns about shareholder capitalism's penchant to create losers and exacerbate inequality. My book *Capitalism at the Crossroads*, published at the height of this crisis, chronicled the transformation that had occurred over the past five decades—from "command and control" regulation in the 1970s–1980s to pollution prevention and product stewardship in the 1990s–2000s to the current realization that more transformational strategies in clean or regenerative technology and inclusive or base-of-the-pyramid business will be required. Indeed, the book set forth a strategic logic for how these challenges associated with sustainability—climate change, environmental degradation, poverty, and inequality—can be converted into business strategies that reduce cost, enhance reputation, build new competencies, and create new markets.[82]

Most recently, the Sustainable Development Goals (SDGs) have starkly revealed the scale and scope of the social and environmental problems faced by the world. The SDGs make clear that incrementalism will no longer suffice. What is required is innovation on a scale that we have not previously experienced. It has become increasingly evident that business will need to step up to the plate—to serve as the catalytic force needed to kick the larger system—including government—into a new gear.[83]

A chorus of voices has also directly questioned the logic and legitimacy of shareholder primacy.[84] In 2006, these mounting critiques spawned the rise of a new business management model—the B Corp—a certification that requires that companies undergo a rigorous review process, overseen by B Lab, and commit to putting social benefits, rights of workers, community impact, and environmental stewardship on equal footing with financial shareholders. There are now over four thousand certified B Corps around the world, and thirty-five states in the US have now passed statutes creating a new legal form—the benefit corporation—based upon this management philosophy.[85]

But perhaps Marjorie Kelly, the cofounder of *Business Ethics* magazine, expressed this perspective best in her pathbreaking book *The Divine Right of Capital*: just as the divine right of kings gave way to democracy in the political sphere, so capitalism must evolve to incorporate the rights of all the key stakeholders, breaking the chains of "economic feudalism." Where would corporations be without their employees in today's knowledge economy? Aren't suppliers crucial partners when it comes to creating quality products and services? Don't corporations depend on an educated public and public infrastructure to conduct business? Shouldn't these key stakeholders share in corporations' success?[86]

We already saw how the advent of distributed stock ownership during the 1920s meant that shareholders no longer played a direct role in the management of public corporations. This trend has only increased over the past forty years with the advent of 401(k)s, and more than half of Americans now owning stock.[87] Holding periods for stock ownership have also become progressively shorter, due at least in part to the rise of automated and electronic investing. During the 1950s, for example, the average stock holding period was eight years, whereas today, the average investor holds shares for less than *six months*. In a very real sense then, shareholders today should more accurately be referred to as *share-traders*.[88]

Furthermore, the bulk of small investors' money is now managed by a new class of powerful players—asset and wealth managers. We have moved from an "ownership" society to an "intermediation" society with managers of endowment, pension, and mutual funds wielding outsized influence over corporations themselves, given the scale of their investments in any given company.[89]

As Amy Klobuchar points out in her book *Antitrust*, horizontal shareholding by big institutional players gives them a disproportionate share of the power in controlling firm behavior. As of 2016, for example, just three players—BlackRock, Vanguard, and State Street—controlled 95 percent of all index fund assets, meaning that just a handful of Wall Street portfolio managers now have large financial stakes in the very same corporations, a prescription for anticompetitive conduct.[90] Quite literally then, today's shareholders command first preference on returns even though, as Berle and Means observed, they "manage not, invest not, nor do they accept liability." This leads to the question, What value do public equities *really* add to today's corporations beyond liquidity for stockholders?

The late Lynn Stout of Cornell Law School supplied the answer to this question with her searing indictment of shareholder primacy in her 2012 book *The Shareholder Value Myth*. Stout examined the empirical evidence for shareholder primacy. The result: there is no consistent connection between investor returns and shareholder-oriented governance structures and business practices.[91] On the contrary, there is substantial evidence to show that firms run according to the logic of shareholder value maximization *underperform* more purpose-driven firms, especially when *long-term* financial performance is the criterion.[92]

A mountain of evidence makes it clear that short-termism and shareholder primacy simply don't work. In the long run, companies that pursue such strategies run themselves into the ground. According to Jensen and Meckling, CEOs were supposed to be agents working on behalf of shareholders to maximize their returns. But decades of excessive executive compensation and gargantuan "golden parachutes" have perverted the incentives in the C-suite. Despite Jack Welch's twenty-year streak of delivering above-market returns, shareholder primacy ultimately destroyed GE: the company fell into a spiral of decline in the 2000s, eventually becoming the *worst* performer in the Dow Jones Industrial Average before coming to its ignominious end in 2021 when company executives decided to break it apart, takeover-style.[93]

As we look ahead, there can be little doubt that shareholder capitalism is under siege and will require wholesale reinvention. History shows us that capitalist reformation is not only possible—it has happened twice before—but inevitable. There is thus nothing whatsoever preordained about shareholder primacy. Yet serious questions remain regarding the focus and trajectory of the next capitalist reformation. Will the reformation happen in time, before we eclipse critical environmental thresholds or experience irreversible societal unraveling? Will the change be sufficiently deep and fundamental to enable a new era defined by sustainable capitalism to emerge?

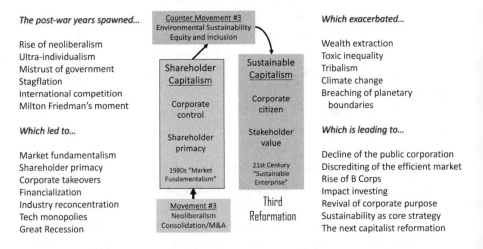

Exhibit 2.1. The Next Capitalist Reformation

Where Do We Go from Here?

While it is certainly true that capitalism emerged in the throes of the New World gold rush fueled by the transatlantic slave trade, the good news is that each new capitalist movement and ensuing reformation has tended to produce comparatively *less* extraction and exploitation, and *more* positive value than the last: our "better angels" seem to be gradually gaining ground on our "animal spirits." To paraphrase (and adapt) a famous phrase attributed to Martin Luther King: the arc of capitalist history is long, but it appears to bend toward sustainability.

As Chapter 1 made clear, mercantile capitalism was state-sponsored imperialism and exploitation—witness India's decline between 1700 and 1950—with the American Revolution and market capitalism representing important turning points for economic and political liberty. And monopoly capitalism, despite its exploitation of labor, rampant pollution, and monopolist profiteering, provided much needed infrastructure, materials, energy, mobility, and, eventually, consumer goods to an urbanizing mass market. Welfare capitalism then redefined the "objective function" for what constituted success for these large corporations, beginning in the 1930s. So there is every reason to believe that the excesses of today's shareholder capitalism can once again be brought to heel.

Francis Fukuyama's claim notwithstanding, the fall of communism, the triumph of neoliberalism, and the rise of American-style shareholder capitalism in the late 1980s and early 1990s were clearly *not* the ultimate forms of political and economic organization—the end of history.[94] On the contrary, the fall of communism *globalized* and *weaponized* capitalism in a way it had not been since before World War I, when the British dominated a liberal world order and America was in the grip of monopoly capitalism. Gone was the need to provide a "fair deal" for the working and middle classes to prevent the advance of communism. It was no coincidence that the height of welfare capitalism also coincided with the height of the Cold War.[95]

After the fall of the Soviet Union in 1991, the neoliberal political order in the US had license to dismantle the labor movement, welfare state, and regulatory apparatus—the institutions built during the New Deal era to tame the harshest aspects of capitalism. The Washington consensus then spread the ethic of free trade; deregulation; and the free movement of capital, goods, and people around the world. "Opening up" in China jibed perfectly with the emerging neoliberal world order, enabling it to become the new "Workshop to the World," riding the wave of offshoring and outsourcing that rose to prominence in the late twentieth century. The Friedman Doctrine of profit maximization and shareholder primacy became a "Holy Grail," replacing welfare capitalism with shareholder capitalism. "Welchism" became the dominant operating system for business.

Unfortunately, four decades of shareholder capitalism has made America the most unequal developed country in the world and aided and abetted a mounting climate crisis. We have also stumbled our way through a series of crises since neoliberalism and shareholder primacy took command in the 1980s: Third World debt crisis; Savings and Loan crisis; 1987 stock market crash; September 11th attacks and subsequent War on Terror; 2008 financial crisis; and most recently, the coronavirus pandemic, a racial reckoning, and the storming of the US Capitol.

The 2008 Great Recession inflicted a mortal wound on the neoliberal order. The rise of Donald Trump and Bernie Sanders during the mid-2010s marked its official demise, with each attacking free trade and free markets from the right and left, respectively. A one-term Trump presidency followed by the election of Joe Biden reflected the ambivalence of our time. Would democracy and inclusion prevail or would ethnonationalism and authoritarianism win out? The former could help usher in a new age of sustainable capitalism; the latter could spell conflict and climate disaster. Paulo Gerbaudo labeled this time the "Great Recoil"—a moment of necessary retreat before moving forward in a new way.[96] Antonio Gramsci described such periods as *interregnums*—times when "the old is refusing to die and the new cannot yet be born."[97]

While neoliberalism in politics has increasingly been overtaken by an emerging form of neostatism, shareholder primacy unfortunately still reigns supreme in business and economics, and industry concentration continues apace. Witness the price gouging, profiteering, and continuing share buybacks by corporations under the cover of the inflation that gripped the world in the wake of the coronavirus pandemic. ExxonMobil's gross profit for the quarter ending September 30, 2022, was $33.969 billion, a 94.85 percent increase year-over-year—far in excess of inflation.[98] Indeed, executives from a range of industries—banking, airlines, hotels, consumer goods, and others—have said the quiet part out loud: consumers have the money to spend and can therefore tolerate higher prices, even prices well above their own inflation-driven costs.[99] Stagflation killed the New Deal political order and welfare capitalism in the 1970s. Will the pandemic-driven inflation spiral and (possible) global recession signal the end of shareholder capitalism in the 2020s?

The bottom line is that shareholder capitalism has made it exceedingly difficult for corporations to behave like the social institutions they are capable of being. The current situation is strikingly similar to the 1930s, when economic catastrophe followed a period of unbridled free-market capitalism. It took a New Deal and a world war to defeat fascism and usher in a new age of welfare capitalism. Will similarly monumental forces by governments be required once again to steer the world away from authoritarianism, corporatism, and environmental oblivion? Can capitalism be remade once again to address the rising tide of social discontent and environmental crises that we now face? Can a different narrative "myth" help change the prime directive and forge the new "operating system" needed to drive sustainable capitalism? What are the leverage points for achieving the necessary corporate and system transformations? Are there lessons we can glean from the past cycles of capitalist reformation that will help us galvanize another reinvention of this venerable institution—this time in a way that is inclusive, just, net positive, even restorative? These questions are the topic of the next chapter, and the balance of the book.

THREE

History Rhymes

ENDURING LESSONS FOR TODAY

As Mark Twain once observed, "History does not repeat itself, but it often rhymes." And so it has been with the evolution of capitalism over the centuries. As we have seen, there is something eerily familiar about each of the three "Enantiodromia Cycles" of capitalism described in the previous chapters: each cycle begins with a significant organizational and financial innovation: Think *joint-stock trading companies, industrial trusts,* and *shareholder-driven corporations.* These organizational innovations then become institutionalized as part of a larger political and economic order—mercantilism and mercantile capitalism, liberalism and monopoly capitalism, and neoliberalism and shareholder capitalism.

As the scope and influence of these new capitalist forms grow, however, they tend toward concentration, monopoly power, and extractive profit maximization—at the expense of society and the environment. Such unfettered release of our "animal spirits" then typically generates a rising tide of resistance, reasserting the voices of excluded or negatively impacted stakeholders such as small business, labor, the poor, minorities, communities, and the environment.

New forms of enterprise then emerge that aim to harness our "better angels" by redressing the shortcomings of the dominant capitalist model through innovation, inclusion, and mutuality: think *invisible hand, corporations as institutions,* and, most recently, *sustainable business.* These innovations also become institutionalized as part of a larger political and economic order—market economy and market capitalism, New Deal and welfare capitalism, and perhaps just emerging—new statism and sustainable capitalism. The "reformed" model then becomes the norm for some period until a new capitalist movement overtakes the reformed approach, and the cycle begins again (Exhibit 3.1).

Perhaps not surprisingly, those capitalist forms that resulted in extraction, exploitation, and overreach were typically characterized by a philosophy of *shareholder primacy*, be they trading companies, industrial trusts, or today's financialized corporations. It was only during periods of shareholder *subordinacy* that reformers harnessed the power of capitalism to produce more positive societal outcomes: entrepreneurship, democratization, and a rising middle class. Today's struggle to reimagine a more inclusive and sustainable form of capitalism is just the latest manifestation of this ongoing dynamic. The good news is that, in the grand sweep of history, the periods of shareholder primacy (when "animal spirits" rule) appear to be shrinking in length compared to the periods when shareholder subordinacy—and our "better angels"—predominate: mercantile capitalism lasted hundreds of years and monopoly capitalism for nearly a century, whereas shareholder capitalism has dominated now for only about four decades. Perhaps the arc of capitalist history really *does* bend toward sustainability and inclusion. Only time will tell.

We have also seen the importance of sociopolitical upheavals as inflection points when it comes to the three capitalist reformations—the American Revolution, the Great Depression, and World War II—and now (perhaps), the coro-

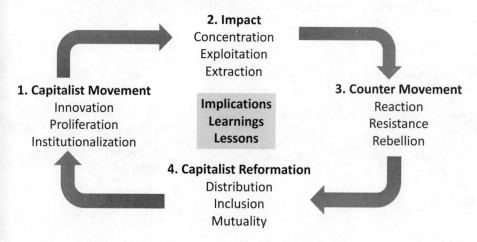

Exhibit 3.1. Capitalism Reformation Cycles

navirus pandemic, racial reckoning, and threats to democracy, in catalyzing change. Exhibit 3.2 summarizes these dynamics for each capitalist reformation, emphasizing the importance of both the *intellectual catalyst*—the source of conceptualization for the transformation—and the *motive force* needed to bring about the transformational change—what John Kenneth Galbraith dubbed as "countervailing power."[1]

For the previous two capitalist reformations, both the intellectual catalysts and the motivating forces were strong, undeniable, and widely shared by the relevant populations. For example, while the work of Adam Smith and Enlightenment thinking, which underpinned the American Revolution, was known only to a relatively small group of educated founders and patriots, the cause of independence from British domination and the yoke of the East India Company was widely shared among the populace. Similarly, while progressivism and the work of John Maynard Keynes may have provided the intellectual basis for trust-busting and the reassertion of governmental power, the widening gap between rich and poor, combined with the impact of the Great Depression, provided a groundswell of public support for the reinvention of capitalism that occurred during the 1930s and in the wake of World War II.

It is also important to note that, in each of the two previous cycles, government played a crucial role in redefining the rules of the game in favor of greater participation, equity, and social responsibility. As economic historian Carlota Perez notes, it typically takes two to three decades for the initial frenzy and disruption of new technological regimes—mechanization, electrification, computerization—to give way to widely shared prosperity, and that occurs only after the establishment of an adequate *socio-institutional* framework.[2]

Exhibit 3.2. History Rhymes

We are now in the midst of the third age of capitalist reformation, turbo-charged by the coronavirus pandemic and its associated societal and economic disruptions. Neoliberalism may be fatally wounded, but its corporate alter ego—shareholder primacy—still rules. Nonetheless, something new *is* clearly emerging—a form of neostatism that calls for stronger government intervention in the economy to protect society. Two competing forms of neostatism have arisen with radically different visions for the future:

- On the right is a populist movement that leans toward authoritarianism focused on restricting trade and immigration, hardening borders, and defending national "purity."

- On the left is a popular democratic movement focused on confronting the world's existential challenges—climate change, environmental degradation, inequality, human rights, social justice—through a "next generation" version of Keynesian interventionism.[3]

The question is, which form will prevail? Can popular support for climate justice, clean energy, social inclusion, and democracy prevail over a rising tide of ethnonationalism, authoritarianism, and minority rule? Can a new sustainable capitalism, one that puts positive societal impact first, outcompete the continued tyranny of shareholder primacy backed by a corporatist state that is complicit in further industry concentration, climate denial, and profiteering?

I believe the past cycles of capitalist reformation offer important and enduring lessons for how to design a capitalist system that delivers an inclusive and sustainable set of societal outcomes. Drawing upon Chapters 1 and 2, I'll address here four key lessons that emerge from the past five hundred years of capitalist pursuit and suggest how we can carry them forward into the third capitalist reformation in which we are currently engaged.

First, I'll trace the historical distinction between *self-interest* and *selfishness* and discuss why the former must take precedence in our current efforts to reinvent capitalism once again. Second, I'll explore the evolution of thinking regarding the separation of ownership and control of large corporations (*agency*) and how an emphasis upon *stewardship* by corporate management must once again predominate over the assumption that managers are self-serving, opportunistic free agents. Third, I'll discuss the historical tendency for capitalist systems to careen toward concentration and *monopoly* control and why this tendency must be overcome if we are to realize the benefits of a *market* system and the promise of sustainable capitalism. Last, I'll examine the historical debate between *reinvestment* of profits versus *extraction* of wealth and why the former is essential if the promise of the profit motive is to truly deliver societal benefits. I'll then close with some thoughts on historical analogues to our present times and how they might inform the unique challenges we face moving forward.

Self-Interest Versus Selfishness

Advocates for today's American-style shareholder capitalism often invoke Adam Smith's famous proposition in the *Wealth of Nations* that the pursuit of self-interest leads to the common good. As we saw, "greed is good" became the battle cry for the neoliberalist revolution in the 1980s, which ushered in an almost religious belief in the rational nature of economic actors and the efficiency of unfettered free markets. Of course, neoliberal thinking also drew heavily upon the work of earlier economists, dating back to the era of British-led liberalism in the late nineteenth century.

It turns out, however, that the entire neoliberal edifice of market fundamentalism, the pursuit of self-interest, and shareholder primacy is constructed on a series of faulty foundations. First, the modern rhetoric about the "invisible hand" represents a fundamental misreading of what Adam Smith and other classical political philosophers were really trying to communicate. His work needs to be understood in the broader context of the Enlightenment thinking of his time. Second, the nineteenth-century economists who converted Smith's classical work on political economy into the mathematically based science of neoclassical economics premised their models on a set of assumptions that simply do not pass the smell test: people are not rational, utility-maximizing machines, and economies are not closed, equilibrium-seeking systems. Finally, Milton Friedman and the Chicago School economists who drove the ascent of neoliberalism beginning in the 1970s took the neoclassical work to new heights of mathematical sophistication and scientific rigor. Unfortunately, the idealized theories and unrealistic assumptions that underpinned this work have meant that the modern era of shareholder capitalism is built on little more than a house of cards. Allow me to elaborate.

CLASSICAL GAS: THE INVISIBLE HAND UP

As we saw in Chapter 1, Adam Smith's first use of the phrase "invisible hand" appeared not in the *Wealth of Nations* but rather in his earlier and deeper work focused on moral philosophy, *The Theory of Moral Sentiments*. He used the phrase to describe what he saw as man's natural instinct to "share the fruits of communal labor" rather than his more infamous observation that the pursuit of self-interest in a competitive market economy can have the positive unintended consequence of increasing the wealth of everyone. The very first sentence of *Moral Sentiments* clearly makes this point:

> How selfish soever man may be supposed, there are evidently some princi-ples in his nature which interest him in the fortunes of others, and render their happiness necessary for him, though he derives nothing from it except the pleasure of seeing it.

Rather than ascribing such selflessness to altruism or benevolence, Smith instead posits that human behavior is driven by an imaginary interaction with what he calls the "Impartial Spectator"—a fellow human being who is look-ing over our shoulders who sees the morality of our actions clearly. If we harm others in order to benefit ourselves, we will be resented and disliked by anyone who is looking on impartially.[4]

These ideas about moral behavior and virtue were part of a larger shift in religious and theological thinking during the eighteenth century. As noted in Chapter 1, the growing rejection of orthodox Calvinism—the original religion of the Puritans—with its dark presumptions of human depravity, predestina-tion, and eternal damnation, opened up new avenues for human agency and good works. More "moderate" Protestants preached that humans' inborn be-nevolence and sociability (rather than depravity), including a desire for the approval of others, fostered moral and virtuous behavior—and eventual sal-vation. It is perhaps no coincidence, for example, that Jonathan Mayhew, an early leader of the "natural theology" movement in America, used language strikingly similar to Smith a full decade prior to his first book. For Mayhew, "God himself is a *Spectator* in this theatre of the universe." The desire for God's approval was thus the most powerful human motivation, offering the prospect of the greatest satisfaction to every person.[5]

Smith's optimistic ideas about how the pursuit of self-interest in a market economy can promote the greater good were thus steeped in the religious zeit-geist of the times. The "cultural soil"—the milieu that a philosopher or scientist lives in—profoundly affects the nature of their thinking. As Albert Einstein observed, "The worldview comes first and the scientific ideas follow from it." Given Adam Smith's post as a professor of moral philosophy at Glasgow Uni-versity, where he regularly interacted with educated elites including clergy, merchants, medical doctors, scientists, and artists, it should come as little surprise that his ideas about market economies and the wealth of nations were part of the more general worldview of the time.[6]

If we widen the aperture even further, it is evident that Smith's ideas about self-interest were embedded in a rich tapestry of thinking that was the Enlightenment. Whereas Hobbes asserted the importance of government in controlling what he saw as man's natural tendency to pursue his urges, appetites, and impulses for short-term gratification (more consistent with the idea of "selfishness"), other well-known Enlightenment thinkers of the time—particularly Locke and Spinoza—emphasized *virtue* when it came to the pursuit of happiness.[7] When the Founding Fathers spoke of "virtue," it was not as we understand the term today, involving personal probity or kindness. For them, virtue meant concern for the *common good*. Indeed, without a virtuous citizenry, they feared the young republic would succumb to authoritarian rule.[8]

It is no coincidence that Jefferson insisted on the phrase "life, liberty and the pursuit of *happiness*" in the Declaration of Independence. Evidence points to the heavy influence of Locke and Spinoza in the development of Jefferson's (and other Founders') thinking. Locke and Spinoza, in turn, were part of a revival of the work of the Greek philosopher Epicurus.[9] Epicurean philosophy espoused the doctrine of *hedonism*—the pursuit of happiness as life's primary aim. The vehicle for achieving happiness was virtue—living a moderate, just, and honest life. Virtue led to peace of mind and a clear conscience, the essence of happiness. Private vice and public corruption—acting on selfish urges and impulses—actually represented a *betrayal* of one's true self.[10]

Only through the pursuit of greater understanding—of self and others— could true happiness be achieved. Epicurus also believed that morality was self-generated, not imposed by a higher power through moral or religious "obligations." Enlightenment philosophers influenced by Epicurean ethics therefore emphasized that virtuous behavior could lead to happiness in *this* life, versus the Christian teaching that such behavior would only be rewarded in the next. Not surprisingly, Epicureanism became the enemy of the Church, which falsely associated hedonism with the pursuit of decadence, gluttony, and promiscuity, a misinterpretation that persists to this day.[11]

The work of Locke and Spinoza also dovetailed with the more "scientific" Enlightenment thinking of their contemporaries—Bacon, Descartes, and Newton. It was not long before a new synthesis emerged—Deism—that blended moral and natural philosophy. Deism arose in Britain around the end of the seventeenth century and arrived in America as the Founders came of age. Deists believed not only that virtue led to happiness, but also that piety was best demonstrated through the study of natural phenomenon—that the pursuit of science and inquiry revealed an understanding of what they referred to as "Nature's God"—the laws governing the universe set down by the creator. The fact that the Declaration of Independence explicitly refers to "the Laws of Nature" and "Nature's God" strongly suggests that America's Founders—particularly Jefferson—were not only Epicureans, but also Deists.[12]

Enlightenment thinkers recognized that the pursuit of self-interest was really a team sport—that banding together in cooperative unity enabled humans to achieve unparalleled feats. They recognized that our species rose to the top of the food chain primarily because of our ability to *cooperate*, not because we could compete against other top predators one on one. Indeed, for tens of thousands of years, humans lived in groups as hunter-gatherers, utterly dependent upon each other for survival. Intelligence and language enabled communication and collaboration, such that the whole was far greater than the sum of the parts. Our big brains required that babies be born small and helpless, requiring years of nurturing prior to maturation. As Hillary Clinton famously observed, "it takes a village" to raise a human child.

Historian Yuval Harari took this a step further in his classic work *Sapiens*: he noted that what truly set humans apart from other species was not just their ability to communicate through language—monkeys, whales, and elephants, for example, also have impressive language and communication skills—but rather the ability to convey *narratives*—practical information about relationships and trust (what he called "gossip"), as well as more abstract ideas in the form of legends, myths, and religion. Gossip enabled humans to bond in stable, relationship-rich groups of up to 150 people with little in the way of formal structure or discipline—the size limit of a typical hunter-gatherer "tribe." Humans managed to overcome this limit, however, founding cities and empires comprising tens of thousands of inhabitants. Such large numbers of *strangers* could cooperate successfully only by believing in what Harari called "fictions"—common myths, narratives, legends, religions, and ideologies.[13]

This uniquely human ability to create imagined realities out of words is in fact what enables many of today's large organizations to function. Witness the corporation: it is no coincidence that lawyers described such entities as "legal fiction." Even though the term derives from the Latin *corpus* (meaning "body"), corporations actually have no physical presence, office buildings and factories notwithstanding. Revenues, profits, share prices, and earnings per share are all abstractions—social constructions—that we have created. They exist only in our imaginations. Indeed, as Lord Edward Thurlow observed in the eighteenth century, corporations have "no soul to damn and no body to kick." Yet today they are considered "legal persons," paying taxes (sometimes) and able to sue and be sued.[14]

In a very real sense, then, human society and culture are totally dependent on cooperation, collaboration, and shared identity. Yet, as we will see, modern economics is based on a caricature of human behavior that is completely misguided—and totally despicable. The "economic man" (*homo economicus*) of modern economics is selfish, greedy, and lazy—a cold, calculating utility-maximizer, seeking to gain the most with the least amount of effort. While such people do exist, we would probably consider them to be sociopaths. Fortunately, most people are actually social beings, neither *homo economicus* nor altruistic saints. We crave esteem and belonging, and these drive our behavior as much as material gain. As Paul Collier notes in *The Future of Capitalism*, people are better described by the term "social man." Social (wo)man is still rational—he (or she) seeks to maximize utility—but his or her utility function is far more multidimensional.[15]

Adam Smith's classical concepts of self-interest and the invisible hand must therefore be understood in this broader context. He stressed, for example, that the "Impartial Spectator" allows us to bring the quality of "sympathy" to our decisions—the ability to put ourselves in someone else's shoes (what we would today call empathy). He urged us not only to seek to be loved, but also to be *lovely*—to earn the respect and appreciation of others. When we earn the admiration of others by being honorable, generous, and kind, the end result is . . . wait for it . . . *happiness*. Indeed, as Russ Roberts perceptively notes, the caricature of Smith as the "Scottish forerunner of Ayn Rand," who in addition to *Atlas Shrugged* also wrote a book titled *The Virtue of Selfishness*, could not be further from the truth.[16]

Self-interest is thus *not* the same thing as selfishness: Smith's invisible hand is really about offering an invisible hand *up*. Happiness and self interest do not mean just doing whatever you like, others be damned. True happiness means having both liberty and justice at the *same time*, which requires a well-developed sense of personal responsibility: wear a mask; make the extra pass; and perhaps most important for business, find your "Impartial Spectator," behave with virtue, and win the admiration of *all* your stakeholders.

NEOCLASSICAL QUANTIFICATION: THE PHYSICS OF ECONOMICS

The "classical" work done by eighteenth-century moral and political philosophers such as Adam Smith left a well-developed conceptual framework for the functioning of a market economy. In addition to Smith's contributions, David Hume and David Ricardo provided a logic for free trade; Jacques Turgot added what would come to be known as the "law of diminishing returns" based upon his observation that farmers' efforts to raise productivity realized less gain for each additional unit of irrigation or fertilizer applied; Jeremy Bentham also helped to operationalize Smith's idea of self-interest by theorizing that people aim to increase pleasure and reduce pain by maximizing "utility" in their decision making. This insight would evolve into what came to be called "utilitarianism"—pursuing the greatest good for the greatest number.[17]

The classical economists' work was premised on a "labor" theory of value— that economic value is created when raw materials are turned into something people want through the work performed. Any surplus created by increasing the productivity of labor should, according to Smith, be reinvested in more production rather than "wasted" on luxuries and "unproductive consumption." I'll address this more later in this chapter. Classical thinkers had clear disdain for those who extracted "unearned income" from the system (for example, bankers, rentiers) but they never directly addressed how labor itself should be appropriately compensated.[18]

With the rise of the First Industrial Revolution and the factory system in the nineteenth century, the labor theory of value came under increasing scrutiny, led by thinkers such as Karl Marx and Friedrich Engels. If labor produced value, they asked, then why were laborers continuing to live in poverty and destitution? If financiers did not create value (as Smith asserted) then how did they become so rich? With such "socialist" critiques on the rise, a new generation of economists, steeped in mathematics, began laying the foundation for a new theory of value—and a more "scientific" approach to the topic. According to this new conceptualization, value was no longer associated with the actual amount of labor committed, but rather was determined by market preferences. Value, in other words, came to be determined *subjectively*, through the price paid by buyers in the market.[19]

This new subjective conception of value was like a hand into a glove for the mathematically inclined economic thinkers of the nineteenth century— Leon Walras, William Jevons, and Alfred Marshall. Drawing upon the classical concept of "diminishing returns," the new-breed economists were able to apply differential calculus to model the behavior of markets. Calculus enabled them to focus on how small ("marginal") changes in one variable (such as price) marginally affected another—the quantity of a product demanded or supplied. Marginal analysis came to provide the conceptual foundation for what is known today as "neoclassical" economics: the price point where the marginal cost of production equals the marginal benefit of buyer utility establishing the "equilibrium" point for the market.[20]

As Mark Carney astutely observed, this combination of subjectivism and marginalism changed perceptions of value from a focus on the *intrinsic* characteristics of goods and services to their *exchange* value—the price in the market. In so doing, the significance of such issues as income distribution and the distinction between productive and nonproductive activities—so important in classical thinking—were downplayed, thereby devaluing considerations of corporate purpose or national ideals.[21]

Neoclassical economists were heavily influenced by developments in the physical sciences, particularly physics. Marshall, for example, borrowed from Newtonian physics to develop his theory of market equilibrium, an idea analogous to Newton's theory of how gravity holds the universe together. Free trade and comparative advantage were seen as living manifestations of harmony in the universe—part of "God's balance."[22] Indeed, the importation of physics concepts such as "balance," "optimum," and "equilibrium" into the neoclassical model had the effect of portraying capitalism as a calm, peaceful system driven by self-regulating competitive mechanisms—a stark contrast to the labor strife and class struggle actually taking place. The shift from a labor theory of value to a price theory of value thus coincided with the major societal disruptions stemming from the Industrial Revolution in the nineteenth century.[23]

The fascination with physics went even further. Walras, for example, explicitly sought to create a "scientific theory of the economy" analogous to astronomers' modeling of the solar system. Similarly, Jevons aspired to establish a science of economics "as predictable as gravity." Iconic twentieth-century economists including Paul Samuelson and Kenneth Arrow continued in this tradition by formulating even more elegant mathematical models, culminating in the neoclassical theory of general equilibrium for the economy as a whole.[24]

To make the equilibrium math work, however, stringent assumptions were required regarding the behavior of both the economy and people. Beginning with Walras and Jevons, for example, arbitrary assumptions had to be made about human behavior—perfect rationality, pursuit of narrow self-interest, and access to complete information. The more sophisticated the economic models became, the more stringent the simplifying assumptions—an unfortunate case of the tail wagging the dog.

Importing these concepts and mathematical methods from physics into economics has actually proved to be apocryphal: it has now become increasingly evident that people don't behave as utility-maximizing robots nor do markets typically have a single price that "balances" supply and demand. In fact, markets in the real world are almost never in equilibrium. The quest to turn economics into physics has ended up setting the field on the wrong course for over a century.[25]

NEOLIBERAL DOGMA: THE HOUSE OF CARDS

The rise of Milton Friedman and the Chicago School of economics beginning in the 1970s took neoclassical economics to a whole new level. *Homo economicus* was no longer just a simplifying assumption in a mathematical model, but rather, a positive role model. Corporate raiders became cultural icons, akin to the larger-than-life heroes of the Old West. Investors became laser-focused on short-term returns and maximizing shareholder value, often to the detriment of such other core constituencies as employees, suppliers, communities, and even customers. Business school became a glorified game of "show me the money," with program success measured more by the starting salaries of graduates than what they learned. Neoliberalism infused the air with the overwhelming scent of "What's in it for me?" Selfishness, individualism, and greed had been put on a pedestal while mutuality, cooperation, and integrity were relegated to the ranks of do-gooders, tree-huggers, and "socialists."

Friedman also took the field of economics in a direction that was increasingly divorced from reality. Faced with growing criticism of the increasingly unrealistic assumptions being used in economic theory, Friedman argued that the assumptions do not matter, so long as the theories make correct predictions. In other words, if the economy behaves "as if" people were perfectly rational and motivated by narrow self-interest, then it doesn't matter whether people really are or not.[26] Yet as Herbert Simon noted, the purpose of science is not simply to make predictions, but rather to *understand* and *explain* how things work; predictions simply test whether such explanations are valid.[27]

A growing body of work in behavioral economics and psychology makes clear that the caricature of *homo economicus* as a selfish, rational opportunist is simply wrong. Psychologists Daniel Kahneman and Amos Tversky poked a hole a mile wide in the assumption of rational utility maximizing with their work on "prospect theory." Their work makes clear that humans use a wide variety of "heuristics and bias" in making decisions that depart significantly from rational behavior—an echo of Herbert Simon's classic work on "satisficing" from the 1960s.[28] Economist Richard Thaler has also been instrumental in creating the new field of behavioral economics by showing that there are not only "anomalies" but "systematic irregularities" when it comes to rational expectations.[29] In short, the human brain is programmed with a whole set of heuristics and biases from our hunter-gatherer past that cause people to overestimate risk, underestimate gain, overweight recent events, and seek confirmation of their preexisting views.[30]

It has also become increasingly clear that the assumptions about equilibria used in neoclassical economics are wildly off base. As Eric Beinhocker explains in his sweeping history *The Origin of Wealth*, the neoclassical economists of the nineteenth century, while enthralled with physics, were not able to incorporate advances in the field once they had established their mathematical models and assumptions. Walras and Jevons, for example, were not familiar with emerging work in physics focused on open systems. Their model was therefore created with the assumption that the economy is a thermodynamically *closed* system, which naturally tends toward equilibrium.

As a consequence, neoclassical economics has been working with a fundamentally misspecified model: the economy is not a closed equilibrium system. Instead, it is an *open disequilibrium* system. As Beinhocker wistfully observed, "For the next one hundred years, as economics and physics each went their separate ways, this assumption [closed system] lay buried in the mathematical heart of [neoclassical] economics." Economies are better conceptualized as complex adaptive systems, rather than closed equilibrium systems.[31] Joseph Schumpeter got it right nearly a century ago when he observed that equilibrium models cannot explain economic growth and innovation; his ideas about "gales of creative destruction" driven by entrepreneurs described exactly the sort of "perturbation" that drives open systems into disequilibrium and adaptation.[32]

Thus, twenty-first-century neoclassical economics is based on nineteenth-century physics, along with similarly outdated assumptions about human behavior. Its "big ideas" are over a century old and seriously out of date. Its unrealistic assumptions about people are contradicted by real-world data—and common sense.[33] Recent critiques of stakeholder capitalism point to the pernicious effects of mixing morality with commercialism.[34] Such reductionism actually flies in the face of Adam Smith and his classical colleagues. It is high time to return to the roots of economic thinking: how "moral sentiments" can and must serve to guide human and economic behavior. We must recognize once again that the idea of "self-interest" is fundamentally different from the idea of "selfishness"[35] (Exhibit 3.3).

If Adam Smith were alive today, how might he draw this distinction? Almost certainly, he would emphasize the importance of reciprocity and mutuality in economic exchange. He would also make clear that a market economy can only function effectively if the actors involved behave with virtue. He would probably be close colleagues with Ed Freeman and others aligned with the stakeholder theory; he would most likely be a leading advocate for what we today refer to as mutual or shared value; he might well be a close advisor to Larry Fink and the Business Roundtable and could have helped draft their recent restatement on the purpose of the corporation. He would no doubt be considered excessively "woke" by some, given his principled opposition to slavery, his disdain for monopolistic corporations, and his empathetic concern for the lives and livelihoods of the common man. In fact, Smith would probably urge that business leaders find their inner "impartial spectators" and trade in shareholder capitalism's selfishness for the classical view of self-interest, once and for all.

Selfish	**Self-Interest**
Assumptions About Human Nature	Assumptions About Human Nature
Greedy Calculating **Rational** Individualistic Opportunistic Lazy	Collaborative Virtuous **Boundedly Rational** Empathetic Creative Self-Motivated
Utility Function: What's in it for me?	Utility Function: Mutual and reciprocal value
Implications for Capitalism	Implications for Capitalism
Maximize Shareholder Value	Optimize Stakeholder Value
Market Fundamentalism	Correct Market Failures
Economy Is a Closed Equilibrium System	Economy Is an Open Disequilibrium System

Exhibit 3.3. **Self-Interested Does Not Mean Selfish**

Stewardship Versus Agency

Whenever the owners of a company (principals) grant authority to others (agents) to act on their behalf, the welfare of the principals may not be prioritized if the agents fail to understand the principals or have different goals, interests, and predispositions. This structural separation of ownership from control in corporations is an age-old conundrum dating all the way back to the very first joint-stock trading companies during the age of mercantile capitalism. The challenge reared its head again as the age of monopoly capitalism gave way to welfare capitalism. Beginning in the 1970s, however, neoliberal economists framed and formalized this challenge in a new theoretical paradigm (organizational economics) composed of two new formulations: *agency theory* and *transaction cost economics*. For the past forty years, these theories have dominated both scholarly and managerial thinking.[36]

Agency theory argues that for corporations with ownership that is widely distributed, managerial (agent) actions will diverge from those required to maximize the owners' (principals) interests—assumed to be the maximizing of shareholder value. Principals, it is theorized, are risk-takers, since they can diversify their holdings across multiple investments; agents, however, are assumed to be risk-averse, since their incomes and livelihoods are tied to the company they work for. Agency theory then specifies a set of monitoring mechanisms (expand the number of independent board members, split the role of board chair and chief executive) and incentives (tie executive compensation to stock price) to control and reduce this disparity.[37]

Transaction cost economics (TCE) is an elaboration of the work of Chicago economist Ronald Coase, who asked the famous question, Why do firms exist? According to TCE, firms exist because of their superior ability to control human opportunism through the exercise of hierarchical control systems that are not available in markets. Both theories begin with the assumption that humans behave selfishly, as *homo economicus*, in their organizational roles. TCE takes it a step further, however, by assuming that agents actually behave with *guile*—that they shirk, mislead, distort, and cheat in the quest to maximize their own utility.[38]

As we saw in Chapter 2, shareholder capitalism and the doctrine of shareholder primacy are premised largely on these two theories, along with the efficient market hypothesis. The ethic of "greed is good" and the market for corporate control are direct outgrowths of the belief that these theories hold— that they both predict and explain outcomes in the real world. Yet as Sumantra Ghoshal notes in his scathing critique of organizational economics, neither theory has actually demonstrated either explanatory or predictive power. There is little evidence that more independent directors, splitting the roles of chairman and CEO, or stock-based compensation of managers (agents), increases shareholder value or corporate performance in the long term.[39]

Such dark, gloomy, and negative assumptions about human behavior also seem extreme on their face. As we saw in the previous section, the enlightenment concept of self-interest is not at all the same thing as *selfishness*, with the latter being a stylized caricature that enables the mathematical models used by economists to function effectively. Combine these unrealistic assumptions with a lack of empirical support and ineffective prescriptions and one would think that the entire edifice of organizational economics would be headed for the dustbin of history. Yet it persists. Indeed, neoliberal economics has proven to be incredibly resilient—continuing to dominate academic research and corporate governance, amplified by the shareholder-primacy-driven financial institutions that have developed on Wall Street over the past four decades.

Yet there has long existed a counter to agency theory and transaction cost economics: the fields of management theory and organizational psychology never bought into the simplifying assumptions about human behavior endemic to the neoclassical economics view. For example, the restrictive and negative assumptions about human nature implicit in organizational economics were long ago characterized as "Theory X" by organizational psychologist Douglas McGregor.[40] His opposing "Theory Y" was more consistent with the Adam Smith view of self-interest—that managers and workers gain intrinsic satisfaction by successfully tackling challenging work and are motivated by a desire to gain the support and recognition of their peers and bosses. In other words, it's as much about psychic rewards as it is money. Building on this foundational thinking, management professor Lex Donaldson and his colleagues developed a direct counterpoint to agency theory—stewardship theory—in which agents' interests can actually *align* with those of the principal, as well as other key stakeholders.[41]

More recent work on higher purpose only serves to reinforce the Theory Y and stewardship views: identification with a mission bigger than oneself is inherently engaging and fulfilling, and enables the melding of individual self-esteem with corporate success.[42] Remember Yuval Harari's observation that what makes humans unique is their ability to collaborate around abstract ideas—myths, legends ... and compelling missions.[43] Of course, it matters what the "something bigger" is—whether it's storming the Bastille or storming the Capitol, but that is a topic for later chapters!

So, when we widen the aperture on the question of separation of ownership and control and the "principal-agent problem," we see that it can be (and has been) framed in very different ways over the years. As noted at the outset, this challenge was on clear display in the case of the British East India Company, when the investors (principals) in England had little direct control over the "governors" (agents) who ran the actual in-country operations, given the distance and time lags in communications involved.

Yet, by the end of the eighteenth century, influential company director Josiah Child had succeeded in changing the mission of the company from one of trade and mutual value creation into one of conquest and extraction—an extension of British imperial interests. With this new intent in place, the attitudes and dispositions of the company's governors naturally changed as well. Governor Robert Clive in India eventually assumed he had the green light to literally take over Bengal and accelerate the process of exploitation, value extraction, and personal aggrandizement. The sacking of India by the East India Company thus occurred partially by design (at the behest of the owners) and partially by default (the result of the autonomy and incentive structure of the governors)—hardly a case of conflict between the goals and interests of the principals and agents.

Adam Smith himself noted that these joint-stock companies provided an impetus for "hazardous speculation." This problem was exacerbated by the corporate incentive system in place—low base salaries for governors with autonomy to pursue personal opportunities—which actually encouraged avarice and corruption on the part of the company's agents. However, the nature of the principal-agent problem at the East India Company was not the one captured by agency theory. In this case, the company's agents took *more* (not less) risk and ended up pushing the organization to the brink; monitoring mechanisms were few and far between and the incentive structure was clearly designed to encourage adventurous behavior by the governors.

As Exhibit 3.4 shows, the nature of the separation between ownership and control has evolved in significant ways over the cycles of capitalism. As noted earlier, mercantile capitalism, characterized by investor groups of owners and hired professional agents, experienced significant challenges but not of the sort propounded by agency theory. Having been on the receiving end of these trading companies, America's Founders acted to prevent the new country from enabling such behavior by severely constraining the corporate form. By creating a high bar for the formation of corporations, the Founders ensured that the commercial sector was composed largely of sole proprietorships and

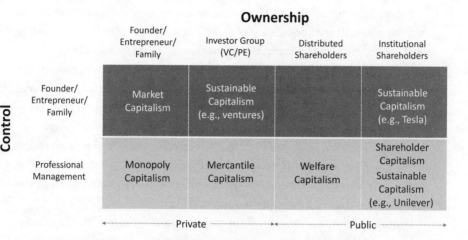

Exhibit 3.4. Separating Ownership from Control:
All the Myriad Ways

partnerships, thereby eliminating any agency problem since ownership and control were once again in the same hands (transition from mercantile to market capitalism).

Even as the legal restrictions on corporations were relaxed in the latter part of the nineteenth century, the large industrial trusts were still mostly owned by their founders, with financing coming from the banking sector. The main difference was their size: as the industrial trusts grew, a whole new category of employee emerged—*the manager.* This was the time when business schools first came into existence to help train a new generation of professional managers able to operate and control the sprawling trusts of monopoly capitalism (transition from market to monopoly capitalism)—much more on this in Chapter 7. Because the tycoons themselves still maintained their leadership positions, however, the principal-agent problem was muted, since ownership was still largely in the hands of the tycoons. Large ownership stakes enabled the tycoons to use their companies' growing market power to drive out competition and create heavily concentrated industries dominated by one or two players.

After the debacle of the Great Depression and the Second World War, however, the character of the large corporations changed in a significant way. By then, the founders of the Gilded Age had left the scene and the industrial corporations were now *entirely* in the hands of professional management—even the senior executive positions. In Exhibit 3.4 this governance change is reflected by the transition from monopoly capitalism to welfare capitalism.

Rather than being viewed as a threat to the interests of ownership, how-ever, the rise of the professional manager was seen by observers as a *positive* development for society: professional managers as "agents" would confer le-gitimacy and good judgment, unlike the Robber Barons" and tycoons of the Gilded Age. Indeed, Berle and Means heralded the arrival of the professional manager in combination with distributed stock ownership as the way for corpo-rations to truly deliver societal value. Distributed, small shareholders were seen as contributing little and were therefore relegated to the position of receiving the "wages of capital."[44] This new age of welfare capitalism, when corporations behaved as societal institutions, persisted well into the 1970s and produced the largest middle class in the history of the world.[45]

Viewed in historical context, then, the transition to shareholder capitalism beginning in the 1980s was an abrupt change from the principal-agent logic of welfare capitalism. Indeed, the neoliberal economists of the Chicago School succeeded in pulling off a virtual "180"—reversing assumptions about manag-ers and agents as positive contributors who kept the avarice of the capitalists in check for the good of society. When seen in this broader sweep of history, agency theory and TCE are really *outliers*, with their assumptions about manag-ers as risk-averse, selfish opportunists. They are also outliers when we consider the broader intellectual landscape, since the fields of management theory and organizational psychology had created a well-developed conceptual framework for "Theory Y" behavior and a stewardship theory, even as the economists hi-jacked the game.

Agency theory and TCE assume that *homo economicus* is the dominant mode of managerial behavior; deviations from the assumption of being risk averse and opportunistic are considered to be exceptions rather than the norm. As a consequence, neoliberal economists consider situations in which agents are risk-seeking or aligned with principals as either special cases or simply un-interesting.[46] Yet evidence increasingly suggests that reality is precisely the op-posite: agency theory does apply in some narrow situations, when principals are dealing with a demonstrably self-centered, opportunistic manager who only cares about him- or herself. But such situations are more the exception than the rule. The vast majority of agents are actually motivated by the desire to collaborate, contribute to the greater good, and be recognized and rewarded accordingly.[47]

Perhaps the problem then really resides with the *principal*—the expecta-tions of ownership—and not the agent: when boosting short-term stock price is viewed as the objective function by the shareholders of public corporations, the result is pressure on agents to engage in a range of such short-sighted practices as stock buybacks and cuts in R&D and new product development, none of which actually enhance the long-term health or positioning of the company. Too often, management accedes under pressure to taking such actions, knowing they are not in the best long-term interests of either the principals or the agents. Perhaps it is time to challenge the entire premise of shareholder primacy!

Drawing upon an extensive body of legal research as a professor of corporate law, Lynn Stout demonstrated clearly that there is, in fact, no legal requirement that corporations maximize profits or shareholder value, nor is there any special fiduciary duty on the part of either directors or senior executives to shareholders. In fact, as Stout's research clearly showed, shareholders of publicly traded companies do not actually *own* the assets of corporations—they are stakeholders with certain contractual rights, claims, and obligations, just like bondholders, employees, and communities. In the case of shareholders, those rights include the ability to vote at board meetings, sue, or sell the stock.[48]

So, despite the ubiquity of principal-agent theory, shareholders of public companies are *not* principals because no one owns publicly held corporations in the traditional sense of the term (since corporations are in fact "legal persons," owning a corporation would constitute a form of slavery!). In fact, shareholders are *residual claimants* in that they get paid after everyone else—creditors, employees, suppliers, and governments (in the form of taxes).[49] The reality is that boards of directors run public companies and, as long as there is no self-dealing or conflicts of interest, courts have not second-guessed boards' decisions about what is best for their companies—a long-standing legal precedent known as the "business judgment rule." The key is to attract a substantial core of investors who share the company's long-term vision and are willing to support the strategies needed to achieve it.[50] Much more about this in Chapter 8.

It is instructive to note that both agency theory and stewardship theory view managers as having significant autonomy. However, through the lens of agency theory, autonomy is framed as a problem to be controlled, whereas stewardship theory views managerial autonomy as positive—a form of empowerment. Indeed, for development economist Amartya Sen, having "agency" meant developing the capacity for a person to act with autonomy by equipping them with the necessary capabilities."[51] If we add Adam Smith's concept of self-interest (stewardship) to this framing, agency becomes a decidedly *good* thing—an "empowered" manager inspired by a greater purpose is not a threat to owners' interests. In fact, empowered agents are actually the *vehicle* for building the unique organizational capabilities that enable enterprises to create shared prosperity and sustained competitive advantage.[52]

The time has thus come to shed the yoke of neoliberal economic logic and go "back to the future" once again. As sustainable capitalism gains momentum, we are beginning to see multiple avenues for better aligning the interests of principals and agents (transitions to sustainable capitalism in Exhibit 3.2). First, the next capitalist reformation is being driven by a new breed of sustainable ventures and B Corps focused on commercializing clean technologies and fostering positive social impact. By 2022, for example, there were more than four thousand certified B Corps around the world; a decade earlier B Corps numbered only in the hundreds.[53]

The ranks of "impact investors"—those seeking societal impact first, along with financial returns—have also swelled in recent years. A decade ago, JPMorgan and the Rockefeller Foundation, together with the Global Impact Investing Network, predicted that this emerging asset class would reach between $400 billion and $1 trillion in assets under management (AUM) by 2020. At the time, this prediction seemed very ambitious, given that impact investment AUM were less than $20 billion. By 2020, however, the impact investing market had reached roughly $715 billion AUM—with the market growing an astonishing 42.4 percent between 2019 and 2020 alone. By comparison, total venture capital investment in 2020 was less than half this size.[54]

In the public equities space, the game has also changed dramatically. As we saw in Chapter 2, stocks are increasingly held by institutional investors, not the individual "distributed shareholders" of the age of welfare capitalism. With the rise of 401(k) retirement accounts and the decline of defined benefit pensions starting in the 1970s, pension funds, mutual funds, endowments, and hedge funds have emerged as the leading "principals." Whereas institutions owned less than 10 percent of the stock during the 1950s and 1960s, by 2020 this number had jumped to over 80 percent.[55]

Activist investors rose to the fore in the 1980s, championing the cause of maximizing shareholder value and driving the market for corporate control through hostile takeovers. Investment advisors also became increasingly oriented toward extracting profits through excessive commissions and fees, abandoning their fiduciary duty to protect and grow their investors' capital for the long term.[56] Increasingly, however, activist investors have begun to focus more on societal impact than on "greed is good" (witness the rise of firms like Engine No. 1 and Generation Investment Management). In addition, large institutional investors such as BlackRock, Vanguard, and State Street have also started to stress the importance of long-term value, sustainability, and climate change— and are voting their shares accordingly.

The result is a more supportive environment for such industry disruptors as Tesla and corporate sustainability leaders as Unilever. Indeed, Tesla's stock price soared in 2020–21, driven by the long-term bet by investors that electric vehicles and electrification more broadly represent the future. Unilever CEO Paul Polman also survived a £115 billion hostile takeover bid by Kraft-Heinz, at least in part because of a groundswell of stakeholder support for the company and its commitment to sustainability.[57] Granted, Danone CEO Emmanuel Faber was ousted by activist investors over complaints that his sustainability initiatives were hurting profitability, but overall, the trend line seems to be in the opposite direction. As a higher proportion of sustainability leaders' stock is owned by not only ESG (environment, social, and governance) investors like Generation Investment Management but also sympathetic institutions like BlackRock, the efficacy of old-school, market-for-corporate-control activists seems to be diminishing.[58]

This new "enlightened" institutional investor environment has also ramped up pressure on resistant incumbents to address sustainability concerns. The recent proxy campaign at ExxonMobil is proof positive: a "new school" hedge fund—Engine No. 1—with a small $50 million stake in the oil giant, along with the backing of BlackRock, Vanguard, and State Street (each holding substantial stakes), pressured the company into appointing two new independent directors focused on the challenge of climate change, sustainability, and corporate transformation.[59]

While there are still real questions about ESG investing's authenticity and financial return, there can be no doubt that "sustainable" finance has gone mainstream, with assets in investment funds focused on ESG and sustainability reaching $2 trillion in early 2021, more than tripling in three years.[60] Overall, sustainability-influenced investing now accounts for one-third of assets under management.[61] More about this in Chapter 8. The days of maximizing the gains for one stakeholder (that is, the shareholder) may be coming to an end, with what Marjorie Kelly calls the "Divine Right of Capital" giving way to the realization that optimizing returns for all stakeholders might actually produce better financial results in the long term. Managers with a slavish devotion to short-term stock price are rapidly becoming a thing of the past, as principals increasingly escape from the straightjacket of shareholder primacy.

The time has thus come to reimagine the principal-agent relationship, from one of monitoring and monetary reward to one of empowerment and steward-ship. We must move beyond agency theory, transaction cost economics, and efficient markets to new ways of addressing the issue of separation of ownership and control in corporate governance. Much more on this in Chapters 5 and 6.

Markets Versus Monopolies

Since the earliest days of the crown trading companies, capitalism has had an uncomfortable relationship with the idea of market competition. While free and competitive markets are typically portrayed as the *sine qua non* for a func-tioning capitalist system, the reality has been anything but. Recall that monop-oly was part of the core DNA of the trading company model. Adam Smith in *The Wealth of Nations* railed against the monopolistic nature of the British East India Company and the other trading companies of the day: "Monopoly of one kind or another, indeed, seems to be the sole engine of the mercantile system." He went on to observe that

> people of the same trade seldom meet together, even for merriment and di-version, but the conversation ends in a conspiracy against the public, or in some contrivance to raise prices.[62]

Given his revulsion to monopoly, Smith's theory of the "market economy" was premised entirely on the existence of many small sellers competing in an open market where neither sellers nor buyers are large enough to influence the market price. As we saw in Chapter 1, the Founders of the United States took his thinking—and their own experience under the thumb of the monopolistic crown corporations—to heart by ensuring that corporations in the new Repub-lic were tightly controlled, monitored, and prevented from becoming too large. Early America was overwhelmingly a nation of farmers, sole proprietors, and small-town entrepreneurs once slavery and the plantation economy were dis-mantled after the Civil War. Indeed, the American tradition came to be defined by *resistance* to centralized power and monopoly.

With the rise of the railroads, however, the constraints on corporations began to erode, and by the late nineteenth century, the tycoons of the Gilded Age had successfully removed all the shackles constraining corporate con-centration and power. The new monopolists of the Gilded Age made the ar-gument that industrial trusts helped to curtail the "ruinous competition" that was driving prices too low and creating boom-and-bust cycles; they thought Adam Smith's ideas about competitive markets had no place in a modern, industrial economy. The US had indeed experienced terrible economic shocks in the latter part of the nineteenth century, with legions of firms thrown into bankruptcy. The tycoons made the case that monopoly was simply a superior form of business organization that could save the economy from such wild swings. The monopolists also liked to portray themselves as part of a movement to build a stronger, better society, using the then fashionable ideology of Social Darwinism.[63]

In politics, the tycoons embraced laissez-faire, opposing any governmental intervention that might prevent the "strong" from displacing the "weak." Law professor Tim Wu described this period as a kind of "industrial eugenics" campaign. William McKinley, president for much of the 1890s, was complicit; his administration effectively ignored the Sherman Antitrust Act, which had been passed in 1890. As a consequence, by the early twentieth century, industrial concentration had reached epic proportions: between 1895 and 1904, over two thousand manufacturing firms merged, leaving fewer than two hundred corporations, most of which dominated their industries. It is important to emphasize that this monopolization movement in the late nineteenth century was actually a radical break—an *aberration*—from the values seen as foundational to the American Republic through most of its first century of existence.[64]

McKinley's assassination in late 1901, however, began the process of restoring competitive markets, bringing Teddy Roosevelt, trust-busting, and the Progressive movement to the fore—much to the dismay of the Republican establishment. Roosevelt's unlikely rise to power would prove crucial, however, in enabling the second capitalist reformation by reasserting the importance of governmental oversight of the industrial behemoths that had come to dominate the commercial landscape.

Indeed, in their sweeping study of economic history, sociologists John Campbell and John Hall show that capitalism's societal performance depends on two primary factors: state capacity and social cohesion. The latter is enabled through political stability and a shared sense of collective interest among the populace: capitalism for the few is unsustainable and almost always ends in catastrophe. State capacity includes the government's ability to both formulate effective, nonpartisan policy and execute it through an array of fiscal, monetary, and regulatory levers to enhance the common good.[65] The Progressive Era was in essence a movement to build both state capacity and social cohesion in industrial America. The Election of 1912 was pivotal in elevating Woodrow Wilson to the presidency and along with him the Brandeis ethic of regulated competition for the common good. Unfortunately, World War I brought a relapse to laissez-faire and during the Roaring Twenties industrial concentration once again became the modus operandi.

It was precisely this concentration of corporate power—and wealth—that produced the preconditions for what would turn out to be one of the most disruptive and bloodiest periods in the history of the world—the Great Depression and World War II. In Germany and Italy (and also Japan), industrial cartels and monopolies rose to prominence during the 1920s, only accelerating during the 1930s. Industrial concentration resulted in rising inequality which then led to the emergence of populist strongmen offering quixotic paths to restoring national greatness. A disaffected and declining middle class came to support these nationalist political figures, often blaming immigrants, foreign influence, and conspiracy theories for their predicament (a rhyme with the 2010–20s). The result? The rise of Hitler and National Socialism in Germany, Mussolini in Italy, and the militarization of Imperial Japan under Emperor Hirohito. In all likelihood, it was FDR's victory during the height of the Great Depression that prevented a similar descent into authoritarianism in the US. The key lesson of the first half of the twentieth century? The road to fascism and dictatorship is paved with the failures of capitalism to serve the common good. Concentration breeds antidemocratic movements and authoritarianism.[66]

It was thus no coincidence that the title Friedrich Hayek selected for his best-known book about these times was *The Road to Serfdom*. Having lived through the horrors of Nazi Germany, Hayek built his economic philosophy upon the singular importance of economic liberty, private enterprise, and entrepreneurship. He saw firsthand what happens when industrial monopolists join forces with fascist autocrats and dictators: the destruction of civilization and the impoverishment of the people. He recognized, in other words, that concentrated power in *any* form—whether big government or corporate monopolies—is dangerous and must be avoided at all costs. It was only later that "modern" libertarians (neoliberals) turned a blind eye to the abuses of monopolies and giant corporations—focusing their wrath exclusively on the evils of "big government."[67]

As we saw in Chapter 1, under FDR's leadership, America emerged from the Second World War a *less* concentrated economy. Aggressive antitrust enforcement during the postwar years was an important factor in enabling the "golden years" of welfare capitalism during the 1950s and 1960s, when inequality plummeted and the country built a strong middle class. It was only during the 1990s and 2000s, after the neoliberals had broken up the conglomerates through the "market for corporate control," that the level of industry concentration—and inequality—began to rise once again, driven by the siren song of shareholder primacy.

The hijacking of antitrust enforcement by Chicago-Schooler Robert Bork during the closing decade of the twentieth century marked the beginning of another radical departure from the long American tradition of economic de-centralization and competitive markets. Indeed, the establishment of the "con-sumer welfare" standard for judging when such enforcement should ensue effectively limited action only to the most egregious cases of price gouging and blatant "mergers to monopoly."[68]

Much like the avoidance of "ruinous competition" was the justification given by the tycoons for industrial concentration during the age of industrial capitalism, so Bork's logic of "consumer welfare" also provided the pretext for another wave of mergers and buyouts. Tim Wu elaborates:

> The contemporary monopolist, it turns out, had been gravely misunder-stood. He was not the threatening brute feared by previous generations, but a well-meaning and timid creature, almost a gentle giant, whose every action was well-intentioned, and who lived in constant fear of new competi-tors. Even though he had already killed his actual competitors, he was none-theless restrained, by just the thought of them. For that reason, he would not dare raise prices or destroy his rivals.[69]

By the early 2000s, antitrust had all but forgotten about concentration and industry structure and instead, in Orwellian fashion, had elevated monopoly to "hero" status. Indeed, Justice Antonin Scalia elevated market power and monopoly to something essential to the advance of the American economy. He asserted that the "possession of monopoly power, and the charging of mo-nopoly prices, is not only *not* unlawful; it is an important element of the free market system . . . it induces risk taking that produces innovation and economic strength."[70]

The result has been epic concentration over the past twenty-plus years, with levels not seen since the Gilded Age and the Roaring Twenties: a full three-quarters of industries witnessed increasing concentration between 1997 and 2012. Monopsony power—when single *buyers* control factor markets—has also exploded in recent years. Companies such as WalMart and Amazon have in-creasingly come to represent the only game in town—for producers and retail employees alike. By 2015, mergers and acquisitions had reached an all-time high of $4.7 trillion, and corporations used their growing market power to reap out-sized profits: mark-ups overall have more than *tripled* since the 1980s and profit margins have risen by 100 percent, driving the stock market to levels never seen before—further enriching the executives who run these companies, along with the richest 10 percent who own 80 percent of the stock.[71] Even with the demise of neoliberalism, and the disruptions wrought by the coronavirus pandemic, price gouging and profiteering continue to this day.

Indeed, nothing can rival the level of market power amassed by the tech industry in just the past decade. In total, Facebook put together 67 unchallenged acquisitions, including its major potential challengers, Instagram and WhatsApp; Amazon closed 91 acquisitions; and Google pulled off 214. In essence, the tech industry now consists of just a few giant trusts, leading observers to describe the 2020s as the *New* Gilded Age.[72] Yet, as corporation scholar Jerry Davis notes, the tech industry does not follow the same script as conventional monopolists in asserting market power. In the old days, monopolists—with a dominant share in their defined markets—had the habit of overcharging customers as well as underpaying their suppliers and workers, driving out competitors, and using their excess profits to accumulate personal wealth and buy off politicians to maintain their positions. The cure was simple: cut monopolistic corporations down to size using antitrust law and encourage more competition.[73]

Few of today's tech companies, however, engage in price gouging. In fact, most offer services for free or offer the deepest discounts—in exchange for using your personal data to sell advertising (and the risks to privacy that accompany it)—thereby passing the Borkian test of consumer welfare. Tech companies also defy easy industry definition. Just what industry is Amazon in after all, and how do you measure its "market share"? The new plutocrats in the tech sector also use the cloud to outsource as much as possible, thereby avoiding full-time employment obligations and asset investments; they wield their market power to preemptively acquire competitors, and (like all monopolists) exploit their wealth and privileged knowledge to all but escape regulatory scrutiny.[74] When it comes to the new tech titans, Davis concludes that *shareholder primacy*—not simply excessive bigness—is really the core problem. So, if we want to tame these new platform-based denizens of corporate power, we need a new set of regulatory tools beyond conventional antitrust enforcement—and perhaps the next capitalist reformation.[75]

Furthermore, as if following a script, rising industry concentration has led to rising inequality—reaching levels by 2020 not seen since just before the great stock market crash in 1929.[76] Where has most of the profit gone during the age of shareholder capitalism? The answer: executive compensation, dividends, stock buybacks, and campaign contributions. As Tim Wu so aptly observes, it is as though we are "trapped in a bad movie sequel." Along with epic industry concentration, slower growth, and rising inequality, we also see the growing disaffection of those left behind, along with the inevitable rise (once again) of populist authoritarian strongmen promising a "return to greatness"—witness Trump, Orban, Duda, Erdogan, and Bolsonaro . . . not to mention Putin. Even University of Chicago economist Luigi Zingales has concluded that we must restore true competition if we are to avoid descent into a corporatist probusiness system run by corrupt politicians.[77]

If Hayek were alive today, what would he think? My guess is he would be extremely scared that we are on the edge of another global catastrophe, aided and abetted by corporatism and monopoly capitalism. With the benefit of historical perspective, it is clear that for most of the nearly 250 years of the American experiment, the bedrock principal has been to foster economic decentralization and competitive markets. Market and welfare capitalism spread opportunity, produced widely distributed benefits, and grew from the middle out. It has only been during two "aberrations"—the "Gilded Age of Monopoly Capitalism" and the "New Gilded Age of Shareholder Capitalism"—that we have violated these principles, with devastating consequences.

Despite the proclivity for monopolists to use the language of markets—prices, supply, demand, competition, and so on—the truth is that monopolies are *anathema* to markets. If monopolists were to have their way, they would establish a centrally directed, planned economy just like the communists—only entirely in *private-sector* hands. Government would exist only to preserve the hegemony of minority rule, in the interest of the monopolists themselves. Truly free markets thus desperately need democratic, transparent government to avoid being captured by monopolists, oligarchs, and kleptocrats.[78]

The Enlightenment thinkers who helped craft today's democratic governments did not contemplate the possibility of a concentrated form of private power that might come to rival that of the government itself—that the corporate form could one day grow to such a scale and scope that it became effectively insulated from the countervailing power of government to keep it in check. This situation happened for the first time at the end of the nineteenth century, and Teddy Roosevelt recognized it for what it was—an existential threat to founding principles of the country. After Wilson and Brandeis launched us on nearly a century of active antitrust enforcement we tragically find ourselves at yet another Roosevelt moment.

The time is now to confront the growing problem of overly concentrated industries and excess market power—now on a global scale. The good news is that the European Union and the Americans now appear willing to take the steps necessary to end the march toward monopoly and excess market power and its inevitable political result—the rise of populist rebellion, ethnonationalism, and authoritarianism. Bork's detour down the road of "consumer welfare" must end and the Brandeisian ethic of "managed competition" be fully restored. Government's capacity to establish guardrails and manage the economy for the common good must once again become a top priority. In many ways, the timing could not be better, since we stand at the threshold of a new era: yesterday's resource- and energy-intensive industries are being creatively destroyed as we speak. So, as tomorrow's renewable energy, sustainable mobility, and regenerative food industries emerge in the years ahead, it is our duty to ensure that they are not captured by neomonopolists.

Reinvestment Versus Extraction

In recent decades, the term "capitalist" has come to mean something quite pejorative in the public's mind: it conjures up the image of business plutocrats and financiers who extract and accumulate personal wealth to indulge their personal fantasies and buy political influence in order to further feather their own nests. Think "capitalist pig." Ironically, nothing could be further away from the original conceptualization of how a businessperson should behave and how a market economy should function.

As Adam Smith stated in *The Wealth of Nations*, a business owner who has more profits than he needs to maintain his own family should use the surplus to "employ more assistants, in order to further increase his profits." The more profits he has, the more "assistants" he can employ, thereby increasing the wealth and prosperity of the entire community. In fact, the core assumption of Smith's notion of the "invisible hand" was that the "selfish" urge to increase private profits was the vehicle for the generation of *collective* wealth.

As Yuval Harari astutely observes, for Smith, greed was good only insofar as becoming richer benefitted everyone—egoism was *altruism*:

> If I am poor, you too will be poor since I cannot buy your products or services. If I am rich, you too will be enriched since you can now sell me something. . . . Being rich meant being moral. In Smith's story, people become rich not by despoiling their neighbors, but by increasing the overall size of the pie. And when the pie grows, everyone benefits.[79]

Of course, there is a giant caveat when it comes to this line of reasoning: it only works if the rich use their "surplus" to develop new products, open new factories, invest in new businesses, and hire new employees rather than spending it on things like lobbying, stock buybacks, luxuries, and personal consumption. Smith, Ricardo, and the other classical economists held a particularly dim view of those who extracted "rents" and squandered gains on nonproductive activities—"collecting books, statues, pictures, or even more frivolous jewels, baubles, and ingenious trinkets."[80] It is why market economies are today described as "capitalist:" *capital* is money and resources invested in expansion and production. *Wealth*, on the other hand, is hoarded in banks, buried in the ground, or wasted on unproductive frivolities. Recall our definition of capital from Chapter 1: "accumulated wealth, *reproductively employed*."[81]

Belief in the core principle of "investing to expand the pie" explains why Smith had such venom for the monopolist trading companies of his day: the *Wealth of Nations* was written during the period when the East India Company's aggression overseas and speculation at home had come to dominate British public life. Smith viewed the European "discovery" of America and the passage by sea to the East Indies as the two greatest events in history. However, in his view, the full potential of these dramatic openings was not being realized due to Britain's exploitation of colonies using crown (monopoly) corporations to extract wealth.[82] As we saw in Chapter 1, the American revolutionaries were heavily influenced by Smith's thinking, which explains why they were committed to entrepreneurship and small business, and placed stringent controls on the chartering of corporations.

The term "capitalism" was coined only in the mid-nineteenth century as the First Industrial Revolution—with its cotton gins and power looms—was reaching its peak and the factory system was driving what Karl Polanyi has called "The Great Transformation."[83] With the advent of the railroads came the emergence of a new generation of large "industrial" corporations owned principally by individual tycoons—and along with it the erosion of the legal controls placed on corporations by the Founders. The extraction of wealth reached new heights during the Gilded Age, with trusts and monopolies (and personal fortunes) once again ruling the day, and inequality reaching epic proportions. As we saw, it took the Great Depression and World War II to once again restore a semblance of equity when it came to income and wealth distribution, ushering in the age of welfare capitalism in the postwar years.

The age of shareholder capitalism and shareholder primacy, however, once again swung the pendulum back in the direction of extraction over reinvestment. Starting in the 1970s, Americans began talking less about the common good and more about self-aggrandizement. The Greatest Generation gave way to the "Me Generation," and *Looking Out for #1* became a *New York Times* best-seller. Even as GDP grew, the share of national income going to labor and capital began to decline. Where did this new income go? Answer: Rents! And the biggest source of rent increase was profits—profits in excess of what would have been earned in a competitive economy.[84]

Leading the way to a new era of extraction was the financial services indus-try. A sector that had traditionally been a means to an end—the more efficient production of goods and services—became an end in itself. Since the founding of the Republic, there has been worry that powerful banks could undermine popular democracy, which is why Andrew Jackson declined to renew the char-ter of the First National Bank in 1836. These worries have proven more than jus-tified in recent years, as financial deregulation has wreaked havoc on not only the economy but the very fabric of society.[85]

Traditionally, banks existed mainly to bring together those who had excess funds (savers) with those who needed more funds (borrowers), providing the necessary credit to drive a healthy capitalist system. Beginning in the 1980s, however, financial deregulation lured the banks into an ever-more-risky set of gambits (yielding higher interest rates or lucrative fees) such as securitiza-tion, junk bonds, subprime mortgages, mergers and acquisitions, and stock buybacks. Eventually, banks descended into the realm of pure gambling with "derivatives"—nothing more than bets on what's going to happen with such things as exchange rates and stock prices.

In short, finance has become the poster child for extraction and rent-seeking—bankers lining their own pockets at the expense of society. They preyed upon the financially unsophisticated and diverted investment capital away from more productive uses, all to maximize short-term profits. As econo-mist Joseph Stiglitz observed:

> Resources that could have gone into wealth creation were devoted to ex-ploitation, as the financial sector grew in size, attracting some of the coun-try's most talented individuals. But all the country had to show for it was slower growth, more volatility, and greater inequality. . . . Bankers' unbri-dled pursuit of their self-interest didn't lead to the well-being of society, but to the largest financial crisis in 75 years.[86]

Stiglitz goes on to chronicle how the greed and moral turpitude of the bank-ers and financial sector spread, literally infecting the broader economy, politics, and society. Indeed, as short-termism and extraction became the norm, corporations and firms inevitably began to imitate this behavior. The financial sector thus played a key role in spreading the ethos of shareholder capitalism to the corporate world, such that short-term profit maximization and shareholder primacy rule, regardless of the societal impacts.

There are five things that companies can do with profits: reinvest in the business, acquire another company, pay down debt, pay dividends to shareholders, or buy back their own stock. Stock buybacks were actually banned following the 1929 Crash due to their extractive nature and were only made legal again in the early 1980s, as neoliberalism was on the rise. The stock that companies buy back can either be used for "incentive" pay to executives and employees or can simply be made to *disappear*. By "retiring" stock, fewer shares are available on the market, artificially driving the value of the remaining shares higher.[87]

In the last decade, corporate profits have reached their highest level as a share of the total economy since the Roaring Twenties, just prior to the 1929 Crash.[88] Yet, over the past forty years, businesses have reinvested less and less in favor of funneling more and more profits to dividends and share buybacks. Despite record profits, we have seen a sharp fall in reinvestment in the workforce, R&D, and capital projects. Such reinvestment averaged more than 20 percent of corporate revenues during the age of welfare capitalism but fell to less than 10 percent after 2000. As we have seen, share buybacks have steadily grown to the point at which they now account for the *majority* of firms' profits on average. For some industries (for example, airlines, pharma), buybacks actually account for more than 90 percent of profits.[89]

History teaches us that there are two fundamental ways to get wealthy: by innovating and creating new products and services, thereby expanding the size of the economic pie, or by exploiting others and extracting wealth, thereby redistributing wealth from lower in the economic pyramid upward. Using market power to generate rents, extract personal wealth, and enrich shareholders is the antithesis of what the classical founders of market economics had in mind. Yet for the past forty-plus years, that is exactly what has happened.

The Upshot

The past four centuries have featured three significant cycles of capitalist reformation with the third in motion as we speak. Through it all, the for-profit, joint-stock, limited-liability corporation stands out as a remarkably robust and resilient organizational form—from the East India Company to Standard Oil, and from General Motors to Amazon. Yet such corporations have *behaved* very differently over the centuries, depending on the values, norms, and intentions of those who own, run, and oversee them. Conclusion? The corporate form is not the problem; the problem is the operating system—the "software" used to run the capitalist endeavor.

History teaches us that capitalism can be run using a variety of different operating systems, and that such systems are little more than *social constructions*, or "myths," if you will. Some operating systems encourage "animal spirits" on the part of capitalists—mercantile capitalism, monopoly capitalism, and shareholder capitalism, for example. Others channel the classical idea of *virtue* described earlier and bring out capitalists' "better angels"—market capitalism, welfare capitalism, and (we hope) sustainable capitalism. Dr. Jekyll versus Mr. Hyde. As B-Lab cofounder Jay Coen Gilbert notes, "If the operating system says business leaders must make decisions in order to maximize profit . . . we will end up in a very different world than if the operating system says we must make decisions in order to maximize benefit to society."[90]

Think about the behavior of the British East India Company *before* Josiah Child versus the years after when the company—and England as a country—became an imperialist, extractive, and occupying force—same company, just a different operating system. Think about Adam Smith's "Impartial Spectator" and invisible hand versus Thomas Hobbes's state of nature dominated by man's appetites and aversions; two entirely different social constructions for how the world works. Think about the Roaring Twenties rapacious General Motors versus 1950s General Motors, when it became known as *Generous* Motors—the beacon for welfare capitalism. Indeed, think about the notable differences between American shareholder capitalism and the Rhine, Nordic, or Asian models. Different myths and operating systems; different values, behaviors, outcomes, and impacts for capitalists.

There is thus nothing preordained about shareholder primacy and industry concentration. Milton Friedman was really just a mythmaker—albeit one adept at wrapping his story in math and the veneer of science; so too were Jensen, Meckling, Coase, Fama, and Bork. Herbert Spencer was also a mythmaker—one also adept at shrouding his story in the trappings of science; in his case it was the pseudoscience of "Social" Darwinism. So too were Walras, Jevons, and Marshall, but in their case the veneer of science was that of physics.

What we really need therefore is a *new myth*—a compelling narrative upon which to build tomorrow's capitalist operating system; a vision for the future that transcends the rising tide of ethnonationalism and corporatism, which will only perpetuate shareholder primacy, drive further division and inequality, and exacerbate the climate crisis. As Louis Brandeis challenged a century ago, we need to clarify and uplift capitalism's *purpose*—given today's world of toxic inequality, social division, and environmental meltdown.

In short, we must redefine what it means to be a "capitalist" for the twenty-first century by creating a new *objective function* for the institutions of capitalism—what Ed Freeman and his colleagues refer to as the "new story of business."[91] My hope is that the balance of this book helps to build this new story—the "myth"—needed for sustainable capitalism to take root and flourish. I will also try to sketch the crucial elements of the new *operating system*—corporate-level transformations and system-level institutional redesigns—needed to catalyze and support this next capitalist reformation.

History makes clear that the situation we now find ourselves in is not entirely unique or without precedent: there have been times in the past that feel strangely similar to our current predicament. For example:

- 1860—a divided country (and now world) with a new president bent on restoring the Union, only to have the whole thing descend into Civil War.

- 1912—on the cusp of a progressive awakening, only to have the entire world order collapse into chaos (World War I–level disaster).

- 1920—after finally emerging from a global pandemic, the urge to "return to normal" produces another period of economic excess prior to eventual collapse.

- 1933—after a financial collapse, the world descends into chaos with the rise of fascist, nationalist, and fundamentalist movements, prior to the emergence of a new age—the age of welfare capitalism.

There are important lessons to be harvested from previous capitalist reformations. Yet, as eerily similar as they may be, none of these historical analogues captures the scale and scope of the challenges we now face. While we have wrestled before with the issues of greed and selfishness, the separation of ownership and control, extraction of wealth, populism, fascism, and the tendency for capitalism to careen toward concentration and corporatism, *never* before has the capitalist pursuit actually threatened the very life support system—the climate and ecosystems—upon which it depends.

Never before has capitalism's unintended consequences and negative side-effects had an impact on so many people and places. Indeed, the external costs imposed by shareholder capitalism have now brought us to the brink of climate collapse, mass extinction, and a toxic inequality on a scale that threatens the very stability of human civilization. Before elaborating on the new operating system for capitalism, therefore, let's explore further the unique and pressing nature of the problems that now present themselves—those world challenges that define the mission for a new age of sustainable capitalism. There is no time to waste.

PART II

Corporate Transformation

**"WIN-WIN" SOLUTIONS WILL
NO LONGER SUFFICE**

FOUR

The Great Race

SUSTAINABLE CAPITALISM'S CHALLENGE

The Great Race is a 1960s comedy film about competing daredevils at the turn of the twentieth century in a race from New York to Paris. The two protagonists—The Great Leslie and Professor Fate—provide the fitting archetypal contrast between the forces of light (The Great Leslie is the classic hero dressed in white) and darkness (Professor Fate is the villain dressed in black with a dark moustache and top hat). Professor Fate wins the race under questionable circumstances, and the film ends with the two embarking on a race rematch, this time from Paris back to New York. Professor Fate lets The Great Leslie start first, then attempts to destroy his car and accidentally brings down the Eiffel Tower in the process!

The Great Race provides a fitting metaphor for our world predicament as we look ahead to 2030 and beyond: Professor Fate (read shareholder capitalism) clearly won the initial race (the past forty years) through the logic of shareholder primacy and market fundamentalism. Unfortunately, Professor Fate has a pernicious dark side in the form of growing fossil fuel use, greenhouse gas emissions, water use, waste generation, and social inequity. Indeed, we have used more energy and resources in the last forty years than in all of the rest of human history. Inequality has also reached levels comparable to the 1920s, just before the 1929 Crash. It cannot be long before the proverbial Eiffel Tower comes crashing down![1]

Fortunately, The Great Leslie (read sustainable capitalism) has emerged as a formidable force in the race rematch (the next forty years). While Professor Fate's dark side has grown exponentially, The Great Leslie's upside has only begun to realize exponential gains. From biomimicry to 3-D printing, and from renewable energy to regenerative agriculture, waves of sustainable technologies are emerging that have the potential to overtake and creatively destroy Professor Fate's industrial-era holdouts. The days of merely seeking to reduce negative impact from existing, unsustainable technologies may finally be drawing to a close.

And so, the real-world Great Race is on. Will the commercialization of next-generation sustainable and regenerative technologies (The Great Leslie) outpace and reverse the continued growth in negative impact associated with Professor Fate? Will a new sustainable and inclusive form of capitalism make obsolete the extractive and inequitable shareholder capitalism that has ruled the world for the past forty years? Will a sustainable capitalism be able to outrun the rise of the authoritarian right with its complicity in continued industry concentration and profiteering, a form of neoshareholder primacy? The next decade will determine the outcome. The fate of humanity—along with other vulnerable forms of life on Earth—hangs in the balance.

In this chapter, I'll first draw the comparison between the Great Race we currently face and the Great Transformation that took place during the nineteenth and early twentieth centuries. I'll then provide a bit of background explaining how we as a society got to where we are today, with a focus on what makes the past forty years truly unique. Since the 1980s, the income and wealth distribution in the world has changed dramatically: while inequality has increased dramatically *within* individual nations, the world as a *whole* has been transformed from a *pyramid*—in which a wealthy elite at the top have long allowed the vast majority of people at the bottom to live in extreme poverty—into a *diamond*, in which a rapidly rising global middle class threatens to overwhelm the world's life support system. In addition, we still face the age-old challenge of extreme poverty in poor agricultural communities around the world, along with a nasty new third threat—the growing nativist backlash among those in the developed world who have been left behind by globalization and deindustrialization.

The chapter explores each of these challenges in depth along with some of the pioneering business initiatives designed to address them. I conclude that the Great Race is an enormous business opportunity—perhaps the biggest in the history of capitalism—but seizing it means nothing less than reimagining the world's inequality and environmental challenges through a new, more integrated and systemic business lens.

The Next Great Transformation

In his classic examination of the societal upheavals created by the Industrial Revolution and British-led economic liberalism in the late nineteenth and early twentieth centuries, *The Great Transformation*, it often seems like Karl Polanyi is speaking directly to present-day issues—albeit as a "rhyme," not a literal replay. Polanyi observed that the rise of the market economy, driven by the Industrial Revolution, brought with it "an avalanche of social dislocation" accompanied by a "vast movement of economic improvement" as well as a "catastrophic dislocation of the lives of the common people." He wondered how best to characterize this transformation: "Was it the rise of factory towns, the emergence of slums, the long working hours of children, the low wages of certain categories of workers, the rise of the rate of population increase, or the concentration of industries?"[2] Sound familiar? It should: liberalism and neoliberalism are blood relatives.

The Great Transformation destroyed existing coping mechanisms and safety nets, while it created a set of new challenges—before new coping mechanisms could be developed. It laid waste to the myth that free markets are "self-regulating." Polanyi recognized that liberalism's impact was not restricted to just the economy; instead, the transformation was societal in scope, requiring government intervention and other forms of protection to cushion the blow. He saw that an entirely new institutional mechanism had been unleashed on Western society, and that actions taken at the time consisted largely of attempts to "protect society against the ravages of this new mechanism," which he described as the "double movement."[3] Even Adam Smith conceded that basic measures of equity and competition were necessary for a market economy to function properly. Polanyi, however, was one of the first to recognize that without the governmental capacity to ensure social cohesion, capitalism spins perilously out of control—the "animal spirits" come to dominate the "better angels."[4]

Polanyi surmised that the era of economic liberalism came to an end not with World War I (which only gave way to a final burst of laissez-faire during the Roaring Twenties), but rather with the Great Depression and World War II. Little did he realize, however, that after a respite from the "ravages" of unabashed free markets during the postwar years—the age of welfare capitalism—a second coming of sorts (neoliberalism) would be unleashed on the world. It would produce a similar but much deeper set of societal and environmental ruptures that only a truly new societal order might be able to ameliorate. With neoliberalism's demise, we now stand at the threshold of such a new order—sustainable capitalism. Will we be able to both grasp the scale and scope of the upheavals caused *and* muster the resolve necessary to mount the transformational response required? The challenges are daunting to say the least.

The soft underbelly of America and other developed countries had been vividly exposed: poverty and inequality were no longer problems just in "poor countries" and the developing world. The plight of refugees, immigrants, minorities, and disenfranchised blue-collar workers had been starkly revealed. The passage of the massive $1.9 trillion Covid Relief Bill in early 2021 constituted a neostatist sea change in the policy agenda in America. Companies ranging from JPMorgan Chase to Target to Ben & Jerry's had also begun to confront directly issues of community disinvestment, social injustice, and reparations for African Americans. A new front in the sustainable business movement had been opened up, and it focuses on our own underserved and disenfranchised backyard.

Yet the reality remained that since the end of World War II, most effort in development and poverty alleviation has been focused on the *developing* world. There, literally *billions* of people still lived in *extreme* poverty, mostly as subsistence farmers in rural areas. Increasingly, however, the rural poor were migrating to cities in search of a better life and livelihood that might ultimately lift their families out of poverty, a true "rhyme" of nineteenth-century industrialization in the now-developed world.

Indeed, by the latter part of the twentieth century, urban migration had already fueled the rapid growth of dozens of emerging "megacities" across the developing world, from Rio de Janeiro to Mumbai to Nairobi, replete with sprawling squatter communities, slums, and shantytowns—an urban and periurban population that could exceed five billion by 2030. As incomes grew, however, consumption of resources, along with associated production of waste and emissions, threatened to overwhelm the planet's regenerative capacity, accelerating the mass extinction of species and runaway climate change.[5]

It was in the context of this mass urbanization movement that the term "sustainable development" first appeared. In their 1987 report, the Brundtland Commission recognized that poorly planned growth and overexploitation of the environment could doom efforts at economic development and poverty alleviation. They defined *sustainable* development as "meeting the needs of the present without compromising the ability of future generations to meet their own needs."[6] Since the Brundtland Commission's report, the challenge of sustainable development has only become more urgent and complex: planetary boundaries have since been eclipsed, inequality has grown, and climate change has become an existential threat.[7] Indeed, there are now *seventeen* Sustainable Development Goals, as articulated in 2015.[8]

These myriad environmental and social issues can be usefully coalesced into three overarching sustainable development *challenges* for 2030 and beyond:

- *End Rural Poverty.* We must alleviate extreme poverty in the *developing* world, by enabling a truly sustainable form of rural and agricultural development, one that simultaneously raises incomes, slows urban migration, and averts environmental meltdown.

- *Revive the "Rustbelt."* We must reverse rising inequality and discontent in the *developed* world, by vanquishing racism and lifting those left behind by neoliberalism, creating a truly inclusive economy, one based upon next-generation technologies that are inherently clean and regenerative.

- *Transform the Aspiring Urban Middle.* We must create a way to meet the needs of the urban underserved and rising global middle class in a way that does not push the environment and climate beyond critical thresholds.

These three challenges are daunting, to say the least. Yet, taken together, they define the Great Race that is sustainable capitalism in the years ahead—the *next* "Great Transformation." Tackling these challenges in the window of time we have available—the next decade or two—will require all hands on deck: bold policy innovation and institutional reinvention on the part of government, an activist civil society dedicated to catalyzing rapid change, and a business sector that sheds short-termism and incremental thinking in favor of long-term transformation—of their own strategies and business models as well as of the larger systems within which they operate. We will focus here on the catalytic role business can and must play in addressing these challenges in the years ahead. But first, before digging into the three "grand challenges" in more depth, allow me to provide a bit more context on how we as a society got to where we are today.

From Pyramids to Diamonds

As neoliberalism tightened its grip in the latter part of the twentieth century, there emerged a governing consensus that regulation was something to be scorned. Environmental and social policy initiatives therefore stalled during the 1990s in the face of coordinated opposition from the economic right. Markets and market forces became the answer to everything. Even the Democrat Bill Clinton declared in the 1996 State of the Union Address that the "era of big government is over."[9] For advocates of environmental and social responsibility, the focus necessarily turned to how best to leverage market forces for good.

As a result, the nascent sustainable business movement was focused on "win-win" opportunities for business—product and process innovations that were eco-efficient and good for the "triple bottom line," ideally even conferring a competitive advantage. This was very much the focus of my own early work in the emerging field, with my 1995 article, "A Natural-Resource-Based View of the Firm" capturing the essence of the win-win logic.[10] As the 1990s progressed, however, it became increasingly apparent that "environmental management" alone would not be adequate to the task, and a focus on the broader challenge of "sustainable development " rose to prominence.[11]

At the dawn of the twenty-first century, the prospect of harnessing the power of business to address the needs of the world's poor was a tantalizing, if counterintuitive, prospect. In fact, when C. K. Prahalad and I first drafted what would become "The Fortune at the Bottom of the Pyramid" in the late 1990s, the vast majority of the world's population (roughly four of the six billion people alive in the world at the time) earned less than $4 per day per capita.[12] The fall of communism a decade earlier had failed to produce the wave of middle-class consumers in developing countries and emerging markets that the world's multinational corporations clamored for. Poverty was still seen almost exclusively as the domain of aid organizations, governments, and philanthropists.

The argument that the poor presented a "prodigious opportunity for the world's wealthiest companies" attracted the attention of many in the corporate senior executive ranks, even as it was clear that "serving the poor" would require radical innovations in both technology and business models. Indeed, the prospect of lifting hundreds of millions out of poverty while simultaneously driving growth and financial performance was sufficient to persuade many business leaders to take the plunge.

In the years that followed, the base of the pyramid (BoP) challenge sparked a flurry of corporate initiatives and experiments aimed at serving the poor profitably. In the process, these large corporations were also awakened to the rich ecosystem of ventures, NGOs, and multilateral agencies already engaged in the space. New terminology emerged to describe the many forms of emerging BoP innovation: inclusive business, hybrid value chains, social enterprise, sustainable livelihoods, opportunities for the majority, and pro-poor business, to name just a few.

At the end of the last century, world leaders also came together to adopt the United Nations Millennium Declaration, committing their nations to a new global partnership and setting forth eight Millennium Development Goals (MDGs) focused on extreme poverty, education, gender equality, child mortality, material health, disease, environment, and global collaboration.[13] Led by Professor Jeffrey Sachs at Columbia University's Earth Institute, the MDGs were headlined by the seemingly audacious goal (MDG #1) of *halving* by 2015 the proportion of people in the world living in extreme poverty in 1990 (defined as per capita income of less than $1.25 per day)—consisting at the time of nearly two billion people.[14]

A surge in MDG-driven development aid focusing on extreme poverty, growing private-sector engagement, and, most important, a burgeoning Chinese economy combined to reduce the number of people living in extreme poverty from nearly two billion in 1990 to fewer than one billion in 2015, enabling the UN to report triumphantly that MDG #1 had been achieved.[15] This dramatic reduction in extreme poverty was accompanied by an unprecedented expansion of the global middle class, defined as those earning between $10 and $100 per day per capita (Exhibit 4.1).[16]

If this trend were to continue to 2030, the global middle class would expand to more than *five billion*, along with a continuing reduction in extreme poverty and an overall decline in the numbers of people at the "base of the pyramid"— those earning less than $10 per day per capita.[17] In the space of three decades, world income distribution would thus be fundamentally transformed from a "pyramid," with the bulk of humanity at the base, to a "diamond," with a burgeoning global middle class and shrinking base.

To be sure, the coronavirus pandemic temporarily reversed some of these long-term trends in poverty reduction. The World Bank estimates that Covid-19 pushed an additional 88–115 million people into extreme poverty during 2020, with the total rising by 150 million in 2021, compounding the forces of conflict and climate change, which were already slowing poverty reduction progress.[18] Indeed, without a renewed focus on the Sustainable Development Goals, the United Nations Development Program forecasts that an additional 207 million

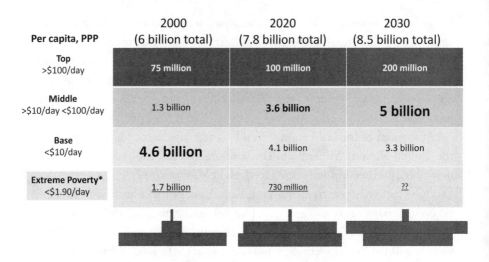

Per capita, PPP	2000 (6 billion total)	2020 (7.8 billion total)	2030 (8.5 billion total)
Top >$100/day	75 million	100 million	200 million
Middle >$10/day <$100/day	1.3 billion	3.6 billion	**5 billion**
Base <$10/day	**4.6 billion**	4.1 billion	3.3 billion
Extreme Poverty* <$1.90/day	1.7 billion	730 million	??

Exhibit 4.1. From Pyramid to Diamond

*Extreme poverty numbers are included in the Base estimate.

Sources: World Bank, World Data Lab, Brookings, and Pew Research Center.

people could be pushed into extreme poverty by 2030, calling the downward trajectory of extreme poverty into question.[19]

Yet, as Exhibit 4.1 makes clear, the world has still undergone significant change for the better over the past two decades when it comes to poverty: while world population has increased from six to eight billion, the proportion of people at the base of the income pyramid has shrunk, in favor of a rising global middle class. And should this trend continue, a rising global middle class of five billion in 2030 would provide clear evidence that we are making significant progress in "making poverty history."[20]

In fact, looking beyond 2030, the population challenge actually turns from one of boom to bust: by mid-century, most of the world's countries will be experiencing *declining* populations. Already in Europe and East Asia, countries such as Germany, Italy, South Korea, and Japan are confronting the reality of fewer workers and more retirees, necessitating infrastructure contractions, facility closures, and incentives for childbirth.[21]

China hit a historic turning point in 2022 when its population declined for the first time since the early 1960s. In the decades ahead, China could experience a sharp decline, with its population expected to fall from 1.4 billion now to around 700 million in 2100.[22] Aside from the obvious disruption to existing governance models, population contraction could have an upside—higher wages for those who work, greater equity, lower carbon emissions, less environmental destruction, and higher quality of life.[23]

Only sub-Saharan Africa appears destined for significant population growth well into the future. Sub-Saharan Africa's population is projected to grow from 1.3 billion in 2020 to 2 billion by the late 2030s, and 3 billion by 2060, making Africa ground zero for sustainable development and eco-innovation. In fact, Nigeria could surpass China in population by the end of the century.[24]

A Train Wreck Ahead?

Despite the "good news" story just articulated, all is not right with the world. Consider Christoph Lakner and Branko Milanovic's famous "elephant curve," which displays graphically the cumulative gains in real household per capita income between 1988 and 2008 (Exhibit 4.2).[25] It shows that incomes indeed have been increasing substantially throughout the bottom half of the global income distribution, but then abruptly drop, bottoming out around the 80th percentile, until suddenly shooting up again at the very top of the global income distribution. As discussed earlier, the substantial income growth from about the 20th to the 60th deciles (the top of the elephant's back) went mostly to people in the rapidly growing emerging economies of the world—China and India in particular.

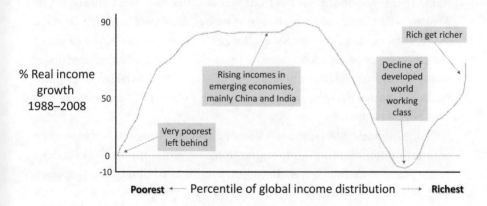

Exhibit 4.2. The "Elephant Curve" of Income Gains

Note: Adapted from Christoph Lakner and Branko Milanovic, "World Panel Income Distribution Data, 2013, www.worldbank.org/en/research/brief/World-Panel-Income-Distribution.

However, the dramatic drop-off in the 80th to 90th decile range (the bottom of the elephant's head) consisted mostly of working-class people in the *developed* countries of Western Europe, America, and Japan who have been negatively impacted by automation, deindustrialization, and globalization. Furthermore, those at the very top of the global income distribution (the end of the elephant's trunk) benefitted from almost as much income growth as the mass of people emerging from poverty at the lower end of the scale. Thus, while a massive new global middle class is indeed on the rise, the "old" middle class in the rich countries is stagnating while a super-rich global elite continues to get even richer, creating a potentially combustible combination of social and demographic extremes.[26]

To make matters worse, the results for MDG #7—"Ensure Environmental Sustainability"—are downright disturbing. Over the past five decades, for example, the use of natural resources has *tripled*, accounting for more than 90 percent of biodiversity loss and water stress and approximately half of climate change impacts.[27] Almost two-thirds of the world's cities exceed World Health Organization standards for air pollution, with many megacities in Asia so polluted that it is unhealthy even to walk outside.[28]

The combination of increasing resource exploitation and pollution has wreaked havoc on the world's ecosystems and threatens to make climate change spin out of control. The Intergovernmental Platform on Biodiversity and Ecosystems Services recently observed that "nature is declining globally at rates unprecedented in human history," with one million of the earth's eight million plant and animal species in danger of extinction. There are about half as many wild animals alive on the planet now as there were in 1970.[29] To make matters worse, after a precipitous decline in fossil fuel use during the height of the coronavirus pandemic in 2020, a "great climate back slide" is now under way. Indeed, financial institutions have poured more than a trillion dollars into the coal industry over the past two years, despite many of them making net-zero carbon pledges.[30]

Bill McKibben has facetiously declared climate change to be humanity's biggest "accomplishment"—the largest thing any single species has ever done to the planet since the Cambrian explosion of life two billion years ago, when blue-green algae flourished for the first time, flooding the atmosphere with oxygen and killing most of the ancient life that existed at the time.[31] In fact, the 2023 Intergovernmental Panel on Climate Change Synthesis Report has warned that the current trajectory of carbon emissions—fifty billion tons per year—will lead to an unstoppable cycle of global warming with major disruptions for life on Earth if significant reductions don't begin by 2025. What we do in the next few years will determine our fate for millennia.[32]

The inability of many people to perceive these massive impacts as the true planetary emergency they represent reminds me of the *crash test dummies* that we have all seen in auto safety testing infomercials: seen in slow motion, as a car gradually crashes into a test wall, the dummies inside appear to be gently and peacefully moving forward into the steering wheel, airbags, and windshield as the front end of the car is gradually turned into an accordion. It all seems innocuous enough to make one think that perhaps such a crash isn't so bad after all—until you see it in real time. Viewed regular speed, the crash appears to be the abrupt and violent event that it really is—sudden, jolting, and catastrophic, for the car and the dummies!

Given our short tenure on this planet, we humans are a bit like the crash test dummies in slow motion: the changes that we see around us appear gradual enough that they do not seem particularly out of the ordinary—we've always had hurricanes, tornadoes, floods, droughts, and wildfires. So, maybe we are just in a bad stretch. Or even if this is the new normal, perhaps it won't be that bad: warmer temperatures mean longer growing seasons. . . .

But when we view this video in "real time"—that is in *geologic time*—the changes that are happening are occurring in the blink of an eye, like the actual crash of the dummies. As far as we can tell, the atmosphere and the climate of the earth have *never* changed this quickly before, in the history of the planet. Not even close. Sure, the climate has fluctuated wildly over the billions of years that life has thrived on our planet. But the changes took place over millennia, not decades. There was time for life to adapt. We, unfortunately, are driving ourselves into the proverbial wall, but we can only see it happening in slow motion.

As a consequence, what economists have traditionally referred to as "negative externalities"—those damages imposed on society by economic exchanges for which no market price is paid—are no longer just peripheral issues. Environmental destruction and climate disruption have reached epic proportions. Recent estimates of the monetary value of unpriced ecosystem services (airsheds, watersheds, pollination, and so on) subject to disruption actually *exceed* global GDP. Imagine the number if we were to also include the costs of poverty and inequality imposed on society by the current capitalist model. In a very real sense, then, dealing with these negative externalities has become the main event. Perhaps today's global economy is better characterized as a market *failure* than an actual market.[33]

There also remains a stubbornly strong relationship between rising incomes and increasing environmental impact. For example, the richest 10 percent in the world currently account for nearly *half* of all consumption-related waste and greenhouse gas emissions.[34] And while an accompanying trend toward urbanization does compensate partially for the greater impacts associated with rising incomes (less transportation, more efficient use of space), we continue to significantly overshoot the carrying capacity of the planet. In fact, by 2030, two-thirds of the world's wealth will be owned by the richest 1 percent, mostly living in cities.[35]

The Global Footprint Network estimates that the current world population of 8 billion requires the equivalent of one-and-a-half Earths to sustain itself. If everyone alive today consumed at the same rate as the average American, it would take more than *five* Earths to support everyone's basic needs. Simply extrapolating current trends to 2030 (a world population of 8.5 billion with an aspiring middle class of 5 billion) would require *two* planets to provide the food, materials, and waste sinks needed for sustained sustenance.[36] Climate change could also multiply the number of "climate refugees." Indeed, the Brookings Institution estimates that there could be as many as 150 million additional climate-related migrants by 2050.[37]

As Exhibit 4.3 illustrates, the sustainability challenges we face vary significantly depending on where in the emerging "diamond" we look. At the top of the diamond, an aging population across the developed world is becoming increasingly unequal: the upper 10 percent have prospered and continue to consume at high rates, whereas the lower 90 percent continue to be threatened with job loss and have experienced flat or declining earning power; many are actually falling out of the middle class entirely, into the category of working poor.[38] Conspicuous overconsumption by the wealthy few combined with declining social and economic status among the majority and growing racial strife makes for a potentially volatile mix as the world experiences the disruptions of the Fourth Industrial Revolution.[39]

At the bottom of the diamond, while extreme poverty has been significantly reduced, many rural villagers (especially the young) are still choosing to migrate to cities in pursuit of better income-generating opportunities. In fact, the share of the world's population living in urban areas is expected to increase from 55 percent in 2018 to 60 percent in 2030. By comparison, just 30 percent of the global population lived in urban areas in 1950.[40]

Rural connectivity via mobile phones has proven a double-edged sword. On the one hand, greater access to information facilitates greater economic efficiency and better access to markets in rural economies. On the other, knowl-

	Pollution	Depletion	Poverty
Top (Developed)	Toxic legacy Greenhouse gas emissions Ecological footprint Overconsumption	Insufficient reuse and recycling Declining tax base Aging infrastructure	Rising inequality Disenfranchised workers Systemic racism Rising extremism
Middle (Emerging, Urban)	Toxic air pollution Lack of water and sewage treatment Solid waste burden	Water shortages Food scarcity Lack of health care Subject to disasters	Exploding shantytowns Inadequate housing Unemployment Rising extremism
Bottom (Poor, Rural)	Animal waste Lack of sanitation Agricultural chemicals Superweeds	Deforestation Overgrazing Soil loss Food spoilage	Family dislocation Aging population Lack of opportunity Community disintegration

Exhibit 4.3. Looking Ahead:
The Major Sustainability Challenges

edge of the wider world and electronic access to personal networks in urban areas fuels the flow of people from country to city, with the aspiration of joining the rising consumer class.[41] Today, approximately 1 billion people live in slums and shantytowns, and if all informal settlements are included in that number, the population of slums and shantytowns rises to 1.6 billion. By 2030, roughly one in four people on the planet will live in an urban slum or informal settlement, most of whom will also be exposed to rising sea levels and flooding due to climate change.[42]

Farming families and rural communities experience significant dislocation as a result: those remaining are faced with the challenge of farming with fewer family members engaged. Such urban migration does, however, have the potentially salutary effect of allowing those remaining to lease the underutilized land of neighbors, thereby enabling more economically viable parcels to farm (for example, five acres versus just one). However, declining rural populations means less aid and fewer services despite the pressure for higher farm productivity to feed the growing urban populations.

As more land is put under the plow or used to graze animals, the environmental consequences continue to mount, thus bringing us to the potential train wreck at the middle of the emerging diamond: an exploding middle-class population is being fueled by rural people migrating to urban and peri-urban areas around the world in search of a better life and livelihood.[43] As the influx of migrants swamps existing infrastructure, the world's megacities are becoming overburdened by waste; lack of adequate sanitation; exposure to toxic air pollution; and shortages of food, water, and access to health care. The proliferation of slums and shantytowns also speaks to the lack of adequate and affordable housing for the hundreds of millions of migrants flooding into the world's cities. But as incomes grow, the consumption of resources, along with the associated production of waste and emissions, will continue to mount.

Can the world build an economy that meets the needs of everyone without further breaching the planetary boundaries—what Kate Raworth calls "Doughnut Economics"?[44] Can we meet the needs of the exploding middle of the diamond *and* reduce carbon emissions and negative environmental externalities sufficiently over the next few decades to make it to what Pope Francis and others call the "Demographic Winter"—the beginning of a long and steady decline in world population—and along with it, environmental footprint— beginning around mid-century?[45] I'll address this question in the next section by delving into the three challenges associated with the Great Race in more depth, and exploring the catalytic role that business can and must play in winning the race.

The Three Grand Challenges for Business

Twenty-some years ago, when C. K. Prahalad and I first published "The Fortune at the Bottom of the Pyramid," the world was focused on the goal of eradicating extreme poverty and business was captivated by the prospect of new markets among the poor and underserved. When I wrote *Capitalism at the Crossroads* in early 2000s, I framed the global challenges we faced in terms of three markets or "economies": (1) *developed markets*, where reducing the corporate footprint was of paramount importance; (2) *emerging markets*, where avoiding the collision between urbanization and environmental degradation was key; and (3) *traditional markets*, where serving the real needs of the poor was of growing concern. Fast forward twenty years and we now appear to be headed for a potential train wreck at the middle of the diamond (MoD), and this potential calamity is being reinforced by the challenges coming from both the top and bottom, where decline and dislocation threaten upheaval (Exhibit 4.4).

Addressing the declining prospects of those in the "Legacy Base"—the remaining farmers in the rural villages of the world—is key to averting the train wreck at the MoD. To stem the flow of migrants from the farm to the city, we

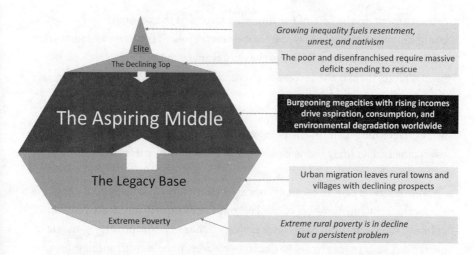

Growing inequality fuels resentment, unrest, and nativism

The poor and disenfranchised require massive deficit spending to rescue

Burgeoning megacities with rising incomes drive aspiration, consumption, and environmental degradation worldwide

Urban migration leaves rural towns and villages with declining prospects

Extreme rural poverty is in decline but a persistent problem

Exhibit 4.4. The Train Wreck Is Being Fueled from Above and Below

must expand successful policies and aid programs for rural development and poverty alleviation.[46] Extreme poverty has been effectively addressed through a combination of aid, philanthropy, economic development, mobilization of resources for social safety-net programs, and natural disaster relief. More recently, such efforts have also included an expanding role for business in serving and lifting the underserved at the base of the income pyramid. The first business challenge, then is as follows:

1. END RURAL POVERTY: How can we best enable a truly sustainable and regenerative form of rural and agricultural development in the "Legacy Base," one that simultaneously raises incomes, slows urban migration, and averts environmental meltdown?

Should discontent and dislocation at the "Declining Top" in the developed world continue to fester, however, continued deficit spending may be required to address the plight of those left behind—and to rebuild the crumbling infrastructure built during the era of welfare capitalism. Such deficits could spell doom for the foreign investment, development assistance, and international collaboration needed from developed countries (particularly the US) to finally vanquish extreme poverty at the base. We already see this tension regarding the continued financial and military support of the Ukrainians by the US and Europe, against the Russian invasion in 2022. Right-wing parties threaten to cut off such support in favor of "our country first" nationalist priorities. Such a retrenchment, in the face of the lingering effects of the coronavirus pandemic, could cause extreme poverty to persist or even grow in the years ahead, further fueling the unprecedented flow of the poor from farm to city in search of opportunity. Here, then, is the second business challenge:

2. REVIVE THE "RUSTBELT": How can we best create a truly inclusive economy at the "Declining Top" in the developed world, one that lifts those left behind, overcomes racial bias, and is based on next-generation, clean and regenerative technology?

While poverty is still a serious concern in slums and shantytowns throughout the world, growing numbers of rural migrants and slum dwellers are succeeding at lifting themselves out of extreme poverty. Once extreme poverty—the struggle for day-to-day survival—has been overcome, people confront new poverty challenges that are more *psychological* and *social* in nature: how to define and pursue a better life. Issues of perceived well-being, social comparison, and status envy become significant, and "poverty" becomes more relative than absolute.[47] As incomes—and aspirations—rise in the emerging, urban economies at the middle of the diamond, it is the former rather than the latter form of poverty that takes center stage. Thus the third business challenge:

3. TRANSFORM THE ASPIRING URBAN MIDDLE: How can we best fulfill the needs and wants of the underserved and rising middle class in the urbanizing "Aspiring Middle" without overwhelming the planet's regenerative capacity and eclipsing planetary boundaries?

Together, these three challenges will require wholesale transformation over the next decade—by governments, civil society organizations, and businesses everywhere—to create the possibility for a sustainable future. For business, this transformation means the shedding of profit maximization and shareholder value as the prime directives in favor of sustainability-driven purpose, innovation-driven strategy, and a commitment to larger system change. Increasingly, companies are seeking to become more purpose-driven—by establishing corporate aspirations and goals focused on *solving* the world's social and environmental problems, not just reducing negative impact from current operations.

The three sustainability challenges outlined here provide companies with potential "North Stars" to help focus their quests for purpose and provide fertile ground for prioritizing strategy and investment in the years ahead. Let's take a closer look at each of the three challenges and some of the pioneering business initiatives to address them both by established companies and by sustainable entrepreneurs.

Ending Rural Poverty: Building a Sustainable Heartland

The rural poor at the base of the income pyramid, while fewer in number than twenty years ago, still number in the billions. Nearly half of humanity still farms, and 70–80 percent of them live and work in smallholder farming households.[48] And as the late Paul Polak, founder of *iDE*, has noted, smallholder farmers are entrepreneurs by nature, but historically they have not been able to afford to take risks like other entrepreneurs do. Their farming has been limited to growing food for the family's survival.

But what if smallholders could grow enough to feed their families, plus more to sell at the market? By actually making a profit from farming, smallholders gain access to better food for themselves, opportunities for education, the freedom to invest in the business, and the ability to buy goods and services that can transform the health and lives of their families.[49]

For business, the opportunity is thus to help create thriving, connected, rural economies that not only sustain the remaining rural population but also point the way to a sustainable and prosperous future. Thriving rural communities would mean fewer of the young flooding the world's megacities in search of better opportunities. Key to this will be strategies that harness distributed energy generation and soon-to-be ubiquitous internet connectivity to bring services and innovations in agriculture, education, finance, and health care aimed specifically at the needs of rural, agricultural populations. It will also be important to think of smallholder farmers as part of families and communities, requiring a *systems* approach, rather than merely sourcing agricultural commodities from farmers or selling stand-alone services. Let's start by looking at a few innovative new ventures and initiatives focused on bringing services previously unavailable to the rural poor.

SERVICE INNOVATIONS FOR THE RURAL POOR

Nearly three billion people worldwide (mostly rural) do not have access to credit or services by banks and other formal financial institutions because they do not have a verifiable identity. Enter BanQu. Founded by Ashish Gadnis in 2015, BanQu uses blockchain to provide a platform where the world's poorest can build a free, secure online profile that provides them with a universal ID and allows them to begin tracking their relationships and transactions. Over time, they build a vetted identity, which is a prerequisite to participating in any form of ownership or transactions in the global economy.[50] BanQu recently launched a new initiative aimed at partnering with global food companies to facilitate commercial access directly to smallholder farmers using their secure, traceable, and transparent blockchain platform, greatly simplifying the quest for the sustainable sourcing of agricultural commodities and ingredients.

Another venture, eKutir, also demonstrates how to leverage the power of connectivity to serve and lift the world's poor, rural farmers. Founded by Ashoka Fellow KC Mishra in 2009 as India's first certified B Corp, eKutir's mission is to eliminate the rural poverty of smallholder farmers by harnessing digital technology and local entrepreneurship to grow farmers' economic, social, and human capital. Using a decentralized network of micro-entrepreneurs and user-friendly smartphone access, eKutir converts an exploitative and fragmented agricultural system into a collaborative and connected soil-to-sale ecosystem. Through a suite of low-cost mobile applications, eKutir extends agricultural services to the last mile, providing affordable soil analyses; reliable, high-quality inputs; education in sustainable agriculture and carbon markets; and key market connections. Concurrently, the company also connects suppliers, aggregators, and distributors to this network of smallholder farmers, providing simplified streams of communication, data, and product among the stakeholders in the value chain. This highly personalized, holistic approach generates rural employment, increases productivity, raises farm income, and generates carbon credits, all while reducing the costs associated with each step of the process.[51]

The good news is that myriad other companies, large and small, have also turned their attention to the needs of the world's rural population with a focus on smallholder farmers: think Mahindra and John Deere in small-scale farm equipment, Tata Group's mKRISHI agricultural platform for smallholder farmers, ITC's e-Choupal market access initiative, Waterhealth International's village-based clean water systems, SELCO's rural household solar electrification, ThinkMD's smartphone-based health platform, and Unilever's Shakti Entrepreneur model focused on rural villages.

Many of the world's global food companies—Unilever, Danone, Nestle, Pepsico, and Griffith Foods, for example—have well-established initiatives focused on the sustainable sourcing of agricultural commodities, which often include a focus on rural livelihoods as well as regenerative farming practices for their suppliers. In fact, the World Benchmarking Institute was recently created to help build a movement to measure and incentivize business impact toward a sustainable future. Their new Food and Agricultural Benchmark measures and ranks 350 keystone companies on key issues underpinning the food systems transformation agenda.[52]

Global food and confectionary giant Mars has taken this approach a step further. Like eKutir, it has recognized the "systems" nature of the smallholder challenge. That's why Mars has launched The Farmer Income Lab, a collaborative "think-do tank" aimed at helping to improve farmer incomes. The Farmer Income Lab invests in research to produce practical insights that can be turned into action. The Livelihoods Fund for Family Farming, as well as Mars's programs in cocoa, mint, and rice, provide a way of testing the insights and implementing new models for significantly improving farmer incomes. The insights and solutions get shared with the industry to help drive wider change and impact across global supply chains. The initiative is also being guided by an advisory panel of experts from academia, nonprofit, and intergovernmental organizations.[53]

COLLABORATIONS FOR RURAL SUSTAINABLE DEVELOPMENT

Recognizing the systemic nature of the rural poverty challenge, several other precompetitive collaborations have emerged in recent years focused on lifting the smallholder farm communities of the world while also creating a truly sustainable food system. The Sustainable Food Lab, for example, organizes safe, creative spaces for precompetitive collaborative initiatives to take root in a specific food chain or region to co-create and implement systemwide solutions. Existing collaborations include the Living Income collaboration, supporting activities to improve smallholder incomes; the Climate Smart Agriculture collaboration, aimed at climate-proofing smallholder agriculture; and the Food Loss & Waste collaboration, focused on high-leverage solutions to food loss and waste in smallholder farm supply chains.[54]

The World Business Council for Sustainable Development has also recently launched its "Farm of the Future" initiative aimed at identifying and scaling farming solutions that are "farmer-positive, nature-positive, and climate-positive." The ultimate goal of this collaboration is to strengthen the resilience of three hundred million small farmers by 2030 by building attractive rural livelihoods, increasing income, supporting access to affordable finance, investing in farming technology, promoting gender equity and social inclusion, scaling up climate and ITC-enabled advisory services, and enabling access to risk mitigation and insurance.[55]

The systemic nature of the rural poverty challenge makes it clear how important it is to engage all the necessary stakeholders when attempting to foment transformational change. The recent farmer protests in India provide an object lesson. On January 26, 2021, as part of India's annual Republic Day celebrations, a rally turned violent. Farmers drove tractors through barricades where they clashed with police and stormed the historic Red Fort in Delhi. It was a dramatic escalation after months of protests by hundreds of thousands of farmers challenging Prime Minister Narendra Modi and threatening the BJP party and the governing coalition of the country.[56]

At the center of the protest were three agricultural reform laws that had been pushed through Parliament by Modi's BJP party in September 2020. The new laws would allow farmers to sell their goods directly to private buyers without going through the state-run wholesale markets known as *mandis*, thus enabling them to negotiate better prices for their crops—a seemingly positive policy change. But because the Modi government rushed the new laws through Congress without significant discussion or engagement of those affected, the farmers feared the reforms would devastate their earnings by removing the Minimum Support Prices set by the government to prevent exploitation by large buyers. Tensions were further heightened as the coronavirus pandemic badly struck the urban economy, sending millions of laborers back their rural villages.[57]

The ensuing protests were met with police in riot gear using water cannon and tear gas to keep the farmers from entering the capitol, New Delhi. Hundreds of thousands of farmers set up camp outside the city. Across India, an estimated 250 million others joined the strike in solidarity, likely the largest organized strike in human history.[58] The government filed sedition charges against nine journalists who reported on the protests and cracked down on social media. Such stifling of dissent brought international attention, with climate activist Greta Thunberg expressing concern about the government's heavy-handed approach.

Whatever happens with Modi's agricultural reforms, the government's attempt to rush the new laws through Parliament without consultation and then to stifle any resulting dissent is not only a cautionary tale with regard to creeping authoritarianism, but also a lesson in how *not* to innovate at the base of the income pyramid. Indeed, as I and my colleagues have argued now for more than a decade, what is required is a truly participatory approach, with active engagement by those in the affected communities and a recognition of the systemic nature of any such innovation.[59] As Robert Chambers makes clear in his classic work on rural development, it is all about "putting the last first."[60]

CO-CREATING SOLUTIONS WITH THE POOR

Contrast the top-down Modi reforms with the development of the agricultural venture Cleanstar in Mozambique.[61] From its inception, the founders of this venture—Greg Murray and Segun Saxena—understood the systemic nature of their innovation and the importance of co-creating the business model and strategy. What began as a research experiment in India in 2005 with the support of USAID, WRI, and local universities soon morphed into an international parent holding company—CleanStar Ventures, which was incorporated in 2007. One of the ventures incubated by this group was a commercial platform to increase the food and energy security of smallholder farmers while addressing the perils of charcoal-based deforestation and cooking rampant across Africa—CleanStar Mozambique (CSM).

Indeed, before clean cookstoves caught the attention of world leaders and became a global priority, this pair of young, visionary entrepreneurs was thinking beyond the clean cookstove silo. They envisioned a vertically integrated business model that would address the challenges of charcoal-based deforestation and improve food security, health, and income for smallholder farming communities living on subsistence agriculture. For CSM, the cookstoves were a small part of a much larger ecosystem of value that included the upstream production of smallholder farmer-based biofuel from cassava, along with an integrated agro-forestry model that generated additional income and food for the farmers. Previously, the farmers subsisted on cassava and made charcoal to sell for cooking in the urban areas, accelerating the problems of deforestation and climate change.

It took significant effort and direct on-the-ground engagement with farmers, but after five years, over a thousand farmers had adopted the integrated agro-forestry model, and a two-million-liter-per-year ethanol-based cooking fuel production facility was built near Beira, Mozambique, to replace charcoal. Partners raised over $21 million from strategic corporate and institutional partners and investors such as Novozymes, ICM, Bank of America, Merrill Lynch, Soros Economic Development Fund, and IFU to grow and scale operations not just in Mozambique but across Africa. These partners also contributed technology, project management skills, connections, credibility, and financial savvy to the venture.

With over thirty-three thousand cookstoves and one million liters of cassava-based ethanol from rural Mozambique (branded as Ndzilo) sold to households in the capitol city of Maputo and elsewhere, CSM was emerging as a game changer. It was a poster child at Rio+20 with the "Screw Business as Usual" award, recognized as the Bioenergy Finance Deal of the Year 2012 by Environmental Finance, celebrated and discussed by sustainability experts, international agencies, and impact investors alike. Here, it seemed, was a true triple-bottom-line BoP ecosystem that created sustainable value for smallholder farmers—and all the stakeholders involved.

However, by late 2013, the story had taken a dramatic turn. Driven by a fresh round of investment capital, the financiers made the decision to "focus" the business by suspending its smallholder agro-forestry and ethanol production. The company also got a new name—NewFire Africa—and was now focused on just the sale of clean cookstoves and generic fuel. Unfortunately, this move proved unsuccessful, and in June 2014, the investors decided to voluntarily liquidate NewFire Africa to staunch the continuing losses.[62]

Nearly a decade of research, co-creation, business model innovation, and funding had gone into building this innovation ecosystem at the base of the pyramid. It was tragic that myopia on the part of financiers ended up destroying what made this venture truly unique and sustainable—the embedded and participatory nature of its business model and the fact that the fuel for the cookstoves benefited smallholder farmers in the countryside and helped to prevent further deforestation from occurring in Mozambique. Fortunately, the founders have been able to leverage their learnings from CleanStar in a new venture based in Kenya—KOKO Networks—that leverages mobile technology to connect users with a network of hundreds of "fuel ATMs" known as KOKO Points, that are installed inside local convenience shops where customers can purchase clean, locally produced biofuel in small quantities close to home to fuel their affordable, easy-to-use cooking stoves.[63]

Another hopeful example of co-creation and engagement with rural communities is the Indian venture Drishtee. The company started its journey as a rural technology solution provider, bringing services offered by the government to the doorstep of villagers. Founded in 2000 by entrepreneur Satyan Mishra as an initial pilot in the remote central Indian district of Dhar, Drishtee has spawned more than 150,000 kiosk centers across the rural Indian subcontinent, Africa, and Southeast Asia.

Mishra soon recognized, however, that simply making services available through an innovative business model did not solve the fundamental problem of livelihood generation in the villages, forcing migration of members of families to cities in search of paid employment. To confront this challenge, Drishtee aimed to build an efficient last-mile distribution network, which also included the most preferred "first mile" out of the village for locally produced goods. Today, Drishtee's mission is "to facilitate development of rural community organizations and delivery of business services to demonstrate a model of sustainable living on the planet."[64]

With growing numbers of companies and ventures realizing the need and opportunity in the Legacy Base, there may be a real chance of building a sustainable rural heartland in the years ahead—and helping slow the looming train wreck at the middle of the diamond. But reducing the influx of people migrating from farm to city serves only to buy time: to avoid the train wreck altogether, we must *innovate* entirely new ways of living and *transform* what people aspire to as they ascend the income ladder. More about that after we consider the challenge at the other end of the diamond—the "Declining Top" in the rich countries of the West.

Reviving the Rustbelt: Overcoming the Zero-Sum Mentality

The Declining Top is the result of a toxic combination of two factors: (1) loss of well-paid, working-class jobs due to globalization and technological change, driven by shareholder primacy; and (2) resurgence of racism and bigotry due to changing demographics, as people of color inexorably trend toward the majority. The coronavirus pandemic has served only to amplify and expose these fissures and trends given the outsized impact it has had on the lower end of the income scale and people of color. While the problem is particularly pronounced in the US, due both to the legacy of slavery and the dismantling of the social safety net over the past several decades, Europe and other developed countries also suffer from this problem, particularly when it comes to the influx of immigrants and refugees.

In *The War on Normal People*, entrepreneur and presidential aspirant Andrew Yang painted the truly grim picture that has been the American blue-collar job market for the past forty years. During that time, US companies outsourced or off-shored millions of jobs, with five million manufacturing jobs lost in just the past two decades alone. Disinvestment and deindustrialization have decimated significant parts of the so-called Rust Belt. Labor productivity grew, but virtually none of the gains were shared with workers in the form of pay increases. In real terms, wages for workers remained essentially flat since the early 1970s. This while the wealthiest 1 percent came to possess more than *half* of the total wealth in the country. So, while *mean* (average) personal income approached $60,000 per year and has continued to rise (given the skewed distribution toward the top), *median* personal income in the US now hovers around just $31,000 per year, meaning that *half* of the American workforce still earns less than $15 per hour.[65]

As a consequence, the labor participation rate (the percentage of working-age adults actually working) has fallen from nearly 70 percent in the mid-1990s to around 62 percent in early 2022. Keep in mind that each 1 percent decline means that 2.5 million people have dropped out of the formal economy. So even though wages have begun to tick up and Covid stimulus has helped drive unemployment to record lows in 2023, the drop in labor participation more than accounts for the drop in unemployment. That's why millions of jobs continue to go unfilled.

To add insult to injury, cutbacks in the social safety net, along with an exploding opioid crisis, have driven nearly 20 percent of working-age adults onto disability.[66] The coronavirus pandemic has only exacerbated this trend, with millions more dropping out of the workforce—twenty-five million in 2021 alone—in what has come to be called the "Great Resignation." With stimulus money enabling large numbers of people to shelter or work from home, many decided that they were no longer willing to sell their souls for uninspiring work.[67]

Whereas FDR presided over a time known as the "New Deal," when opportunities were dramatically increased for the poor and unemployed, social commentator Kurt Anderson has aptly labeled the last forty years as the era of the "Raw Deal."[68] I believe a root cause of this state of affairs has been the dogmatic adherence to zero-sum thinking by policymakers, capitalists, and disenfranchised whites—a coalition of strange bedfellows that has contributed to the downward spiral of the past four decades (Exhibit 4.5).

Policy during the neoliberal era has been guided by an assumption that *property owners* (read: monied interests) should take precedence, given their presumed outsized contributions as "job creators." Strategies such as raising taxes to fund public goods, providing health care for all, and fully supporting public education presumably violate the rights of the property-owning minority to do with their wealth as they please—an unfair taking. "Economic freedom" means countering the tendency of the majority to elect officials willing to raise

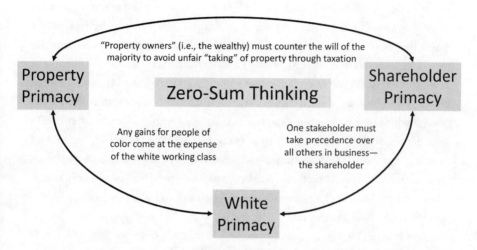

Exhibit 4.5. The Vicious Circle Driving the Decline at the Top

taxes on the wealthy minority in order to provide the "pork" demanded by their constituency—minorities, the poor, the disadvantaged, college students, and educated urban elites.[69] In my view, this is zero-sum thinking at its best: it ignores long-term, positive feedback loops that investment in public goods and services provide by reducing toxic inequality and raising overall demand for privately provided goods and services. A sea of poverty punctuated by islands of wealth surrounded by gates and barricades does not a sustainable economy nor desirable society make.[70]

Similarly, shareholder primacy in business is premised on the idea that *one* stakeholder should take precedence over all the others—*the shareholder*. Higher wages for workers, more spending on R&D, and environmental responsibility are expenditures that will presumably serve only to reduce the bottom line and lower the short-term return to shareholders—a sign of undisciplined management and cause for hostile takeover.[71] Again, zero-sum, short-term thinking at its best: shareholder primacy ignores the fact that optimizing results for *all* stakeholders—employees, suppliers, customers, communities, environment, and the future—is key to the generation of ongoing, long-term returns, even for the shareholders themselves.[72]

Finally, the erosion of the middle class and deindustrialization of entire working-class communities over the past forty years has exacerbated the problems of racism and hate. White primacy (in other words, systemic racism) is premised on the idea that African Americans, people of color, and immigrants are inherently inferior—members of a lower *"caste"*—a relic from the era of Indigenous and African enslavement in America.[73] The result is the belief that any gains for people of color come at the expense of white people. Even as the white working class has been decimated by globalization and automation, there is at least some relief in the knowledge that some are worse off than them. Indeed, it was Lyndon Johnson who, in the mid-1960s, noted that "if you can convince the lowest white man he's better than the best colored man, he won't notice you're picking his pocket." Again, zero-sum, trade-off thinking at its best: racism and bigotry, especially for disenfranchised whites, serves only to cut off their proverbial noses to spite their faces. Adhering to white privilege serves only to validate and enable a regressive policy agenda and shareholder primacy, thereby perpetuating the vicious cycle.

As Heather McGhee notes in her pathbreaking book *The Sum of Us*, it is high time that we rise above such zero-sum thinking.[74] The good news is that the idea of moving beyond trade-off thinking has actually been one of the core underpinnings of the sustainability movement. Indeed, "win-win" solutions have been the lodestar for sustainable business strategies from the very beginning: think eco-efficiency, pollution prevention, mutual, shared, sustainable, and stakeholder value. And while there are limits to "win-win" thinking—sometimes hard decisions and trade-offs do have to be made—the time has come to widen the aperture. Systemic racism and bigotry make it impossible to live sustainably. We must expand non-zero-sum thinking not only to overturn shareholder primacy, but also to reverse the policies and shift the institutions that reinforce racism and discrimination.

The loss of well-paid, working-class jobs due to globalization, automation, and digitalization has taken a heavy toll. Focusing on those left behind at the top of the pyramid will therefore be key to avoiding further societal upheaval, nativism, and extremism. Only by reversing the trend toward greater inequality that has plagued the developed world for the past forty years can we effectively address the problem of the Declining Top. Certainly, the aggressive new stance being taken by the Biden administration to provide for the short-term needs of those at the lower end of the income scale is a step in the right direction. So too are the bold policies for reinvestment in infrastructure and clean energy. We must seize the once-in-a-lifetime opportunity created by the coronavirus pandemic to truly change course in business as well, to create the sustainable economy—and capitalism—of the future.

CREATING TOMORROW'S JOBS WITH TOMORROW'S TECHNOLOGY

A key to the successful rebirth of deindustrialized regions and communities will be investment in the "exponential" technologies that will create the jobs of the future, as part of the "Fourth Industrial Revolution" (see Exhibit 4.6).[75] As Peter Diamandis and Steven Kotler have noted in their book *Abundance*, exponential technologies are those that increase in functionality at an exponential rate (for example, doubling every year) while simultaneously reducing cost.[76] Coincidentally, many exponential technologies also happen to be dramatically more environmentally sustainable than their predecessors (such as 3D printing, distributed energy generation, precision agriculture, the internet of things, artificial intelligence, nanotechnology). In the years ahead then, these emerging, exponential technologies will inevitably "creatively destroy" today's incumbent players in the energy, food, materials, construction, and health care industries.

Automation and digitalization have been used by companies to accelerate the *outsourcing* of production (for example, Alibaba), distribution (such as Amazon Fulfilment), and labor (for example, Uber) resulting in *downward* pressure on full-time employment. In fact, half or more of the increasing gap in wages among American workers over the last forty years is attributable to the automation of tasks formerly done by human workers. Economist Daron Acemoglu has made the case against what he describes as "excessive automation"—technologies that replace workers but do not yield real gains in productivity (such as self-checkout kiosks and automated customer service over the phone). Conclusion? We can and must harness automation and digitalization to help people do their work better rather than replace them.[77]

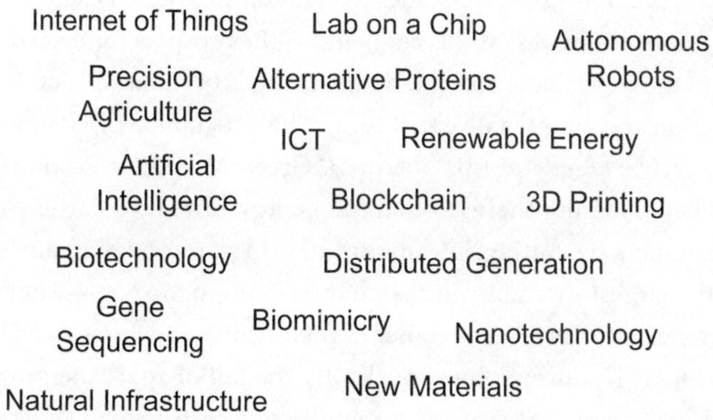

Internet of Things   Lab on a Chip

Autonomous Robots

Precision Agriculture   Alternative Proteins

ICT   Renewable Energy

Artificial Intelligence

Blockchain   3D Printing

Biotechnology   Distributed Generation

Gene Sequencing   Biomimicry   Nanotechnology

Natural Infrastructure   New Materials

Exhibit 4.6. **Next-Generation "Exponential" Technologies**

Other exponential technologies enable the creation of tomorrow's jobs.[78] In the energy domain, for example, electrification of end-uses in the transportation, building, and industrial sectors coupled with renewable electricity generation has been identified as one of the key pathways to achieving a low-carbon future in the US and other industrialized economies. Think electric vehicles, HVAC, industrial pumps, as well as home appliances powered by solar and other renewables rather than coal or oil. Indeed, a recent study by the National Renewable Energy Lab found that by 2050, end-use electrification combined with power sector decarbonization could achieve reductions nearly 75 percent below the 2005 level of economy-wide fossil fuel combustion emissions.[79] Deep electrification could help turn the developed world toward the path to climate stabilization—and a sustainable future. Trane Technologies, for example, through its well-known brands Trane (HVAC) and Thermo King (refrigeration), has set its sights on cooling the world's cities and providing much-needed refrigeration without destroying the climate in the process—an audacious and crucial mission, to say the least.

Large-scale wind and solar power were the first renewable generating sources to achieve commercial viability, due at least in part to their fit with the existing utility model. But exponential improvements in both the performance and cost of *distributed* solar and other renewable sources means that they already outcompete coal-generated power, and soon the same will true for natural gas. While the number of US jobs in the coal industry is small (approximately 60,000) and continues to shrink, the Solar Foundation estimates that solar already employs more than 250,000 Americans—a number that has tripled since 2010. Witness the recent growth of solar financing and installation companies such as SolarCity, SunCommon, and Sunrun. Once the cost of energy storage is sufficiently reduced—and companies like Tesla, Ambri, BYD, and others have focused serious resources on this challenge—the prospect for even more rapid conversion to renewables is bright, with hundreds of thousands of skilled jobs in installation and maintenance that cannot be outsourced as a bonus.

As an early example of this potential, Green Mountain Power (GMP) in Vermont is pioneering the use of stored energy to reduce carbon and costs for all customers by cutting the amount of grid power needed during peaks. It offers the largest discounts in the country—up to $10,500—when customers buy home batteries from a retailer of their choice and agree to share stored energy with GMP during power peaks. By the fall of 2020, the growing network of stored energy reduced about $3 million in costs for all GMP customers by cutting power demand during energy peaks, especially during the hot, dry summer. This network includes home batteries, utility-scale Tesla Power Pack batteries at solar sites, and carbon-reducing devices such as electric vehicle smart chargers.[80]

Putin's barbaric war in Ukraine may have the unintended consequence of actually *accelerating* the transition away from fossil fuels. As the world's largest exporter of total fossil fuels, Russia is being systematically cut out of markets, creating a supply-side shock, driving up fossil fuel prices, and speeding the penetration of renewable power of every variety.[81] The tipping point is coming first in Europe, where Russian fossil energy accounted for a fifth of total energy use. Renewables now beat coal, oil, and gas; electric vehicles win on life cycle costs in most cases; heat pumps are the new instruments of security and resilience; and green hydrogen made from solar and wind power has also become competitive. Even more significantly, the Global South can now leapfrog directly to cheap, stable, domestic renewable energy, avoiding the fossil-fuel stage of development entirely.[82] The "green leap," as I have called it, is now full speed ahead.[83]

Indoor agriculture also appears to be hitting the steep part of the exponential improvement curve, with great potential to lift the Declining Top. Vertical farming, in particular, is especially well-suited to urban environments and may finally be reaching a tipping point. Its virtues, relative to conventional agriculture, have long been clear: indoors, the climate can be controlled year-round; pests can be minimized, and with them pesticides; water and nutrients can be applied in precise quantities; and nutritious fresh vegetables can be grown for local markets year-round, with minimal transportation costs.[84]

The indoor farming technology market is also projected to grow by nearly 10 percent compound average growth rate, with a projected market of $40 billion by 2022.[85] And while growth of technology players such as Philips Lighting (Signify), Argus Controls, Everlight Electronics, and Lumigrow will certainly result in job creation, the biggest employment gains will come at the production level, where players such as FreshBox Farms (Crop One), AeroFarms, and dozens of other new urban farm entrants will, like the solar installation industry, produce thousands of skilled jobs in the years ahead, none of which can be exported abroad. With the proper investment incentives, many of these jobs could also come in the deindustrialized cities and communities left behind that need them the most.

And when it comes to housing and construction, we may be on the cusp of a game-changer: 3-D printing technology's exponential development now makes it possible to literally "print" a house at a fraction of the time and cost of conventional construction. Indeed, the venture ICON partnered with the nonprofit

New Story to build the first permitted 3D-printed home in America. The home was unveiled in March 2018 in Austin, Texas, and was built using a prototype of a mobile printer the group was creating for the developing world (where this could also be a game changer). The production version of the printer will have the ability to print a single story, 600 to 800 square foot home in under twenty-four hours for less than $4,000. As a part of this effort, ICON has developed cutting-edge materials tested to the most recognized standards of safety, comfort, and resiliency and is designed to function with nearly zero waste production methods and work under unpredictable constraints (limited water, power, and labor infrastructure) to tackle housing shortages.[86]

And imagine the possibilities as exponential innovation makes even more revolutionary new materials possible in the years ahead. Calera Corporation, for example, has used the emerging technology of "biomimicry" to make a cement-like material the way that coral make reefs—by sucking carbon out of the air, rather than spewing massive quantities of greenhouse gases to make conventional cement. Affordable housing that is carbon-negative? Not such a far-fetched idea.

PROMOTING ANTIRACISM THROUGH BUSINESS INVESTMENT

The majority of those left behind by shareholder capitalism over the past forty years have been members of the white working class. Yet the impact on communities of color has been even more extreme, with Black and Latino households holding dramatically lower assets across the board. Environmental injustice, including the proliferation of climate change, has also had a disproportionate impact on communities of color in the United States and low-income communities around the world. Toxic facilities, including coal-fired power plants and incinerators, emit mercury, arsenic, lead, and other contaminants. Many of these same facilities also emit carbon dioxide and methane—the number one and number two drivers of climate change. As it turns out, race, even more than class, is the number one indicator for the location of toxic facilities in America. And communities of color and low-income communities are often the hardest hit by climate change.[87]

Systemic racism accounts for much of this disparity, with long-standing policies of exclusion and discrimination in housing, finance, education, health care, law enforcement, and environmental protection leading the way. However, growing resentment among whites has also fueled a resurgence of racism toward minorities and immigrants in recent years, making the need to confront this challenge a key to addressing the problem of the Declining Top.

The coronavirus pandemic and its ensuing economic meltdown laid bare the extreme inequities that exist in the world, particularly in the US. Long-standing policies designed to exclude (housing and education discrimination) and other forms of systemic racism (for example, racial profiling, mass incarceration) had already resulted in gross imbalances in terms of income and wealth. The Brookings Institution estimated, for example, that African American wealth per capita in the US was *less than 10 percent* that of white wealth even before the pandemic hit.[88]

The Black Lives Matter (BLM) uprisings that swept the world in the wake of the brutal murder of George Floyd at the hands of the police were a clarion call for change. Indeed, the BLM movement has shined a bright light on the inhumanity and brutality that is systemic racism in the US and around the world. While such discrimination cries out for sweeping policy changes to remove the structural biases that have long existed with such practices as redlining in housing, mass incarceration in criminal justice, and injustice in environmental protection, the time is now for the private sector to also step up to this challenge.

Stepping up means more than philanthropy and commitments to diversity and inclusion in hiring and promotion within the company—it means making *proactive investments* in communities of color with the aim of redressing the historical deprivation these communities have experienced. As Ibram X. Kendi makes clear, the opposite of racism can no longer be a neutral claim of simply *not* being racist.[89] The fight against racism by business must thus be championed by strategies and behaviors that are explicitly antiracist.[90]

For example, JPMorgan Chase, along with the mayor's office and a range of local groups, entered into a public-private partnership in Detroit, Michigan—a city that is 80 percent Black—to help fuel the recovery from decades of deindustrialization and disinvestment. Their strategy focused on stabilizing neighborhoods, retraining the workforce for today's job market, and bolstering local small businesses, all while attracting new investors. JPMorgan Chase was among the initial investors in this strategy, committing $100 million in 2014 with plans to expand that to $200 million by 2022. Even more important, JPMorgan Chase's work in Detroit provided proof of concept of a model that could be applied to other deindustrialized, minority-heavy cities in the US, as well as in Europe and other parts of the industrialized world now experiencing technological dislocation.[91] Citigroup, for example, has recently launched the

$200 million Citi Impact Fund, which makes equity investments in double-bottom-line private-sector companies with a focus on women and minority entrepreneurs.[92]

In partnership with Black women-led organizations, Goldman Sachs also recently launched a new investment initiative—One Million Black Women—which will commit $10 billion in direct investment capital and $100 million in philanthropic support to address both the gender and racial biases that Black women have faced for generations, which have only been exacerbated by the coronavirus pandemic. Areas of investment focus will include health care, education, housing, and small business development, all aimed at narrowing opportunity gaps and having a positive impact on the lives of at least one million Black women. The company estimates that reducing the earnings gap for Black women has the potential to create 1.2–1.7 million US jobs and increase annual GDP by $300–400 billion.[93]

Cascade Engineering makes a wide variety of plastic injection-molded parts used in myriad products, including cars, furniture, and manufacturing equipment. As one of the larger B Corps, with more than a thousand employees and revenues of $200 million, the company is guided by a "true north" strategy that is defined by long-term objectives focused simultaneously on people, profit, and planet. For two decades Cascade has also been hiring people almost no one else would hire and has made a healthy profit doing it. Cascade is committed to hiring ex-felons and welfare recipients (the majority of whom are people of color) from around its hometown of Grand Rapids, Michigan. So far, some eight hundred men and women have found jobs through Cascade's Welfare-to-Career program, a model that has been replicated at fifteen other companies in southwest Michigan and has drawn interest from agencies in three other states.[94]

Ben & Jerry's has taken strategies for antiracist reinvestment even a step further.[95] As an aspiring social justice company, Ben & Jerry's believes in a greater calling than simply making a profit for selling its goods. As most people know, the company produces a wide variety of super-premium ice cream, yogurt, and sorbet using high-quality ingredients. Lesser known is the fact that Ben & Jerry's incorporates its vision of "Linked Prosperity" into its business practices in a number of ways including a focus on inequality and racism. Ben & Jerry's also cares deeply about its environmental impact on the planet, which is why they have not only set aggressive targets for greenhouse gas emissions, but also seek to take responsibility for all of their *historic* climate impact. They have begun to think about what reparations for slavery might look like for the company and have creatively integrated this with the offsetting of their historic carbon by investing specifically in sustainable innovation in Black communities.[96]

The Sustainable Innovation MBA Program at the University of Vermont worked with Ben & Jerry's to develop a pilot program to launch this innovative investment initiative that combines the offsetting of historic greenhouse gas (GHG) emissions with investing in Black communities, businesses owned by Black Americans, and other social justice initiatives associated with their supply chain and consumer market. The key here is that they are not interested in just planting trees or purchasing offsets; instead, they want to *invest* in antiracist business development projects so as to simultaneously realize both carbon reductions *and* social and environmental justice benefits.

The hope is that this pilot project will give Ben & Jerry's a clear path to be able to scale up to a full-blown program intent on offsetting 100 percent of historic GHG emissions, set a public goal, create a clear timeline, estimate total investment and create an investment plan, and establish a long-term program to systematically address their historic climate impacts and, at the same time, commit to a greener future steeped in justice. They just might also create a model for how other, much larger corporations can shatter the perceived trade-off between social justice, environmental sustainability, and financial viability.

As important as proactive investment is to overcoming racial bias in the years ahead, of equal importance is *how* these investments are actually implemented. As noted earlier in the chapter, I have personally been engaged over the past twenty years in developing effective business strategies for reaching the base of the income pyramid, mainly in the developing world. There is now extensive experience in how to effectively *co-create* business models with those in underserved communities rather than simply seeking to sell low-cost goods and services from the top down.[97] The importance of partnering to create new business ecosystems to realize more systemic change has also become increasingly well understood in the developing world context.[98]

Much of this experience can be productively transferred to the underserved and left behind in the Declining Top. The time is now to leverage this experience to increase the probability of success with antiracist investments and to accelerate the rate of change. Being a good ally means resisting the temptation to engage in heroic initiatives to "save" people of color from their plight. Instead, it means standing up for and supporting communities of color in their struggle to improve their own lives and communities.[99]

With some guts, persistence, and investment, business financiers and innovators can spearhead the rebuilding of the world's postindustrial cities—and economies—in the developed world. Like the proverbial phoenix rising from the ashes, the Declining Top can be transformed into a bottom-up, antiracist innovation engine featuring new jobs and careers focused around renewable energy, electric mobility, sustainable agriculture, and affordable homes made of materials that reverse climate change. Which now brings us to the third and most daunting poverty challenge of all: How can we avoid the impending train wreck at the middle of the diamond?

Transforming the Aspiring Urban Middle: Enabling Five Billion to Flourish

The good-news development story of the past twenty years is that we have (1) dramatically reduced extreme poverty, and (2) succeeded in lifting the mass of humanity further up the income scale. But how can we reconcile the material demands of the soon-to-be massive swell of five billion people in the rising middle class with environmental constraints and planetary boundaries? Will we fall prey to the same material overconsumption of the past or can we promote environmental sustainability as the new fashion? We have the opportunity— perhaps the duty—to set a new tone for what constitutes status and success with the rising middle classes in emerging economies. And sustainable innovation will be the vehicle for making it happen.

Producing sufficient quantities of food to nourish five billion increasingly discerning consumers presents perhaps the biggest challenge. Even with indoor agriculture and a concerted effort to reduce food waste, there will simply not be adequate land to produce the feed necessary to supply protein to these five billion if they all become avid meat-eaters. Beef cattle are especially inefficient producers of protein, requiring nearly seven pounds of grain for every pound of meat, not to mention the water, chemicals, and fossil energy involved in growing the grain itself. Plant-based and alternative proteins will almost certainly be required. Unfortunately, life-long meat eaters at the top of the pyramid are tough to convert—the result of too many years of indulging in juicy steaks on the grill and hamburgers from McDonald's. Unlearning is always a difficult proposition.

But the new, aspiring meat-eaters among the recent rural migrants and urban slum-dwellers are not as set in their ways. What if we can produce tasty, appealing, nutritious, and affordable forms of meat and dairy substitutes that rising middle class consumers clamor for? This is precisely the mission of the innovative Silicon Valley–financed Eat Just, founded by Josh Tetrick in 2011. Indeed,

Eat Just aspires to nothing less than playing a prominent role in ending world hunger by 2030 and ensuring that every family, in every community, has access to delicious, nutritious, and affordable food.[100] By combining state-of-the-art technology, including computational biologists, food engineers, and chefs with culturally relevant product development to suit local tastes and decentralized low-cost production facility design, they just might be on to something.

The company's initial products have been items such as eggless mayo and mung-bean-based egg substitute for upscale Americans, helping to drive the business to unicorn status in 2016, surpassing $1 billion in market value. Eat Just has also raised nearly $100 million in venture capital to fund cultured meat production. Indeed, its lab-grown chicken became the first cultured meat to receive regulatory approval, in Singapore in 2020.[101] From this base, their ultimate aim is to tackle the global meat substitute challenge—and change the world for the masses. It is only a matter of time before other alternative protein innovators such as Beyond Meat, Impossible Foods, Oatly Group, Tattooed Chef, and BlueNalu, not to mention such food companies as Unilever, Danone, PepsiCo, and Nestle, recognize this same need—and massive opportunity. In fact, Chicago-based food product development partner Griffith Foods has begun to devote increasing attention to the creation of alternative protein dishes that are simultaneously delicious, nutritious, and affordable. Much more about this in Chapter 5.

Garbage and waste are also massive problems in the exploding megacities of the world: the typical shantytown consists of densely packed, make-shift dwellings surrounded by wall-to-wall trash. Waste pickers are omnipresent, but with predatory middle men as buyers, they usually end up earning only meager, informal wages for dangerous and dirty work. High-value metals are the first to be picked, but the remaining mix of plastics and low-grade paper litters communities and roadsides across the developing world. But what if we really could turn this garbage into gold—and living-wage jobs at the same time?

Enter the Inclusive Waste Recycling Consortium (iWrc). Launched in 2015 by former Johnson & Johnson executive Michael Maggio, the iWrc brings together global and regional companies (for example, J&J, HP, Kimberly Clark, Dr. Reddy's), NGOs, key government agencies, academic partners, and technical collaborators to build an ecosystem focused on achieving multiple objectives, including (1) promoting social inclusion, better working conditions, living wage, and formalization for waste pickers; (2) creating market value for "worthless" or low-value materials; (3) integrating new technology (for example, the Internet of Things) as part of the collection infrastructure; and (4) helping avoid plastic waste making its way into water bodies and landfills. The iWrc has already launched successful initiatives in both Brazil and India and is seeking to scale its model to other countries in the future.

Plastic waste is no small problem: over three hundred million tons of plastic is produced annually, and less than 8 percent of that plastic is recycled. Plastic chokes the environment in places that do not have waste collection infrastructure, like the world's burgeoning megacities, which usually means the plastic is burned or ends up along roadways or waterways, with growing amounts finding a final resting place in the ocean. If we keep producing (and failing to properly reclaim) plastics at current rates, the World Economic Forum projects that plastic in the ocean will outweigh fish pound for pound by2050.

Another venture—ByFusion—could be a game-changer when it comes to the plastic waste scourge that is choking the world's cities and oceans. Currently only three categories of plastic waste can easily be recycled, types 1, 2, and 5. ByFusion offers a unique value proposition by enabling all categories of plastic to be given a new productive life. The new technology, called the Blocker, was first developed in the year 2000. In 2015, entrepreneur Heidi Kujawa purchased the rights for the Blocker technology and became ByFusion's new CEO. The Blocker uses pressurized medical grade steam, in combination with compression, to mold and reset waste plastic into functional forms such as interlocking blocks, the size of standard cinder blocks. These bricks, called ByBlocks, have many potential uses, including infrastructure projects, sound barriers, wall partitions, warehousing, housing construction, and landscaping.[102]

Imagine for a moment the world's exploding cities being built, at least in part, with blocks made from recycled plastic waste, employing hundreds of thousands of people in living-wage, safe, and formalized employment. And now imagine the existing polluting and exploitative brick-making industry, which "employs" millions in dirty, seasonal, low-paying jobs in places like India and Bangladesh, being creatively destroyed by this next-generation sustainable technology.

Sustainable food and shelter are critical if we are to sustainably accommodate five billion in the rising global middle class in the years ahead. But many of the world's swelling megacities—Lagos, Jakarta, Shanghai, Rio de Janeiro, Mumbai, Kolkata—are threatened by climate change, with sea level rise and increasing storm intensity leading the threats. To be sure, some hard infrastructure (for example, seawalls, levees, dikes) will be necessary to avert disaster in many of the most threatened locales. But much can be done through the building of natural "green" infrastructure, such as reclaimed or expanded wetlands, marshes, floodplains, dunes, and coral reefs.

The Nature Conservancy has led the way on this global quest, but recently global companies and banks, such as JPMorgan Chase, Dow, and Caterpillar, have stepped forward with business models and financing that could take this approach to the next level. Caterpillar, for example, has launched a new corporate initiative focused on natural infrastructure as a business of the future. Indeed, as core businesses of the past like coal mining equipment show serious decline, the company is looking to position itself for the future. And what better way to apply its core competencies in earthmoving and vehicle automation than solving the world's challenges around coastal resilience, storm protection, and water management?

As we move more people out of extreme poverty in the years ahead and the trend toward urbanization continues, the biggest challenges—and business opportunities—will be those of creating the sustainable livelihoods and lifestyles for the burgeoning middle class of the world. Will the world's entrepreneurs and business innovators be up to the challenge?

Pulling Out All the Stops

The magnitude of the challenges we now face calls for nothing less than "all hands on deck." The years ahead will, of necessity, be disruptive and transformational times. In all likelihood, many of today's incumbent corporations—especially those in resource- and waste-intensive industries—will not survive the next decade. If you think the Great Recession was wrenching in the last decade, just wait for the Great Extinction in the next one. Yet, with many national governments under duress and civil society already overburdened, the world desperately needs the private sector to step up in a way previously considered unfathomable.

I believe the companies that will succeed in making it to the future will be those that focus their resources and creative energies on *transforming* themselves to solve the pressing social and environmental problems we now face. The time is now to move beyond "sustainability" as a set of separate company initiatives and programs to one of core purpose and strategy. The current situation calls for nothing less than dedicating corporations' formidable resources to addressing world challenges and building the capabilities, strategies, and partnership ecosystems necessary to making it happen. But even total transformation by individual companies will not be enough.

Twenty-six years ago, I wrote a piece in the *Harvard Business Review* titled "Beyond Greening: Strategies for a Sustainable World."[103] In the article, I drew the distinction between strategies for "greening"—incremental reductions in negative impact through process or product innovation—versus "beyond greening" strategies, which involve commercialization of inherently clean or regenerative technologies and inclusive business models that serve and lift the underserved. Had we executed on the beyond-greening agenda starting back then, we might be in a position now for a purely business- and market-driven approach to prevail in the quest for a sustainable economy and world. But alas, a quarter century has gone by and most of what passes for "sustainable business" is still firmly rooted in the *greening* category—what Bill McDonough calls being "less bad" versus aspiring to be "more good"—even while Rome burns.

Consequently, we have now—sticking with the Roman metaphor—crossed the proverbial Rubicon. We have, for the first time, begun to cut off our own lines of retreat. Averting the train wreck will now require a more fulsome commitment by business than simply voluntary, market-based sustainability initiatives and impact investing. As Duncan Austin points out in his provocative essay "From Win-Win to Net Zero," we are now literally in a race against time. Remaining within planetary boundaries—climate stability, ecosystem integrity, water availability—now requires emergency response, placing the entire global economy on deadline. Science-based targets and net zero commitments mean working *back* from real-world thresholds and limits to identify proportionate commitments for companies and other organizations over finite time frames. As Austin notes, the days of "more sustainable than before" must give way to "enough sustainability before it is too late."[104]

Even "beyond greening" initiatives will not be enough to bend the curve when it comes to climate change or biodiversity loss—let alone toxic inequity. Our circumstances now demand that business take the lead in transforming not only its *own* house but also the larger system in which it operates, including the policies and institutions that define the game of capitalism itself. As Paul Polman and Andrew Winston argue in their landmark book *Net Positive*, business must become a *catalytic* force for redefining the very conception of value across the entire value chain . . . and beyond.[105]

The Great Race is thus an enormous business opportunity, perhaps the biggest in the history of capitalism. But seizing it means nothing less than reimagining the world's inequality and environmental challenges through a new, more integrated business vision. Think of the three sustainability challenges described in this chapter as the fulcrums for the future, and the company pioneers highlighted as early examples of what must become a tidal wave of transformation. These challenges must serve to inspire and inform compelling company aspirations and define business goals and impact metrics that really matter.

The times demand commitment not only to corporate transformation but also to larger system change and institutional redesign. In our work focused on harnessing the power of business to lift the base of the pyramid, for example, the "first generation" of thinking focused on simply *selling* affordable products and services to the poor whereas the "BoP 2.0" approach recognized the importance of *co-creating* new products and markets *with* the poor. Current thinking—BoP 3.0—however, takes it a giant step further—to achieve the desired developmental impacts in underserved communities, it is necessary for business to orchestrate change in the local *socioeconomic system* in which the poor find themselves.[106]

A similar challenge now faces tomorrow's corporations. Wholesale changes at the policy, system, and institutional levels will be necessary to usher in a new age of sustainable capitalism. The strictures of shareholder primacy continue to make it difficult for individual companies to make the necessary long-term investments and wholesale transformations needed. Sustainable capitalism will require not only corporate innovation, but a new narrative and objective function for business—an entirely new operating system. It is to these more pragmatic matters that we turn our attention in the remainder of the book, beginning with the necessity for wholesale corporate transformation.

FIVE

Re-Embedding Purpose

"Purpose and sustainability are our primary objectives. Our aim is to do the right thing in the world, to use our knowledge and capability to make the world a better place. We are organizing for impact. Goals that measure progress in this regard are really our effectiveness measures—they tell us how well we are doing as a company. Financial measures are indicators of how efficiently we are pursuing these societal objectives—how well we are converting societal needs into business reality. They are target locating tools, means to an end. They are not the end in themselves."

BRIAN GRIFFITH, EXECUTIVE CHAIRMAN,
GRIFFITH FOODS

The Great Race should sound the alarm bell inside corporate boardrooms around the world: the social and environmental challenges we now face require nothing short of a fundamental reorientation of business in the years ahead. As we have seen, the world is not on track to achieve the Sustainable Development Goals by 2030, and Force for Good, a UK-based NGO focused on sustainable finance, concludes that most companies still see the SDGs as "worthy causes" rather than business opportunities to invest in.[1] Indeed, for the past forty years, business purpose—to the extent that it has existed at all—has been primarily aimed at maximizing profit. As we look ahead, we must literally flip the script: profit must be returned to its rightful place in the capitalist pantheon—as a *means* to a greater end for business—solving the existential world challenges that we now all face.

There is some momentum toward such reorientation. Over the past decade, the ideas of sustainability and purpose have become increasingly prominent in the public rhetoric of firms, but while purpose statements and sustainability goals abound, serious investments in portfolio and business strategy transformation are still few and far between. Re-embedding purpose back into core business strategy thus represents one of the most important challenges—and opportunities—for realizing the promise of sustainable capitalism. In this chapter, I'll develop a practical framework and approach for re-embedding purpose in companies, and illustrate it through the "living" case of Griffith Foods, where I have been working with senior management the past several years to make sustainability part of the core DNA of the company.

You may wonder why I use the phrase "re-embedding" purpose rather than simply "embedding." I quite consciously select this phrase because the last forty years have represented a detour—a radical departure from the age of welfare capitalism—when corporations were viewed as institutions and societal contribution was paramount—albeit with blind spots. Allow me to briefly refresh your memory about how we went off track before focusing our attention on the task at hand—re-embedding purpose.

The Great Transactional Detour

University of Chicago economist Ronald Coase wrote a piece during the 1930s that would eventually become a pillar for the shareholder primacy movement that gathered momentum in the 1980s—and serve to blunt the significance of societal purpose in business for a generation.[2] Coase's article, "The Nature of the Firm," served as the foundation for what came to be known as transaction cost economics and, by implication, the Friedman Doctrine of profit maximization.[3]

As noted in Chapter 3, Coase asked the following provocative—and existential—question: Given that "the price mechanism should give the most efficient result . . . why do firms exist?" His answer was that firms exist because they are more efficient in reducing transaction costs (for example, search, bargaining, and enforcement costs) than the market. In other words, were it not for the inherent superiority of firms to execute transactions more efficiently than through the market, there would be no need for firms to exist![4]

So much for the idea that people working together in firms might be motivated by the societal mission of the organization, or a sense of professional dedication and shared purpose, or being part of a team with a unique constellation of capabilities. The consequence? Beginning in the 1980s, corporations came to be viewed (at least by many economists and Wall Street investors) as little more than efficiency machines—vehicles through which profits (and shareholder value)—could be maximized. Indeed, by the 1990s, shareholder primacy had become a "Holy Grail," with company purpose devolved into the crafting of corporate "mission" and "vision" statements, most of which were narrowly technocratic, usually focused on vanquishing competitors or dominating markets.

We had entered the era of the "laminated corporate mission card"—with competitive shibboleths formulated by executives distributed to management and the rank and file on cards for their wallets and purses to ensure "buy in." I still have wistful memories of teaching executive education programs at the University of Michigan during the late 1980s and early 1990s and listening to the company participants commiserate about just how disingenuous this exercise was. They noted that, despite the laminated cards, few managers or employees in their firms could actually tell you what the corporate vision and mission was or how it connected to their jobs. They simply knew that making the numbers was all that mattered.[5]

With the new millennium, however, came a growing resistance to this logic, particularly after the Great Recession, questioning the legitimacy of market fundamentalism and shareholder primacy. Business ethics, corporate responsibility, and sustainability emerged as front-and-center issues on the corporate agenda.[6] The latest round of capitalist reformation is witness to a rebirth of corporate purpose focused on *societal* contribution and not just competitive dominance. Growing numbers of companies are seeking to bring their purposes to life by articulating a set of long-term sustainability goals and commitments and making positive contributions to and impacts on society and the world. While this trend toward societal purpose and long-term sustainability goals is clearly positive, it comes with a hitch: companies have often overpromised and underdelivered.

Beyond Sustainability Hyperbole

Given the scale and scope of the environmental and social problems we now face—witness the three "grand challenges" outlined in Chapter 4—sustainability has appropriately become a central focus for the renewal of purpose among today's corporations. The Sustainable Development Goals (SDGs)—adopted in 2015 by the United Nations—have been used increasingly by corporations aiming to rekindle their sense of societal purpose: the 17 goals and 169 associated targets provide a roadmap that enables companies to identify which of the myriad sustainability challenges they are best positioned to address. Many corporations have even adopted specific SDGs as core to their purpose and societal focus.[7]

Yet challenges remain when it comes to making corporate societal purpose something genuine and authentic, rather than just window dressing for analysts, critics, and observers. A recent study by PricewaterhouseCoopers, which included 729 companies from twenty-one countries, found a significant gap between corporate intention and operating reality. Indeed, the study found that while 72 percent of the companies mentioned the SDGs as key in their corporate and sustainability reporting, only 27 percent of the companies said that the SDGs were core to their business strategy. The study concluded that while there appears to be a clear appetite to embrace sustainability as part of corporate purpose, most companies still lack the capability, tools, and culture needed to embed it into core strategies and initiatives.[8] Indeed, a 2022 Capgemini study of over two thousand senior executives found that a majority still view sustainability initiatives as obligatory and largely unprofitable.[9]

The launch of the meat-free "McPlant" burger at McDonald's is a case in point. On the surface, it appeared to be a bold strategic move—to stake out a future position in the emerging "alternative proteins" space and lead the transformation to a more sustainable food system. But a deeper dive into the company's strategy revealed that it did not seem to be part of a bigger corporate agenda to reduce beef consumption or shape consumer demand for the future.[10] Indeed, the pledge by McDonald's to cut its climate impact to "net zero" by 2050 has been called into question by environmentalists given its global growth strategy of "tapping into customer demand for the familiar."[11]

Smoothie maker and B Corp Innocent provides another object lesson. A recent ad campaign featured animated characters encouraging people to "get fixing up the planet" by buying Innocent drinks. They were immediately called out by the activist group Plastics Rebellion over the fact that the drinks were packaged in single-use plastic. The additional fact that parent company Coca-Cola used three million tons of plastic packaging each year certainly did not help matters.[12]

Too often, corporate sustainability initiatives have been guilty of what I call "sustainability hyperbole"—grandiose marketing statements that adorn company websites and sustainability reports but offer little in the way of integration into long-term corporate strategy, investment priorities, and operating plans. For purpose-driven brands, the temptation to go public with halo-inducing sustainability messaging might be even more problematic. Unilever CEO Alan Jope has gone so far as to say that such "woke-washing" from brands is undermining people's trust in advertising and marketing.[13]

Lofty statements of corporate purpose have become increasingly *de rigueur* for large public corporations, with more than 90 percent of them now filing sustainability reports—a hundredfold increase in the past two decades.[14] The problem is that many such purpose statements turn out to be little more than disembodied catchphrases that neither describe current reality nor effectively serve to guide future investment or strategy. Increasingly, corporations are being called out for "purpose washing"—failing to practice what they preach.[15] In his provocative book *Winners Take All*, journalist Anand Giridharadas contends that in their efforts to portray themselves as making the world a better place, many corporations have actually "changed things on the surface so that in practice nothing changes at all."[16] Entrepreneur Vivek Ramaswamy takes this critique a step further. In *Woke, Inc.*, he asserts that corporate "elites" prey on our innermost insecurities about who we really are: "They sell us cheap social causes and skin-deep identities to satisfy our hunger for a cause and our search for meaning, at a moment when we lack both."[17]

A recent Harris Poll of 1,491 C-suite or VP-level executives at large global companies found that while 74 percent agree that sustainability can drive powerful business transformation, 58 percent said their companies were guilty of greenwashing, including 72 percent of respondents in North America.[18] Former Generation Investment Management director Duncan Austin notes that the sustainable business movement has long faced the problem of *greenwash*—promoting token sustainability initiatives to divert attention from unsustainable core businesses—but now faces the potentially even more damaging affliction of *greenwish*: inauthentic sustainability goals that are set and reported primarily for the "optics."[19] It is important therefore to distinguish between those companies that genuinely commit to stretch sustainability goals (but may fall a bit short) and the larger number of firms that never expected to achieve them in the first place. In fact, many companies in the former category, increasingly wary of blowback, are avoiding public-facing communication on sustainability matters, engaging in what has come to be known as "greenhush."[20]

Harvard Business School professor Rebecca Henderson reinforces the prevalence of sustainability hyperbole with data, observing that 85 percent of the world's largest public companies now claim to be guided by a societal purpose. Yet few of these corporations have been able to effectively integrate purpose into strategy and operations. The number one reason cited for this disconnect? The unrelenting pressure on executives to meet quarterly earnings targets and fear of activist investors and raiders.[21]

Consider the venerable Johnson & Johnson's recent stumbles in this regard. With a proud history of being run according to a multistakeholder "Credo" written nearly eighty years ago, CEO Alex Gorsky served as the Business Roundtable's lead author for the recent "Statement on Corporate Purpose." Unfortunately, this statement was released just a week before J&J was found guilty of exacerbating (and profiting from) the opioid crisis. The irony could not be more delicious . . . and tragic. So how do we move beyond the sustainability hyperbole that consigns the recent revival of corporate societal purpose to little more than a marketing ploy to enhance legitimacy in a world that increasingly demands more than simply maximizing shareholder value? The answer is we must *re-embed* purpose by returning it to its rightful place as the "North Star" that guides investment, strategy, and operations.

Sustainability Goals: The First Step

In an effort to make societal purpose more concrete and accountable, many corporations have adopted the practice of setting *sustainability goals*—specific social and environmental commitments the company aspires to, usually accompanied by a set of metrics to measure progress toward them. The roots of sustainability goal-setting date back to the 1990s, when pioneering companies such as Dow, DuPont, and 3M set specific "eco-efficiency" goals for reducing energy use, water use, and waste from their own operations—what I have elsewhere characterized as strategies for "pollution prevention."[22] As we entered the twenty-first century, companies gradually expanded these goals to include impacts across the entire value chain and life cycle—supply chain and sourcing as well as the impacts of products-in-use and end-of-life considerations, what I have referred to as strategies for "product stewardship."[23]

Beginning in 2012, Andrew Winston began tracking the state of the art of corporate sustainability goal-setting through the Pivot Goals Project.[24] The project has systematically posted and analyzed the sustainability goals of all the world's largest companies (US Fortune 250, Global Fortune 200). Winston and his colleagues find that over the past decade, corporations have indeed further expanded the scope and ambition of their sustainability goals, including more science-based targets (particularly those related to renewable energy, water, and greenhouse gas emissions) and more commitments to social impact (for example, employee engagement, societal health and well-being, diversity and inclusion, and human rights).[25]

But as sustainability pioneer John Elkington has noted, the coming decade will almost certainly prove to be a transformational one for business—what he calls the "Exponential 20s." Companies will need to shift their focus from achieving the *10 percent* continuous improvement that has characterized the past two decades of corporate sustainability to realizing *10x* change through innovation and the creative destruction of unsustainable core businesses.[26] A veneer of lofty corporate purpose coupled with the obligatory set of sustainability goals focused on reducing negative impacts from operations and making the value chain more sustainable and inclusive will simply fall short of the challenges we face.

We have now crossed the proverbial Rubicon: as explained in Chapter 4, given the scale and scope of the challenges we face—runaway climate change, mass extinction, degradation of ecosystem services, toxic inequality, and the steady erosion of democracy around the world—nothing short of wholesale transformation will suffice. *Transformational* sustainability goals change the direction of core business strategies and call for the development and introduction of new, innovative technologies, product offerings, and business models— what I have referred to as "beyond greening" innovation.[27] Transformational goals also aspire to shift the institutional landscape by building collaborations for the policy and institutional innovations needed to accelerate the transformation process.

The experience at Dow over the past thirty years illustrates how sustainability goals have evolved, and how the motivation for transformation is just now beginning to emerge. Former Dow Chief Sustainability Officer Neil Hawkins has tellingly referred to the first-generation (1996–2005) environment, health, and safety goals at Dow as "Footprint" (operational) goals, the second-generation (2006–2015) sustainability goals as "Handprint" (product system) goals, and the third-generation 2025 goals as institutional "Blueprint" (societal) goals.[28] Yet in a recent assessment of fifty Fortune 250 companies, analysts Jeff Gowdy and Jessica Forrest conclude that truly transformational goals—aspirations to change the fundamental direction or technology of the company, innovate the entire value chain, or shift the institutional landscape—are still rare. Instead, most corporate sustainability goals are still incremental in nature, aimed at reducing the negative impact of existing company operations or improving the value of existing product offerings to stakeholders.[29]

Even seemingly transformational sustainability goals have come under increasing fire. Case in point: the recent fashion for corporations to set goals for "net zero" carbon emissions, in alignment with the 2015 Paris Agreement to limit global warming to 1.5 degrees Celsius. A recent study by Accenture found that while more than 90 percent of global GDP is now covered by net-zero climate commitments, upwards of 90 percent of those same companies will likely *fall short* of their targets.[30] Such sustainability goals are often set for 2050, without any clear interim goals for emission reduction, enabling companies to effectively "kick the can down the road" while still claiming to be proactive and responsive—"greenwish" at its best.[31]

Furthermore, as audacious as the goal sounds, there is growing concern among scientists and environmentalists that the net-zero craze is little more than a smokescreen, enabling corporations to use the purchase of carbon offsets to delay taking more fundamental action to reduce actual carbon *emissions* from their own business operations and products. As the author of a recent report from Friends of the Earth notes, "Fake zero strategies rely on offsets, rather than real emission reductions."[32]

The hyperbolic nature of many corporate sustainability goals should come as little surprise since, historically, they have been spearheaded by corporate sustainability staff. Large corporations have been staffing up with sustainability professionals in recent years to meet the growing demand for corporate sustainability goal-setting, metrics, and reporting.[33] Unfortunately, overly ambitious sustainability goals developed primarily by staff can breed frustration and cynicism if they fail to effectively connect to the real-world reality of business strategy. The realization of truly transformational sustainability goals requires direct engagement not only with senior management, the board, and investors, but also business leadership—and ultimately employees—throughout the company.[34]

Bringing Purpose to Life

A few leading-edge public corporations have begun to crack the code of how to effectively re-embed purpose into operating reality. They have developed specific, impact-oriented, aspirational goals for the business looking out a decade or more, and they have engaged executive and business leadership to develop this necessary "connective tissue," which integrates societal purpose into strategy development, resource allocation, and operating plans.

Launched in 2010 under the leadership of then new CEO Paul Polman,

Unilever's purpose—"to make sustainable living commonplace"—is perhaps the most often cited example of embedding purpose in core strategy. Three "Big" 2020 goals—"Improving Health and Well-Being for More than 1 Billion," "Reducing Environment Impact by Half," and "Enhancing Livelihoods for Millions"—were operationalized with specific business targets and metrics, providing both the vision and roadmap for corporate transformation over the course of the decade, as part of the Unilever Sustainable Living Plan (USLP). While the USLP met with significant early success, some of the truly bold objectives—halving the environmental footprint of Unilever *products*, for example—proved difficult to achieve.[35]

Undaunted, the company doubled down on its commitment to sustainability once again in 2020, setting aggressive new goals for 2030 through its "Unilever Compass" strategy.[36] A key element of the strategy was the elevation of purpose-led brands. Such "Sustainable Living Brands" (SLBs) embodied a strong environmental or social purpose, with products that contributed materially to the company's "Big Goals." By 2020, *half* of Unilever sales came from SLBs. Perhaps more important, SLBs were growing nearly 70 percent faster than the rest of the business, delivering 75 percent of the company's total growth.

Such success gave new CEO Alan Jope the confidence to declare that the company will *dispose* of brands that "don't stand for something," with the goal of earning 80 percent of company revenue from SLBs in "a few years' time."[37] Unilever encountered some headwinds with the onset of Covid in 2020 and the ensuing spike in energy and food costs. With a flat stock price and a bungled attempt to buy GSK's consumer health care business in 2022, Jope announced that he would retire at the end of 2023. Nonetheless, the company remains undeterred in its commitment to Unilever's long-term strategy.[38]

Unfortunately, beyond a few "usual suspects" like Unilever, not many large public corporations (especially American corporations) have taken this step: most still operate with a "veneer" of purpose and set of sustainability goals designed primarily to improve current operations and build legitimacy with existing customers, suppliers, and stakeholders.[39]

The opposite is true, however, when it comes to benefit corporations, B Corps, and purpose-driven companies: to be certified as a B Corp, for example, companies must clearly articulate their societal purpose, enshrine this purpose in their corporate charter, and publicly disclose their performance against clear goals and metrics designed to measure societal impact.[40] Purpose constitutes the *objective function* for B Corps—the "North Star" for prioritizing strategic and operating decisions in the business. As a purpose-driven company, Tesla's aim is "to accelerate the world's transition to sustainable energy." It has been their audacious pursuit of this purpose that drove their stock price to stratospheric levels—not quarterly earnings—despite a recent market pull-back, amid recession fears. Put bluntly: a company cannot be purpose-driven and subscribe to the Friedman Doctrine of short-term profit maximization at the same time since these are fundamentally incompatible ideas and operating principles.

The key to purpose is *authenticity*—the willingness on the part of corporate leadership to put purpose above short-term profit. Only then will purpose truly engage and inspire the rank and file, thereby unleashing the power of the whole organization.[41] A recent study by Porter Novelli/Cone Communication made clear the power of embedding authentic purpose: truly purposeful brands connect with consumers on an emotional level, trumping the more rational appeal of traditional marketing. Authentic purpose builds a relationship with customers that goes deep, so deep that it changes their entire perception of the company.[42]

We can learn a great deal from such benefit-driven innovators about how to effectively embed purpose in larger, public companies. Sustainability goals are not the same thing as strategic or operating goals. To become truly embedded, bold *business* aspirations must be developed to serve as the prime directive for the business leaders within companies—senior executives, business unit heads, and regional presidents. This directive means nothing less than setting business and financial goals *in service* to purpose and its transformational aspirations, rather than the other way around, as is the typical framing in today's large public companies.

It is instructive to examine how the very first B Corp—Seventh Generation—developed this much needed "connective tissue" between lofty purpose and operating reality in order to translate purpose into business strategy. Recently acquired by Unilever, Seventh Generation was founded in the late 1980s. From its inception, the company embraced the Iroquois belief in caring for the next seven generations. The company's original purpose, "to inspire a consumer revolution that nurtures the health of the next seven generations" has evolved and is now an equally inspiring "to transform the world into a sustainable, healthy, and equitable place for the next seven generations." No one argues that the company's purpose isn't audacious, bold, and emotionally appealing; it clearly serves to attract (and retain) people to the company with a passion for sustainability. However, on its face, it provides little in the way of constructive guidance for what managers and employees in the company should actually focus their attention on.[43]

The result at Seventh Generation was a schism or bifurcation between the company's societal purpose and its business and financial performance. By the early 2000s, two "camps" had emerged, with some advocating that purpose should take precedence and others arguing that purpose could not be effectively pursued without sound business and financial performance. Indeed, this internal struggle for the "soul" of the company relegated it to chronic underperformance from both a growth and a profitability perspective for much of its first two decades of existence.

To address this apparent conflict and lack of clarity, Seventh Generation made the momentous decision to bring on new senior management in 2011. In 2012, twenty-five company stakeholders were engaged in an "aspiration-defining" exercise for the company. This participatory process identified four focused company "Aspirations" that served to animate the "Purpose" and provide a sense of guidance and direction for developing company goals and business strategies: "Nurturing Nature"; "Enhancing Health"; "Building Communities"; and "Transforming Commerce." Each of these Aspirations, in turn, was operationalized through two to four specific "Goals and Metrics" used to track progress toward the Aspirations, consistent with the Purpose. For example, the "Enhancing Health" Aspiration was operationalized with the goal of creating exclusively healthy products for healthy homes, free of chronic toxicants. This exercise effectively resolved the bifurcation and returned the company to both growth and profitability, making the acquisition by Unilever in 2016 even more attractive.[44]

While there is much to learn from Seventh Generation's experience, the reality is that few existing large public corporations today started as passionate, purpose-driven companies. For the vast majority of existing corporations, the reality is that "sustainability" is still seen as a separate activity with specialized staff focused on reducing company risk, burnishing reputation, or, at best, driving new technology development that might generate long-term growth. Tragically, for many existing corporations, the most tangible product of the corporate sustainability staff is the annual Sustainability Report that they produce touting progress on eco-efficiency goals and featuring a few, high-profile CSR projects or clean tech experiments.

The journey of Atlanta-based carpet and flooring leader Interface demonstrates just how challenging—and important—it is for a public company to truly embed sustainability as part of core purpose and strategy. Interface's commitment to sustainability began nearly thirty years ago when founder Ray

Anderson had an epiphany after reading Paul Hawken's book *The Ecology of Commerce*. The result was "Mission Zero"—the bold quest to eliminate negative impact from the company's products and processes by 2020, with the ultimate aim of becoming a "regenerative enterprise" and "leading industry to love the world."[45]

Ray's audacious purpose was bolstered by a high-profile "Dream Team" of outside sustainability advisors including Paul Hawken, Amory Lovins, and Janine Benyus. Not surprisingly, these bold moves raised the profile of Interface in the emerging sustainability community—but not the stock price. Indeed, with Ray Anderson giving hundreds of inspiring speeches each year about "Mount Sustainability" and "regenerative enterprise," the external expectations for sustainable innovation and reinvention at Interface went through the roof, while the company's financial performance predictably deteriorated. Indeed, at one point, the stock price fell by 40 percent in one day.[46]

Few in the rank and file initially grasped Ray's visionary thinking; some even thought he had lost his mind. Many in the management ranks felt the notion of regenerative enterprise was more than the company could actually deliver on. Indeed, as a public company, senior management necessarily had to be concerned with the company's stock price, which had chronically underperformed during the 1990s. Most of the focused sustainability effort from the mid-1990s into the 2000s was therefore focused on the more operational aspects of "Mission Zero"—waste and emission reduction and closed-loop strategies for product take-back. There was a rather wide gap between Ray's inspirational overtures and the reality on the ground inside the company. Over time, however, Interface built up strong capabilities in eco-efficiency and product stewardship, realizing significant cost savings and reputation gains with positive impacts on financial performance.

By the early 2010s, Interface was coming close to actually achieving the zero-impact goal set back in the mid-1990s. The company had also developed a strong sustainability culture and capabilities in clean technology and biomimicry and, with the passing of Ray Anderson in 2011, a successor management team that shared the commitment. By 2016, the company was actually ready to begin to craft a strategy to deliver on the transformational (restorative) part of the original mission. Focusing attention on a truly pressing challenge facing the world, Interface declared that its next mission would be "Climate Take Back:" The quest to build a business that is *carbon negative*—and influence other companies and employees to take their own actions to reverse global warming.

Former Chief Sustainability Officer Erin Meezan explained that the company identified four pillars to make this new mission more tangible, with even more specific goals and metrics for each:

- *Live Zero*: aim for zero negative impact on the environment

- *Love Carbon*: stop seeing carbon as the enemy and start using it as a resource

- *Let Nature Cool*: support our biosphere's ability to regulate the climate

- *Lead the Industrial Re-Revolution*: transform industry into a force for the future we want

Three of these pillars—"Live Zero," "Love Carbon," and "Let Nature Cool"—can be realistically achieved through process and business innovation, along with the engagement of suppliers and customers: "Live Zero" is simply a continuation of the original "Mission Zero" goal seen to its logical conclusion. "Love Carbon" has recently been demonstrated through the introduction of new carpet backing and tile products that actually sequester carbon; made exclusively from plant-based materials, this new carpet product stores more carbon than is emitted during its production. "Let Nature Cool" involves mimicking the functioning of the ecosystems where Interface plants and facilities are located. Can such facilities be designed to purify water, cycle nutrients, and sequester carbon if they better integrate the lessons of nature?

"Lead the Industrial Re-Revolution" is bigger than any innovation or initiative that Interface can muster on its own or through its value chain. Realizing such a big, hairy, audacious goal will require building partnership ecosystems with NGOs, government, academia, and other corporations to actually transform the way business and manufacturing gets done in the years ahead. For example, the company's Net-Works program, which focused initially on recycling ocean plastics for use in its own carpet, has expanded into NextWave Plastics—a wider coalition of manufacturers and NGO leaders dedicated to reclaiming ocean plastics for use in global supply chains. In this sense it is more of a *corporate quest* than a process or business innovation. I'll expand on these important distinctions in the next section. It turns out that achieving clarity—and accountability—for internal stakeholders when it comes to societal impact is key to making corporate purpose truly part of the company's DNA.

Making It Real: Aspirations and Quests

Most incumbent corporations will need to completely reinvent themselves over the course of the next decade—think renewable energy, electrification, sustainable mobility, regenerative agriculture, alternative proteins, circular materials, and inclusive business models capable of sustainably serving and lifting the poor and underserved. This transformation process is actually well under way already—witness that ExxonMobil and Tesla essentially traded places over the past decade in terms of market value, post-Covid price spikes in fossil energy notwithstanding. The fact that even General Motors has now declared its intent to phase out all internal combustion engines by the middle of the next decade should serve as all the proof we need that transformation will be the watchword in the decade ahead.

To drive such transformation, as we saw from the experiences at Dow, Seventh Generation, and Interface, it is crucial to translate and embed broad statements of societal purpose into strategic and operating reality in a way that is meaningful and inspiring for executives, managers, and employees. Bringing purpose to life means defining what *specific* positive impacts the company seeks to make in the world, looking out a decade or more. Think of this as a process of "double clicking" on purpose—making it clear to external stakeholders what the transformational intent of the company is and making it tangible for the internal stakeholders who will be held accountable for making it happen.

It is also important, however, not to allow the articulation of the corporation's desired societal impact to get out of hand. As Benoit Leleux and Jan Van Der Kaaij note in their excellent book *Winning Sustainability Strategies*, less is more when it comes to selecting impact goals. Indeed, they found that the corporations delivering the most positive impact focus on a *limited number* of critical, relevant, and material sustainability impacts and aim to deliver on them *through* the business. Laggards, on the other hand, typically proclaim a wide variety of sustainability goals, many often unrelated to core competence or business strategy, and focus their efforts on reporting activities as part of their customer nonfinancial information cycle.[47]

To help develop a sharper focus, it is useful to distinguish among *three levels* of specific positive impacts that companies might pursue (Exhibit 5.1). First, "Foundational Goals" are those functional elements that underpin everything a company seeks to achieve when it comes to sustainability and societal impact. Without such Foundational Goals in place, a company may lack the necessary

Corporate Quests
Bold, Compelling, and Enabling
- Transforms the **institutional landscape**
- Outward-facing "battle cry" for positive change
- Requires broad **partnership/ecosystem/coalition** building
- Goes beyond company's areas of control

    Enterprise (Business) Aspirations
    Unique and Authentic to Company
    - Brings Purpose to life through the business
    - Works within company's value chain and locus of control –
      products, customers, suppliers, revenue, and profit
    - Driven through **business** innovation and investment
    - Leads customers/suppliers/stakeholders to the future

        Foundational Goals
        Critical Foundational Elements
        - Focuses on **functional excellence** and building **new capabilities**
        - Driven by **functional** leaders
        - Supports key business and innovation initiatives
        - Enables Aspirations and Quests

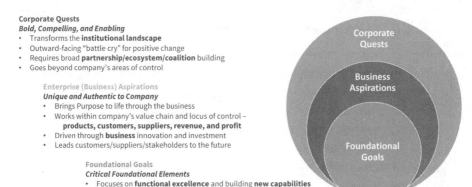

Exhibit 5.1. Bringing Purpose to Life:
Goals, Aspirations, and Quests

capabilities to deliver on its purpose and risk being perceived as hypocritical, particularly if it is asserting a truly transformational purpose.

Foundational Goals are primarily *internal* in scope, so accountability can be meaningfully assigned to functional leaders in operations, R&D, sourcing and procurement, and HR. For example, operations can be tasked with continuing the journey on eco-efficiency and waste reduction, R&D can be challenged to build new capabilities and develop new sustainable or regenerative technologies for the future, sourcing and procurement can be held accountable for the traceability and sustainability of the supply chain, and HR can focus on employee engagement and education, well-being, and fulfillment as well as issues of diversity, inclusion, and gender equity. Foundational Goals are similar to what Dow called "Footprint" goals, since they are oriented primarily toward impacts "within the fence line" of the company itself. They ensure continuous improvement and legitimacy in current businesses, but also enable the more transformational aims the company aspires to by building new competencies and capabilities for the future.

For Seventh Generation, the "Nurturing Nature" Aspiration is largely foundational in quality—focused on eliminating waste, sustainable sourcing, and conversion to nonfossil energy. So too are several of the goals associated with "Building Communities," particularly those having to do with creating a vibrant workplace. Similarly, two of the four "pillars" of Interface's Climate Take-Back Mission also include Foundational Goals: "Live Zero" is essentially a continuation of the original "Mission Zero" which was focused on company operations—Scope 1 and 2 in sustainability jargon. And despite its innovativeness, the "Let Nature Cool" pillar is also foundational in quality since its focus is on innovating its plant and facility model to embrace nature's services in the surrounding ecosystem; it is all about building a new corporate capability.

The second level of impact—"Business Aspirations"—is distinctly different from the first in that it requires the direct engagement of the commercial side of the company to be successful. Business Aspirations are *external* in scope, focused on customers and the company's value chain—Scope 3 in sustainability parlance. Business Aspirations are similar to what Dow described as "Handprint" goals, since they focus on life cycle impacts beyond the fence line of the company itself. Societally oriented Business Aspirations seek to *lead* customers and other key value chain stakeholders toward a future vision of true sustainability and inclusion. Business Aspirations should be unique to the company making them, enabling a truly authentic articulation of purpose to come to life, and they can *only* be realized through business investment and innovation—new products, strategies, and business models.

It is crucial, therefore, that accountability for Business Aspirations be assigned to the company's product managers, business executives, and regional presidents, since they are the only ones capable of championing the customer-facing and revenue-generating innovations required. Too often companies make the mistake of articulating grandiose sustainability goals without effectively engaging and empowering the commercial side of the company, thus placing an unrealistic burden on sustainability staff and functional managers, leading to sustainability hyperbole, greenwish, and purpose-wash. Effective Business Aspirations define clear business and financial metrics (along with the societal impacts) so the company can measure progress toward its transformational aspiration—and recognize the business leaders responsible.

For Seventh Generation, "Enhancing Health" is their central Business Aspiration—a commitment to developing and selling *only* healthy products for healthy homes—products free from chronic toxicants. And for Interface, the "Love Carbon" pillar constitutes its central Business Aspiration: it aims to shift the company portfolio toward carpet and flooring products that actually *sequester* carbon, rather than aiming only for reductions in climate impact or carbon neutrality across the value chain. "Love Carbon" captures the essence of the commercial strategy for Carbon Take-Back.

The third level of impact is "Corporate Quests." Like Business Aspirations, Corporate Quests are *outward-facing* and geared toward transformational change in the world—literal "battle cries" for positive change. Quests require what Rosabeth Moss Kanter describes as "outside-the-building thinking"—work beyond their silos and sectors.[48] Unlike Business Aspirations, which can be driven through company efforts across the value chain, Corporate Quests are bigger than any single product, business, company, or value chain. They seek to fundamentally transform entire industries through issue-focused partnerships, collective action, and policy innovation. Quests thus seek to catalyze *system change*—a metaphorical "Scope 4" impact that shifts and transforms entire markets and industry landscapes.[49] Beyond industry-level Quests lies what I call "Scope 5" impact—the quest to create a truly *sustainable capitalism*—and world—through redesign of the institutions underpinning and animating capitalism itself (Exhibit 5.2).

Quests for system change and redesign thus recognize the complex and interdependent nature of sustainability.[50] No man is an island, as the poem by John Donne famously enjoined. Companies and industries are embedded in systems of issues, policies, and institutions, all of which affect the ability of individual firms to deliver on their business aspirations. Selecting among the various issues (for example, deforestation), policies (such as carbon pricing), and institutions (for example, equity markets) to focus on is thus key in defining a material and impactful corporate Quest.

In their landmark book *Net Positive*, Paul Polman and Andrew Winston articulate a similar hierarchy of corporate sustainability initiatives, distinguishing between company (four walls) initiatives, which can be done working alone

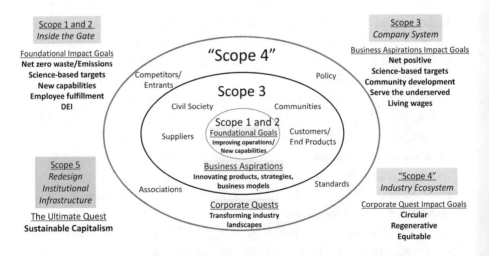

Exhibit 5.2. Levels of the Business Sustainability Game

(like Foundational Goals), and those requiring partnership and collaboration. This second type of initiative includes action at the level of the company's *value chain* (similar to Business Aspirations), *sector or industry* (similar to Corporate Quests) and *full systems* (similar to the idea of "Scope 5" impact) which requires what they describe as "system reset."[51] Much more about such system-level redesigns in Part 3 of this book.

Given their bold and encompassing character, responsibility for Quests must necessarily rest with corporate leadership—the C-suite and the board—since it is all about using the corporate platform as a megaphone to "punch above the weight" of the company itself. Typically, Quests require the building of partnership ecosystems and coalitions to be effective. Think of Quests as a form of *positive* lobbying or what Polman and Winston describe as "net positive advocacy," rather than the traditional lobbying efforts to preserve the status quo or block reform.[52] Corporate Quests support and enable the realization of Business Aspirations, just as Business Aspirations build upon and leverage the Foundational Goals. Exhibit 5.2 summarizes the differences among these different levels of the business sustainability game, including the appropriate impact goals and accountabilities associated with each.

The most effective Quests are those that *leverage* the unique position and capabilities of the company itself. For example, in the late 1980s, on the heels of the first scientifically backed consensus linking CFCs to ozone depletion, DuPont committed to cease CFC production and led an orderly global industry transition to alternatives via the Montreal Protocol. Of course, it certainly helped that DuPont had already developed the next generation of refrigerants to replace CFCs, leveraging its position as industry leader.

Similarly, Walmart used its monopsony power to leverage the formation of the Sustainability Consortium in 2007, with the aim of transforming the consumer goods industry to deliver more sustainable products. It should come as little surprise then that most of the active participants in the Consortium were Walmart suppliers! JPMorgan Chase has also used its position as large-scale financier for certain activities (such as mountain-top coal mining, palm oil development) to leverage industrywide collaboration for prohibition or reform.

Seventh Generation's Aspiration of "Transforming Commerce" has all the hallmarks of a Corporate Quest: exerting influence beyond its size to effectively change the institutional landscape. The company's commitment to "Building Communities" is also Quest-like in quality. For Interface, "Lead the Industrial Re-Revolution"—transforming industry into a force for the future we want—is a very audacious Quest. Seeking to lead an industrial re-revolution as a $1 billion flooring company is a tall order, but given the company's outsized impact in the past, we should not discount the possibility.

Indeed, Interface's quest to transform industry builds on the example set by company founder Ray Anderson going all the back to the 1990s, when his pioneering voice served to elevate the entire carpet industry with regard to sustainability. His public persona and charismatic speaking also changed the way entire generations of students, citizens, and business leaders thought. I still have vivid memories of Ray coming to speak in my MBA core class in strategy at UNC's Kenan-Flagler Business School in the late 1990s. And I'll bet many of the students in the class also remember it to this day.

Taken together, Foundational Goals, Business Aspirations, and a compelling Corporate Quest provide the infrastructure to bring Purpose to life and connect it in a meaningful way to the strategy and operating plans of the company. As Salesforce founder and CEO Marc Benioff notes, "Fighting for a cause that matters to our stakeholders is just as much a CEO's job as preparing for a quarterly analyst call."[53] But since embedding purpose means disrupting business as usual, it requires a process of both external engagement (to stimulate new thinking) and internal participation (to ensure engagement and commitment). It must transcend the usual analytical and staff-driven approach to sustainability goal-setting that has typified corporations in the past.[54]

Let's take a close look at a company where sustainability is being actively embedded into core strategy real time: Griffith Foods. This "living" case provides insight into not only the *content* of Foundational Goals and purpose-driven Aspirations and Quests, but perhaps more important, the *process* needed to effectively develop and embed them. Creating effective goals, aspirations, and quests is a journey, and the Griffith Foods story provides a useful roadmap.

Griffith Foods is a century-old, fourth-generation, family-owned business with a strong commitment to the greater good as part of its corporate culture. As a B2B company, Griffith does not *make* the food you eat, they make the food you eat taste, feel, and smell better . . . and be more nutritious. Despite being privately held and family owned, Griffith's experience is relevant for large, public corporations given its size (annual sales in excess of $1 billion) and global scope (it operates in more than thirty countries around the world). Indeed, I believe Griffith Foods provides a model for other corporations seeking to embed purpose and embark on their own journeys of transformation—and still realize strong financial performance. Griffith Foods demonstrates what is *possible* for public companies, should they develop the courage of their convictions to actually pursue a consistently transformational path, rather than being buffeted and controlled by the short-term demands of current public equity markets.

I first met the executive chairman of the company, Brian Griffith, in 2017. From the very first phone conversation, it was evident to me that he was committed to the sort of transformation at his company that the world demanded. After several conversations and a kick-off meeting in Chicago with Brian and CEO TC Chatterjee, we began a collaboration that continues to this day. The intent from the start was to devise a process to elevate sustainability at Griffith Foods—to embed it as core to purpose and strategy. As part of this work, we benchmarked fifteen recognized sustainability leaders to better understand how some of the most innovative companies went about achieving such integration. It was through this experience that I was able to crystalize the distinctions among Foundational Goals, Business Aspirations, and Corporate Quests— and use them to make sustainability part of the DNA for Griffith Foods.

Embedding Sustainability at Griffith Foods

For Brian Griffith, the journey began in earnest in 2013.[55] Several of the company's biggest customers had been inquiring about Griffith's philosophy and strategy with regard to sustainability. Brian's father (and then company chairman) Dean Griffith, however, never connected "sustainability" to his personal belief that business should serve as a force for the greater good. As a result, the company took little action beyond responding to basic customer expectations and complying with environmental and sustainability requirements.

However, at a senior management meeting in early 2013, Brian (now a senior executive at the company) was "struck to the core" when the topic of customer sustainability surveys was treated as a pesky nuisance: "I felt we had lost our way at that moment." While he had only a "general awareness" of what sustainability in a business context might actually entail, he sensed its potential to reinvigorate the company's family values and humanistic approach to management: "I sensed sustainability was a powerful connection to the idea of being a 'vehicle for greater good.' I realized that sustainability could be *the way* in which we could demonstrate this ideal in the decades ahead."[56]

Brian assembled a team consisting of TC Chatterjee, regional VPs, and functional leaders in supply chain, HR, marketing, strategy, finance, and operations and began work on a sustainability initiative for Griffith. At the next senior management meeting in May 2013, Brian asked his father to speak about what the company meant to him. Dean spoke of the importance of responsibility, of being engaged in something bigger than one's self, and of using the company as a vehicle for the greater good.

Brian then stood up and introduced the "People, Planet, and Performance" model that the sustainability team had drafted. He made the case that confronting the environmental and social challenges associated with "sustainability" for Griffith—malnutrition, supply chain transparency, soil loss, waste, energy and water use—actually captured the essence of Griffith's commitment to being a force for the greater good—that it represented "who we are." Sustainability was, in short, the bridge to the future. It represented the sort of company that the next generation of Griffiths and employees could be proud of.

The Sustainability "Platform"

Following that pivotal meeting in 2013, Brian Griffith led a team to create a sustainability "platform" for the company. He initiated a stakeholder engagement process that included dialogue with customers, suppliers, and external experts in the food and agriculture space. Griffith also conducted a "Materiality Assessment," leading to the identification of several issues that were both important to key stakeholders and had potentially important business impacts and implications.

On the basis of this work, Griffith established a set of sustainability goals and metrics in 2014 focused on "People, Planet, and Performance (*Triple Bottom Line (3BL) Framework*)." Key metrics included the following:

- *People*: employee safety, employee engagement, ethical employment, talent development, family support, and community involvement

- *Planet*: solid waste reduction, energy efficiency, water conservation, emissions reduction, transportation efficiency, and sustainable sourcing

- *Performance*: customer growth; financial improvement; food safety; risk management; ethics or integrity; and healthy, nutritious and innovative products

One of the first areas of focus associated with the 3BL Framework was the company's supply chain, which manifested itself in the "Griffith Sustainably Sourced (GSS) Program." By offering support to smallholder farmers and spice cultivators around the world, Griffith helped producers generate higher yields and safer work environments, and it provided full traceability and transparency for customers through a newly created spices and herbs certification through the Rainforest Alliance.

Griffith's "Sustainably Sourced" initiative later led to the launch of a new company—Terova—focused not only on sustainable sourcing for Griffith but also improving the livelihoods of the smallholder farming communities from which Griffith sourced raw materials and spices. By aiming to not only serve Griffith Food's own captive needs but also expand the broader external market for sustainably sourced raw materials, Terova enabled the company to multiply its positive impact in farming communities around the world—and to create a new revenue source at the same time. Ultimately, the aspiration was for Griffith to source 100 percent of selected spices, herbs, and botanicals from Terova.

In 2015, upon his father's retirement, Brian Griffith assumed the helm as executive chairman of the company. With the 3BL Framework now established, he realized that the company was missing a clearly articulated *Purpose* that answered the higher-level question, "Why do we exist?" He felt there was a real need to articulate the connection between what was unique and authentic about Griffith and the significant needs in the world that the company could address. A participatory process was set in motion in 2015, and Brian asked TC Chatterjee, now the COO of Griffith, to lead the "Purpose Project," engaging the employees in the development of a concrete expression of Griffith's Purpose. The result: *"We blend care and creativity to nourish the world."*

The intent was for the new Purpose to do more than simply increase employee "engagement"—a motivational gambit to boost financial performance. Instead, as Brian Griffith so aptly put it, the objective was to increase the level of employee *fulfillment*: to harness the power of positive impact to make good on Dean Griffith's commitment that the company provide the opportunity for people to learn and grow, and to serve the greater good. Griffith Foods seemed to be particularly well-positioned to take on this challenging new purpose. As Brian Griffith stated, "We don't have the problems faced by publicly held companies—a couple of down quarters and you are forced to abandon your long-term game plan. As a privately held and family-owned company, we have no excuse not to do the right thing. We have the capacity, and it is our duty to tackle these challenges. It is our family's legacy that is at stake; we are compelled to do so."

The new company Purpose led to the development of a framework known as the Griffith Foods "House" (Exhibit 5.3). The "House" built upon Griffith's new Purpose, pulling together the stakeholder engagement, materiality assessment, and 3BL work, and it visually reinforced the importance of sustainability as

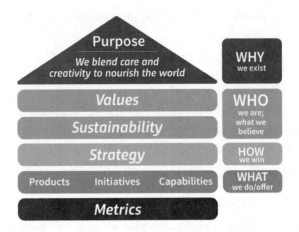

Exhibit 5.3. The Griffith Foods "House"

the core platform for the company's values and strategy. As Brian emphatically stated, "Sustainability became the lens through which Griffith Foods sees the world and the 'filter' that informs all our decisions."

Purpose-Driven Strategy

In 2016, the company officially changed its name from Griffith Laboratories to Griffith Foods. The new name aligned more directly with the Purpose. While the "Laboratory" designation spoke to the company's first century of food safety and science (more on this below), the new name spoke to the company's aspirations for food innovation and sustainable nutrition—what customers would demand for the future.

TC Chatterjee also became CEO of Griffith Foods Worldwide Inc. in 2016. To complement and reinforce the work on the 3BL Framework, "House," and Purpose, Chatterjee initiated a process to translate Griffith Foods' sustainability commitments into a portfolio of new strategies and capabilities worldwide. The "Purpose-Driven Strategy" initiative kicked off in February 2016. A strategy working group comprising business leaders from across the company assumed the responsibility of coalescing the results of a series of working sessions and began communicating the findings and expectations for next steps over the summer of 2017. Local business units worked with regional leadership to develop new products, launch new strategic initiatives, and build new capabilities from the ground up. Said Chatterjee, "We have made a commitment that everything we do as a company will be driven by and connected to our Purpose. The Purpose-Driven Strategy focuses the organization on 'where to play' and 'how to win' to best serve our Purpose."

The Purpose-Driven Strategy leveraged existing Griffith Foods capabilities in consumer insight, culinary, food, and sensory science, as it also sought to build new layers of competence for the future through work streams focused on health and nutrition, leveraging technology, shared value, and partnership ecosystems. Examples of strategic initiatives associated with these four work streams included the following:

- *Health and Nutrition*: nutritional products, botanicals, plant-based or alternative proteins

- *Leveraging Technology*: 3D printing, blockchain, AI, Internet of Things

- *Shared Value*: affordable nutrition for the underserved at the base of the pyramid, building smallholder farmers' capacity and knowledge along with local processing capabilities and community development

- *Partnership Ecosystem*: customer partnerships, startups and venture investments, and waste stream and food loss commercialization

The Purpose-Driven Strategy became a key driver of the company's future growth and expansion. The initial goal was that these four domains and their associated initiatives should account for no less than 25 percent of both Griffith's revenues and profits by 2022, with continued geographic expansion into underserved markets.

The new Purpose and Strategy were game-changers for Griffith Foods. Yet something was still missing: a clear articulation of what *specific* external sustainability challenges—such as regenerative agriculture, farmers' livelihoods, affordable nutrition, and proactive health—the company was committed to tackling through its Purpose, Strategy, and 3BL Framework sustainability platform.

Griffith's Purpose explained "why we exist" and provided the proverbial "North Star" for the company. The Purpose-Driven Strategy addressed "where to play" and "how to win" by specifying a new set of strategies and capabilities consistent with the Purpose. Left unanswered, however, was the question of "what problems we seek to solve in the world"—problems that Griffith could uniquely and authentically tackle. Griffith also needed goals and metrics to hold accountable the business leaders and employees tasked with delivering on these challenges. The question became: How could Griffith Foods build on the work already accomplished to clarify and sharpen its societal impact and financial targets to more fully express its commitment to change the world for the better in the years ahead?

Origins of Purpose

As Dave Stangis and Katherine Valvoda Smith wisely observe in their book *21st Century Corporate Citizenship*, history can often productively inform future direction-setting, especially for long-established companies.[57] Even if it has been many decades (or even centuries), since a company's founding, recalling the *original* company purpose can be clarifying for current business leaders aiming for bold and authentic future directions.

Griffith was founded in 1919 by Enoch Luther Griffith (E. L.), a Chicago sales executive, and his son, Carroll Ladd (C. L.) Griffith, a pharmacologist. From the beginning, E. L. and C. L. sought to infuse safety and reliability into a flawed food system. They named their company Griffith Laboratories to underscore their focus on food science.

At the time, the nation's food supply couldn't be trusted. Upton Sinclair's *The Jungle* had exposed the unhealthy conditions of the Chicago Stockyards in 1906, but rancid beef, inedible sausages, and unpurified spices continued to find their way into American homes.[58] Both C. L. and E. L. Griffith wanted to help change that by introducing food science to the food industry. They believed they could improve food safety and help create healthier, better-tasting food using new technologies, food science, and innovative manufacturing processes.[59]

Griffith Laboratories' original purpose was thus to enhance the *safety and taste* of food products, while at the same time *reducing cost and food waste*. From the beginning, Griffith "punched above its weight" by launching "win-win" innovations that were good for the food producers *and* good for end consumers. The company's motto was, "Help customers prosper and Griffith will prosper." Griffith also developed an early reputation for being most creative when times were most difficult. By partnering with large meatpackers such as Armour and Swift, Griffith helped to transform the meat industry at a time when food safety lapses, unsanitary conditions, and waste were rampant.

If Upton Sinclair's *The Jungle* was the clarion call a century ago in Chicago, perhaps Michael Pollan's *The Omnivore's Dilemma* serves that purpose today, making clear the unsustainable and unhealthy nature of today's global food and agricultural system.[60] Might Griffith be able to use its creativity once again to address this daunting global challenge?

Food Becomes an Industry

In many ways, the journey of Griffith Foods parallels the industrialization of the food industry itself. A key turning point in this regard occurred in 1909 when Fritz Haber invented a way to make synthetic nitrogen (commercialized as the Haber-Bosch process), enabling the manufacture of synthetic fertilizer. Although nitrogen makes up about 80 percent of the earth's atmosphere, nitrogen atoms are tightly paired and nonreactive until they can be split apart and bound to hydrogen. Until Haber figured out how to artificially "fix" nitrogen from the atmosphere, all the useable nitrogen on Earth was fixed by soil bacteria living on the roots of leguminous plants (for example, peas, beans, lentils, pulses). Before Haber's invention of synthetic fertilizer, in other words, the amount of life on Earth—plants and animals—was limited by the amount of nitrogen fixed by natural processes.[61]

Before Haber-Bosch, a farmer could grow enough food to feed his family and perhaps a dozen or so other people. Farmers would nurture a variety of different plants and animals—fruits and vegetables, as well as corn, oats, hay, alfalfa, and other grains to feed pigs, cattle, chickens, and horses. Crops would be rotated so as to replenish the soil with legumes and animal manure. Not surprisingly, the *majority* of Americans (and the vast majority of the world population) farmed prior to the twentieth century, but with the advent of Haber-Bosch, that number quickly dwindled in the developed world: by the end of the twentieth century, for example, *less than 1 percent* of Americans farmed, but they were able to grow enough to feed the rest of us—and export as well.[62]

Having acquired the power to fix nitrogen, humankind was effectively liberated from biological constraints. Indeed, Vaclav Smil estimates that two out of every five humans on Earth today would not be alive if not for synthetic nitrogen. Fixing nitrogen artificially enabled the development of "modern" industrial agriculture—monoculture crops fed with massive quantities of chemical fertilizers and pesticides manufactured from fossil fuels, planted and harvested with mechanized equipment. Large quantities of food could now be produced by far fewer people, accelerating the shift from farm to city that was already occurring during the late nineteenth and early twentieth centuries due to industrialization.[63]

The "Green Revolution"—with its high-yield cereal hybrids and irrigation technologies—then spread the intensive, industrialized form of agriculture to the developing world, averting mass starvation in many countries experiencing population booms in the postwar years, but also extinguishing many of the age-old agricultural practices that had served societies reliably for thousands of years. The transition to Green Revolution agriculture required the purchase of chemical inputs and an increased level of mechanization, making it difficult for smallholder farmers and landless farm workers to survive, leading to increased urban migration in the developing world.[64]

Despite the Green Revolution, however, nearly *half* of those in the developing world still farm—with the vast majority still tending small plots with low productivity and incomes. The result is that today we have a two-tiered farming system in the world, each with its own sustainability challenges: (1) a relatively small number of large, industrial farmers growing monoculture row crops using intensive agricultural methods, often enabled by subsidies; and (2) a large number of smallholding, subsistence farmers using unsophisticated methods, primarily in the developing world, often living in poverty. The opportunity for creating a truly "sustainable" or "regenerative" system of agriculture therefore requires strategies for addressing the challenges of both industrial row crop producers and smallholder farmers.[65]

Since the end of the Second World War, a food *industry* has developed, supported by the industrialization of agriculture—an industry that has become both increasingly specialized and concentrated in recent decades. For example, the *agricultural inputs industry*—seeds and agrochemicals—is now dominated by three global players—Bayer (formerly Monsanto), Corteva (formerly DuPont and Dow), and Syngenta (part of ChemChina).[66] *Agricultural commodity processing and trading* has become concentrated with a few large players such as Archer Daniels Midland (ADM), Cargill, ConAgra, and Bunge. Similarly, *meat processing and packing* has become highly concentrated with just a few large-scale producers—Cargill, Tyson Foods, JBS, Smithfield, Perdue, and National Beef Packing—controlling the hog, cattle, and chicken markets.[67]

As food production became more industrialized, food itself changed. A flood of inexpensive, subsidized corn, soybeans, and other agricultural commodities made it profitable to raise cattle on feedlots instead of pastures and raise chickens in factories rather than farmyards. Agricultural commodities also enabled the large-scale production of inexpensive, processed foods, and the emergence of a vast *retail food industry*.[68] A few large corporations such as PepsiCo, Unilever, Mars, Kraft-Heinz, Nestle, and Danone came to prominence in the food industry, with *quick service restaurants* like McDonald's, Restaurant Brands International Inc., Wendy's, and Yum Brands Inc. growing into a market that is now worth nearly a half-trillion dollars.[69]

Unfortunately, there are potential negative health effects with over-consuming processed foods. Heightened levels of fat, sugar, sodium, and excess calories have caused obesity, heart disease, high blood pressure, and diabetes to run rampant throughout the world in the postwar years, particularly in developed countries.[70] At the same time, malnourishment remains a pervasive problem throughout the developing world: nearly a quarter of the world's population is food insecure, with almost 10 percent of the population seriously undernourished.[71]

Industrial agriculture has also taken a toll environmentally: agriculture consumes nearly two-thirds of all water drawn from the world's rivers, lakes, and aquifers, although only about 20 percent of the world's croplands are irrigated.[72] Poor agricultural practices (for example, overapplication of agricultural chemicals, heavy tilling) have contributed to the degradation of billions of acres of farmland, with soil loss on a massive scale.[73]

It takes *more* than a calorie of fossil fuel energy to produce a calorie of food using synthetic fertilizers and monoculture methods. Industrial production of animals is also reaching a breaking point: the world now contains more than a *billion* cattle, pigs, and sheep, and more than twenty-five billion chickens. The cattle population alone takes up nearly a quarter of the land mass of the planet and consumes enough grain to feed billions of people. Since it takes nearly seven pounds of grain to produce just one pound of beef protein, it is simply not physically possible (let alone ethically acceptable) for eight or ten billion people to become eaters of industrial meat in the decades ahead.[74]

Not surprisingly then, pressure is mounting on the food and agriculture industry to address the environmental and social challenges just described through calls for *sustainable and regenerative* agriculture, *alternative proteins*, and *more nutritious and affordable* foods. Most of the large players, including Cargill, Unilever, PepsiCo, Mars, Danone, and McDonalds, have now launched significant initiatives in this regard.

Postwar Global Expansion

Griffith became an international company during the second half of the twentieth century, as agriculture became industrialized and food became increasingly processed and marketed as a branded product. Under the leadership of Brian's father, Dean Ladd (D. L.) Griffith, who joined the company in 1950, Griffith not only established a global presence but also expanded its culinary capabilities with regard to both flavor and nutrition. As families fanned out into suburbs in the US after World War II, quick meals and convenience became priorities, increasing interest in frozen foods, ready-made dinners, and boxed cake mixes. Using soy protein concentrates, Griffith helped pack nutrients into breakfast cereals and ushered in the age of Salisbury steaks, while the company's iconic Mince Master® equipment allowed commercial customers to produce sausages at an astounding rate of five hundred pounds a minute.

Flavor boosters made from vegetable proteins, like Vegamine, added body and umami to once-pallid soups. Bottles of natural smoke and Pepperoyal seasonings infused bold tastes into the otherwise bland diet of 1950s and early 1960s America. These innovations supported the viability of Griffith's unique business model, which aided its partners by ensuring consistency and improving the quality and taste of their products.

The blending of knowledge from first-rate chefs and food scientists allowed Griffith to expand into the restaurant industry and further improve the quality of its products. Indeed, Griffith has acted as a "development partner" with various customers in the creation of some of the most iconic fast food and fast-casual creations ever produced, always aiming to improve not only the taste, but also the nutritional profile of the products.

Griffith Laboratories acquired Custom Food Products®, located in Chicago, in 1991, which was rebranded into Custom Culinary. Custom, which was acquired to expand Griffith's soup, base, sauce, and gravy offerings, then launched its Innova®Flavors division in 1997, greatly diversifying its catalog of natural flavorings. Griffith worked with partners to create authentic regional (native) flavors as diverse as its expanding footprint, from red Thai curries and shawarmas to chimichurri and tandoori pastes.

By the 2000s, Griffith had formed truly multidisciplinary teams focused on innovation. While its regional chefs ensured authenticity, its food scientists developed novel ways to replace MSG, reduce sodium, eliminate trans-fats, and create clean-label products. Meanwhile, sensory scientists calibrated textures and aromas throughout the process, and Griffith's consumer insights and marketing specialists researched the trending dishes, consumer preferences, and flavor profiles around which its customers could build new products and recipes.

The company developed the capabilities to make food not only *fast* and *convenient*, but also *nutritious* and *delicious—anywhere in the world*. And with the ascent of Brian Griffith to the chairmanship, sustainability became a core company priority as well. Such a unique combination of skills and capabilities made Griffith one of the food ingredient and product development partners-of-choice in the industry.

Indeed, Griffith has only a few direct global competitors—primarily Kerry Foods, Newly Weds Foods, and McCormick. As a result, Griffith has performed very well financially over the years. Indeed, the company's third-party evaluation of stock value has outpaced the S&P 500 stock index for more than thirty years.[75]

Remember, however, that Griffith also has a long history of focusing on innovation, reducing cost and food waste, suggesting the possibility of a food industry "trifecta"—nutritious and delicious, sustainable, and affordable. Might this skill set hold the key to helping catalyze another industry transformation—toward a truly sustainable and inclusive food system?

Sustainability 2.0

By 2017, Griffith Foods had put in place a number of important puzzle pieces for embedding sustainability into the DNA of the company: the 3BL Framework (with its People, Planet, and Performance metrics), the new corporate Purpose, and a Purpose-Driven Strategy. The challenge that remained was to devise a way to bring them all together into a coherent whole. The Griffith "House" went a long way toward providing such integration, but still did not answer the question of what *specific* problems in the world Griffith Foods would concentrate on addressing.

Beginning in 2017, my nonprofit organization, Enterprise for a Sustainable World (ESW), began working with Griffith Foods to help them pursue this next level of embedding—"Sustainability 2.0." Along with my colleagues Priya Dasgupta and Kate Napolitan, we began facilitating workshops with the board and the senior leadership team to develop a deeper understanding of and shared perspective about the world's sustainability challenges that might operationalize Purpose and define strategic priorities for the company, beginning with the Sustainable Development Goals.

SUSTAINABLE DEVELOPMENT GOALS ASSESSMENT

The 17 SDGs include 169 *specific* targets and subgoals (88 of which we determined to be directly relevant to business). We surveyed key senior leadership and staff to assess their perceptions of Griffith Food's potential for having a material impact on the SDGs and subgoals both for a "current" and a possible "future" state. We defined the current state as simply continuing with the sustainability initiatives already under way, looking out to 2030. For the future state, we asked respondents to focus on the positive impacts Griffith might be able to achieve on the SDGs and subgoals if it chose to expand on its current sustainability platform and pursue a more transformational strategy. We focused our attention on the 88 *subgoals*, that are quite specific in nature, rather than the 17 more general SDGs. The results helped both to "take the pulse" within the organization and to identify the most relevant potential world challenges on which the company might focus its attention in the future (Exhibit 5.4).[76]

For the "current state," seven subgoals emerged as the most highly rated, most relating to the incremental reduction of negative impacts in the current business—eco-efficiency, waste reduction, efficient water use, and labor rights—reflective more of the 3BL Framework than the Purpose-Driven Strategy. In fact, there was only *one* item that related in any way to a more transformational aim—sustainable food production systems.

Not surprisingly, the "future state" yielded much more ambitious results. Indeed, it was apparent that the people at Griffith saw the potential for the company to have a much broader and more substantial impact than the current sustainability platform would suggest. Only four items carried over from

Top 7 Subgoals: Current State		
12.2	Efficient use of natural resources	3.1
12.3	Reduce food waste and loss	3.0
12.5	Reduce waste generation	3.6
2.4	Sustainable food production systems	3.2
8.8	Labor rights / working conditions	3.1
6.3	Improve water quality	3.0
6.4	Water use efficiency	3.1

Top 9 Subgoals: Future State		
2.1	*End hunger/ ensure access by all*	4.7
2.2	*End malnutrition*	4.1
2.3	*Productivity of small holders*	4.3
2.4	Sustainable food production systems	4.6
1.1	*Eradicate extreme poverty*	4.1
9.5	*Technology and innovation in developing countries*	4.0
12.2	Efficient use of natural resources	4.2
12.3	Reduce food waste and loss	4.8
12.5	Reduce waste generation	4.3

Exhibit 5.4. **SDG Priorities: Current Versus Future State**

Note: The numbers to the left of each sub-goal item represent that number assigned in the SDGs, while the numbers to the right of each item are the ratings assigned by the respondents, on a 1 to 5 scale.

the "current state" assessment. The rest (in italics) focused on more aspirational aims like ending hunger and malnutrition, eradicating extreme poverty, improving productivity of smallholder farmers, and improving technology and innovation in developing countries—impacts that could only be achieved through transformational new business models and strategies.

These results made clear the importance of setting clear *Aspirations* for transformational change and business innovation when it comes to embedding purpose and making sustainability part of core strategy. Indeed, as Lewis Carroll once said, "If you don't know where you are going, then any road will get you there."

TRANSFORMATIONAL SUSTAINABILITY BENCHMARKING

The SDG work then led to an initiative launched in 2018 to benchmark leading-edge practices in companies focused on sustainability as core strategy. The project focused on "outliers"—a sample of those companies in the world pushing the envelope of truly transformational sustainability. Ultimately, we selected fifteen companies for further study—a mixture of American and European as well as public and private firms. We were particularly interested in better understanding how such companies went about setting clear Business Aspirations as part of their sustainability strategies. The companies were examined comparatively in order to identify patterns and create a framework for presenting the key elements and "next practices" for transformational sustainability.[77]

Through our study, we came to understand that a societally relevant purpose was insufficient to the task of focusing company attention on the actual, on-the-ground challenges that the company sought to address. It became clear that another layer of specificity would be required to embed lofty purpose into operational reality—what we came to call *Aspirations* and *Quests*. As explained earlier in this chapter, Aspirations and Quests (as distinct from Foundational Goals) serve as the "connective tissue" between purpose and actual business strategy—they answer the question, "What problems will we solve?"

Unlike the outlier companies we studied, most large corporations adopt sustainability goals and targets as a set of commitments separate from their primary goal, which is *financial* performance. For Griffith, however, Sustainability 2.0 meant turning this logic on its head—making the company's sustainability-based Aspirations the *primary objectives*, with financial metrics serving to support the societally driven purpose.

Building on the insights from the Transformational Sustainability Bench-

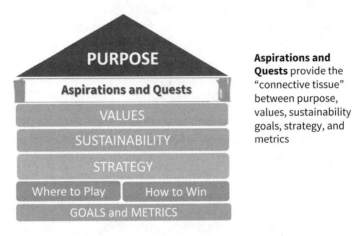

Aspirations and Quests provide the "connective tissue" between purpose, values, sustainability goals, strategy, and metrics

Exhibit 5.5. Adding Aspirations and Quests to the Griffith "House"

Source: Griffith Foods. Reprinted with permission.

marking, Griffith committed to developing a set of 2030 Aspirations and Quests to provide clarity regarding the positive impacts the company sought to create in the world through its business. Such clarity would then serve to *prioritize* and *sequence* investments and strategic initiatives—what came to be called "Big Bets"—and establish metrics to track progress and better align rewards and incentives. The Griffith executive team envisioned this as adding another layer to the Griffith "House" (Exhibit 5.5). In addition to operationalizing purpose, the team emphasized that such Aspirations and Quests should be bold and compelling, but also unique and authentic to Griffith Foods.

Building Aspirations and Quests

Recognizing that the world had moved forward since the setting of the original 3BL metrics in 2014, Griffith first sought to upgrade its internal infrastructure to support the tracking and reporting of sustainability-related metrics throughout its global operations. Increasingly, large food company customers were demanding that Griffith show evidence for performance on a more robust set of sustainability metrics, especially when it came to sustainable sourcing and climate. With the assistance of the consulting group Corporate Citizenship, the company embarked on the process certification by both EcoVadis and CDP.[78] This "foundational" work on sustainability goals served as important input into what was to come next: the development of a set of bold, authentic, unique, and compelling Aspirations and Quests to truly embed sustainability into core purpose and strategy.

To assist and inform this process, Griffith Foods formed an external sustainability advisory council (SAC). The council was composed of six experts (including me) from business, government, civil society, and academia with extensive experience in environment, social impact, health and nutrition, sustainable agriculture, and business model innovation.[79] Typically, sustainability advisory councils are convened by corporations as a separate group, led by the sustainability staff, with little interaction with business leadership or the board. Brian Griffith, however, was intent on breaking down these artificial boundaries.

He created a unique new hybrid governance structure for the company that included the board, the SAC, and selected executives from the company with functional responsibility for delivering on sustainability commitments—supply chain, R&D, operations, environment, and HR. To reinforce its central role in guiding the company's future, Brian himself, along with the senior management team—TC Chatterjee (CEO), Jim Thorne (Chief Strategy Officer), and Matt West (Chief Financial Officer)—led the convenings of this group.

Senior management created four workstreams or "verticals" deemed central to Griffith's future to move this process forward: "Health and Nutrition," "Sustainable Sourcing," "Climate Action and Environment," and "Well-Being and Fulfillment." A board member chaired each vertical, and each team included appropriate members of the SAC, along with key functional leadership and staff from Griffith.

Each of these four verticals worked to brainstorm about and develop a set of potential 2030 societal impacts, including specific goals that the company might commit to pursue in their area of focus. Not surprisingly, the interconnectedness across these four workstreams quickly became apparent. For example, it is not possible to innovate a healthy new plant-based protein food product without simultaneously addressing the sustainable sourcing of the ingredients, the well-being and income of the farmers involved, and the life cycle environmental and climate impacts of the entire product system.

To address these points of intersection and interdependency, vertical teams met jointly several times to encourage the *cross-fertilization* of ideas. For example, the Health and Nutrition team met with the Sustainable Sourcing team to compare notes and discuss areas of interaction and coordination. Periodically, the entire hybrid governance team would meet to hear progress reports from all four verticals, further stimulating interaction and integration.

By the fall of 2020, each of the four verticals had converged on a set of proposed 2030 impact areas. Exhibit 5.6 shows the twelve impact areas proposed by the four vertical teams. Each of these impact areas was accompanied by a detailed set of proposed 2030 goals and targets—over forty in all. As we assembled all these goals and targets, it became apparent that they were quite diverse in nature: many were foundational and internal (for example, achieve zero waste to landfill across all sites), while others could only be accomplished through business innovation (for example, become the most sought-after producer of food ingredients for healthy and nutritious food products). Still others were even broader in scope, requiring a partnership ecosystem to achieve (for example, mainstream regenerative farming practices).

The issue of differing levels arose repeatedly during the work of the vertical teams. We would often hear a functional manager from Griffith comment as an SAC or board member waxed poetic about an aspiration to "shift the company's product portfolio" or "transform agriculture" that "there is really no way that I can be held accountable for delivering on that goal." We then realized the importance of distinguishing between the three levels of impacts defined earlier in this chapter—Foundational Goals versus Business Aspirations and Corporate Quests—each category with its own locus of control and appropriate accountability, ranging from functional management to corporate leadership.

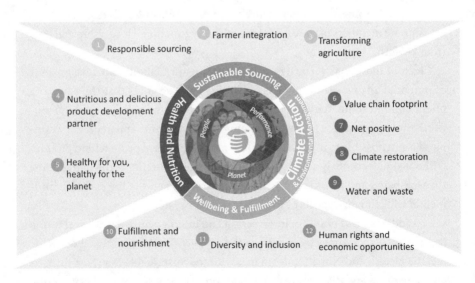

Exhibit 5.6. Proposed Impact Areas from the "Vertical" Teams

Source: Griffith Foods. Reprinted with permission.

It became clear that we needed to "convert" the organization of the proposed items from vertical impact areas to the three levels of impact. To facilitate this process, ESW and the executive team took the forty-plus goals and targets and categorized them into the three levels—Foundational Goals, Business Aspirations, and Corporate Quests. It turned out that nearly half of the items were foundational in nature. Functional leaders were assigned accountability for these goals. The fifteen Foundational Goals for 2030 included

- Aligning our ingredient portfolio with globally recognized standards (Health and Nutrition)

- Purchasing 100 percent of major raw materials from fully certified sustainable sources (Sustainable Sourcing)

- Achieving net zero in operational GHG emissions (Climate Action and Environment)

- Ensuring a living wage across our operations (Well-Being and Fulfillment)[80]

We then took the remaining twenty (or so) items and clustered them together according to theme. After several working sessions with the board, SAC, and key Griffith executives using Miro and other collaborative innovation tools, we converged on a set of three Griffith Foods Business Aspirations, with proposed impact and financial metrics for each. As Exhibit 5.7 shows graphically, the Foundational Goals were seen as supporting and enabling the Business Aspirations, while the Corporate Quest—still yet to emerge—would be an extension of the Business Aspirations, aiming to transform the broader commercial and policy ecosystem.

The first Business Aspiration—in the spirit of the first "grand challenge" described in Chapter 4—related to opportunities focused on the *upstream* portion of Griffith's value chain—scaling positive impact by championing a sustainable agricultural future, both for the smallholders who grew Griffith's spices and herbs and for the row crop farmers who grew the commodity grains used in Griffith products. Financially, Griffith aimed to derive 25 percent of its profit by 2030 from ingredients and products grown using regenerative agricultural practices.

Examples of proposed impact goals for 2030 included

- Partnering with suppliers and smallholder farmers to develop X million acres using regenerative agriculture practices

- Enabling X percent of customers to achieve net zero supply chains

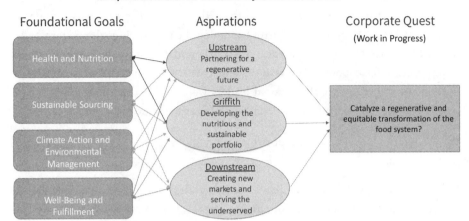

Purpose: We Blend Care and Creativity to Nourish the World

Exhibit 5.7. Foundational Goals, Business
Aspirations, and (Emerging) Quests

The second Business Aspiration—corresponding roughly to the second "grand challenge" in Chapter 4—focused on the transformation of Griffith Food's own technology and product *portfolio*, aiming to scale positive impact through more nutritious and sustainable finished goods and customer end products. Financially, Griffith aimed to derive 50 percent of its profit by 2030 from customer products that meet or exceed external global nutrition or sustainability standards.

Examples of proposed impact goals for 2030 included

- Meeting or exceeding external global nutrition and sustainability standards for X percent of raw materials and X percent of finished products

- Having a positive impact on the nutrition profile of products for X percent of customers globally

Finally, the third Business Aspiration—reflecting the third "grand challenge" in Chapter 4—related to business opportunities focused on the *downstream* portion of Griffith's value chain—scaling positive impact by creating new markets and serving the economically and nutritionally underserved. Financially, Griffith aimed to derive 10 percent of its profits by 2030 from business serving the underserved.

Examples of proposed impact goals for 2030 included

- Building new businesses in X new geographies that serve the underserved

- Enabling X percent of our customers' products to deliver affordable and accessible nutrition in underserved markets and communities

The work continues to finalize the Griffith Business Aspirations. As the process matures, the Aspirations are being incorporated into the company's long-term strategic and operating plans. The newly defined Business Aspirations will also be used to determine where to target the company's capital investments for the future—what CEO TC Chatterjee refers to as the "Big Bets"—to enable the aspirations to become reality.

The final step will be the crafting of Griffith Foods Corporate Quest. Given Griffith's long-standing reputation in the industry as a trusted and innovative partner for new and innovative food products and processes, a *downstream* focus is probably where the leverage for true transformation lies. Might Griffith return to its roots and dedicate itself to the quest of revolutionizing the food industry once again? Perhaps the Quest could revolve around accelerating the commercialization of alternative proteins and affordable nutrition in the world? Griffith has already created *Nourish Ventures* as an organizational vehicle for tracking—and acquiring—key new technologies in this space.

By leveraging existing customers and building new relationships with food innovators and NGO partners, Griffith is in a position to truly "punch above its weight" by catalyzing a new commercial ecosystem aimed at accelerating the availability of healthy, sustainable, delicious, and affordable food for all. In the words of Brian Griffith,

> While our history demonstrates we can innovate, adapt, and gain new relevance in the food industry, we are not content merely to evolve from where we've been. Rather, moving forward from here will take transformational change as we remake our business. . . . I believe the greatest challenges before us are not the scale and ambition of our 2030 Aspirations but our own capacity to change. To me, evolutionary incrementalism may be the greatest threat we face. To deliver on our Purpose and reach our Aspirations, we must free ourselves of the constraints of a traditional evolutionary mindset. With boldness and conviction, we are choosing this path because we recognize Griffith Foods' potential as a catalyst for a regenerative and equitable transformation in the food system and beyond.

Isomorphic or Iconoclastic?

When it comes to sustainability and purpose, large, publicly held companies are often heavily influenced by the behavior of their peers—what academic institutional theorists call "isomorphism"—mimicking the "best practices" of the companies you want to be associated with so as to be viewed as legitimate, both by Wall Street and key stakeholders.[81]

A key to realizing isomorphism is imitation: rather than necessarily innovating their own strategies and practices, companies look to their peers for cues as to appropriate behavior. For "corporate sustainability," this often means being ranked highly by the "right" outside evaluators (for example, Dow Jones Sustainability Index, MSCI, Sustainalytics), adopting industry standards for sustainability reporting, goals, and metrics (for example, Global Reporting Initiative, SASB, EcoVadis, CDP, TCFD, SBTi), complying with emerging reporting requirements (for example, CSRD, SEC) or working with highly visible partners, consultants and NGOs. Such mimicry has the effect of raising the mean for entire sectors and industries, which is valuable and important, but fails to push forward the leading-edge tail of the curve—the "positive deviants"—which will be crucial if we are to realize the transformational change required in the years ahead.

When asked if the logic of isomorphism necessarily held for Griffith Foods, Brian Griffith replied, "While achieving 'best practice' is not our goal, we are interested in learning everything we can from the experience of others. But at the end of the day, our aim is not legitimacy or acceptance. Instead, our goal is to be true to ourselves—to do the right thing. We are duty bound to step out—to innovate—for the betterment of society and the world." Asked if this looked more like being iconoclastic than isomorphic, Brian responded simply, "Yes."

Salesforce CEO Marc Benioff put it in even starker terms: "Over time, I've become convinced that there are two types of CEOs: those who believe that improving the state of the world is part of their mission, and those who don't feel they have any responsibility other than delivering results for their shareholders."[82] It has now become increasingly clear that the future belongs to the former.

So, when it comes to re-embedding purpose, let this serve as an object lesson for all the corporate fast-followers out there: blending in with the crowd with "best practice" sustainability goals is not the same thing as doing the work to develop your own unique and authentic Purpose realized through bold Business Aspirations and a compelling Corporate Quest. And it will not be long before sustainability hyperbole, greenwishing, and purpose-washing catch up with those companies seeking safety in numbers. Yet, as we will see in the next chapter, the process of re-embedding purpose does not end with the declaration of authentic and compelling Aspirations and Quests. The ultimate challenge—and necessity—is to engage the entire organization in their effective realization.

SIX

Redesigning the Corporate Architecture

"The system was strained when [the former CEO] lost support of the people in the organization. Although everyone believed in the ultimate sustainability vision, it was how it was being executed and the timing of it that were not ideal. . . . The new CEO focused on rebuilding the culture and communication especially around accountability and ownership."

JESSICA SANDERSON, FORMER DIRECTOR
OF SUSTAINABILITY, NOVELIS

Establishing a higher societal purpose animated by tangible Business Aspirations and a compelling Corporate Quest is becoming increasingly important as we move deeper into the third capitalist reformation and a new era of sustainable capitalism. Yet even with this directional infrastructure in place to guide strategy and resource allocation, there is still the danger that companies end up off course: since most corporate efforts to re-embed purpose involve only a relatively small number of more senior people in the company—C-suite, functional, and business leaders—the potential of fully engaging and aligning the entire organization, including middle management and front-line employees, remains unfulfilled. In fact, without focus on *organizationwide* transformation, there is a risk that the "head" of the organization (that is, senior management) becomes disconnected from the "body" (organizational members), rendering the entire effort ineffective and potentially counterproductive.[1]

To understand the potential for such a disconnect in greater depth—and how best to address it—my colleagues Priya Dasgupta, Kate Napolitan, and I took a close look at some truly innovative corporate "outliers"—the selection of fifteen companies noted in the previous chapter as pushing the envelope when it came to societal purpose, sustainability, and corporate transformation.[2] We found that a clear Purpose was necessary but not sufficient to the task of focusing company attention on the actual, on-the-ground challenges that the company seeks to address. Even tangible Business Aspirations and a compelling Quest were not enough: embedding societal purpose into the DNA of the company requires a truly systematic approach that includes everyone, everywhere in the company.

Our examination revealed that effectively embedding a transformational societal purpose requires a complete *rewiring* of the company. Actually, it entails more than just an upgrade to the electrical system: achieving transformational societal purpose means nothing less than a renovation of the entire corporate architecture—a new, and upgraded, "House."[3] There is an integrated set of building blocks and elements that appear to be essential if companies are to successfully chart the course for transformational purpose. Taken together, these constitute a *new architecture* for corporate transformation with Purpose serving as the "North Star."[4]

Before delving more deeply into this integrated approach to transformational sustainability, let's take a look at the historical roots of this challenge— the question of how best to organize for strategic change and transformation.

Historical Roots of Strategic Transformation

There is a long and venerable history of models and tools focused on strategic change and transformation, dating back to Alfred Chandler's classic work in the 1960s professing that organizational structure must follow strategy to be effective.[5] In the early 1970s, Kenneth Andrews's pathbreaking work *The Concept of Strategy* added the important dimensions of corporate purpose, personal values, and social responsibility to strategy-making, while still emphasizing that the accomplishment of purpose and strategy be achieved through the design of organizational structure, processes, and behavior.[6]

Jay Galbraith's work on strategy "implementation" has also been highly influential.[7] His "Star Model" of organizing for success has been particularly useful for those aiming to implement innovative new programs and initiatives within companies.[8] Dave Stangis and Katherine Valvoda Smith in *21st Century Corporate Citizenship* devoted a section to Galbraith's Star Model as an important tool for sustainability leaders in achieving alignment among the many organizational elements necessary to ensure success—structure, formal systems, processes, people, rewards, and incentives.[9]

However, as important as these frameworks and tools have been, most of them are based on the presumption that a "strategy" already exists and is waiting to be implemented. They make the implicit assumption that there is a separation between strategy *formulation* and strategy *implementation*—that the former is an analytical task and the latter is an organizational one. Similar assumptions are often made about societal purpose—that it descends from "above" (that is, from senior management) in fully articulated form, similar to the logic of strategy formulation.[10]

It turns out that these "bifurcation" assumptions are contestable at best since there are numerous ways that purpose and strategy can be formed in organizations. Henry Mintzberg, for example, famously documented what he called "emergent" strategy-making—strategies that emanate from unintended patterns of smaller decisions and initiatives, which emerge from below and are simply recognized and affirmed by senior management—quite the opposite of analytically derived or deliberate strategy-making.[11] Indeed, the McKinsey 7-S Framework described a constellation of interrelated factors—strategy, structure, systems, shared values, style, skills, and staff—that influence an organization's ability to effectively change direction. The framework emphasized the lack of hierarchy among these factors, which meant *all* of them need to be aligned as an integrated system.[12]

I began teaching strategy in business schools in the mid-1980s and was troubled by the formulation-implementation split, which reigned supreme at the time. It seemed that the *process* used to craft strategy appeared to have real and significant implications for company performance, yet it was not given the attention it deserved. Was it better to determine strategy through a formal and analytical planning process and then implement it, or was it more effective to guide the process with a broad vision and let the actual strategies emerge from within the organization? I was motivated to delve more deeply into this question. The result was a couple of scholarly journal articles that, I believe, resolved the seeming dilemma.[13]

After an extensive review of the literature, both academic and practitioner, it became clear to me that there were actually *multiple* modes of purpose-setting and strategy-making, that could be combined in various ways, with significant implications for performance. I developed an Integrative Framework consisting of five modes: "Command," "Rational," "Transactive," "Symbolic," and "Generative" (Exhibit 6.1). The framework was based on the varying roles top managers and organizational members can play in the strategic process and how they interrelate.[14] I observed that the role played by senior executives can range all the way from that of a *commander*, consciously formulating strategy at the top and issuing it to the rest of the organization, to what might be called a *sponsor*, when strategy emerges from below and is merely recognized and supported by the top—Mintzberg's "emergent" strategy. Correspondingly, the role played by organizational members can range all the way from *good soldier*, members who execute the plans formulated by top managers, to *entrepreneur* (or intrapreneur), members who are expected to behave autonomously in the pursuit of new strategic initiatives.

The *Command* mode of strategy-making, in which a strong leader or top team formulates the strategy and organizational members execute it, is often found in startups. Founders frequently play the role of "commander" as they passionately pursue their founding vision. As organizations grow, however, the Command mode usually ceases to be an effective means of strategic management and other modes take shape that involve more formal analysis or enable more engagement by organizational members.

With the *Rational* mode, for example, formal planning systems and hierarchical relationships come to predominate. Strategy is seen as the execution of plans produced through comprehensive analysis and systematic procedure.

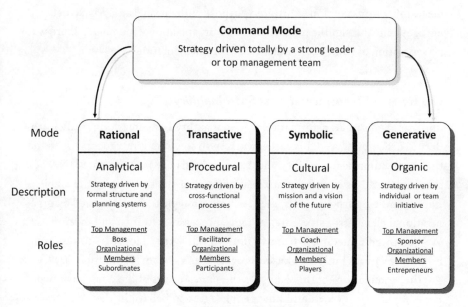

Exhibit 6.1. Five Faces of Strategy-Making

Top managers and staff determine strategic direction through a formal planning process and organizational members are held accountable for results. The *Transactive* mode, however, entails a higher level of engagement by organizational members in the strategic process. In this case, top managers' role is to facilitate an interactive, cross-functional process of strategy formulation; the resulting strategy flows from organized interactions among organizational members, suppliers, customers, and key stakeholders.

In contrast, with the *Symbolic* mode, senior leaders focus primarily on developing and articulating a compelling purpose, mission, or vision to help guide the actions of organizational members toward a set of common goals. Top managers serve more as "coaches" to inspire and focus organizational members in the strategic process. Finally, with the *Generative* mode, central direction gives way completely to internal entrepreneurship, and top management adjusts the strategy to fit the pattern of innovations emerging from below.

I reasoned that companies need not adhere to a single mode of strategy-making. Instead, I hypothesized, the more companies develop a higher level of "process capability"—skills in multiple modes of strategy-making—the higher their performance. In a survey-based research study of 285 firms, this hypothesis was borne out: firms with the highest process capability indeed outperformed single-mode or less process-capable organizations across multiple dimensions, including growth, future positioning, and social responsibility.[15] The highest-performing firms combined inspired purpose with rational analysis, structured engagement, and significant autonomy for organizational members. There was no separation of strategy formulation and implementation.

The House of Transformational Sustainability

The results of the Transformational Sustainability Benchmarking study introduced earlier reinforced this earlier work on strategy-making process: we found that embedding sustainability and a societal purpose into the core DNA of a company requires the systematic realignment of the *entire corporate architecture*, including purpose, goals, metrics, and strategies, as well as the key organizational elements—structure, systems, processes, rewards, and incentives.[16] We borrowed a metaphor from Griffith Foods—the "House"—to represent how these various building blocks fit together as a system (see Exhibit 6.2).[17]

The "foundation" of this House is the *shared values* of the company—what the company believes in and how people agree to behave in their daily work life. The "roof," which serves to shelter, protect, and enclose everything else

Exhibit 6.2. Embedded Purpose:
The New Corporate Architecture

inside the House, is the company *Purpose*—a clear articulation of *why* the company exists. The corporate *Aspirations and Quests* then serve to give texture and clarity to the purpose—*what* specific positive impacts the company seeks to make in the world through the business. The middle floor of the House is then composed of the core elements of *Strategy*, which define *how* the company will aim to succeed in delivering on the Aspirations and Quests: "Structure and Governance," "Experiments and Initiatives," "Technologies and Capabilities," and "Partnerships and Platforms." Finally, specific *Goals and Metrics* serve to track progress, both internally and with regard to the external Aspirations and Quests, as operationalized through the strategies; *Rewards and Incentives* are then developed for everyone in the company to enable both engagement and fulfillment. Let's examine each of the elements of the corporate architecture in more depth, along with examples from the fifteen companies we studied.

WHAT WE BELIEVE: VALUES

The transformational companies we examined established a strong *foundation* built on their organizations' *Values*. These lived values, whether stated or unstated, make up the culture of the company and encompass what the company believes and how people behave toward each other and their stakeholders. A house with a poor foundation will not last—regardless of how large, visually appealing, or expensive the house may be. The foundation must be strong enough to support everything else the organization aspires to become. For example,

SC Johnson has been guided by a strong set of principles and values since its founding in 1886. These principles were first summarized in a 1927 speech by H. F. Johnson Jr: "The goodwill of the people is the only enduring thing in any business. It is the sole substance . . . the rest is shadow." The values were more formally stated in 1976 in "This We Believe," which sets forth five sets of stakeholders to whom the company holds itself responsible: employees, consumers and users, general public, neighbors and hosts, and the world community. Everything at SC Johnson flows from these core values and principles—they pervade the culture at the company and influence day-to-day behavior and decisions in fundamental ways.[18]

WHY WE EXIST: PURPOSE

With values serving as the foundation, the "roof" of the "House" consists of a clear articulation of corporate Purpose. As we saw in the previous chapter, a compelling societal purpose is distinct from past efforts to articulate corporate vision and mission, which were often competitive or technical in nature, emphasizing the company's strengths and how these would lead to competitive success in the future. Think: "Our vision is to be the world's premier provider of [fill in the industry]" or "We will become number 1 or number 2 in every market we serve." Transformational purpose, in contrast, gives voice to *why* the company exists—what positive impact it seeks to have in the world. It is a moral call to action, a higher purpose, that fosters emotional connection and commitment on the part of organizational members.

The Unilever Purpose, for example, "to make sustainable living commonplace," is realized through its "Sustainable Living Plan"—a ten-year mission to improve the health and well-being of one billion people, reduce environmental impact by half, and enhance the livelihoods of millions. At DSM, "our purpose is to create brighter lives for people today and generations to come." Campbell's Soup recently adopted a new corporate purpose: "*real food* that matters for life's moments." But perhaps the Purpose espoused by Ben & Jerry's is the most missionary: "to courageously advance the global movement for social, economic, and environmental justice through linked prosperity." For Ben & Jerry's, ice cream is merely a means to a more noble set of ends.

Such a sense of higher purpose signals a return to the roots of leadership thinking from the 1930s such as from Chester Barnard[19] and Philip Selznick,[20] which emphasized the moral, normative, and philosophical aspects of leadership and drew a sharp distinction between an *organization*—a rational instrument engineered to accomplish specific tasks—and an *institution,* which is infused with values and meaning beyond the instrumental and technical aspects.

Virtually all of the leading-edge companies we studied proclaimed Purposes that focused on their roles in the world and provided the *why* behind everything they did. Among this group of "outlier" companies, Purpose also served to inform and guide strategy through a compelling set of Aspirations and Quests.

WHAT WE SOLVE: ASPIRATIONS AND QUESTS

As Chapter 5 made clear, lofty statements of purpose can breed frustration and cynicism if they appear as mere platitudes or fail to connect to the real-world reality of managers and employees. To overcome this potential for disconnect, the companies in our study developed Aspirations and Quests to bring corporate purpose to life and serve as the "connective tissue" for strategy development, goals, metrics, rewards, and incentives.

In addition to the examples of Seventh Generation and Interface discussed previously, most of the companies in our study also demonstrated the importance of Aspirations and Quests to the realization of Purpose. For example, family-owned food and confectionery giant Mars unveiled its new corporate purpose in 2017, "the Sustainable in a Generation Plan," with an initial commitment to investing $1 billion to tackle urgent threats facing the business and society, such as climate change, poverty in the value chain, and resource scarcity. Mars created strategies around three main Business Aspirations: "Healthy Planet," "Thriving People," and "Nourishing Well-Being." They then operationalized each of these Aspirations with specific goals and metrics. For the "Thriving People" Aspiration, for example, the goals were increasing income for farmers, respecting human rights, and unlocking opportunities for women, each with specific quantitative metrics (targets) to be met over time.

The transformation of Ingersoll-Rand is also a compelling story of escalating Aspirations. After ramping up a significant set of initiatives in sustainability over the past decade, including an aggressive set of sustainability goals for 2020, they made the decision in 2019 to *de-merge* the corporation in order to create a purpose-driven "climate" company focused on sustainability as core strategy—Trane Technologies.[21] The new company is dedicated to providing access to cooling, refrigeration, and healthy food, all without warming the planet. The company's new purpose, "to boldly challenge what's possible for a sustainable world," speaks to their quest to transform the entire industry.

To bring this new purpose to life, Trane Technologies has crafted and publicly announced three new 2030 aspirational commitments:

- *The Gigaton Challenge.* Reduce one billion tons of carbon emissions from their customers' footprint by 2030 by innovating clean technologies, advancing system level energy efficiency, reducing global food waste, and making the transition to next-generation refrigerants.

- *Leading by Example.* Reimagine company operations and the supply chain so as to have a restorative impact on the environment.

- *Opportunity for All.* Achieve workforce diversity reflective of their communities, gender parity in leadership roles, and pathways to green and STEM careers.[22]

The expectation is that these 2030 commitments will change every facet of the existing business, from operations to supply chains to products to employee and community development and governance. Aspirations and Quests thus serve as the fulcrum for change in leading-edge companies, translating purpose and intention into strategy and operating reality.

HOW WE WIN: STRATEGIES AND INITIATIVES

To live the Purpose and realize the audacious Aspirations and Quests, strategy and execution are key.[23] It takes organizational focus (Structure and Governance), innovation and iteration (Experiments and Initiatives), investment in core competencies for the future (Technologies and Capabilities), and reaching out to the broader ecosystem (Partnerships and Platforms) to make Aspirations and Quests a reality.

A Structure and Governance system with sustainability embedded within (as opposed to hanging off the side) establishes clear roles and responsibilities to enable the setting of priorities, decision making, and execution of strategy. Governance helps to embed the sustainability efforts, starting with the board and CEO and supported by a dedicated staff. At Unilever, for example, every board-level committee has a purpose-related mandate to fulfill, with the CEO being ultimately responsible for delivery on the Purpose. An engaged and aligned board is crucial in order to overcome the inevitable pressures for short-term performance that may serve to block the investment and commitment required to realize transformation. In Unilever's case, the board stood behind former CEO Paul Polman's bold initiative to abolish quarterly earnings reporting, which served to open the door to longer-term thinking at the company, consistent with its purpose.

At Trane Technologies, the company's governance structure includes both internal and external sustainability advisory councils, along with the Center for Energy Efficiency and Sustainability. Trane Technologies is also one of the first industrial companies to have a CEO-level sustainability target focused on GHG reduction. This CEO target serves to frame the climate targets for the entire senior team, which then trickle down to all levels across the company, effectively making it a companywide key performance indicator (KPI). And as we saw in the last chapter, Griffith Foods also created a unique governance structure—a hybrid entity that combined members of the board, the sustainability advisory council, and functional leadership in the company to drive its process of setting Aspirations and Quests and guide its broader mission and strategy.

Such clear governance then enables the pursuit of Experiments and Initiatives—be they pilot projects or small-scale market probes, new products and services, or an overhaul of existing business models—in line with the company Purpose and Aspirations. For example, Essilor created a completely new "Mission Division" focused on bringing vision correction to the world's underserved. This new strategic initiative has catalyzed the development and launch of dozens of new technologies and business models aimed at reaching those 2.5 billion lower-income people in the world with uncorrected poor vision.

Cemex has long been known for its strategic initiatives focused on serving the underserved at the base of the pyramid. Beginning with Patrimonio Hoy in the 1990s, Cemex has launched a series of new business experiments— Construyo Contigo, ConstruApoyo, Yo Construyo—all aimed at developing new business models in affordable and sustainable housing beyond the reach of the current business. By doing so, Cemex is building the network of partners and business models needed to shape tomorrow's construction ecosystem.

When it comes to Technology and Capabilities, it is all about identifying and investing in the new, sustainable core competencies and technologies the company will use to transform the business in line with its Purpose and Aspirations—the "Big Bets" on the future. It may also be necessary to shed legacy products and technologies that are not in line with the future Aspirations. Our research showed that leading companies typically invest 5 to 15 percent of revenue in R&D in the quest to transform themselves into tomorrow's sustainable enterprise. Over the past two decades, for example, DSM has transformed itself from a mining and petrochemical producer (DSM initially stood for Dutch State Mines) into a science-based company with a focus on nutrition and innovating for the bio-based, circular, and low-carbon economy of tomorrow.

Our exploration also shows that leading-edge companies are realizing that it is not possible to drive the transformational change required purely through changes in competitive or corporate strategy. Indeed, strategic Partnerships and Platforms appear increasingly to be key to delivering on the wider, societal value propositions associated with Corporate Quests. Partnership ecosystems and engagement in broader collaborative platforms can address *systemic* changes beyond the capabilities of the firm itself—an approach Dow has deftly described as "Blueprint" strategy. As we saw, Mars established the Farmer Income Lab—a collaborative think-do-tank aimed at elevating smallholder farming communities as a whole, thereby ensuring sustainable supply chains for the company well into the future.

Novozymes illustrates all these elements of transformational strategy. With more than 10 percent of sales dedicated to transformational R&D, the company has launched a stream of new "game changer" products in bioenergy and sustainable agriculture. Novozymes has also forged alliances and partnerships aimed at advancing its sustainability goals, working with large customers, NGOs, and other players to shift the policy dialogue in the world toward more sustainable solutions.

WHAT WE TRACK AND *HOW* WE ACCELERATE: GOALS AND METRICS, REWARDS AND INCENTIVES

Companies with truly embedded purpose develop an *interconnected system* starting with Purpose, which cascades to Aspirations and Quests, which in turn are tracked through specific Goals and Metrics, and reinforced through the Rewards and Incentives system. Purpose is forever; Aspirations and Quests are enduring and serve as beacons for the development of strategy and business plans, but can also evolve as necessary; Goals and Metrics are expected to be updated, revised, and amended periodically as the world (and business conditions) change; and Rewards and Incentives are updated every year. Aspirations and Quests serve as the "connective tissue" that connects the broad and enduring corporate Purpose to the more immediate and practical business realities operationalized through the ever-evolving Goals and Metrics and Rewards and Incentives.

For example, once Seventh Generation had developed a set of company Aspirations and Quests with associated Goals and Metrics (see Chapter 5), leadership then took the step to connect these directly to organizational members' Rewards and Incentives. At Seventh Generation, *every* employee is part of the bonus-incentive system. Depending on position and level in the company, bonuses constitute between 10 and 50 percent of total compensation. Business and financial goals constitute 80 percent of the bonus; the remaining 20 percent is focused on progress toward the four Aspirations.

Each year, one metric from each of the four Aspirations is selected to be part of this bonus calculation. For these sustainability-related metrics, there is a "target" and an "exceed" goal for each year. If the company exceeds on these metrics, then the bonus can be increased by another 10 percent. To qualify for the bonus, every employee must participate in a community volunteer program and an annual "Leadership/Sustainability" education and awareness program. Such participation also helps inform the setting of individual employee performance targets, Goals and Metrics, done jointly by employees and their managers.

Seventh Generation stands in stark contrast to the typical corporation of today. Indeed, for most companies, Goals and Metrics are disconnected from purpose: metrics, along with Rewards and Incentives, are typically focused on *near-term* business progress—what was achieved this quarter or this year— while almost never addressing long-term Goals and Aspirations. These short-term-only objectives demotivate people, narrowing their focus and diminishing their creativity, and sapping the passion and commitment desperately needed to solve the enormous global challenges we face.

DOING A HOUSE INSPECTION

The "House" metaphor captures the elements and building blocks required for companies to effectively embed purpose and transform themselves to ensure a sustainable future. The first step toward such radical reconstruction is to do a comprehensive "house inspection" to determine which elements are outdated, missing, or most in need of renovation. For most companies with a stated societal purpose, this inspection will reveal that the best place to begin is by developing the few Aspirations and Quests upon which to focus strategic and organizational attention, as we saw in Chapter 5. Once there is clarity about these priorities, the company can then develop the specific Goals and Metrics against which progress can be measured and articulate the "How" elements described earlier—where to play and how to win—including what new technologies, capabilities, initiatives, and partners will be needed. Finally, the company can devise the means to most effectively integrate these elements with Rewards and Incentives and ensure the alignment needed with other key company management systems to ensure that the "head" and the "body" are completely in sync.

This last element of the "House"—Rewards and Incentives—requires special attention, since the effective embedding of purpose requires authenticity and emotional commitment, not just monetary rewards and financial incentives. With this in mind, let's take a closer look at the challenge of effectively engaging middle management and the rank and file in the realization of the company's Purpose, Aspirations, and Quests.

Motivation for Good

A growing body of research indicates that an inspiring organizational purpose or mission can result in greater personal identification, organizational commitment, engagement, creativity, capability development, and need fulfillment among organizational members and employees.[24] For example, Self-Determination Theory identifies multiple kinds of motivation, ranging from lower to higher levels of "Motivation Quality" (MQ).[25] On the lower end of the spectrum are conventional means of motivation such as "External Pressure" ("carrots and sticks") and "Internal Pressure" (guilt or ego involvement). These motivators are typically imposed from the outside and are thus characterized as "extrinsic" in nature. On the higher end of the MQ spectrum are more internally driven forms of motivation such as "Personal Value" (goal alignment) and "Intrinsic Motivation" (flow experience on the job or enjoying the work itself).

As Exhibit 6.3 shows, Aspirations and Quests can serve to catalyze the high MQ potential implicit in corporate Purpose. Without Aspirations and Quests, Purpose can be seen as inauthentic by employees—an attempt at PR—and result in cynicism and skepticism. Goals and Metrics can also appear disconnected (forced from "on high") rather than the natural outgrowth of a shared sense of Aspirations and Purpose within the company. And if Goals and Metrics appear arbitrary, any attempt to connect them to individual rewards and incentives will be seen as External or Internal Pressure. The result is either demotivation or, at best, short-term motivation for a financial reward that cannot be sustained in the long term.

Contrast this situation with one in which there is a strong set of Aspirations

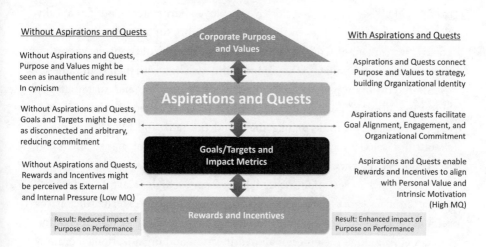

Without Aspirations and Quests

Without Aspirations and Quests, Purpose and Values might be seen as inauthentic and result In cynicism

Without Aspirations and Quests, Goals and Targets might be seen as disconnected and arbitrary, reducing commitment

Without Aspirations and Quests, Rewards and Incentives might be perceived as External and Internal Pressure (Low MQ)

Result: Reduced impact of Purpose on Performance

Corporate Purpose and Values

Aspirations and Quests

Goals/Targets and Impact Metrics

Rewards and Incentives

With Aspirations and Quests

Aspirations and Quests connect Purpose and Values to strategy, building Organizational Identity

Aspirations and Quests facilitate Goal Alignment, Engagement, and Organizational Commitment

Aspirations and Quests enable Rewards and Incentives to align with Personal Value and Intrinsic Motivation (High MQ)

Result: Enhanced impact of Purpose on Performance

Exhibit 6.3. **Aspirations and Quests as Catalyst for Purpose**

and Quests in place. Here, Purpose is clearly connected to strategy and goals, creating a sense of goal alignment and organizational commitment. Rewards and Incentives based upon such goals can also result in a higher MQ if the employee has a strong emotional commitment: striving to achieve such goals will be seen as having Personal Value and Intrinsic Motivation for the work involved. The result is enhanced effort, commitment, and company performance.

Consistent with this line of thinking, Robert Quinn and Anjan Thakor proposed an *economic theory of higher purpose*: "The adoption of an authentic higher purpose creates a bond between employees and the purpose and motivates them to work harder, be more entrepreneurial, and subordinate their self-interest for the common good, all in order to help the organization serve its higher purpose. This sense of purpose results in better economic performance. However, these things happen only if employees believe that the purpose is *authentic*."[26]

Authentic purpose is thus paradoxical: it results in higher motivation and better business results only when it is *not* undertaken with the intent of generating better business results! To create this belief, higher purpose must be the arbiter of all major business decisions—not just when it is convenient or serves short-term performance needs. Leaders must regularly communicate the higher purpose, integrate it with business strategy, and effectively weave authentic higher purpose into the day-to-day work and decisions of middle management and line employees.[27] In fact, a new survey of four thousand workers in the US and UK—the 2023 Net Positive Employee Barometer—found that fully *three-quarters* of employees in the US want to work for a company that has a positive impact on the world, and about *half* said they would consider resigning from their job if the values of the company did not align with their own values.[28]

Many corporations have attempted to drive purpose and sustainability by setting "stretch" goals and tying executive compensation to them. Unfortunately, those in middle management and the rank and file often respond skeptically to lofty statements of purpose drafted by senior management and to demands from their managers to change their day-to-day work routines on the basis of new expectations passed down from on high. "Carrots and sticks" may produce a short-term change in behavior, but such external incentives seldom produce the change in mindset needed for large-scale transformation to happen, let alone the emotional identification and organizational commitment desired.

The leading-edge companies in our study recognized that the most powerful incentive is *meaningful* and *fulfilling* work and have therefore aimed to *activate* employees through initiatives focused on awareness and understanding about the companies' Purpose and Aspirations, incorporation of Purpose into job descriptions and performance evaluations, and Rewards and Incentives systems. Indeed, these companies typically asked *all* managers and employees to personally contribute to the corporate purpose as a KPI (personal purpose) and often linked these contributions directly to the bonus system.

Atlanta-based carpet and flooring leader Interface exhibits an especially well-developed system for bringing Purpose and Aspirations to life by activating employees' *personal* purpose to increase internal motivation and commitment.[29] Recognizing that the pursuit of "Climate Take Back" as a mission would mean transformation of the entire company—its products, processes, competencies, technologies, materials, business models, and partnerships—the company sought to motivate, activate, and engage its employees through a variety of means. First, Interface reset and reaffirmed its core values: "Design a Better Way," "Be Genuine and Generous," "Inspire Others," "Connect the Whole," and "Embrace Tomorrow Today." These core values were then codified as behaviors and incorporated directly into job descriptions and included in performance evaluations for everyone throughout the company.

But the company did not stop with these more "extrinsic" forms of motivation (that is, via rewards and recognition). In addition, leadership sought to truly *activate* and *engage* employees, starting with an awareness campaign about the significance of the climate crisis. Next, middle managers were given a set of guidelines for talking with their direct reports about the mission—and how to make it real for them on the job. This engagement was complemented by workshops about the four Aspirations (see Chapter 5) for all employees with a focus on understanding how what every employee does relates and how they contribute to the mission.

The ultimate aim was to shift employees from simply understanding the company's mission to taking individual actions—both on the job and at home. To achieve this larger shift in mindset, Interface explored the use of "Handprinter" and the "Good Life Goals," an individual version of the SDGs, as sources of inspiration enabling individuals to identify, initiate, and spread actions—and track their associated positive impacts. By combining awareness, education, and personal engagement, Interface seeks to engage the "whole person" in the quest to slow and ultimately reverse the climate crisis.

Looking forward then, the transformation to sustainability will not just be a matter of how to "motivate" or "incentivize" employees from the *outside*, but instead, how to effectively foster and nurture a higher quality of employee motivation from *within*.[30] The development and nurturing of a strong sense of societal purpose, manifested through a set of compelling Aspirations and Quests, appears crucial to building the internal motivation and emotional commitment required. Indeed, it seems that turning the business into a compelling "cause" is the best way to capture the imagination—and dedicated work effort—of employees and organizational members.

Let's take a close look at a company where transformational sustainability has been the watchword for the past decade: Novelis. I was able to observe—and participate in—the transformation process there up close, having served as a member of the company's sustainability advisory council from 2012 through 2016. Novelis was also one of the fifteen companies we studied as part of our Transformational Sustainability Benchmarking project. This case provides insight about the challenges of embedding purpose and making bold aspirations actually "stick" with organizational members. It brings the entire "House" into clear focus and demonstrates the importance of aligning all the elements and building blocks of the corporate architecture.

The Renovation of Novelis

Phil Martens experienced one of those turning points that fundamentally alter the course of a person's life, an entire industry, and perhaps even the future trajectory of the planet.[31] As he sat in his Atlanta office in early 2015, he pondered the chain of events that had led to the creation of Novelis, his decision to join Novelis as its CEO, and the development of a disruptive new strategy based on closed-loop recycling of aluminum, the radical reduction of greenhouse gas emissions, and the pursuit of a more sustainable world. By choosing to be an industry revolutionary, he knew that the future held tremendous potential and opportunity but was also filled with potential pitfalls and challenges.

It began in 2005. As part of the mergers and acquisition wave of the time, aluminum industry titan Alcan was split apart, with the upstream mines, alumina production facilities, and smelters separated from the downstream rolling mills and customer-facing assets. The idea was to "unlock value" by creating a pure play mining company. Mining giant Rio Tinto later scooped up these upstream assets, paying a substantial premium. The downstream portion (viewed as noncore) was spun off into a new company—Novelis—which was listed on the New York Stock Exchange. With nearly $10 billion in sales, it instantly became the largest aluminum rolling company in the world.[32]

Unfortunately, Novelis floundered in the immediate aftermath of the demerger. As a highly decentralized collection of downstream mills and sales offices, the new company was now almost completely dependent on the purchase of primary or "prime" aluminum from upstream producers. And with largely former Alcan divisional managers now serving as senior executives, they failed (among other things) to hedge aluminum prices, resulting in the rapid accumulation of more than $1 billion in debt, which all but crippled the company. Eighteen months later, the board decided to put Novelis up for sale. While a potentially attractive asset, it would take a special buyer to see the value. The Aditya Birla Group (ABG), one of the oldest and most respected Indian conglomerates, surprisingly emerged as the suitor. By bidding 30 percent higher than anyone else, ABG became the proud owner of Novelis in 2007.

The search began for a new CEO. Enter Phil Martens. Martens had a long history in the auto industry, serving in various engineering and leadership positions at Ford Motor Company from 1987 to 2005. After leaving Ford, Martens served as a senior executive at Plastech Engineering and ArvinMeritor, Inc., before becoming president of Arvin Innovation. He was hungry to be an entrepreneur. But as Martens said, "If I can't start my own company, then I would love to have the opportunity to fundamentally reshape an existing one."

Novelis appeared to be the perfect opportunity: it was effectively a "$10 billion start-up," being only three years old in 2008. It was also in dire need of reshaping. As Martens commented, it was "an incredible ship at sea" with "investment grade assets and junk bond results." The idea of a global downstream aluminum company was new, so perhaps there was an opportunity to turn things upside down and "reboot the software." Novelis was a $10 billion startup owned by a $40 billion Indian conglomerate. ABG, led by its chairman, Kumar Birla, was in it for the long term, which offered a fighting chance to build a new kind of aluminum company.

ENVISIONING THE CLOSED-LOOP ALUMINUM COMPANY

Phil Martens took the helm as CEO of Novelis in 2009. His first challenge was to unify the company and repair the broken balance sheet. He launched the "One Novelis" initiative to integrate the various decentralized parts into a single operating company. Symbolizing this move was the transition from twenty-three separate websites to a single Novelis corporate website. By 2011, the financial health of the company had been restored, with EBITDA growing from $400 million to $1.6 billion. The time had come to unite the company around something even bigger.

Martens's intuition and experience told him that climate change (and the challenge of global sustainability more broadly) would soon become core drivers of strategy for any industry with a large energy and resource footprint. Aluminum was clearly such an industry. The mining of bauxite and the production of "prime" aluminum used enormous amounts of energy and produced vast quantities of greenhouse gases and waste. He wondered if Novelis's perceived weakness (lack of upstream mining assets) might actually be turned into a strength: the production of aluminum from recycled scrap consumes 95 percent less energy and produces 95 percent fewer greenhouse gas emissions than the production of "prime" aluminum.

Martens wondered if the company might pursue a corporate purpose focused on reducing climate change, using the power of business to drive toward a more sustainable world. Might it be possible to create a "closed loop" aluminum company effectively severing the tie to the mining of bauxite? If so, where and how would they find and source such vast amounts of scrap aluminum?[33] How would competitors react if Novelis sought to disrupt the dominant industry business model, effectively locking up the world's supply of scrap aluminum? Would core customer segments such as beverage can, automotive, and electronics welcome such a strategy, especially if Novelis sought brand recognition for their environmental achievements?[34] Would employees unite around such a vision?[35] Would their owners, the Aditya Birla Group, support such a strategy, given that they also owned an upstream aluminum company (Hindalco) focused on "prime" aluminum? Might such a strategy actually deliver superior returns?[36]

Amidst all these questions, Novelis made the strategic decision in 2011 to pursue the "closed loop" strategy. At that point, Novelis used about 33 percent recycled scrap (mostly used beverage cans) in its production of rolled aluminum. They set the goal of *80 percent recycled scrap* for 2020, while simultaneously *doubling* revenues. Achieving this aspirational goal would require more than *four times* the amount of scrap aluminum currently used by the company. No one in the company knew how to make this happen at the time—a truly "big hairy audacious goal."[37] By adopting such a transformational strategy, Novelis effectively aimed to turn itself, and the aluminum industry, upside down. The company sought nothing less than to reinvent itself—to become "above-ground miners." If successful, not only would they dramatically reduce greenhouse gas emissions and put in place a global aluminum cycle, but they would also lower cost and double profitability in the process. The road ahead would be filled with great challenges, and opportunities.

THE ALUMINUM INDUSTRY

For most of human history, aluminum was thought to be an extremely rare and exotic metal—the most valuable metal in the world, fit only for kings and conquerors. Aluminum's rarity is a matter of chemistry.[38] After oxygen and silicon, it is the third most abundant element in the earth's crust. But because of aluminum's high affinity for oxygen, it never appears in nature as a pure metal. Instead, it is tightly bound as oxides and silicates in a claylike material called bauxite.[39]

Separating out the pure metal ore is a difficult task. But in the late nineteenth century, two inventors discovered a new breakthrough technology known as electrolysis. The Hall-Heroult process, as it is now known, uses electricity to separate aluminum from bauxite. The alumina ore is then refined into a liquid metal, which is then cast into large slabs of solid aluminum known as "ingots" and then "rolled" into coils of different alloys for various uses. With this breakthrough, virtually everyone on the planet now had access to this strong, light, pliable, corrosion-resistant metal.

The aluminum industry grew steadily through the twentieth century. With real prices falling significantly during the first half of the century, the industry achieved a compound annual growth rate of 10 percent between 1945 and 1972. By the early 1970s aluminum had become a commodity used in a wide range of products, including beverage cans, automobiles, foil, packaging, electronics, and buildings.

However, the global aluminum industry has changed significantly since the 1970s.[40] What was originally the International *Primary* Aluminum Institute in 1972 is today known as the International Aluminum Institute, reflecting a broader agenda, including the recycling of scrap and increased attention to the entire industry value chain. In the early 1970s, the international aluminum industry was dominated by the "Six Majors"—Alcoa, Alcan, Reynolds, Kaiser, Pechiney, and Alusuisse. The industry was vertically integrated, with the majors operating bauxite mines, alumina refineries, and smelters, which supplied downstream fabricated aluminum production facilities. Bauxite production was dominated by four countries—Australia, Jamaica, Suriname, and the USSR, and the vast majority of aluminum consumption was concentrated in the industrialized countries—US, Western Europe, and Japan. Given their dominance, the majors could use their market power to effectively stabilize prices.

Forty years later, major structural changes have occurred. The energy shocks of 1973 and 1979 and the growth of the emerging markets of China, India, and Brazil have fundamentally changed industry dynamics. Those nations endowed with hydropower, oil, or low-cost coal have been able to prevent energy costs from rising as sharply, shifting aluminum production away from the industrialized nations to regions such as Australia, Canada, Russia, China, and the Middle East.

In addition, a host of new players have entered the industry over the past forty years—new private producers, conglomerates, and state-owned enterprises from around the world. Among the most significant are UC Rusal (Russia), Chalco (China), Hongqiao Group (China), Hindalco (India), Rio Tinto Alcan, Dubai Aluminum Company, Aluminum Bahrain, CVG Venezuela, various Chinese state-owned companies (such as Wanfang Group, Xinfa Group), and, of course, Novelis. Significantly, many of these new players are not fully integrated, creating for the first time distinctive strategic groups, with particular configurations of assets.

Some aluminum companies focus on bauxite mining and the production of primary aluminum while others focus more on aluminum rolling and the production of aluminum products. And while aluminum recycling is still fundamentally a business-to-business industry, its rise has allowed some players (such as Novelis) to become more actively engaged with end-users, since aluminum's light weight, pliability, and corrosion-resistance make it increasingly desirable for brand-holders in the beverage industry (packaging waste and environmental footprint), automobile industry (fuel economy, material reuse), electronics industry (light weight), and the construction industry (for example growing pressure for "green building"). The growth in recycling has also caused aluminum companies to become increasingly engaged with the highly fragmented and informal world of metal scrap merchants, recyclers, and waste pickers.

By 2010, the global aluminum industry was growing at a 5 percent rate—faster than other metals such as nickel, copper, steel, zinc, and lead, which were in the 2–3 percent range. Even with this growth, however, aluminum prices continued to decline, since there is no shortage of bauxite, compared to other metal ores. The growth of BRIC—Brazil, Russia, India, and China—had driven the most significant structural changes in the industry. Indeed, China alone accounted for over 80 percent of the increase in global production between 2002 and 2010, making it the world's largest producer of primary aluminum. World aluminum demand was expected to nearly double by 2020, from eighteen million tons to more than thirty million tons, with the bulk of this growth coming in China, which now accounted for over 40 percent of world aluminum consumption.

While the rise of aluminum was generally a good news story for the world, there was also a dark side to the growth of the global aluminum industry: it requires massive amounts of electricity to produce "prime" aluminum and the process generates enormous quantities of waste in the form of mine tailings, since roughly four kilograms of bauxite are required for every kilogram of pure aluminum produced. In a very real sense, primary aluminum is like "solid electricity." Indeed, the aluminum industry is responsible for more than 1 percent of all man-made greenhouse gases in the world. And 80 percent of Chinese aluminum (the fastest growing source) is produced using low-cost coal.[41]

THE AUDACIOUS 80 PERCENT GOAL

John Gardner had been with Alcan since 1986, serving in various roles in Europe including marketing, strategic analysis, operations, and corporate affairs. Importantly, he was also responsible for establishing the aluminum can recycling programs in Europe over the previous ten years. At the time of the de-merger, Gardner could have easily stayed with Alcan (what was seen as the smart choice at the time), but instead chose to join Novelis because he could see the potential for a new kind of aluminum company focused on the downstream aspects of the business. He assumed the post of Vice President, Human Resources and Communications for Novelis Europe and began to pitch recycling for the company as soon as Martens took the helm. This made implicit business sense, since, as Gardner so aptly put it, "How could Novelis stand alone and depend on prime producers for three million tons of aluminum each year?"

Recycling dovetailed well with Martens's search for a compelling mission for Novelis. While at Ford Motor Company, he served on the Climate Change Task Force in 2001–3 under Bill Ford, and he came to realize the looming threat— and opportunity—presented by climate change. It had become increasingly clear to him that the challenges associated with global sustainability—energy, climate, biodiversity, poverty, and inequality—would soon become central to corporate strategy, especially in material- and energy-intensive industries.

By January 2011, Martens had persuaded Gardner to join the senior management team in Atlanta as Chief Sustainability Officer. Initially, Gardner resisted, thinking that "sustainability officers in corporations are not really focused on core business strategy." Rather than seeking to build a large staff of environmental, energy, and corporate social responsibility specialists, Gardner instead made the choice to build a small team focused on embedding sustainability into every aspect of corporate and competitive strategy. Accordingly, he hired two MBA-trained colleagues: Brooke Beadle and Jessica Sanderson.

In mid-2011, Novelis made the strategic decision to make sustainability the core of its strategy for the future by seeking to "close the loop" in aluminum. Martens challenged Gardner and other senior executives to come back with a compelling corporate goal for the recycling of scrap aluminum. One hundred percent recycling would probably never be possible because of the need to mix some "prime" (pure) aluminum with the various alloys making up the scrap waste stream. Given the 2011 rate of 33 percent recycling, initial discussion began in the 60 percent range, but soon rose to the 70s. Martens ended the discussion by declaring 80 percent as the corporate goal, to be reached by 2020!

Achieving the 80 percent goal would require nothing short of transformative change—in product portfolio, customer relations, marketing, operations, product take-back, and scrap recycling. No one knew how to achieve such an audacious goal. But if successful in this quest, Novelis could literally turn the aluminum industry upside down. At the time, scrap aluminum provided a significant cost advantage over prime aluminum—perhaps as much as a 25 percent advantage on a per ton basis.[42] The vast majority (more than 80 percent) of available scrap aluminum came from used beverage cans (UBCs). But UBCs accounted for less than 20 percent of the scrap aluminum available in the world.

Achieving the 80 percent goal thus meant moving well beyond UBCs, which would require an entirely new global infrastructure of scrap aluminum collection and recycling, for aluminum in automobiles, electronics, buildings, even landfills.

Yet even with all the time, effort, and energy expended in collecting and recycling scrap aluminum, not only was it cheaper, but it also used only a fraction (5 percent) of the energy required for the production of prime aluminum from bauxite—a 95 percent savings in energy use and greenhouse gas emissions. And when the "life cycle" benefits (such as downstream savings in automobile fuel efficiency) were included, the environmental sustainability case became even more compelling.

Recognizing this virtuous cycle, Martens and the senior team put in place an aggressive set of linked business and sustainability goals for 2020: double revenues from $10 to $20 billion; double profits from approximately $1.1 billion to $2 billion; quadruple the use of scrap from one million tons to more than four million tons; and increase recycled content from 33 percent to 80 percent. The "roof" of the Novelis "House" seemed to be in place, along with a focused set of Business Aspirations, manifested through the clarion call of the 80 percent recycling goal.

Beginning in 2011, Martens and team also set in motion an unprecedented series of Strategic Initiatives to realize these goals. Derek Prichett assumed the role of Vice President for Global Recycling in 2011, and he knew he was in for a challenge. Now that the 80 percent goal had been set, the question became how Novelis would actually achieve what seemed to be an impossible task—moving from 33 percent to 80 percent recycling—in less than a decade. Initially, people were skeptical that such a goal was even possible. The first step was to inventory the existing recycling assets and then develop a plan to expand this *capability* in North America and around the world, in Europe, Asia, and South America.

A six-point plan was developed in 2011 to break down this huge challenge into more manageable, interim steps. Prichett built a team of about two hundred people and got to work, realizing that they would still be dependent on hundreds of other people across the company to make the recycling goal a reality. They set their sights first on achieving 50 percent by 2015, to provide a "line of sight" for people in the organization. Over the next three years, hundreds of millions in recycling investments in *technology* were made to make the 50 percent interim target a reality, including $250 million in Europe, $75 million in Asia, $40 million in Brazil, and $50 million in the United States.

The company had achieved a 46 percent recycling rate in fiscal year 2014 and had a clear line of sight to achieving more than 50 percent by fiscal year 2015. The "low-hanging fruit" in UBC recycling and recovery of automotive aluminum scrap had already been achieved. Now the question was how to move from 50 percent to 80 percent. For that, entirely new skills, capabilities, strategies, and partnerships would be required. The development of such an infrastructure was a daunting task but had the potential to help organize and formalize what was a fragmented and largely informal sector of recyclers, scrap merchants, waste management companies, street and community collectors, and waste pickers, thereby helping to foster income-generating opportunities and more sustainable livelihoods for many at the "base of the income pyramid" around the world.[43]

By 2014, Novelis had invested more than $500 million in recycling infrastructure in the US, Europe, Brazil, and Asia. They had shed or divested several products that were not easily recycled (for example, aluminum foil). They invested hundreds of millions more in the ability to produce closed-loop aluminum for the automobile industry. With Novelis as partner, for example, Ford Motor Company unveiled the all-aluminum F-150 pick-up truck in early 2014, which marked the first of a burgeoning list of automotive aluminum clients.[44] In addition, the company had developed a new aluminum can body sheet with better than 90 percent recycled content as a first step toward its goal of an "up to 100 percent recycled content" can, enabling endless closed-loop recycling of beverage cans—the evercan™.[45]

DISRUPTIVE BY DESIGN

Under Birla ownership and *governance*, Novelis had not just survived, but had thrived and had been able to become a disruptive industry leader with a unique positioning. Hindalco, Novelis's parent company, and the ABG allowed Novelis to operate with long-term strategic thinking with minimal demands for quick wins or short-term results—something a private equity buyout would not have allowed. The 30 percent premium paid by Hindalco also gave the necessary cushion to allow Novelis to start being profitable by 2010.

Not being under pressure to answer shareholders' quarterly expectations also allowed Novelis to plan big and invest for the long term, a circumstance that did not exist in the 2005–2007 time frame, prior to the Birla purchase, when Novelis was a publicly traded company on the New York Stock Exchange. Indeed, between 2011 and 2014 alone, Novelis had invested well in excess of $1 billion in recycling infrastructure, closed-loop production, and international expansion. The Novelis leadership unanimously agreed they could not have pursued the closed-loop recycling vision as a public company.

Novelis consciously sought to be "disruptive by design." Competitors were shocked when Novelis announced the 80 percent goal and left the US National Association of Manufacturers—in favor of a proactive stance on climate change and the need for carbon policy. Customers were both surprised and delighted, depending upon their position in the value chain and orientation toward aluminum recycling. For example, some can makers were fearful of being held hostage by a single aluminum supplier should closed-loop aluminum become the consumer preference of beverage companies; automobile makers, on the other hand, were lining up at the door to make the move to all-aluminum vehicles.

To help accelerate the strategy, John Gardner launched a Novelis sustainability advisory council in 2012, made up of experts and thought leaders from diverse backgrounds in the sustainability field.[46] The objective of this new *structure* was to provide a regular channel for Novelis to solicit external advice, expertise, and critical analysis of the company's sustainability goals, strategies, performance, and reporting. Council members were also challenged to help Novelis identify and understand emerging sustainability issues and opportunities. Rather than merely seeking endorsements or testimonials for the Annual Corporate Sustainability Report, the SAC members were urged to provide frank and direct advice on some of the most important issues facing the company. To ensure that the members had a direct line of communication to the most senior decision makers, the SAC also included CEO Phil Martens, the Chief Commercial and Strategy Officer, and the Chief Sustainability Officer.

Given the existing size and scale of Novelis, the capital investments required, and the amount of scrap aluminum available globally, it was possible that only *one company in the world* might be able to deliver on the promise of closed-loop recycling of aluminum. This appeared to be first mover strategy at its best, since it effectively preempted future competitors from entering the game. And as climate and sustainability issues grew in significance, customers would be under growing pressure to use climate-friendly, sustainable aluminum in their products, enabling Novelis to differentiate their aluminum from the competition. As the new corporate tagline stated: "Not Just Aluminum, Novelis Aluminum."

Birla ownership, however, as important as it had been to rescuing and reorienting the company, had not come without its challenges. Being a subsidiary of Hindalco—a primary aluminum company—could be confusing and sent mixed signals to the market and the external world. Being privately owned had enabled Novelis to take a long-term view, but not being public had also kept the spotlight away from its success. By any measure, Novelis was a leader in corporate sustainability, but since it was not publicly held, it was also not eligible for industry sustainability benchmarking and recognition by the Dow Jones Sustainability Index, Global 100, and others.

Raising the $1.6 billion to execute the new strategy was greatly facilitated by Birla ownership, but might Novelis be better off going public again if it was to take another big step forward toward realizing its audacious goal? Martens pitched this idea, but Birla was less than enthusiastic about selling the company, especially given that their investment had just recently begun to pay off.

THE HUMAN AND ORGANIZATIONAL CHALLENGE

A key to Novelis's reinvention strategy had been its senior management team. The corporate headquarters in Atlanta, Georgia, and the 160,000 square-foot R&D center at Kennesaw, Georgia, were completely aligned to, motivated by, and working toward the 2020 goal. The sustainability vision was also very important when it came to recruiting MBAs and engineers—a clear differentiator. Engineers in particular were attracted by the technical challenges associated with the 80 percent goal—doing something that had not been done before. And with a turnover rate in the 2–4 percent range, the company's commitment to sustainability was also a key factor in retaining good people as well as attracting new talent.

The problem was that the corporate and technical units constituted less than 20 percent of the total workforce. In FY13, approximately 63 percent of the employees were represented by labor unions in twenty-five facilities across nine countries. Getting eleven thousand employees to adopt and embrace a sustainability vision without a clear line of sight does not come easily. Indeed, as Phil Martens openly acknowledged, "We are proud of the progress we've made, and the path to 50 percent recycled inputs by 2015 is clear. To be candid, however, achieving the remaining 30 percent is less clear. It will test the limits of our company and require us to move even more aggressively toward a closed-loop model across all of our operations and products."

For plant-level employees and contractors on the ground with more of an operating focus, the big picture was not as compelling as it was for those at corporate headquarters. As Leslie Joyce, Chief People Officer, observed, "It is far easier to just melt prime and make rolled aluminum. The 80 percent goal creates work and change at the plant level. People are not used to innovation as a cornerstone of plant operations." Rather than getting excited about global sustainability and preventing climate change, most employees were more motivated by the kind of "sustainability" that has an impact on their daily lives and their communities.

Novelis had indeed made substantial progress toward the 80 percent goal in a short period of time—achieving a nearly 50 percent recycling rate by late 2014. But moving from 50 percent to 80 percent in the next five years would prove to be a much more difficult task. Relationships with some suppliers and customers had become strained. Signs of frustration had also begun to appear in the company among middle management and front-line workers. How would Novelis get all its employees to buy into the closed-loop vision and strive toward achieving the 80 percent goal? Were there ways to reconcile more immediate operational and environment, health, and safety goals with the larger corporate vision of closed-loop aluminum? If so, how could this be implemented at the plant and facility level?

The big question, however, was, had Martens moved too aggressively too quickly? While a coalition of senior management and staff were fully on board, had the rest of the organization been left in the lurch? Had the "Foundation" of the "House" been sufficiently laid at this point—a set of shared values and culture? Was sufficient attention given to the "people" and motivation issues— Rewards and Incentives? Were the necessary external Partnerships and Platforms being developed, or was Novelis attempting to "go it alone" in its quest to transform the aluminum industry?

CONNECTING THE BODY AND THE HEAD

In 2015, amid growing tensions with the Birla Group, suppliers and customers, and Novelis employees, Phil Martens stepped down as CEO and was replaced by Steve Fisher, the former CFO of the company. Fisher surmised that his most important immediate task as CEO was to "slow down" a bit in order to (1) better engage the middle management and the rank and file by building a more inclusive culture, and (2) mend the fence with key constituencies by building strong external partnerships and relationships.

In 2016, the audacious 80 percent goal was put on hold to allow the organization time to absorb the changes that had already taken place. A "Say Anything" work environment initiative was launched to encourage employees to speak up and take ownership at all levels, with the aim of building collaboration and teamwork. This initiative was complemented by four other cultural beliefs and Values introduced in 2017 to deepen employee engagement and improve strained relationships: "Do It Right," "Own It", "Get Focused," and "Win Together." The new CEO also championed five Metrics critical to operations as part of the cultural turnaround: "Safety," "Customer Centricity," "Quality," "Operational Excellence," and "Return on Capital Employed (ROCE)."[47]

External Partnerships were also prioritized, extending to all stakeholders across the aluminum value chain. Community engagement projects were launched focusing on three pillars: making communities safer; supporting science, technology, engineering, and math (STEM) education; and increasing recycling by consumers. Given the nature of the company's products, its position in the value chain, and the scale of its Aspirations, it became clear the company simply could not "go it alone."[48]

A new, more externally focused statement of Purpose was adopted in 2018: "Shaping a Sustainable World Together," with the core principles being care, trust, and innovation. Efforts were initiated across the company to connect *personal purpose* with company purpose. The new Purpose was also woven into everyone's business objectives and *performance reviews*, with each employee explaining how they contribute to the new company Purpose and core principles each year. The trust built by leadership through the "Say Anything" culture helped with adoption and integration of this new Purpose.[49]

The role of Vice President and Chief Sustainability Officer, established in 2011, was dissolved in 2017. A newly defined role—Director of Sustainability—was filled by Jessica Sanderson, who had been a member of the sustainability staff team under former VP John Gardner. Rather than concentrating on the achievement of the 80 percent goal, the new role focused on integrating a wider range of targets—especially energy use, water use, waste to landfill, and greenhouse gas emissions—into operating units globally. Jessica left the company in 2020 and her role was filled by an external hire—Suzanne Lindsay-Walker, who had previously been Chief Sustainability Officer at UPS.

By 2020, Novelis had solidified its position as the global leader in aluminum recycling, having created the first and largest closed-loop recycling system for automotive aluminum in the world. The company achieved a 61 percent recycling rate in 2019, only to have that number fall slightly to 59 percent in 2020 with the acquisition of Aleris—a major player in the aerospace and construction markets.[50] Novelis also delivered record financial and operating results in 2020: $11.2 billion in sales and $1.5 billion in EBITDA.[51]

The Covid times have also been quite favorable for Novelis: for its full fiscal year 2022, the company reported that net sales increased 40 percent to $17.1

billion compared with $12.3 billion in 2021, driven by higher average aluminum prices and record shipments in every product end market. Adjusted EBITDA increased 19 percent to a record $2 billion in 2022 compared with $1.7 billion in 2021.[52]

LESSONS LEARNED

The Novelis experience teaches us many important lessons about transformational sustainability in business. First, it makes clear that business and sustainability goals that are exclusively "top down," regardless of how audacious or compelling, eventually run into headwinds, both within the organization and without. While leadership can have a clear logic for establishing aggressive Goals and Aspirations, if employees (and other stakeholders) do not understand why these goals have been set and how the organization will work toward achieving them, it is highly likely that leadership will lose their commitment. As an old African Proverb wisely observed, "If you want to go fast, go alone; if you want to go far, go together."

Second, a single quantitative goal does not a Higher Purpose make. Setting a goal of 80 percent recycling, while audacious and challenging, falls more into the category of sustainability goal than it does a Corporate Quest or Purpose. A single goal fails to provide the necessary coverage—the "roof" for the "House"—that includes and enables everyone associated with the company to become engaged. When Steve Fisher became CEO, he established a more inclusive and outward-facing Purpose: "Shaping a Sustainable World Together." This higher Purpose, along with a set of new values, principals, and internal processes to engage organizational members, made it possible for *everyone* in the company to connect their personal purpose with the company's Purpose.

Finally, the Novelis experience demonstrates the importance of dispelling the idea that strategy formulation should precede implementation. While the work of establishing a transformational Corporate Purpose, Aspirations, and Quests can and should begin with the senior ranks (along with some outside advisors to stimulate creative thinking), the process of crafting the necessary Strategies, Goals, and Metrics must engage middle management, and the appropriate Rewards and Incentives must be co-created with front-line workers. Interconnection and iteration are the rule when it comes to redesigning the corporate architecture.

In short, the "House" is a *system* that must be designed and built simultaneously, in a manner that is internally consistent with elements that are mutually supportive. Let's close with a few recommendations for how best to make this happen.

Reconstructing the House

Assuming a company has already developed a statement of societal purpose that focuses broadly on the positive impact the organization seeks to have in the world, the next step is to bring that purpose to life in a way that

- Defines what specific positive impacts—Aspirations and Quests—the company seeks to make in the world through the business (Raising the Bar)

- Integrates the Aspirations and Quests with the company's strategic and operating systems and processes (Walking the Talk)

- Inspires middle managers and employees by aligning their personal values and motivations with the company's Purpose, practices, and processes (Living the Purpose)[53]

RAISING THE BAR

The first step is to develop a compelling set of Business Aspirations and Corporate Quests that make the Purpose operational. As was described more fully in Chapter 5, I recommend the following steps:

1. *Stimulate Thinking.* Participants in the Aspiration and Quests setting process should be drawn from key internal (corporate, functional, and business leadership) and external (content experts, customers, suppliers and NGO/government representatives) constituencies for the company.

2. *Distinguish Between Foundational Goals, Aspirations, and Quests.* Engage participants in a process to identify the key sustainability challenges and opportunities for the company. Separate the Foundational Goals from the Business Aspirations and Corporate Quests that serve to define and operationalize the company's broad statement of Purpose. Once finalized, accountability for the Foundational Goals can be given to functional leaders in the areas of R&D, sourcing, operations, environment, and HR.

3. *Propose Metrics.* Define the expected *financial* metrics and positive societal *impacts* for the Business Aspirations and Corporate Quests that will be used to track progress.

WALKING THE TALK

The next step is to "socialize" the Goals, Aspirations, and Quests with organizational members and begin to integrate them with the strategies, formal systems, and processes in the company.

4. *Engage Business Management.* Seek business and middle management inputs on how best to realize (Strategies and Initiatives) the Goals, Aspirations, and Quests to increase their level of engagement on the transformational change being developed. Rather than assuming that middle managers are capable only of implementation and transactional exchange, engage them as though they are owners (principals) rather than simply agents (employees).[54]

5. *Build Awareness and Understanding.* Launch employee awareness, education, and training programs focused on sustainability, purpose, and the new Goals, Aspirations, and Quests. Build a cadre or coalition of managers and employees with a common knowledge base about sustainability and passion for change.[55]

6. *Unleash the Positive Energizers.* Identify the managers from step 4 and the employees from step 5 who exhibit the highest level of positive energy regarding the new Foundational Goals, Business Aspirations, and Corporate Quests. Convene them as a group to harness their energy in helping to walk the talk throughout the company. Have each develop their personal purpose statement and lead the charge in building a "bottom up" network of "positive deviants" within their immediate spheres of influence.[56]

LIVING THE PURPOSE

The final step is to "activate" employees' emotional commitment to the company's Purpose, Goals, Aspirations, and Quests.

1. *Encourage Employees to Bring Their "Whole Person" to Work.* Provide means and incentive for employees to take individual action at home and in their personal lives that connect to the company's Foundational Goals, Busi-

ness Aspirations, and Corporate Quests. Individual actions at home can then translate into creative and innovative ideas at work.[57]

2. *Connect Personal Purpose to Corporate Purpose.* Encourage front-line workers and employees to share their own accounts of how they currently make a difference when it comes to the corporate Purpose. Challenge employees to tell their stories publicly by offering some additional companywide paid holidays if a certain number submit their stories by a given date.[58]

3. *Engage Employees in Individual Goal-Setting.* Provide managers with guidelines for talking with employees about the implications of the new Foundational Goals, Business Aspirations, and Corporate Quests for their roles in the company. Empower managers to provide opportunities for choice and input as to employees' individual goals and metrics; such engagement will increase employees' level of creativity, commitment, and satisfaction.[59]

4. *Integrate Purpose into Rewards and Incentives.* Include elements of the Goals, Aspirations, and Quests in job descriptions, performance criteria, and Rewards and Incentives. Ideally, all employees should be included in the bonus system and a nontrivial portion of the bonus system should be focused on the Foundational Goals, Business Aspirations, and Corporate Quests.[60]

By taking such steps to "Raise the Bar," "Walk the Talk" and "Live the Purpose," it is possible to create a virtuous circle connecting Purpose, Aspirations and Quests, Goals and Metrics, Rewards and Incentives together into an integrated and self-reinforcing system. Such an interconnected *purpose system* serves as the infrastructure from which all the company's transformational strategies, initiatives, innovations, and partnerships then flow.

For public companies, the challenge is justifying such bold actions in a world still dominated by a stock market driven by short-term thinking and a lack of recognition of the massive and growing external costs imposed on the world by "business as usual." To enable and accelerate these necessary corporate transformations, companies will need to become more actively involved in transforming the larger, institutional system within which they operate—the public policy regime, the financial system, and of course, the business schools that supply companies with the people that currently perpetuate the status quo. It is to these institutional challenges that we turn our attention in the third and final section of the book.

PART III

Institutional Redesign

BUSINESS'S INDISPENSABLE ROLE IN SYSTEM CHANGE

SEVEN

Reinventing Business Education

"How do I summarize the payoff of my MBA education? '100 Gs for 20 Bs'"

ANONYMOUS MBA GRADUATE, CIRCA 2005

Few institutions have been more complicit in the care and feeding of shareholder capitalism than business education. For the past forty years, MBA programs have churned out *millions* of graduates, most of whom aided and abetted (either wittingly or unwittingly) the cause of market fundamentalism. If we are to overthrow the ideology of shareholder primacy and usher in a new age of sustainable capitalism, then business education as we know it must be creatively destroyed and reinvented. Corporate transformation cannot proceed quickly enough without the legions of financiers, managers, and business people involved possessing the necessary knowledge, tools, skills, capabilities—and mindset—to make it happen.

Fortunately, we already have some models for what business education needs to look like in the decades ahead, but they are few and far between. Indeed, as William Gibson famously said, "The future is already here, it's just not very evenly distributed." I've personally been involved in the development and launch of a completely new "clean sheet" program at the University of Vermont—the Sustainable Innovation MBA program (SI-MBA)—which I will describe in depth in this chapter. Our challenge—and opportunity—is to amplify, multiply, and scale these "next practice" MBA programs such that they become the norm within the next decade.

Given the current scale and scope of the MBA "industry," such a transformation may seem daunting. Indeed, there are over five hundred accredited business schools and a thousand MBA programs in the US alone, churning out more than two hundred thousand MBAs each year. Perhaps it is heartening to realize that this is not the first time that business education has undergone fundamental reinvention. In fact, just fifty years ago, business education had nary a whiff of shareholder primacy or market fundamentalism as part of its curriculum. A small group of neoliberal advocates were intent on changing that state of affairs. They succeeded beyond their wildest dreams.

Mighty Oaks from Little Acorns Grow

In 1973, Professor James Buchanan—a leading intellectual force behind the growing neoliberal campaign for "economic liberty"—hosted a retreat at his cabin in the Virginia mountains. It was attended by a small but influential group of fellow academics, Mont Pèlerin Society Fellows, business executives, and government representatives. The topic: "how to put the manacles back on Leviathan."[1]

The retreat came on the heels of Milton Friedman's famous 1970 essay, "The Social Responsibility of Business Is to Increase Profit" and the 1972 release of the "Powell Memo"—a battle plan by future Supreme Court justice Lewis Powell to counter what he saw as an assault on the free enterprise system. At the retreat, Buchanan and his colleagues hatched a plan to create a massive counterinsurgency movement that would turn the tide in favor of free enterprise and economic liberty. He presciently commented at the retreat that "large things can start from small beginnings."[2]

From this retreat sprang a multidecade campaign fought on multiple fronts: in academia, think tanks, the media, politics, and the legal system. It brought to the fore a new breed of wealthy conservatives who were ready to commit their philanthropic giving over decades to fight this multifront war. Among them: Richard Mellon Scaife, Joseph Coors, John Olin, and a young Charles Koch, who had recently taken over his family oil company.[3]

On the academic front, Buchanan and his University of Chicago economics and law colleagues created a Society of Fellows—a growing network of like-minded academics, donors, business executives, and political leaders—that would ultimately change the course of both business and legal education and usher in the era of shareholder capitalism that began in the 1980s.

As it turns out, however, the neoliberalist insurgency was actually the *third time* that a small coalition of academics, capitalists, and donors had fundamentally changed the course of business education—and society. The birth of business schools in the late nineteenth century was catalyzed and bankrolled by the industrial tycoons of the time, in an effort to legitimize and professionalize the massive industrial corporations they had created. The Great Depression and World War II catalyzed another cycle of transformation in business education, this time led by two foundations—Carnegie and Ford—that had been created from the largess of their industrial founders.

The business schools the Carnegie and Ford Foundations bequeathed to us were once again transformed by the insurgency described above, resulting in forty years of market fundamentalist ideology and shareholder primacy as the prime directive that continues to this day. Tragically, this version of business education has led us to the brink of oblivion: toxic inequality, democracy under threat, and the prospect of runaway climate change and mass extinction. The time is now to fundamentally alter the DNA of business education to address the social and environmental challenges we now face. Will a new coalition of enlightened capitalists step up once again to accelerate this process of reinvention and relegitimation?

After further tracing the historical evolution of business education and need for transformation, I'll describe one such next-generation program—the SI-MBA program at the University of Vermont—and suggest how this program might help to catalyze the creative destruction—and reinvention—of business education for the twenty-first century. The SI-MBA experience also offers some important insights into the most useful and important leverage points for the transformational change of business education in the years ahead.

What Goes Around Comes Around

University-based business education dates back only to the 1880s in the US, paralleling the rise of industrial monopoly capitalism and the need for a new breed of professional manager for the large corporate "trusts" that had come to predominate: railroads, telegraph, oil, and steel. In fact, the impetus for formal business education was a growing realization on the part of the capitalists *themselves* that for their large corporations to endure, they needed to be imbued with a sense of legitimacy as institutions contributing to the greater good of society. They saw university-based business schools and the professionalization of management as a key means to this end.[4]

Yet since their inception in the late nineteenth century, business schools have been in a constant struggle with themselves—a sort of ongoing identity crisis—as to what constitutes their primary purpose. This struggle has been driven by periods of rapid expansion and exploding demand (such as the years after World Wars I and II) followed by periods of societal crisis and retrenchment, when business schools have come to question their very existence. Just like capitalism itself, business education has gone through its own series of 180-degree shifts, or "Enantiodromia Cycles." Indeed, business schools have alternated between periods when they conceive of their role as preparing graduates for (1) a *profession*, with a focus on societal contribution and standards of professional conduct, or (2) a *vocation*, with a focus on technical skill development, career networking, and job placement.

For the past four decades, business schools have been decidedly focused on the vocational model of education—the building of functional skills, career networking, and job placement, ruled by the paradigm of shareholder primacy and market fundamentalism.[5] For much of that period, I served on the faculties at three different "top twenty" business schools—Michigan (Ross), University of North Carolina (Kenan-Flagler), and Cornell (Johnson). I witnessed finance and economics taking over business schools in the 1980s. With their focus on theory-driven mathematical modeling, empirical research, and neoclassical assumptions about human nature, these fields literally redefined the culture of business schools.

The primary criterion for faculty promotion and advancement became publication in a select few scholarly journals within each function, with a focus on how best to maximize shareholder value. The narrow focus necessary for "scientifically" rigorous research in article format typically precluded interdisciplinary research and broad, reflective thinking on societal issues of fundamental importance. Methodological rigor took precedence over managerial relevance.[6] The time- and energy-consuming nature of publishing in discipline-based, scientific journals also made the formulaic teaching of simple paradigms attractive to faculty members trying to "optimize" their time in the classroom.[7]

Indeed, with such intense pressure for scientific publishing, faculty sought to minimize their "new preps" in teaching, making predictable loads in MBA core courses, including finance, accounting, operations, marketing, strategy, and HR, highly sought after. As Dartmouth's Sydney Finkelstein has noted, if you look at core courses *across* business schools, most are now generally the same, making it easier for faculty to move from one school to another. The business core curriculum has effectively become a commodity business.[8] The result has been rigidly defined and carefully guarded functional turf and a resistance to change that would shame most self-respecting government bureaucrats!

For most business school students, the MBA experience has become synonymous with these first-year "core courses"—a rite of passage not unlike military indoctrination—with shareholder primacy at its root. In the words of the University of Michigan's Tom Lyon, "It's like the MBA core is the inner sanctum of the religion of business schools. . . . [E]very functional area says I have my sacred concepts I must teach, and I cannot make room for these nice, but superfluous ideas" having to do with societal contribution and sustainability.[9]

The tragic reality is that most MBA students graduate with a *narrower* idea of business than when they started the program. I've personally known scores of MBA students over the years who started their business education with the best of intentions to harness business for the greater good, only to graduate touting the gospel of shareholder value. In fact, by the time most MBA students complete the core, they are so preoccupied with job search to repay the massive debt they have accumulated that there is little time for elective courses that might broaden their bandwidth or allow for critical self-reflection.

For most business students, the focus has been on "getting their tickets punched": harnessing their school's alumni network and on-campus recruiting for job opportunities in the highly prized (and lucrative) fields of consulting, marketing, investment banking, hedge fund management, and private equity. And while the guarantee of a high-paying job has taken a bit of a hit since the Great Recession, value continues to be measured by starting salary and size of the bonus for the graduates. The idea of business as a profession or a vehicle for societal contribution has taken a back seat to the acquisition of the technical skills needed for job placement.[10]

Since the 1980s, business schools have produced upwards of three million MBA graduates, many of whom have gone on to leadership roles in big banks, investment firms, hedge funds, and consulting firms, the very institutions that have perpetrated shareholder capitalism on the world and subjugated the world's companies with short-termism.[11] History teaches us that *systemic* and *institutional* change is required to fundamentally transform the nature of the capitalist pursuit. If we are to realize the next capitalist reformation, we must therefore return business education to its roots—an institution dedicated to developing leaders with a commitment to the common good who use business as their instrument. We must exorcise the demons of shareholder primacy from our business schools if we are to develop a generation of business leaders who bring a more multidimensional perspective to the role of business in the world.

Beyond "Saddlebag" Sustainability

Over the course of my career, I've watched this "financial-vocational" business education model—with its shareholder primacy ideology, emphasis on scholarly publishing, and functional core courses in the MBA program—spread across the world. In a very real sense, US business schools are responsible for institutionalizing the culture of short-termism and quarterly returns—the shareholder capitalism that has pervaded business since the 1980s with dire societal and environmental consequences.

Countervailing forces, however, have been growing. A majority of college students now say companies should take public stances on issues, and over 80 percent of Gen Z employees want to work for a company that has a positive impact on the world.[12] Business schools have come under increasing fire, and conventional, shareholder-primacy-based MBA programs have experienced declining applications, especially since the Great Recession in 2008. Even the highest-ranked business schools in the US have experienced declines in MBA applications in recent years. Indeed, the top ten MBA programs saw an average drop of nearly 6 percent in applications in 2018 and 2019, although most experienced a significant "COVID bump" in applications in 2020.[13] Despite this temporary recovery, observers predict that 10–20 percent of the top one hundred MBA programs in the US could be shuttered within the next few years, with even more attrition among the second- and third-tier business schools.[14]

Business schools have sought to cope with the rising tide of discontent in part by applying a veneer of legitimacy through the creation of centers, institutes, and programs focused on corporate citizenship, ethics, sustainability, social entrepreneurship, and positive leadership.[15] I have personally been involved in creating three such initiatives over the past thirty years—the University of Michigan's Corporate Environmental Management Program (now the Erb Institute's Dual Master's Program), the University of North Carolina Kenan-Flagler Business School's Center for Sustainable Enterprise, and Cornell University's Johnson School Center for Sustainable Global Enterprise.

The problem is that virtually all of these initiatives merely hang off the side of the existing business school corpus. Like the proverbial "saddlebag" on a horse, these initiatives are contained within separate compartments that are readily visible from the outside, but have little impact on the behavior of the animal itself.[16] Sustainability has joined other business school "saddlebag" issues such as ethics, entrepreneurship, and emerging markets; such content is increasingly present in the curriculum, but usually in the form of electives, stopping short of full integration into the core DNA of the institutions.[17]

Indeed, save for cosmetic changes, the MBA curriculum at top-tier business schools remains startlingly unchanged from what it was when I started teaching nearly forty years ago: functional core courses in finance, accounting, marketing, operations, OB, and strategy still rule, with the "saddlebag" issues addressed as elective courses after students have completed the "real" content. Despite the fact that many of the challenges associated with sustainability seem to sit at the core of what business school research is all about—strategy, leadership, business models, marketing, supply chains, incentives, and governance— tenured research faculty remain focused more on theory-driven questions within established functions and disciplines, not on the challenges contained in the saddlebags (which are unruly and therefore difficult to study). Faculty focused on the saddlebags are often untenured adjuncts, lecturers, or clinical professors with little say in the governance of the schools. As a result, institutional inertia reigns supreme.[18]

It is high time to move beyond saddlebag sustainability in business education. Given its centrality to our current predicament, business education represents a high-leverage, systemic target of opportunity if we are to transform capitalism in the years ahead. We desperately need new models of business education appropriate to the challenges we face in the twenty-first century.[19] We need transformative change and revolutionary new business models, not just adjustment around the edges. We need a focus once again on business for the greater good and the nurturing of business as a profession—what University of Michigan professor Andrew Hoffman refers to as management as a "calling"— and we need to emphasize the skills required to imagine, co-create, launch, and scale game-changing new ventures that simultaneously lift the poor and leap- frog to new environmentally sustainable and regenerative ways of living.[20]

Not unexpectedly, the few pioneers who have thus far sought to integrate the "saddlebag" challenges into a new MBA model have been independent players with no prior baggage, such as the Presidio Graduate School and Bard's Sustainable MBA. But unfortunately, these upstarts lack the institutional legitimacy to mount a serious challenge to the status quo in research universities. Duquesne University's Palumbo Donahue School of Business has launched an important new MBA in sustainable business practices, and Colorado State University's College of Business has christened a new "Impact" MBA, but both of these programs stand alongside traditional MBA programs that still adhere to the traditional program design.[21]

This is why the University of Vermont Grossman School of Business's new SI-MBA program is such an important milestone: it represents the first time (to my knowledge) that a major US research university has sought to fundamentally reinvent business education and the MBA degree to address the looming social and environmental challenges we face in the twenty-first century. If you want an MBA degree from Vermont, SI-MBA is the only option—we are "all in."

I have spent the past decade of my professional life dedicated to the design, launch, and scaling of this radical experiment in reinventing business education, as cofounder, codirector, and chaired professor at the University of Vermont's Grossman School of Business. I believe it represents a model that can be replicated and adapted by others in the years ahead.[22] Our mission must be nothing short of "creatively destroying" the shareholder-primacy-driven model of business education that has predominated for the past four decades. We will turn our attention to the SI-MBA program in more depth, as a living case. But let us first learn from the past incarnations of business education. We have been here before.

The Historical Evolution of Business Education

Apart from a few "Schools of Commerce" in Europe, the growth of business schools has been a largely American phenomenon.[23] The first university-based business school in the United States was founded in 1881 by industrialist Joseph Wharton at the University of Pennsylvania. A devout Pennsylvania Quaker, Wharton saw a need for something more than apprenticeship and technical training in business, both of which were prevalent at the time—a *university* education for "wellborn youth in the knowledge and in the arts of modern Finance and Economy."[24] Wharton was the tip of the spear of what became an important trend: by the 1930s, there were nearly two hundred business schools in the US alone, most started by wealthy industrialists providing funding in return for naming rights.

These business schools were created to provide certification and legitimacy for what was then a *new profession*—the manager. While companies for most of the nineteenth century had been organized as sole proprietorships or partnerships, the advent of large industrial corporations meant the rise of hierarchies and a new cadre of administrative workers involved with directing personnel, organizing work, defining procedures, and selling products. Furthermore, as stock ownership of these corporations became more widely distributed, managers gradually appropriated the authority of the entrepreneurs who had started the businesses, leading to a new form of "managerial capitalism."[25]

As Rakesh Khurana points out in his sweeping and authoritative history of business education, "When these salaried managers appeared in large corporations for the first time in the late 19th century, then began to proliferate, it was not obvious who they were, what they did, or why they should be entrusted with the task of running corporations."[26] University-based business schools thus served the purpose of bestowing social and moral legitimacy for this new profession, linking management to existing institutions of higher learning dedicated to the common good.

THE LEGITIMATION OF BUSINESS SCHOOLS

As we saw in Chapter 1, the industrial tycoons of the Gilded Age such as Vanderbilt, Rockefeller, Carnegie, and Wharton succeeded in removing the legal shackles (strict public purpose, limited life, geographic bounds) from corporations that had been put in place by the Founding Fathers in the late eighteenth century. With the facilitation of financiers such as J. P. Morgan, they led a process of industry consolidation—into so-called "trusts"—in an effort to blunt what they described as "cutthroat" competition. Most trusts, for example, the Sewer Pipe Trust or the Thread Trust, provided a well-deserved exit and liquidity event for founding families of smaller industrial firms started after the Civil War. A few, however, evolved into massive corporations—think Standard Oil and US Steel—that integrated scores of smaller players and came to dominate entire industries.[27]

These tycoons were increasingly seen by the general populace as monopolists who exploited workers by paying the minimum possible and offering workplaces that were often unsafe, unsanitary, and oppressive. Indeed, labor and social unrest were a central feature of the late-nineteenth-century industrial landscape. It was in that world that Wharton foresaw the need for a new breed of "professional" manager on a par with doctors, lawyers, and clergymen— businessmen dedicated to the public good, capable of attacking the "social problems incident to our civilization." He, like other capitalists during this era, sought to gain respectability in society by giving away substantial portions of his accumulated personal wealth, some of it dedicated to the cause of university-based, professional business education.[28]

Wharton's vision of business as a profession would become the paradigm for scores of new business schools founded over the next forty years by successful industrialists such as the Tuck School of Business at Dartmouth in 1900 (first graduate business program); Harvard Business School in 1908 (first MBA); and the University of Chicago Business School in 1920 (first doctoral program in business). The American Association for Collegiate Schools of Business (AACSB) was founded in 1916 in an effort to provide standards and raise the bar for what by then constituted an accredited, university-based form of business education (Exhibit 7.1).

It was also during this time that neoclassical economics gained ascendency, with the more qualitative and integrative field of institutional economics receding to the background. Neoclassical economics, with its mathematical bent and emphasis on rational self-interest, became the paradigm around which business schools developed curricula emphasizing utility and profit maximization. Many of the same industrialists that supported the creation of business schools also financed economics departments with a neoclassical bent, including Leland Stanford (Stanford), Cornelius Vanderbilt (Vanderbilt), John D. Rockefeller (Chicago), Andrew Carnegie (Carnegie-Mellon), and J. P. Morgan (Columbia).[29] Frederick Taylor's new "Scientific Management" also provided the practical management tools and methods needed to increase efficiency and productivity in the large, industrial corporations that had risen to dominance.[30]

The Roaring Twenties unleashed a wave of demand for business education, as World War I and the 1918 flu pandemic gave way to rapid growth, unfettered free markets, and wild speculation in the stock markets. Unfortunately, many of

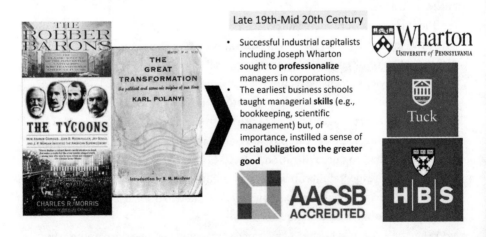

Exhibit 7.1. The Legitimation of Business Schools

these new business programs were of questionable quality, with poorly trained faculty and underqualified students, leading many to question the value of business education, despite AACSB's best efforts.

The 1929 stock market crash and ensuing Great Depression in the 1930s ushered in another time of soul-searching regarding the role of business in society and the purpose of business education. The emergence of the New Deal and the increasing importance of the government in rescuing the country from catastrophe gave pause to the explosive growth of business schools in the 1920s, even causing some business school leaders to question the uncritical acceptance of laissez-faire, rational self-interest, and free markets. It was also during this period that Adolph Berle and Gardiner Means proclaimed the primacy of "managerial capitalism" over the dominance of shareholder interests that characterized the 1920s, as discussed in Chapter 1.[31]

THE MECHANIZATION OF BUSINESS SCHOOLS

The period of business school introspection and soul-searching during the 1930s came to an abrupt end with the attack on Pearl Harbor and the US declaration of war against Japan and Germany in 1941. The mobilization for war drew upon the best and brightest in American universities, with major advancements in management science—linear programming, systems analysis, queuing theory, survey methods, and statistics—helping to win the war. In the postwar years, the federal government became a major player in both the funding of research at universities and, through the GI Bill, the provision of scholarship support to the millions of veterans returning home.[32]

Business schools were once again inundated with demand, and the application of the quantitative methods that had been developed during the war became the primary focus. The objective: to train the returning soldiers for managerial jobs in the nation's large corporations, which had emerged from the war as the unquestioned leaders in their industries—automobiles, electronics, energy, and chemicals.

With a new generation of business school deans now in charge, the focus turned to how best to accommodate this postwar surge in demand. With rapid growth, quality once again became a serious issue in business education, with regard to both faculty training and applicant standards.[33] Unfortunately, the AACSB had receded from the scene in the postwar years, creating a vacuum with regard to the oversight of business schools. Flush with large endowments from the passing of their industrialist founders, corporate foundations—in this case the Ford and Carnegie Foundations—assumed the leadership position in guiding the evolution of business education in postwar America.[34]

Just as the capitalists had provided the impetus and resources for the founding of university-based business schools for the generations following the Civil War, the Ford and Carnegie Foundations provided the resources and focus that determined the trajectory of business education for the generations following World War II—the Greatest Generation and the Baby Boomers (Exhibit 7.2).

The two foundations conducted a comprehensive review of business education in the 1950s. The scathing results were published in two companion reports in 1959. They observed that with a few notable exceptions, business schools were regarded as the "slums" of the educational community. Their conclusion: the poor quality of many of America's business schools jeopardized not only the industrial corporations that were the well-spring of employment in the postwar years, but ultimately, the health of the economy and even American Democracy, with the Cold War now in full swing.[35]

The Ford Foundation in particular focused on the state of MBA education; its approach was to focus on a small number of business schools as "centers of excellence" and invest intensively and consistently in those institutions, particularly the Harvard Business School and the newer Carnegie Institute of Technology's Graduate School of Industrial Administration. The effort emphasized increasing the intellectual quality of business education by increasing the pro-

Post-WWII Years

- **1959 Ford and Carnegie Foundation reports** criticized the weak scientific foundation of business education
- Suggested that professors were more like **quacks** than serious scholars
- Advocated for **research-driven decision science**

Exhibit 7.2. **The Mechanization of Business Schools**

portion of faculty with doctoral degrees and integrating far more content focused on quantitative analysis and the behavioral sciences.

The Ford Foundation also focused on expanding doctoral programs at these schools, so as to expand the number of well-trained business school faculty. These interventions created the model for what business schools and MBA programs would come to look like for the next half century—a quantitatively oriented "core curriculum" focused on the business functions taught by research-oriented faculty at the frontier of knowledge.[36] It would also inadvertently set the stage for what was to come next—the rise of neoliberalism and the ascent of shareholder capitalism.

THE FINANCIALIZATION OF BUSINESS SCHOOLS

Business schools, staffed with more and more PhD-trained researchers, were gradually taken over by financial economists with their strong theoretical and quantitative bent. By the end of the 1980s, business schools had been transformed into bastions of market fundamentalism, with shareholder value as the "objective function" for business. By the 2000s, business had become the most popular bachelor's as well as master's degree in the United States.[37] With manufacturing on the decline and finance on the rise, MBA programs became training grounds for Wall Street and consulting jobs, rather than their historical focus on educating students for managerial positions in industrial corporations. Increasingly, the MBA degree became seen as a way to "get your ticket punched" to make more money.[38]

As we saw in Chapter 2, managers and executives were portrayed as selfinterested "agents" with no fiduciary or stewardship duties for the greater good. Indeed, shareholder primacy effectively delegitimized managerial judgement as a crucial element in the conduct of the business enterprise. The idea that business education was about steeping students in a set of professional ethics for a career in the "management profession" dedicated to the common good effectively went out the door (Exhibit 7.3).[39]

I personally lived through this transformation, having joined the faculty at the University of Michigan Business School in 1985 as an assistant professor of strategy. By then, the "economics perspective" had already come to dominate the areas of finance, strategy, international business, and negotiations. I spent the next thirty years seeking to produce a counternarrative through my research and writing. I developed the "Natural Resource-Based View of the Firm"

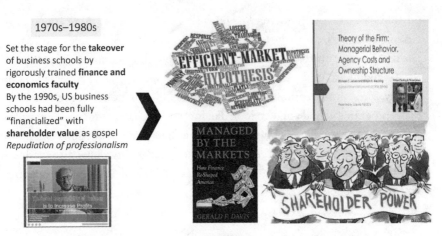

1970s–1980s

• Set the stage for the **takeover** of business schools by rigorously trained **finance and economics faculty**
• By the 1990s, US business schools had been fully "financialized" with **shareholder value** as gospel
• *Repudiation of professionalism*

Exhibit 7.3. The Financialization of Business Schools

and "Sustainable Value Framework" as conceptualizations to demonstrate how environmental and social challenges could be harnessed strategically as sources of competitive advantage and shareholder value creation.[40] The simple truth, however, is that this sort of work has done precious little to fundamentally alter the core DNA of business education. We have produced a number of high-quality "saddlebags" but have done little when it comes to reenvisioning and reimagining the proverbial "horse."

Relegitimizing Business Education

In many ways, we find ourselves now in a position not unlike that in the late nineteenth century—industry concentration has once again enabled large corporations to gain monopoly power in many key sectors such as information technology, fossil fuels, pharmaceuticals, food and agriculture, and financial services. The very legitimacy of "free market" capitalism is again under fire given the unprecedented levels of income and wealth inequality, unfolding climate crisis, and reassertion of the importance of government in the wake of the coronavirus pandemic. The question is, will the capitalists themselves step into the breach again to help guide the ship into calmer waters?

Just like today, the excesses of the Gilded Age were countered by the Progressive movement, which focused on quelling the growing labor unrest and rising environmental concerns. But it was the tycoons *themselves* who took the initiative to create the new institution known as university-based business education, with a focus on professionalization and the greater good. Has the time now arrived for business leaders to once again intervene to relegitimize business education?

Recall that the 1929 stock market crash and ensuing Great Depression prompted serious soul-searching and reflection on the part of business leaders—and business school deans. Many even attributed the crash to the blind acceptance of the laissez faire, free-market ideology that drove the Roaring Twenties. The emerging view that corporations should be institutions with responsibilities to society and that shareholders deserved only the "wages of capital" helped drive the age of welfare capitalism and the postwar boom of the 1950s and 1960s. Is it time to flip the script once again in the quest to unseat shareholder primacy as the prime directive? I believe that it is, and that society's very survival depends on it.

COUNTERVAILING FORCES

Even as large corporate institutions came to dominate the economy in the postwar years, societal criticism of business began to accelerate in the 1960s. Many of the returning veterans from World War II—armed with the business education of the day—became the quintessential "organization men," populating the middle-management ranks of corporations and raising middle-class families in the largely white suburbs.[41] Their children—the Baby Boom generation—increasingly rejected such conformity and segregation, giving rise to a growing "counterculture." A key part of this rebellion was growing opposition to the Vietnam War and the role played by business in supplying the military.

In response to this growing societal criticism, business schools began to add courses in business ethics and corporate social responsibility (CSR) in the 1970s. However, these courses were usually solitary elective courses taught in the second year. The first-year core curriculum—as prescribed by the Ford and Carnegie Foundations' reports—focused exclusively on the functional areas of finance, accounting, marketing, organization behavior, human resource management, operations management, and business policy or strategy, taught with little integration of the ethics and CSR concepts.[42]

Furthermore, the elective courses in business ethics and CSR were often developed and taught by faculty members trained in nonbusiness disciplines such as philosophy or sociology. During this period, business schools did not provide the option to pursue doctoral training in these topics. Junior faculty were discouraged by senior colleagues from pursuing research and developing courses in these fields. Focusing on ethics, CSR, or other areas of social and environmental impact was almost certain to destroy any chances for tenure and promotion in most business schools.[43] I was personally told this by many senior colleagues during the early stages of my academic career starting in the 1980s.

By the late 1980s, however, the situation began to change. The 1987 report of the World Commission on Environment and Development, *Our Common Future* (popularly known as the Brundtland Commission Report), argued for a more significant role for business in achieving sustainable development. This shift manifested in corporate initiatives during the late 1980s and the 1990s to reduce negative social and environmental impacts through eco-efficiency and environmental management, and it further expanded the domains of corporate social responsibility and business ethics.[44]

Faculty members at business schools began offering more electives in these areas, and by the 2000s, centers and institutes focusing on business and sustainability, social entrepreneurship, and positive impact began to flourish. Faculty members in the areas of organizational behavior, technology management, operations, and accounting were naturally more inclined toward the sustainability challenge compared to those in finance, business economics, strategy, and international business. Given the diverse backgrounds of the faculty involved, a wide range of initiatives aimed at confronting these massive societal challenges emerged, each with its own distinctive label and branding, resulting in a proliferation of "buzzwords" and "tribes" focused on slightly different aspects of the same set of underlying societal challenges (see Exhibit 7.4). The grassroots nature of this counternarrative stood in stark contrast to the centrally directed and deliberate strategy of the neoliberalist and shareholder primacy agendas.[45]

Sustainable Value	Blended Value	For Benefit
Mutual Value	Impact Investing	Social Entrepreneurship
Sustainable Brands	Hybrid Value Chains	Green Leap
Clean Technology	Shared Value	Social Innovation
Conscious Capitalism	Regenerative Technology	ESG
Sustainable Innovation	Closed Loop	Base of the Pyramid
Purpose-Driven	Inclusive Business	Circular Economy

Exhibit 7.4. **Countervailing Forces: Tribalism and Buzzwords**

THE POWER OF INERTIA

Even though the accreditation body for business schools, the AACSB, had begun to stress the need to include content on ethics, CSR, and, more recently, sustainability, in the MBA curriculum, business schools typically did not respond, other than by adding elective courses and centers.[46] Most established business school rankings—*Financial Times, Fortune, US News and World Report, Bloomberg Businessweek*—still emphasized job placement and postgraduation starting salaries as their primary metrics for success, all but ignoring such things as research relevance or societal contribution.[47]

Around 2010, however, AACSB began organizing a sustainability conference to share knowledge and best practices in integrating sustainability into business school curricula. Unfortunately, these conferences and a related initiative called PRME (Principles for Responsible Management Education)—to which most leading business schools had become signatories by the late 2000s—have done little to truly motivate business schools to integrate sustainability fully into their core curricula.[48]

In 2020, AACSB incorporated a new requirement in its accreditation standards—Standard 9. It read as follows:

STANDARD 9: ENGAGEMENT AND SOCIETAL IMPACT 9.1 The school demonstrates positive societal impact through internal and external initiatives and/or activities, consistent with the school's mission, strategies, and expected outcomes.

The success of this new standard in catalyzing transformational change in business schools and MBA programs remains to be seen. Why is institutional change so difficult and why can't business schools overcome this inertia? There appear to be three major reasons:

1. As noted above, tenured faculty members are typically trained as researchers focused on theory-driven questions within the functions and disciplines, not on the interdisciplinary challenges associated with sustainability. Faculty focused on societal and sustainability questions are typically untenured adjuncts, lecturers, or clinical professors with little say in the governance of the schools.

2. Leadership at the decanal level with regard to sustainability is weak. Deans usually emerge with a personal foundation in one of the core functional disciplines with limited or no knowledge of sustainability or soci-

etal impact. Hence, they are less comfortable becoming champions for radical change in these domains.

3. University career progression systems for promotion and tenure are based on publishing in top tier, peer reviewed journals that do not encourage or readily accept new ideas or less rigorous research on complex issues such as sustainability.[49]

The persistent inability of business education to move beyond "saddlebag" sustainability is what makes the University of Vermont's Sustainable Innovation MBA Program so important and timely. It represents one of the few attempts by a major research university to fundamentally reinvent business education and the MBA degree to address the very real challenges we face in the twenty-first century—environmental degradation, climate change, poverty, and inequality. Sustainability is the core DNA of the program. It can serve as a model for those business schools seeking to move beyond shareholder primacy in the years ahead. Let's take a closer look.

Going All In: The University of Vermont's Sustainable Innovation MBA

When my long-time colleague Sanjay Sharma joined the University of Vermont (UVM) as the dean of the business school in 2011, he had reinvention on his mind.[50] The business school had a traditional MBA program that dated back to the 1970s and catered to mid-level managers at area companies and UVM employees looking to "get their ticket punched." By 2011, the largest company in Burlington, IBM, had cut its headcount by more than half, and enrollment in UVM's MBA program had declined significantly.

Facing declining enrollments and revenues, Sharma convened an ad hoc faculty committee to analyze the situation and explore options. Ultimately, he and the faculty committee decided the best option was to shut down the program and develop a new specialized MBA program focused on addressing the world's sustainability challenges. Such a program would not only be distinctive, but would also be entirely consistent with the culture and ethic of the university and the state of Vermont. Although Sharma had to deal with pushback at the level of the university board, he ultimately received the green light to proceed. The faculty unanimously approved this recommendation in 2012, and planning for the new program, then called the Sustainable Entrepreneurship MBA (SEMBA), began.

STARTING WITH A "CLEAN SHEET"

When Dean Sharma asked me to be involved, I leapt at the opportunity. For the previous twenty years, I had been working to bring environment and sustainability concerns into MBA programs at Michigan, UNC, and Cornell, but had succeeded only in developing "saddlebags"—centers, elective course sequences, and dual-degree programs—without ever fundamentally changing the core DNA of the MBA. SEMBA offered the chance for the first time to fundamentally alter the "horse" itself.[51]

It was the opportunity I had been waiting for: the chance to start with a blank sheet of paper with the aim of creating a model for the purpose-driven MBA program of the twenty-first century, focused entirely on the knowledge, skills, and capabilities needed to harness the power of business for a sustainable world. Appointed as a part-time "adjunct" faculty member by the dean in 2013, I started making regular visits to UVM to work with the faculty on this new enterprise. Initially, Professor Willy Cats-Baril had been selected as the faculty director of the new program, as he was one of the few members of the existing faculty with entrepreneurial experience. I worked closely with Willy during the 2013–14 academic year to design the curriculum while simultaneously building and developing the faculty team to deliver it.

We set out to create a one-year (twelve-month) program, rather than the typical two-year-with-summer-internship MBA, since it had become widely recognized that the second year of most MBA programs had become little more than an "unmanaged smorgasbord" of elective classes.[52] We knew that the design of the curriculum would have to depart significantly from the norm. In fact, all the course work would need to be completed in just *nine months*, since the program culminated with a three-month experiential learning project— the practicum—as its capstone experience. To break the mold even further, given the constraints of the graduate school, the program would start and end in August, which meant that the students would miss the usual MBA recruitment cycle that followed the conventional academic year calendar.

The 2013–14 "design year" turned out to be an exercise in "building the bridge as you walk on it" since the existing business school faculty lacked the full spectrum of knowledge and experience needed to deliver on the program's vision. To identify prospective faculty and courses, we took an inventory of current course offerings and titles both within the business school and across the university. This effort included faculty from the Rubenstein School for the Environment, Community Development and Applied Economics, the Engineering College, the Gund Institute for the Environment, and Vermont Law School.

We also identified people from the world of practice who had a history and/ or passion for teaching and working with students. We engaged these individuals in workshops about our vision for the program and worked with them to explore how their teaching might be adapted to the program's needs. We realized that if we kept the typical three-credit-hour course structure, then the tendency for faculty would be to simply rename their existing courses, without significantly altering the course design.

Instead, we broke the traditional mold by organizing the curriculum around a larger number of intensive one- and two-credit courses, which would require faculty to innovate their course designs and would allow for more diversity in content. Ultimately, we conceived of four half-semester modules, two in the fall and two in the winter-spring, with the experiential learning-based practicum as the capstone experience during the summer. While the courses and sequencing have evolved, this basic program structure has endured.

To strengthen the program further, the dean recruited additional key faculty members, funding some of their appointments through a donation from alumnus Steven Grossman. Among other things, the Grossman gift created three endowed chairs within the school—one in sustainable business (which was offered to me); one in finance, which enabled the recruitment of Professor Chuck Schnitzlein; and one in entrepreneurship, which brought Professor Erik Monsen to the school. A subsequent large gift by Grossman also resulted in the naming of the school as the Grossman School of Business.

We launched the program in August 2014 with an initial cohort of twenty students—most either from Vermont or with some prior connection to the university. The ecosystem of well-known Vermont-based sustainable brands were very much engaged—Ben & Jerry's, Seventh Generation, Casella Waste Systems, Keurig-Green Mountain, Native Energy, Vermont State Employees Credit Union, Burton Snowboards, and Cabot Creamery, to name a few. As the year progressed, however, it became increasingly clear that such a strong Vermont focus would not be sustainable: not only did this narrow geographic focus limit the career opportunities for graduates, but perhaps even more critically, it made recruitment efforts for future student cohorts very difficult. Indeed, the program nearly died after the first year: We had *zero* enrolled students for the second class as late as February 2015.

It had become clear that the program needed a more aggressive marketing strategy to expand its reach beyond its Vermont roots. It would need to become not only national, but *global* in scope, with regard to both program focus and student recruitment. Professor David Jones, who had been part of the original ad hoc committee, assumed an increasingly important profile with the fledgling initiative, as did Casella executive Joe Fusco. By the early spring of 2015, David Jones and I were appointed codirectors of the program, with Joe Fusco taking responsibility for the leadership development track. It required an "all hands on deck" mobilization to assemble a critical mass of sixteen students to enable a second cohort of the program to go forward. Indeed, without strong support and commitment from the dean, this program may have quietly disappeared after its inaugural year.

We also realized that the original name of the program—the Sustainable Entrepreneurship MBA—was limiting potential student interest. The next year, we changed the name to the Sustainable *Innovation* MBA (SI-MBA) to better recognize that the program was focused not only on startups and ventures, but also on purpose-driven business and corporate transformation. This wider program scope was captured by the tag line, "Transforming Today's Business, Creating Tomorrow's Ventures." The rather audacious mission of the new SI-MBA program was stated thus: "To reinvent business education, and develop and launch a new generation of leaders who will transform capitalism to solve the world's most pressing sustainability challenges."

Since the "near death" experience in 2015, the program has steadily ramped up in numbers, both in applications and enrollments. SI-MBA continues to be a small, intimate MBA program with cohort size in the forties, but now operates in the black, with the prospect of expanding to two sections in the not-too-distant future. During the Covid "bump" year of 2020–21, the program received an outsized bump in applications. Indeed, the program's new directors Caroline Hauser and Professor Chuck Schnitzlein received more than *double* the applications compared to the previous year.

Such growth needs to be viewed in the context of the trajectory of "conventional" MBA programs which, aside from a Covid "bump" of about 20 percent, have experienced declining applications—even among the top twenty "incumbent" players such as Harvard, Stanford, Kellogg, MIT, Cornell, Tuck, Wharton, and Michigan. Several second-tier MBA programs have even been forced to shut down due to declining enrollments. We interpret the increasing applications for SI-MBA to mean that we must be on to something. Indeed, new SI-MBA director Kim Nolan has been able to maintain the overall upward trajectory. As a result, we believe we are at the beginning of a wave that will sweep business education in the years to come: the creative destruction of the shareholder-primacy-based MBA from the 1980s.

SI-MBA has also gained growing external recognition. The program received the 2015 Page Prize for Innovating Sustainability Issues in Business Curriculum and has been ranked the number 1 Best Green MBA Program in the US by Princeton Review in 2018, 2019, and 2020. Corporate Knights also ranked SI-MBA number 1 in the US and number 4 globally in their Better World MBA Rankings in 2019, and it has remained in the top ten globally since. In addition, Professor Chuck Schnitzlein led a team of SI-MBA students to victory in the inaugural Wharton School Total Impact Portfolio Competition in 2019. Prospective students who align with the program's focus and values pay attention to these rankings and achievements even more than the conventional MBA rankings by *Fortune, Business Week,* and *US News and World Report,* which place primary emphasis on how much more money students make after graduating. To be clear, SI-MBA is not opposed to money or profit. We simply view them as means to a greater end—positive impact in the world—rather than an end in themselves.

DOING MORE IN HALF THE TIME

Traditional full-time MBA programs take *two* years—and sixty credits—with the first year dedicated largely to "core" courses and the second year dedicated to electives in an area of functional specialization. So how does the SI-MBA program, which received AACSB accreditation in 2015 (and was reaccredited in 2021), deliver the obligatory core MBA content in *one* year (and forty-five credits) while also developing the twenty-first-century knowledge, skills, tools, and capabilities needed to achieve sustainable innovation?

Designing the SI-MBA program from a "clean sheet" allowed us to select the most critical sets of core knowledge, skills, and capabilities that every MBA graduate must know, while infusing the curriculum with the perspective of sustainable innovation (Exhibit 7.5). We begin by requiring all SI-MBA students to complete a suite of self-paced, online tutorials before they start in-person classes in late August. This preenrollment coursework enables us to bring all our incoming students up to speed on the basics in accounting, statistics, economics, and finance, regardless of their prior education or business experience. Such foundational material typically occupies an inordinate amount of time in the first-year core curriculum of traditional MBA programs.

SI-MBA then takes a critical perspective with regard to the traditional tools and techniques of business: functionally oriented courses not only ensure competence but also examine the *toxic side effects* of applying traditional busi-

Removal of Legacy MBA Content

- We eliminate legacy content of the past, and focus on tools for the present and future
- Instead of preparing managers for functional execution and administration, we develop visionary leaders for innovation and transformational change

Core MBA Toolkit

- Accounting
- Finance
- Economics
- Statistics
- Marketing
- Operations
- Management
- Strategy

The SI-MBA Difference

- We integrate sustainability and innovation in everything we do, and students learn from top leaders in sustainable business
- Graduates gain project-based experience via practicums hosted by world-class companies and ventures

Exhibit 7.5. An MBA for the Twenty-First Century

ness tools such as industry analysis, competitive strategy, marketing strategy, supply chain optimization, discounted cash flow, internal rate of return, and financial reporting. We ask, What do the traditional tools miss? What are the blind spots? What unintended negative consequences result from their uncritical application?

Next, the SI-MBA curriculum adds courses focused on the emerging knowledge, skills, and capabilities that will be crucial for creating the sustainable and inclusive businesses of tomorrow. These courses include content that would typically not be found in traditional MBA programs, such as world challenges, the Sustainable Development Goals, planetary boundaries, climate change, natural capital, circular economy, poverty, inequality, ESG, and DEI, as well as "next practice" tools and capabilities such as materiality assessment, climate accounting, life cycle design, systems thinking, data analytics, AI, biomimicry, impact investing, benefit corporations, base-of-the-pyramid business models, deep dialogue, appreciative inquiry, and co-creation skills.

What makes SI-MBA truly unique is the integration of sustainability and innovation content throughout the entire program rather than just a few elective courses. In other words, sustainable innovation is core to *every* course taught in the program, and every course taught in the program is "core." Indeed, there are *no* electives in SI-MBA. Students experience the entire curriculum—twenty-three courses across four modules—together, as a cohort, building strong bonds and gaining deep experience in teamwork and leadership in the process (Exhibit 7.6). Courses are supplemented by "Toolkit Workshops" that provide

• Fall Semester	• Winter Semester

• Module 1
  • Business Strategy for a Sustainable World
  • Finance for Innovators I
  • Sustainable Brand Management
  • Teamwork for Sustained Innovation
  • Business Economics
  • Cost Models for the Transformational Enterprise
 	
• Module 2
  • From CSR to Creating Shared Value
  • Business Sustainability and Public Policy
  • Marketing Decision Making Under Uncertainty
  • Family Business for Sustainability
  • Leading Sustainable Innovation
  • Finance for Innovators II
	• Module 3
	  • Sustainable Operations and Green Supply Chains
	  • Crafting the Entrepreneurial Business Model
	  • Data Analytics for Sustainable Business
	  • Financing a Sustainable Venture
	  • Driving Sustainable Change I
	  • Sustainability Toolkit I
	
	• Module 4
	  • Driving Sustainable Change II
	  • Driving Innovation from the Base of the Pyramid
	  • Innovation Strategy: From Idea to Market
	  • Accounting for a Sustainable Enterprise
	  • Systems Tools for Sustainability
	  • Law as a Framework for Entrepreneurial Business
	  • Sustainability Toolkit II
	
	• Practicum Project

Exhibit 7.6. 2021–22 SI-MBA Curriculum

intensive training in emerging tools and methods, along with visits by "Innovators in Residence," practitioners who can speak to the challenges and opportunities of pursuing a career focused on purpose and sustainable innovation.

This entire curriculum is delivered in nine months, preparing students for the capstone integrative experience of the practicum project in the final three months of the program. So, how are we able to deliver all this content in *less* than a year? Traditional two-year MBA programs have significant amounts of "legacy" content. Indeed, many of today's established MBA programs have been in existence for well over a half a century, so the core courses include content that is akin to a vestigial organ in the body—it served a purpose in the distant past, but has outlived its usefulness yet still takes up space. Since core courses, including the teaching materials, are often "passed down" from one professor to another, it is easier to simply adapt the existing material than to reinvent it. Taking this vestigial short-cut allows faculty to focus their time and attention on research and peer-reviewed publishing, since that is where the rewards lie.

For example, today's traditional core course in "Operations" still includes two-plus weeks of material on "Queuing Theory and Factory Optimization," often including problem sets with hand calculations. Do MBA students need to know what "Queuing Theory" is? Yes. Do they need to know where to go and who to consult should this ever become an issue for them in their professional lives? Yes. How long might it take to accomplish this in the classroom? Maybe fifteen minutes rather than two weeks.

Because we designed SI-MBA from scratch, we weren't beholden to any such nonessential legacy content. Starting with a "clean sheet" enabled us to include only that material and content that is relevant to our mission of sustainable innovation. The SI-MBA design process unfolded like zero-based budgeting: faculty had to justify why a particular course or topic should continue to exist rather than simply rubber-stamp the continuation of the status quo. This "all in" redesign approach enabled us to *remove* nonessential legacy content of a bygone business era in order to make room for the next-generation content that is critical to a sustainable and inclusive future.

We made extensive use of workshops and retreats so that SI-MBA faculty had a clear understanding of the entire program, and so they would know exactly how their courses fit into it. We asked each faculty member to "storyboard" their course and present it to their colleagues. The process accomplished several objectives: (1) It created peer pressure for faculty to truly innovate their course designs, (2) It enabled us to collectively optimize the sequencing and pacing of the content and the workload so as not to overload the students, and (3) It allowed us to identify redundancies as well as complementarities so as to optimize the delivery of the content in an integrated and coherent manner.

SI-MBA also helped to stretch faculty members' intellectual agendas. Since business school faculty normally conduct research and teach only in their functional areas, the SI-MBA curriculum development process helped broaden faculty from the different disciplines and functions, enabling them to examine their research and teaching from different perspectives, through the lens of sustainability. This stretching opened up avenues for new research ideas, encouraged new and interesting research questions, and increased the potential for collaborations across disciplines.

PRACTICUM: THE CAPSTONE EXPERIENCE

Experience-based learning is a central component of the SI-MBA curriculum. Most courses include project-based work, some of which is organized in conjunction with site visits and interactions with executives and entrepreneurs. But the capstone experiential learning element of the program is the practicum, constituting six credits toward students' degrees. The practicum affords the opportunity to consolidate and apply the learnings from all the courses and workshops in a real-world setting.

Practicum is a full-time, hands-on, three-month experiential engagement with established companies and organizations or early stage ventures (host organizations) from Vermont, the US, and around the world. Projects are carefully curated by faculty and staff to ensure their appropriateness to the SI-MBA mission. During the practicum, teams of two to four students work with the host organization to create an action plan related to starting a sustainable venture, expanding an existing initiative, or working within a corporation to address a specific sustainability-related business challenge or opportunity. The student practicum teams are supported by faculty advisors and a "Clinic," providing consultation on how best to scope and frame the projects using systems thinking and tools.

Practicum hosts have included PepsiCo, Facebook, SAS, Cemex, Microsoft, Philips, Novelis, Trane Technologies, Interface, REI, Caterpillar, Griffith Foods, Seventh Generation, Ben & Jerry's, Native Energy, Burton Snowboards, Keurig Green Mountain, Casella, Resonance, Dalberg, Care Enterprises, Morningstar, EDF, and the Rainforest Alliance.[53] Some students have also utilized the practicum as a vehicle for advancing their own venture idea. Indeed, a handful of growing ventures have already been launched through this process.

Ideally, practicum projects give momentum to an important initiative or strategy that the host organization would like to continue beyond the three-month practicum time frame, thus opening the potential for continued engagement or even employment for the students after graduation in August. The deliverable for the practicum is a detailed and comprehensive business or action plan for the host organization. In early August, students pitch their business or action plans to representatives of the host organizations, fellow students, and SI-MBA faculty. A week later they graduate, but relationships endure well beyond their completion of the program. As you might imagine, the intense, "boot camp" like character of SI-MBA forges close ties among both students and faculty. Indeed, alumni have become an amazingly tight community that serves not only an important networking function, but also as a source of social and emotional support, as well as a source for future practicum projects and job opportunities.

THE SI-MBA VALUE CHAIN

When we first embarked on the adventure of creating a completely new MBA program focused on sustainable innovation, I thought the most significant challenge would be the design of the curriculum and the recruitment of the faculty to deliver the program. Make no mistake, doing so was (and continues to be) a real challenge.

But I did not realize at the time how significant the *system design* challenge would be when it came to the creation of such a disruptive new program. Once David Jones and I became the SI-MBA codirectors in 2015 (and we weathered the "near death" experience of the recruitment of the second cohort), we realized that the curricular innovations were just the beginning of our work. Most business school faculty don't give much thought to where the students come from or where they go after graduation. Those issues are the concern of Admissions and the Career/Placement Offices.

But SI-MBA was a whole new ball game. We were on our own. Where would we find the reservoirs of purpose-driven prospective students who were essential if the program was to thrive? And, how would we create the necessary opportunity horizons postgraduation for the students to justify their time and investment in the program? In short, we had to develop the entire value chain of the program.

Our colleague Joe Fusco created a wonderful way of framing this larger system challenge: SI-MBA was really composed of three interconnected elements: (1) "Attract"—recruit and enroll inspired students from around the world who were truly aligned with the purpose of the program; (2) "Develop"—build their sustainable innovation knowledge, skills, and capabilities through the SI-MBA program itself; and (3) "Launch"—enable students to find and embark on their "best" path for having positive impact in the world.

At first, we thought we were in direct competition with other traditional MBA programs for students. But it did not take us long to realize that many of the students who were most attracted to our program were often those who were not even initially thinking about business school. Instead, they were from diverse backgrounds—education, engineering, policy, social work, civil society, finance, ventures, business—who were in search of a graduate program that would further their desire to do something truly positive in the world. Often, this meant programs in public policy, social work, design, environment, or law. SI-MBA attracted their attention because they did not think that such MBA programs actually existed and that business could be such a powerful driver of positive change.

We realized that a key to "Attract" was to position our program in those places and with those people who were motivated by a sense of purpose to do something positive in the world, such as the Peace Corps, the Idealist Grad Fair, or Net Impact, and then to microtarget particular demographics on social media. Gradually, as the program's reputation grew, we crossed a threshold, when the number of applications each year began to grow significantly year-over-year. Rather than competing for a declining number of applicants like the traditional MBA programs, we had succeeded in opening up an entirely new reservoir of prospective students that should be sustainable well into the future.

LAUNCH VERSUS PLACEMENT

Attracting the right students to the program—those with the ambition to be positive change agents rather than passive recipients of job offers—is critically important to SI-MBA's success. We aim to attract a new breed of business student, one more concerned with using profitable business models to solve societal problems, rather than just maximizing profits. If a student comes to SI-MBA primarily with the expectation that they will "get their ticket punched" for placement in a high-paying job, they will leave dissatisfied with the program's value proposition.

Traditional MBA programs focus on training graduates for "executional" roles in established firms, and preparing students for traditional jobs in finance, marketing, operations, and consulting (Exhibit 7.7). SI-MBA, in contrast, endeavors to create *changemakers* rather than implementers of the status quo. Our emphasis is on entrepreneurial and purpose-driven ventures focused on clean technology and social inclusion, "impact" investing, consulting, and the transformation of existing large corporations. It would be completely disingenuous if we attempted to "bolt on" a conventional MBA placement office, since our students have very different career aspirations.

Recognizing the need to innovate the back end of the program, we began benchmarking existing MBA programs in 2016 to see if there were any best practices we could adopt when it came to the career development of business students focused on business for good. What we discovered was both predictable and disconcerting. Most established MBA programs have "saddlebag" initiatives in sustainability, social entrepreneurship, or positive impact. To deal with the students with these interests, the Career and Placement Offices in these business schools typically assign just one of their career development people to work with these so-called "impact students."

I spoke with several of the career counselors who had been given this assignment at a handful of top-twenty MBA programs and discovered that, as a rule, these individuals were exceedingly frustrated: they generally had no background in the "impact" space, but yet were expected to be expert in the full range of potential career avenues, such as corporate sustainability, social entrepreneurship, CSR, impact investing, and NGOs, as well as industry sectors, such as energy, food and agriculture, mobility, apparel, and IT. It was clear we

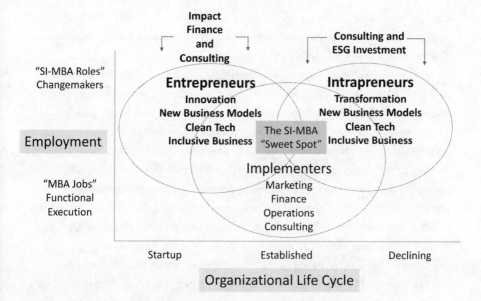

Exhibit 7.7. Placement Versus Launch

had little to learn from these experiences since, once again, they were "saddle-bags" rather than truly integrated solutions.

Just as we did with "Attract" and "Develop," therefore, we had the opportunity (and obligation) to create a completely new approach to career development for SI-MBA, since *all* of our students are "impact" students. We again developed a "clean sheet" approach, which we labeled "Launch" (rather than "Placement") since it is designed for people who take an active part in discovering and creating their own opportunities, rather than being pursued by campus recruiters for conventional MBA jobs. SI-MBA career advisor John Kim now runs a robust process for helping our students find their best path forward post graduation.

The career launch process has three phases: "Discover," "Focus," and "Customize." The initial "Discover" phase starts immediately upon arrival on campus for the start of the program in August. Students complete career assessments and receive individualized career counseling; they prepare a personal vision and action plan with the aim of identifying their career "North Star"— how they think they can best harness their strengths and passion to have maximum positive impact in the world—as well as their immediate next step—what pathway they will pursue upon completion of the SI-MBA program. Students can also now choose among several additional "extracurricular" tracks in particular areas of focus such as sustainable finance or impact investing, sustainable branding, and sustainable sourcing.

In the "Focus" phase, students participate in career panels and workshops, and they attend networking events where they interact with business people and entrepreneurs working in their target pathway. To enable this process, we have developed an active, committed "ecosystem" of companies and individuals who share our vision of sustainable capitalism: "the SI-MBA Changemaker Network." With well over a hundred committed practitioners engaged at this point, the Network provides mentorship for our students, availability for informational interviews, in-reach into their organizations, and referrals for opportunities in related areas. A smaller number of these Network members spend more focused time with our students as "Innovators in Residence."

During the "Customize" phase, students work with advisors to tailor their pitches, personal brand, and resumes. They also begin to identify specific organizations of interest and line up interviews and scope out postgraduate opportunities. Since we made a strategic choice as a program to dramatically reduce tuition for SI-MBA—$32,000 for Vermont residents and $52,000 for out-of-state students—students have more degrees of freedom to pursue professionally worthwhile opportunities that may not be as lucrative from the outset. It helps to graduate with the equivalent of a car loan rather than a home mortgage of student debt. SI-MBA alumni can now be found driving sustainable innovation and change in organizations such as Ben & Jerry's, Seventh Generation, Anthesis, Trane Technologies, Morningstar, Rainforest Alliance, FSG, the Corporate Eco-Forum, and the Long-Term Stock Exchange, among many others.

Over the past decade, the Grossman School of Business itself has been fundamentally transformed: SI-MBA has helped to attract several new faculty members with a professional interest and passion in environmental sustainability and social inclusion. We now have a critical mass of faculty in all the functional areas with a common focus on sustainable innovation and reinventing business, allowing this perspective to spread and gradually transform the undergraduate business program in the school as well. Sustainable innovation has been baked into the culture of the school, enabling the establishment of stronger ties with other units around campus with a focus on sustainability.

Disrupting Business Education for the Twenty-First Century

Our mission in creating the SI-MBA program was to build a "clean sheet" model of what business education needs to look like in the twenty-first century. The Grossman School of Business deans and faculty remain absolutely committed to seeing this program grow and thrive. But our aspirations were never limited to innovating a single MBA program. The challenge—and opportunity—is much bigger than that. Our *audacious* goal is to creatively destroy shareholder-primacy-based business education writ large and usher in a new dominant model that helps to actually regenerate natural capital, avert the climate disaster, lift the poor, and foster racial justice, all while making money in the process. Millennials and especially the rising Gen Z demand nothing less.[54]

While many see top-tier business schools as the bellwethers for the industry, the truth is that most continue to milk the cash cows of their conventional MBA programs while building legitimacy through "saddlebag" centers, institutes, and programs.[55] That is why I believe, like my colleague, the late Clayton Christensen, that the reinvention of business education will come from the *bottom up*, through a process of disruptive innovation. Already, traditional MBA programs are being shuttered due to falling applications and enrollments, mostly among the legions of "second tier" business schools. The deans of many of these schools recognize that the time has come to either innovate or die—and they are increasingly motivated to consider such transformation as a result.

SI-MBA has already influenced several such business schools to develop and launch new MBA programs focused on sustainable innovation, such as the University of Victoria's new MBA in Sustainable Innovation and Colorado State's new Impact MBA. Organizations such as the Globally Responsible Leadership Initiative, One Planet Education Network, Positive Impact Rating for Business Schools, Principles for Responsible Management Education, Net Impact, Good Worldwide, Global Movement, White Men for Racial Justice, and Paul Polman's Imagine have also begun to focus on the reinvention of business education as part of their core missions.

As in any industry, the large, incumbent players—in this case, the "top fifty" MBA programs—will be the last to change as they have the most to lose. Having spent twenty-five years of my academic career in such programs, I understand this all too well. That is why we need the SI-MBA model to multiply exponentially in the years to come, such that a decade from now, sustainable capitalism is the norm and shareholder primacy is a distant memory. Experience points to a few key areas on which motivated corporations and individual donors can focus their attention and resources to accelerate this much-needed reinvention of business education:

- *Support deans and faculty champions from business schools that are intent on transforming their MBA programs.* Corporate sustainability leaders and donors spend inordinate amounts of time and money at name-brand, top-tier business schools where visibility is high but saddlebag sustainability still reigns supreme—and money is not a limiting factor. Providing program funding and sponsorship to less visible (and less well-resourced) but more highly motivated schools will produce greater impact on actual curriculum than comparable resources given at the top fifty, which will mostly result in more saddlebags and academic journal articles published.

- *Encourage reinvention not integration.* For corporate sustainability leaders and donors committed to change at top-tier business schools, support deans and motivated faculty leaders in the launch of *new* MBA or master's programs focused entirely on sustainable business. New programs help build a cohort of faculty across functions with a shared interest in sustainability and innovation. Businesses launch new products all the time with the intent of making existing offerings obsolete, so why not business schools as well? Continuing the quixotic quest to "integrate" sustainability into the core courses of incumbent MBA programs is the definition of insanity: doing the same thing over and over and expecting different results. After thirty years of failed "integration," we should abandon ship on this strategy once and for all.

- *Commit to recruiting and hiring at the business schools that have truly transformed their MBA programs.* Most corporations have well-established MBA recruitment systems that are limited to a few of the elite, top-tier business schools. For companies committed to sustainability, wouldn't it make sense to also recruit at the business schools that are fully focused on developing and equipping their purpose-driven graduates with the knowledge, tools, and skills to deliver on the sustainable business promise? This is one of the biggest challenges for innovative new programs like SI-MBA: creating "pull" for the graduates of these programs sends a strong market signal, attracts more students, and encourages more business schools to take the leap. It will also help shift the rankings more in the direction of the real innovators.

- *Steer university donor capital toward sustainable business transformation.* Development organizations in universities have their own agendas for where they would like to steer donors, and seldom does this include the business school unless the donor demands it. In my experience, donors focused on such societal issues as environment and poverty are often steered to other schools and departments, the result being that "business school" donors are disproportionately those devoted to the continued care and feeding of shareholder primacy, thus perpetuating the problem. Donors committed to the vision of sustainable capitalism must insist that at least some of their donor capital be targeted toward the support of transformational initiatives at business schools.

Stepping Up to the Plate

In the 1950s, it was the Ford and Carnegie Foundations that determined the nature and trajectory of business education for the generations following World War II—the Greatest Generation and the Baby Boomers—helping to drive the age of welfare capitalism. But beginning in the 1970s, a small group of capitalists on the economic right—Scaife, Olin, Coors, Koch—orchestrated an investment and intervention strategy that redefined the agenda and established market fundamentalism and shareholder primacy as the prime directives, at least in part by transforming the nature of both business and legal education.[56]

If we are to establish the new "story" and "operating system" of sustainable capitalism as the dominant logic—the new *myth*, if you will—it is crucial that business education be reinvented once again before it is too late. Business schools and MBA programs have been the *progenitors* of the shareholder primacy ideology, the keepers of the market fundamentalist flame. Business education is the system that has trained and propelled millions of MBAs into the finance and business worlds as shareholder primacy's true believers. The next capitalist reformation will not be possible unless the High Church of Shareholder Capitalism itself undergoes a reformation.

The questions are thus: Will a new generation of enlightened capitalists and donors now step up to the challenge to reinvent and relegitimize business education for the twenty-first century, much as the industrialist founders of the business school movement did in the late nineteenth and early twentieth centuries? Should the Business Roundtable's call for the end of shareholder primacy also include a commitment to reinvent business schools, so as to accelerate the transformation to sustainable capitalism? Might those companies committed to sustainability take a more activist role in accelerating the transformation of business education? Do we need a twenty-first-century version of the Society of Fellows that spearheads the spread of sustainable capitalism's DNA rather than the virus of shareholder primacy? I believe the answer to these questions must be yes, and we now have early proof-of-concept as to what the next generation of business education needs to look like. The time is now to make it happen.

The world faces existential challenges that desperately need the collective brainpower of business researchers and professors to help create solutions that generate business performance on the triple bottom line and a pedagogy to train and develop a new generation of purpose-driven, sustainable business-people. Only by transforming the *system* of business education itself can one of the root causes of our current predicament—the ideology of shareholder primacy—be banished from the business landscape. If that can happen, we will have come full circle and returned to the roots, when business education was oriented toward developing ethical professionals focused on the greater good. The ultimate aim: to redefine the very meaning of value itself.

EIGHT

Redefining the Meaning of Value

"In the field of modern business, so rich in opportunity for the exercise of man's finest and most varied mental faculties and moral qualities, mere money-making cannot be regarded as the legitimate end."

LOUIS BRANDEIS (1912)

History has sold Louis Brandeis short. Most people remember him only as a prominent Supreme Court justice who stood up for First Amendment and privacy rights. Some (particularly those in Boston) recognize that his life's work was also significant enough to have a university named after him. Few, however, realize that what he was truly passionate about was bending capitalism to serve the needs and aspirations of people and society, rather than the other way around—and that he achieved considerable success in doing so.[1]

Perhaps most significant was Brandeis's thinking about the role of the market economy in a good society. Today, we increasingly expect corporations to behave "responsibly" or even pursue a societal purpose, but we still tend to think the primary objective for the economy is simply to *grow*. Brandeis stood this thinking on its head. He asked, "*What is the purpose of the economy in a good society?*" For him, the ideal was a market-based economy that served as a "cauldron for character and self-development"—the right to *live* and not merely exist. A good economy was one that provided everyone sufficient liberties and support to live meaningful, fulfilling lives, including protection from monopoly domination, exploitation, and economic insecurity.[2]

After four decades of market fundamentalism, it is high time that we restore—and update—the Brandeisian vision of what constitutes a good economy for our time. The focus can no longer be simply increasing GDP and controlling inflation (although the latter is clearly important); instead, we must shift attention to the *direction* and *quality* of such growth. To achieve this aim, we must restore the capacity of government to act with purpose since individual companies—even with the best of intentions—cannot tackle the world's grand challenges alone. As economist Mariana Mazzucato argues, we must reestablish government's commitment to *mission*—like the moon landing in the 1960s—but this time focused on developing next-generation technologies and low-carbon infrastructure, thereby shaping the sustainable markets of the future and delivering societal outcomes that people truly want and need.[3]

To make this happen, given the polarized state of our politics, business leaders will have to rise to the challenge—by becoming champions of institutional reinvention and system redesign. Indeed, in their commissioned study of the state of capitalism, three prominent Harvard Business School professors concluded that "if market capitalism cannot be made to work for almost everyone, then it will eventually not be allowed to work at all."[4] Their overarching conclusion: government cannot do this alone, business must step up to the plate. "The private sector has enormous potential to drive positive change—if its leaders commit to do so—and leadership by business is crucial to solving the problems at hand."[5]

As we saw in the last chapter, reinventing business education is a crucial requirement in accelerating the transformation to sustainable capitalism. But no system or institution has a more pervasive impact on the conduct of capitalism than the *financial infrastructure* that underpins it. Incremental improvements such as sustainability ratings, reporting, and ESG investing, while important, will not be nearly enough. They are finance's version of "saddlebags:" they look good from the outside but do not change the fundamental DNA of the underlying system. Nothing short of the outright overthrow of shareholder primacy and market fundamentalism will suffice. Indeed, the entire financial infrastructure will need to be redesigned with a different *objective function*: the creation of an inclusive and sustainable economy.

After reviewing the importance of government and role of finance in historical context, I'll focus on why the financial infrastructure is so important and how we can and must transform it if we are to realize the next capitalist reformation. The Long-Term Stock Exchange is featured as an example of the kind of disruptive innovation needed to creatively destroy current public equity markets that—despite the recent trend in ESG investing—are still ruled by shareholder primacy and short-termism. The lesson? If we get the "objective function" of the market right, the desired business behavior will follow, and the building of a sustainable and inclusive economy based upon our "better angels" will be the inevitable result. We will have redefined the very meaning of what drives and constitutes "value."

From Demonization to Elevation

The age of shareholder capitalism mired us in the groundless and counterproductive belief that government is little more than a drag on the economy and an added cost burden. Indeed, the neoliberal era—while now in retreat—delivered an ongoing assault on the credibility and importance of government, such that many *still* see "tax" as a dirty word, regulation as something to be eliminated, and government programs as little more than distortions of free markets.[6]

The truth, of course, is that government and institutions play a crucial role in determining the trajectory of entire nations and societies. Indeed, as Daron Acemoglu and James Robinson make clear in *Why Nations Fail*, inclusive (versus extractive) political and economic institutions largely determine whether nations realize sustained increases in living standards or descend into downward spirals of autocracy, poverty, and inequality. The plight of Korea over the past seventy years offers a vivid example: while a remarkably homogeneous culture, the people of North Korea are now among the poorest on Earth while their brethren in South Korea are among the richest. The differences between the two Koreas are due almost entirely to the starkly different political and economic institutions adopted by each in the wake of the Second World War.[7]

Government has also played a crucial and catalytic role in past capitalist reformations and will need to once again.[8] When we examine the history of the US, for example, we see the importance of inclusive *political* institutions reinforcing inclusive *economic* institutions in the form of a series of policy "redesigns" that roughly parallel prior capitalist reformations. As we saw in Chapter 1, the founding of America catalyzed the first reformation—market capitalism—along the lines of Adam Smith's vision for a market economy. Next came Alexander Hamilton, the architect of industrial development and the nurturing of the "American System" of manufacturing, which enabled the rise of industrial (monopoly) capitalism in the late nineteenth century.[9]

Along the way, Abraham Lincoln ensured that the growth of the railroads and other large corporations was met with the countervailing democratizing forces of the Homestead Act and the Morrill Land Grant Act, enabling a generation of aspiring settlers to pull themselves up by the bootstraps, albeit with dire consequences for the native population and newly freed slaves. Teddy Roosevelt, Woodrow Wilson, Louis Brandeis, and Franklin Roosevelt then engineered the Progressive Era and New Deal reformations of monopoly capitalism, which led to more than three decades of welfare capitalism, a rising middle class, and shared prosperity (albeit with continued racial bias). Indeed, during the postwar years, the US federal government was the world's most successful R&D organization, helping to develop, through its early stage investment muscle, jet aviation, semiconductor technology, computing, and the core technologies that would underpin the digital age.[10]

Tragically, we "missed the boat" when it came time to reinvigorate capitalism once again in the 1970s. Rather than charting a proactive course of government R&D and public investment to pull us out of the stagflation curse and accelerate the economy into the twenty-first century, the country (and the world) were hijacked by the neoliberal agenda which, through its vilification of government and deregulation of the financial sector, led us to four decades of market fundamentalism and shareholder primacy.

The core assertion that has underpinned the era of shareholder capitalism has been the presumed superiority of the "free market" in delivering prosperity—the belief that "government" serves only to *distort* the market, causing it to be less efficient. Recent events—the Great Recession and the global pandemic—have clearly overtaken this view. Indeed, as Robert Reich makes so vividly clear in his book *Saving Capitalism*, such a caricature serves mainly as a smokescreen enabling monied interests and corporations with market power to manipulate government in their own interests.

The idea that a "free market" exists somewhere out there on its own into which government "intrudes" is an absurdity. As Reich explains,

> There can be no "free market" without government. The "free market" does not exist in the wilds beyond the reach of civilization. Competition in the wild is a contest for survival in which the largest and strongest typically win. Civilization, by contrast, is defined by rules; rules *create* markets, and governments generate the rules.[11]

Economist and banker Mark Carney concurs:

> The market does not exist in a vacuum. It is a social construct whose effectiveness is determined partly by the rules of the state and partly by the values of society. . . . Unchecked market fundamentalism devours the social capital essential for the long-term dynamism of capitalism itself. . . . Capital-

ism loses its sense of moderation when the belief in the power of the market enters the realm of faith.[12]

A truly *free* market would look like a Hobbesian "state of nature" in which "animal spirits" predominate and life is "nasty, brutish and short." Government *makes* markets, by establishing the rules of the game and holding participants accountable. Societies at different times have adopted different rules that mirror their norms and values. I have referred to these as different *myths, narratives, stories,* and *operating systems* for capitalism. The three cycles of capitalist reformation recounted in Chapters 1 and 2 are a tale of how *differently* societies and cultures have chosen to define the rules of the game over time—and the implications they have for prosperity, equity, and quality of life.

The most central of these rules are those defining the market mechanism itself—property rights, contracts, antitrust, bankruptcy, and enforcement. However, as Reich warns, these decisions about markets are often hashed out behind closed doors, in negotiations influenced disproportionately by giant corporations, big banks, and wealthy individuals. Their money buys lobbyists, experts, lawyers, campaign contributions, public relations campaigns, and quiet promises of future jobs for the politicians and regulators. The *Citizens United* decision by the US Supreme Court and the ensuing tidal wave of "dark money" in politics have only made this problem worse.[13]

The fact that money buys access has created a vicious cycle—market power feeds political power, and political power further expands economic dominance. The smokescreen of the "free market" has served as a foil for those that do not want the design of the capitalist infrastructure brought into the light of day.[14] Market fundamentalism has also effectively blunted efforts to institute progressive policies that would ensure a more equitable distribution of wealth or steer economic development in a more environmentally sustainable direction. Witness, for example, the continuing tax cuts for the wealthy and subsidies for fossil fuels but the absence of a price on carbon or serious action to address the climate crisis.

I've spent the past thirty-plus years of my life making the case for how corporations and enterprises can themselves innovate for sustainability in the *absence* of a meaningful and proactive government policy framework. Indeed, most of the "sustainable business" movement during this time has been an attempt to accommodate environmental and social objectives within the constraints and demands of shareholder primacy, resulting in a potpourri of monikers such as triple bottom line, sustainable value, social innovation, blended value, hybrid value chains, and shared value. A growing chorus of voices, however, makes it clear that the logic of "win-win" will simply not be adequate to address the transformational challenges that lie ahead. In fact, virtue signaling and claims of corporate purpose can ring hollow or worse when the prime directive of capitalism still dictates quarterly earnings growth to maximize shareholder value.[15]

In *Reimagining Capitalism in a World on Fire*, Rebecca Henderson makes a strong and compelling argument for why free markets must be balanced by free politics: free markets need democratic, transparent government to avoid the corruption associated with those states captured by small groups of oligarchs and kleptocrats.[16] She goes on to call for business leaders to take a much stronger leadership role in ensuring the legitimacy and functioning of core institutions of democratic government—judicial independence, a free press, voting rights, and getting money out of politics. In this perilous time, there is no question that business leaders must stand up for democracy to counter the growing authoritarian momentum in the world.

The truth is, however, that such prodemocratic advocacy by business leaders will be necessary but not sufficient. The coronavirus pandemic has made crystal clear just how badly we need competent, open, and assertive government. Indeed, without proactive public investment in tomorrow's technology and infrastructure, it may not be possible to extricate ourselves from our current predicament of toxic inequality, social injustice, and climate crisis, perpetuated by the outsized influence of incumbent firms and industries lobbying to preserve the status quo.[17]

The Business Roundtable and the U.S. Chamber of Commerce, for example, both lobbied against the Build Back Better bill in 2021, which included $555 billion earmarked for addressing climate change—public investments which would eliminate more than a *billion* tons of carbon dioxide by 2035. So, while corporate sustainability teams at these very same companies poured their creative energies into cutting their companies' emissions by perhaps a million tons over the next decade, their lobbying colleagues were working to prevent government from enacting legislation that would have achieved a *thousandfold* greater reduction. The tragic irony here is that companies actually need climate legislation to hit their targets, particularly for Scope 3 emissions in their value chains.[18]

Thus we must now embark on a new governmental "redesign" that will serve to catalyze a truly sustainable and inclusive economy—in keeping with the Brandeisian ethic.[19] Mariana Mazzucato provides the ultimate vision of proactive government restored to its former role in her ground-breaking book

Mission Economy. She notes that the challenges the world now faces require governments to do much more than just react to market failures—they require "imagining new landscapes, not fixing existing ones, and aligning policies to inspire different actors who can spot opportunities for investment that they did not see before . . . which begins with the question: what sort of markets do we want?"[20]

Government must no longer limit itself to reactively *fixing* markets but must instead *co-create* markets with the private sector to fulfill a public purpose and deliver the outcomes society needs. The recent passage of the Infrastructure Bill and the Inflation Reduction Act in the US represents a step in this direction. The question is, How can we more fully restore and elevate the role of government in co-creating shared and sustainable prosperity? After four decades of market fundamentalism, money in politics, and the scourge of hyper-partisanship, it does not appear that government *itself* has the capacity to reestablish its historical role. A proactive private sector and citizenry can and must provide the impetus needed to literally *pull* government into the future. Only then can the system-level redesigns that are so desperately needed actually be realized.

Some sectors are probably in too deep—too wed to the status quo—to provide the necessary influence and activism for transformation—Big Tech, Big Pharma, and Big Banks come to mind. However, it is in the direct interest of other industries and sectors to become advocates for change—food and agriculture, forest products, materials, HVAC, construction, mobility, and renewable energy, for example—or risk oblivion in the decades ahead. Some have already begun to step up to the plate, as we have seen in earlier chapters of this book.

While many important reforms have been made to the global financial system in the wake of the Great Recession, many other policies and laws still need transforming at the country level—tax laws, corporation laws, antitrust laws, bankruptcy laws, intellectual property laws, regulatory and subsidy regimes—to name just a few.[21] Indeed, if we had to pick *one* domain that would provide the greatest leverage for system change it would have to be the redesign of the *financial infrastructure*. It provides the foundation for American-style shareholder capitalism, aided and abetted by MBA programs as discussed in the previous chapter. Even with neoliberalism in retreat, the shareholder-primacy-driven finance industry continues to be a major part of the problem. We must rethink—and redefine—the financial infrastructure before it is too late.

Financialization Through History

For the past forty years, a large and growing financial sector has been touted as a resounding positive by advocates for shareholder capitalism—credited with picking up the slack at a time when the manufacturing sector was declining into net import status. Indeed, for market fundamentalist believers, finance has been seen as nothing less than the *engine* of innovation: "what was good for Wall Street was good for America"—despite unprecedented volatility, environmental destruction, and increasing levels of inequality.[22]

As we saw in Chapter 7, business schools have served as an accelerant, teaching shareholder primacy and financialization as ideology. Millions of the most talented young people have chosen finance rather than other careers that might more effectively strengthen the *real* economy. Countries aspiring to US levels of prosperity have been advised to make deregulation and expansion of banks and financial markets a central part of their development strategy. Living in this moment, many of us would simply assume that the primacy of finance is the natural order of things.

However, the elevation of finance and the financial sector as key to growth and prosperity is actually quite new—it has happened only a few other times in history, roughly coinciding with the emergence of capitalism around four hundred years ago.[23] Indeed, for most of recorded history, finance has been seen more as a necessary evil—a cost of doing business. Such a perception, however, belies finance's massive historical plunders as well as its monumental contributions to economic development.

Indeed, as Edward Chancellor notes in *The Price of Time*, the advent of commercial *credit* was one of the most important innovations in human history. For thousands of years, humankind was trapped in a zero-sum game: credit was virtually nonexistent because people did not trust that the future could be better than the present. It was hard to get a loan in the premodern world, and if you got one, it was usually small, short term, and subject to *high interest rates*. So, while money lending dates to the time of the Sumerians and Babylonians, most cultures viewed it as being extractive, even sinful. In fact, the Hebrew word for "usury" is *neschek*, which means "to bite." As Jesus said, "It is easier for a camel to pass through the eye of a needle than for a rich man to enter into the kingdom of God" (Matthew 19:24).[24]

Nonetheless, lending systems flourished in Rome, and later in China, India, and throughout the Muslim world in the first millennium. While Islam rejected usury as immoral it still built a system of banking and finance which would become a mainstay of Western finance.[25] Europe was slow to emerge from feudalism, so commercial credit took longer to develop. But by the fourteenth century, finance as we think of it today had begun to develop in northern Italy, given the importance of long-distance trading to such places as Venice, Genoa, and Pisa. Since the Roman Church also banned usury, however, those providing credit for overseas trade had to resort to more creative forms of financing, involving compensation for risk, rather than the charging of interest.[26]

The emergence of bond markets helped provide the financial basis for the Italian Renaissance. Adventure capital and stock markets helped give rise to the Dutch and British empires. Banks, insurance, and corporate finance played pivotal roles in accelerating the First Industrial Revolution and enabling the emergence of fully "commercial societies." Today's financial world is thus the result of more than four centuries of evolution. Credit and lending have been essential building blocks for economic development. Indeed, as Niall Ferguson notes in *The Ascent of Money*, economies that combine *all* the financial innovations developed over this period—banks, bond markets, stock markets, insurance, and corporate finance—generally perform better over the long run than those that do not because financial intermediation enables a more efficient allocation of resources than say, feudalism or central planning. Poverty has more to do with a *lack* of financial institutions than with their presence.[27]

Yet the ascent of finance has been anything but uniformly positive. As Niall Ferguson also observes, financial history is replete with "bubbles and busts, manias and panics, shocks and crashes."[28] In fact, Mark Carney notes that across eight hundred years of economic history, financial crises occurred roughly *once a decade!*[29] Historian Jacob Soll helps explain this phenomenon: he reminds us that finance is not the same thing as financial *accountability*. His sweeping history of accounting in *The Reckoning* makes clear that when the books don't balance, accounts are not well-maintained, and oversight is lacking, corruption festers and empires fall.[30]

For example, revelations about dishonest accounting and shoddy bookkeeping regarding the infamous "Mississippi Company Bubble" in eighteenth-century France ultimately led to royal bankruptcy and provoked a public outcry that helped to fuel the French Revolution. In contrast, once transparent accounting took hold in nineteenth-century England, it helped enable the expansion of their global empire.[31] The willful misuse of accounting combined with corrupt political influence and lack of accountability led to catastrophic crashes, first in 1929 (ending the age of monopoly capitalism) and then again with the S&L Crisis, the Tech Bubble, and the Great Recession of 2008, leading to our current predicament.

Much like the cycles of capitalism itself, the evolution of finance over the past four hundred years can be seen as consisting of alternating episodes of *financial hubris* (when "animal spirits" are ascendant) and periods of *financial accountability*, when our "better angels" take hold (Exhibit 8.1). During the periods when financial hubris rules, the ideology of shareholder primacy typically reigns supreme as well. Conversely, when financial accountability is ascendant, shareholders typically assume a more subordinate position, with societal objectives taking precedence.

Let's take a closer look at finance's role in driving the evolution of capitalism so we can better appreciate the unprecedented nature of the challenge we now face. As we saw in Chapter 1, finance first ran amok during the age of mercantile capitalism, when financiers, merchants, and kings conspired to monopolize the world through global trading companies—and get rich in the process. So-called "adventure capital" ruled the day. European kingdoms— England and the Netherlands in particular—rose to prominence and became wealthy through the blending of private financing, royal charters, and imperial aspirations. Advocates for market economies such as Adam Smith and David Ricardo, however, had little regard for these financiers and monopolists; they viewed them as "rentiers"—*extractors* of wealth—prone to corruption and exploitation. Americans fought a revolution to escape from the clutches of these

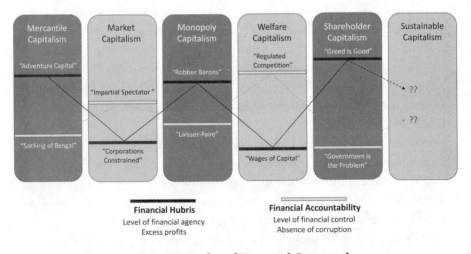

Exhibit 8.1. Episodes of Financial Overreach

monopolists.[32] Market capitalism and strict control of corporations and banking were the eventual result.

The Industrial Age brought another resurgence of finance. By the latter part of the nineteenth century, industrial "Robber Barons" were using tariff protection and monopoly power to generate unprecedented profits . . . and extract surplus with impunity.[33] Industrialists and financiers used the *lack* of government oversight and accountability to exploit labor, drive out competition, and amass huge personal fortunes in the process. Yet even during the height of the Gilded Age, the cost of the financial system—the fortunes of the bankers at the top and the paper-pushers who kept track of the transactions—was small by today's standards, perhaps 1.2 percent of total financial assets per year versus closer to 3 percent today.[34]

The efforts of progressives including Roosevelt, Wilson, and Brandeis to bring the large corporate trusts to heel notwithstanding, the financial sector continued to proliferate, especially in the wake of World War I, when public shareholding became widely distributed for the first time. During the 1920s, trading in financial instruments actually outgrew trade in real products, and finance became an *end in itself* rather than simply facilitating growth in the real economy. Corruption and influence peddling also became rampant once again. Speculation spread from the rich to the wider population, creating the bubble that ultimately resulted in the 1929 Crash.[35]

The cataclysm of the Great Depression caused thinking about the role of finance to undergo another dramatic transformation. John Maynard Keynes stressed the crucial difference between financial speculation (value extraction) and actual productive investment (value creation). A comprehensive set of financial regulations and institutions was put in place, with administrative oversight sufficient to the task, for the first time. Investment banking was separated from commercial banking. Indeed, the Glass-Steagall Act of 1933 effectively forced banks to choose between taking customer deposits and playing the markets.[36]

In the wake of the Great Depression, the financial sector was constrained again to its historical role as a *facilitator* of business, not a growth sector unto itself. During the age of welfare capitalism, commercial banks made their money by acting mainly as intermediaries—offering credit to borrowers and capturing value by charging fees and interest. Investment banks and venture capitalists made capital available for business expansion through new ventures and stock issues during one of the most rapid economic expansions in the world's history. Yet all of this was done with a much smaller and less expensive financial sector than today's behemoth. During the age of welfare capitalism, commercial banking in the US remained a heavily regulated industry and was considered by many to be a rather boring profession. Perhaps not coincidentally, however, it was also during this time that the economy boomed, and a broad middle class was built—the "golden age" of capitalism.[37]

The Neoliberal Aberration

Beginning in the 1970s, however, finance asserted itself once again, this time in a truly revolutionary manner, as the centerpiece of neoliberalism and tip of the spear for the emergence of shareholder capitalism. Perhaps the most authoritative work on this period is Gerald Davis's book *Managed by the Markets*. Davis likens the financialization of capitalism over the past forty years to a "Copernican Revolution," under which the large corporations central to the welfare capitalism era were replaced by financial markets as the primary organizing principle for the economy. In the process, wage-holders and employees were converted into shareholders and "free agents," with few of the benefits and little of the security characteristic of the previous era.[38]

As we saw in Chapter 2, stagflation and sagging stock performance heightened concerns that the conglomerate behemoths that had emerged during the 1960s were no longer being managed with the interests of investors in mind. A few influential Chicago financial economists and legal scholars asserted that Berle and Means must have been wrong since the "strong management and weak shareholder" model of the welfare capitalism era no longer seemed to be producing acceptable financial results. Their solution was to make executives and managers directly accountable to investors by tying their rewards to stock performance. The neoliberals reasoned that by creating a "market for corporate control," managers would be persuaded to run their companies for the benefit of the shareholders or risk being taken over and broken up.[39]

Fueled by "junk bonds," corporate raiders exploded onto the scene and captured the national imagination in the 1980s. Private equity, activist investors, and "bust-up" takeovers emerged as a growing part of the finance landscape. Information and communication technologies got cheaper and more powerful, opening new potential financial products and markets, for example, securitization and high-speed trading. Banks and the financial sector assumed an increasingly significant role in the economy, aided and abetted by government itself. Indeed, as manufacturing began its precipitous decline, finance was both deregulated and redefined to be part of the "productive" economy as a way of compensating for lost GDP from manufacturing.[40]

Financial deregulation began in earnest in the early 1980s, when the laws prohibiting interstate banking were systematically repealed, resulting in a wave of interstate banking mergers and the emergence of the first truly *national* banking players (for example, Citi, Bank of America) since the nineteenth century.[41] It was the introduction of the *tax-advantaged* 401(k) Individual Retirement Account (IRA), however, that really blew the top off in the 1980s, spawning a whole new financial industry segment—asset management. Corporations, pressured by foreign competition, began shutting down their defined benefit pension plans to stay competitive, replacing them with defined *contribution* plans—effectively outsourcing employee pensions. The number of IRA accounts exploded, creating a lucrative new business advising individuals on how and where to invest their 401(k) money. Overnight, employees became shareholders.

By the early 2020s, the asset management industry boasted more than $100 *trillion* in assets under management. Industry behemoth BlackRock alone managed assets of $10 trillion, with the fifteen largest asset managers accounting for nearly *half* of the world's invested capital.[42] Driving this growth was the explosion of mutual funds, with a business model featuring attractive management fees of as much as 2 percent of assets under management, compounded annually. Financial advisors were further compensated through transaction fees, encouraging the "churn" of clients' portfolios rather than actual returns. Vanguard founder John Bogle decried this business model as a betrayal of capitalism, lining the pockets of Wall Street fund managers (and executives) without any obligation to deliver returns to the *owners* of the shares—the IRA account holders themselves.

Bogle's introduction of index funds and other passive instruments during the 1970s and 1980s took asset management in a whole new direction. By the 2010s, investment funds featuring "active" management had declined significantly, with passive investing and exchange traded funds accounting for nearly half of all assets under management.[43] Indeed, by the 2020s, passive investing had reached the point at which a small number of giant asset managers—perhaps a dozen or so CEOs—exercised outsized control over most public companies in the US, and increasingly, the world.[44]

Beginning in the 1990s, investment banks also created a massive new market in derivatives that were sold "over the counter"—off any exchange and out of public sight—amounting to trillions of dollars in trading. As noted by Michael

Hirsh, "The geniuses on Wall Street were always finding ways to repackage assets and sell them to new customers, and derivatives were the means." Those charged with monitoring such transactions, however, were "ideologically opposed to regulation—ex-Wall Street men like Robert Rubin (Treasury), Alan Greenspan (Federal Reserve), and Arthur Levitt (SEC). Efforts to monitor derivatives trading by the Commodity Futures Trading Commission (CFTC) were rebuffed." With no controls on leverage or speculation, it was only a matter of time before problems arose: in the fall of 1998, Long-Term Capital Management collapsed under the weight of trillions of dollars in options and derivatives bets gone bad.[45]

Financial deregulation culminated with the repeal of the Glass-Steagall Act in 1999, eliminating the separation of commercial and investment banking that had been in place since the 1930s. Banks were once again free to use depositors' money to engage in trading and market transactions. The Glass-Steagall repeal meant the banks could effectively play with "house money" since deposits were insured by the FDIC. By the 2000s, a significant portion of big banks' profits came from activities such as writing options and futures contracts, and trading in derivatives for capital gain. In effect, banks now made money by taking advantage of the guarantee provided by the government: if they succeeded, they pocketed the profits; if they failed, the taxpayers footed the bill.[46]

Banks also began targeting riskier (read: lower income) prospects offering higher rates of return. This included everything from subprime home mortgages to high-interest credit cards, home improvement loans, and car loans to the tune of nearly $1 trillion by the late 2000s.[47] Banks then developed exotic derivative instruments based on these assets, such as collateralized debt obligations and credit default swaps, to hedge the risk. Between 1999 and 2008, the market for derivatives exploded from $27 trillion to more than *$600 trillion*. Abuse of derivative instruments would ultimately become the proximal cause of the financial crisis in 2008.[48]

By the 2000s, "financial services" had become a mega-industry, encompassing a surprising range of players—commercial banks, investment banks, asset managers, hedge funds, private equity firms, insurance companies, and freestanding financial specialists. The result: over the past forty years, the financial sector in the US (and most of Europe as well) had increased dramatically in size. Finance has come to dominate the economy rather than serve its traditional role as supplier of capital to the "real" economy of goods and services.[49] A brief comparison of the financial sector during the era of welfare capitalism versus that of shareholder capitalism illustrates this transformation all too clearly:

- During the 1950s–70s, finance accounted for just 10–15 percent of corporate profits, but ballooned to nearly *half* of all corporate profits just prior to the Great Recession.

- During the 1950s–70s, finance represented just 3–4 percent of the economy, but by the 2000s it had grown to 8 percent of GDP.

During the age of welfare capitalism, IPOs, stock issues, mergers and acquisitions, and other forms of primary investment accounted for 30–40 percent of investment bank transactions. However, by the 2000s, primary equity investing came to represent less than 1 percent of all financial transactions. In other words, the finance industry was now geared almost exclusively toward *secondary market activity*—asset management and trading—none of which involved *new* investment. And when the lucrative business of financing share buybacks by corporations (to the tune of nearly $1 trillion per year) was included, the financial sector had become *net-negative* regarding capital—it now *extracted* more capital than it provided.[50]

With such outsized revenues and profits, the financial sector had also come to wield increasing influence and lobbying power in Washington, with five lobbyists for every congressperson. Wall Street became a revolving door, with executives from the big banks—Goldman Sachs in particular—appointed to such key oversight posts as treasury secretary, Fed chair, and head of the SEC, virtually insuring favorable treatment for the industry. The failure of the federal government to regulate over-the-counter derivatives until after the financial crisis in 2008 was just one example.

The bank bailout following the crisis demonstrated even more clearly the power of the banks: they *caused* the crisis, yet government bailed them out to the tune of nearly a *trillion* dollars, without so much as a single prison term for the bankers who created the mess. This included the $180 billion bailout of a single company, AIG, which amounted to more corporate welfare than had been provided to America's poor through all welfare programs aimed at children for more than a decade. However, millions of ordinary borrowers caught up in the catastrophe ended up losing their homes and being treated as little more than collateral damage.[51]

Tragically, most of the financial innovations that were originally touted as democratizing finance, diversifying risk, and boosting upward mobility—derivatives, securitization, junk bonds, and subprime mortgages—ended up turbocharging greed, corruption, and speculation. We have entered what Mark Carney calls the age of "disembodied finance," when markets have grown apart from the people, households, and businesses they ultimately serve. And when those offering financial products are doing so only to "sell them on," their duty of care diminishes. Recent financial innovations have also ended up magnifying risk and heightening volatility. It is interesting to note that there were virtually no bubbles or crashes during the age of welfare capitalism save for the "Nifty Fifty" down-draft in the wake of Watergate and the Arab oil embargo. Since then, however, we have had the S&L Crisis, the Tech Bubble, and in 2008, the Great Recession, along with slower growth and rising inequality.[52]

It is also important to remember that more than a third of the world's population remains effectively *unbanked*—outside of the formal financial system—without access to credit or, in many cases, even legal identity. Innovations such as microfinance and microlending have helped to bring the poor into the formal economy, but even this presumably purpose-driven form of financial service has met with mixed success.[53] And as noted in Chapter 3, however, impact investing, which exceeded $700 billion in 2021, has helped to fund and spawn a new generation of ventures, many of which are focused on financial inclusion and serving the underserved.[54]

The application of information technology to finance—"fintech"—has also shown promise in serving the underserved. Witness the success of startups such as mPesa in Africa and bKash in Bangladesh in providing access to "mobile money" for the underserved using smartphones.[55] Blockchain technology has also shown promise in providing the unbanked with both a digital identity and a credit history, with ventures like Banqu, described in Chapter 4, leading the way.[56] Most of these innovations, however, prioritize impact and social inclusion over financial returns and are therefore only tangentially connected to the incumbent finance industry.

In short, the twenty-first-century financial sector has become a monster that eats profits yet adds little if any real value in the form of new investment, sustainable growth, or social inclusion. Think of it this way: if finance were truly creating value, then an expanding financial sector would account for a *decreasing* share of GDP; instead, it is precisely the opposite—finance has accounted for an increasing share of GDP over the past forty years—indicating that it has become increasingly extractive rather than wealth creating.

Wall Street has become the master of Main Street rather than its handmaiden.[57] We are approaching the extremes of commodification where "the price of everything is becoming the value of everything."[58] The "evil geniuses" described in Kurt Anderson's book by the same title have been singularly effective over the past forty years in transforming finance from a highly regulated "workhorse" industry focused mainly on intermediation and capital allocation to one focused on short-term trading and hedging along with predatory consumer and mortgage lending targeted at those least able to repay.[59] Not since the age of mercantile capitalism have we seen government and finance in cahoots to this extent, with the result being a financial Leviathan run amok.

Such extreme financialization led naturally to shareholder primacy becoming the "objective function" for capitalism. Corporations sought to emulate the high pay and incentive schemes of the finance industry, contributing directly to the disease of short-termism. The financial sector has thus effectively imposed market fundamentalism and shareholder value maximization as the dominant corporate management philosophy. As Duncan Austin wryly notes, finance has become in essence a "profit enforcement agency," taking the place of governmental guardrails in the age of deregulation.[60]

The fact that the stock market rebounded to *new highs* in the face of the global coronavirus pandemic during 2020 is all the proof we need of how utterly disconnected the current public equities market and financial system have become from the real world. As environmental devastation, climate meltdown, and inequality continue to mount, it has become increasingly clear how woefully inadequate shareholder primacy has been in recognizing and rewarding what is truly important for societal well-being. Wall Street booming while Main Street decays and the world burns tells the story: in a very real sense, the market (not the press) has become the "enemy of the people."

Recognizing the growing unsustainability of shareholder primacy and financialization, the Business Roundtable's recent change of heart in favor of corporate purpose and stakeholder capitalism represents an important milestone. While largely symbolic, it is still significant that the top two hundred corporate CEOs have reversed a position held since the 1990s that the purpose of business is to maximize returns to shareholders. Unfortunately, while the Roundtable's new statement of corporate purpose is important, it changes little in and of itself. Even if it results in a flurry of new corporate statements of purpose, proxy votes, and ESG investment funds, these actions in no way change capitalism's prime directive—its *objective function*.

The recent experience of ESG pioneer Generation Investment Management is a case in point. After minting some of the biggest profits in sustainable investing over the past two decades, Generation's largest (tech heavy) fund slumped nearly 30 percent in 2022, while *half* the companies in the portfolio simultaneously *increased* their carbon footprints. Lesson: it's easier to "do well by doing good" when high-growth but comparatively clean industries (such as technology) are leading the market. When technology stocks slumped in 2022, however, Generation's refusal to invest in fossil fuel companies (which surged with the price of oil) laid bare the dilemma of sustainable investing when shareholder primacy still reigns supreme.[61]

Capitalism will thus only be truly transformed when the financial infrastructure on Wall Street that perpetuates the current short-term, shareholder primacy model has itself been transformed—when the analysts, asset managers, investment bankers, and hedge fund managers pay attention to a *different* set of value drivers. It is now increasingly clear that the paradigm of shareholder primacy, which has dominated business theory and practice for nearly a half-century, must give way to a new consensus about what constitutes *sustainable* value creation. As Mark Carney quips, it is time for society's *values* to determine once again what defines *value*.[62] We need a new "myth"—a compelling new narrative—which can drive the adoption of a new operating system for capitalism. There can be no single metric—no "Holy Grail"—for corporations; business is too complex and embedded in society to have anything less than a *multidimensional* objective function. If we are to truly reinvent capitalism for the twenty-first century, therefore, we must overhaul the financial infrastructure that underpins the capitalist endeavor itself.

The Inverted Logic of Shareholder Capitalism

Since the onset of the shareholder primacy era in the 1980s, CEOs of large public companies have bemoaned the fact that they have become slaves to quarterly earnings and short-term performance: deliver on the numbers or risk the wrath of activist investors and raiders waiting in the wings to acquire the firm in the name of shareholder value. Such "discipline," they say, often prevents them from making necessary investments for the long term and encourages expedient decision making that cuts off companies' proverbial noses to spite their faces. The result has been disinvestment in things that matter in favor of maximizing short-term earnings. Examples abound of corporations cutting back on R&D, negotiating cutthroat deals with suppliers, shelving strategies for new business development, outsourcing labor, and skimping on employee pay, all in the name of maximizing shareholder value.

Since peaking at around eight thousand in the mid-to-late 1990s, the number of corporations publicly listed on US exchanges began to steadily decline. By the second decade of the twenty-first century, only about *half* the number of companies were listed on the NYSE and NASDAQ compared to two decades prior. Because traditional initial public offerings (IPOs) are increasingly expensive and time-consuming, the IPO market has become heavily skewed toward large, later-stage corporations—companies able to afford the cost and deal with all the reporting requirements and expectations that come with a public exchange listing. The short-term demands of shareholder capitalism have taken their toll on the public equity market as well.[63]

Yet there is more to the capital market story of the past four decades than a simple decline in exchange-listed companies. In just the past few years, for example, Special Purpose Acquisition Companies (SPACs) have exploded onto the scene, accounting for the majority of new listings in 2021—about $100 billion of the $135 billion IPO market, with most listings being done on "over the counter" exchanges.[64] In fact, the number of nonexchange-traded public companies has more than *doubled* over the past decade. What accounts for this increase? Answer: the rise of *private equity*. But not so much the traditional "buy-out" variety of private equity made famous during the 1980s. Instead, the largest private equity managers are now rushing to meet investor demand for *growth and venture* plays, with a focus on tech-enabled firms. So, with more ventures and early stage companies able to raise money in private markets, it's easier to stay private longer.[65]

In fact, the private equity market has actually *tripled* in size over the past decade, from $2 trillion to over $6 trillion (compared with about $90 trillion for public equities). Like the traditional IPO market, private equity deal size has also increased, with the average deal exceeding $1 billion in 2021. Private equity's traditional focus on cost and efficiency is thus giving way to the realization that technology-enabled growth, disruption, and even sustainability are more potent drivers of value.[66] Investors are responding with trillions in new capital to fund insurgent innovators and incumbent players intent on bolstering their impact and competitiveness.[67]

As one might expect, early stage ventures have also become increasingly adept at spinning audacious stories about their company's growth potential and lofty social missions as justification for private equity and venture capital (VC) investment. Many of these ventures are eventually taken public (increasingly through the SPAC vehicle) with sky-high IPO share prices. Most, however, see their market values come crashing down once they encounter the "real world" of the public equities market. Witness the fate of high-visibility IPOs such as Uber, Peloton, and Etsy as examples. More recent SPAC-IPO collapses include Uphealth, 23andMe, and Blade Air Mobility.[68]

The story of WeWork, now dramatized in the Apple TV+ miniseries

"WeCrashed," is particularly illustrative.[69] A decade ago, amidst a jumble of startups all seeking to capitalize on the emerging "co-working" trend, entrepreneur Adam Neumann was able to elevate his venture above the rest. He passionately promoted his new company, WeWork, as the vehicle for building a "community that can change the world." In 2012, when the New York–based company was less than two years old, he self-assuredly asserted that WeWork would be "all over the country very, very soon." With a massive infusion of venture capital, WeWork was indeed expanding at a feverish pace. Neumann's audacious promises of becoming the "biggest office space provider in the world" were so compelling that venture capitalists could not shower enough money on the venture.

Rapid expansion became a self-fulfilling prophesy: with a war chest of capital, WeWork came to new towns, opened facilities near competitors, and undercut them on price, eventually driving them out of business—behavior reminiscent of the industrial tycoons of the nineteenth century. By the end of 2014, WeWork had raised more than half a *billion* dollars from VCs—all while losing approximately $6 million each month. The venture capital industry traded on fantasy—they all wanted to find the "next Zuckerberg."[70]

With the rise of shareholder capitalism in the 1980s, venture capital began to stray far from its roots in the 1950s–60s in much the same way that banking became unrecognizable compared to its postwar years. Back then, venture capitalists framed their profession as an elevated calling—they were not speculators but rather "midwives of innovation," as Charles Duhigg aptly put it.[71] In many ways, venture capital was the heart of America's economic strength, and it was thanks in good part to visionary financiers. VCs made money by identifying and supporting the most promising startup technologies and ideas, providing both funding and strategic advice to nascent entrepreneurs resulting in the Silicon Valley phenomenon and companies such as Fairchild Semiconductor, Genentech, Sun Microsystems, Compaq, and later Amazon and Google.

The VC industry has grown exponentially since the early days but has also become increasingly concentrated—with a few dozen firms now controlling hundreds of billions of dollars—and more avaricious, in search of the next "unicorn." Venture capitalism has transformed into speculative fever.[72] In recent decades, the gambles made by VCs have grown dramatically larger, enabling money-losing firms to get big fast by undercutting smaller (and often better run) competitors.

In the case of WeWork, there were obvious problems that should have concerned the VC investors on the company's board (for example, the company spent $60 million on a corporate jet). However, by 2019 WeWork had 528 locations in twenty-nine countries, had raised in excess of $12 billion, but was losing nearly $300,000 per *hour*. The "Holy Grail" was the IPO, when everyone could get cashed out at many multiples of their original investment. Morgan Stanley, for example, estimated that WeWork could go public at a valuation of more than *$100 billion*.

In the end, however, the fantasy crashed and burned. Neumann was forced to step down as CEO and more than twenty-four hundred employees were laid off. The coronavirus pandemic presented both problems and opportunities for WeWork. The company restructured and went public via a SPAC company, BowX, valued at $9 billion; by February 2022, WeWork was valued at just $5 billion—a far cry from the sky-high valuations of just a few years before.[73]

Charles Duhigg concludes that "VCs seem to now embody the cynical shape of modern capitalism, which too often rewards crafty middlemen and bombastic charlatans rather than hardworking employees and creative businesspeople."[74] The collapse of crypto exchange startup FTX and its charismatic founder, Sam Bankman-Fried, is the most recent—and egregious—case in point: he sold investors on the pipe-dream that FTX would "change the world" by empowering the little guy and sticking it to the big, established financial players. His stated commitment to "effective altruism" justified his extraction of massive wealth in the short term, making him an overnight billionaire, at least on paper. The 2022 collapse of the exchange, however, left investors holding the bag, making FTX the latest poster child for such startup overreach.[75]

There seems to be something terribly wrong with this picture: Shareholder capitalism seems to have completely *inverted* the logic of investment and business performance. Startups funded with private equity invest *real money* to grow the companies of the future. Shouldn't their executives and boards be held accountable to demonstrate the viability of their business concepts and produce realistic business plans for the future? While some investors are perhaps willing to gamble their money on a pipe dream, most would probably prefer the chance to realize a real return on their investment within a reasonable time frame. To the extent that societal impact and environmental sustainability are keys to such strategies, entrepreneurs should demonstrate them through actual performance—or at least show a trajectory to profitability in the not-too-distant future. In other words, in the *primary capital market*, there should be discipline imposed to demonstrate business viability within some reasonable (not short-term) time frame.

But once a company goes public—after the IPO—it has entered a new realm. Public stock trading is a *secondary market*—it does not value new capital raised but rather the trading of existing equity among shareholders of already established companies; it simply provides an exit for the primary (private) investors who took the actual risk when the companies were being built and makes it possible for retail (public and institutional) investors to participate in the market. In fact, even though it was a record year for IPOs in 2021, with over $100 billion in new listings, equity issues were still swamped by share buybacks, which hovered around $1 *trillion*.[76]

Given their detachment from real investment, the drivers of share price in the public (secondary) market are therefore, by definition, entirely *socially constructed*—they are little more than narrative "myths." There is nothing sacred or preordained about quarterly earnings, return on equity, and price-earnings ratios. The idea that short-term profits and earnings growth are the best metrics for determining share price is nothing more than a convention—an imagined reality that has become deeply embedded into the routines of the financial sector—and hard-wired into the system through innovations such as high-speed trading. Business schools and MBA programs have created and perpetuated this convention for the past four decades by preaching the Friedman Doctrine and the gospel of shareholder primacy. But as we saw in Chapter 3, this artifice is really nothing more than a house of cards, supported by questionable theory and assumption-driven mathematical models from the academic field of financial economics.[77]

Like any narrative or social construction, therefore, it can be changed—transformed into something more conducive to the long-term well-being of society. Once companies graduate to the level of issuing public stock, shouldn't they be treated more like *institutions*, the way they were back in the 1950s and 1960s? The time has come to establish a new set of conventions—and metrics—when it comes to valuing public companies and their performance. No one questions that companies need to be profitable to be sustainable; that goes without saying. To create the positive societal impacts that should be expected of public companies, profitability is necessary . . . but not nearly sufficient.

Reinventing the Financial Infrastructure

Efforts to reform the capital and financial infrastructure to better reflect societal impact and value date all the way back to the nineteenth century but have ramped up significantly over the past half-century in response to the age of shareholder capitalism. As Laura Asiala and Neil Hawkins note in their thought-provoking piece "System Change Is Harder Than It Looks," system transformation seldom happens through a "big bang" but rather is enabled over time by a set of smaller changes—what they call "system shifts"—that set the stage for larger transformative change.[78] A sudden dam burst is a bad way to let a river run free—it results in catastrophic damage downstream. It is better to gradually build up pressure behind the dam while simultaneously protecting and preparing downstream communities, before allowing the dam to be breached.

Serious efforts to shift the financial system began in the 1960s in the form of socially responsible investing, with financiers using "negative screens" to create investment portfolios free of activities such as tobacco production, nuclear power, or involvement in the South African apartheid regime. More proactively managed funds focusing on social or environmental performance soon followed in the 1980s and 1990s, led by social investing pioneers such as Domini Social Index, KLD, Winslow Capital Management, and Trillium Asset Management.[79]

In 1997, the Coalition of Environmentally Responsible Economies launched the Global Reporting Initiative (GRI) out of the need for greater corporate transparency about sustainability and to establish the first reporting guidelines. As demand grew, GRI was spun off as an independent NGO in 2002 and established the first global standards for sustainability reporting—a practice that has become all but required for corporations over the past twenty years.[80] The Sustainability Accounting Standards Board was then formed in 2011 with a mission of establishing industry-specific standards for corporate reporting on ESG issues, helping companies to establish and report such metrics.[81] Then in 2015, the Financial Stability Board established the industry-led Task Force on Climate-Related Financial Disclosures, which developed a comprehensive protocol for disclosures on climate-related financial risks and opportunities that has since been adopted by over thirteen hundred of the world's largest companies.[82]

The terms "sustainability" and "ESG" have now come to mean different things to different people, although ESG factors are generally considered to be that subset of all sustainability issues that matter to investors. The US Securities and Exchange Commission is currently working to determine what corporate disclosures regarding ESG should be required, particularly regarding climate risk, while the European Union enacted the Corporate Sustainability Reporting Directive in 2022, establishing the world's most comprehensive ESG reporting framework. Political battle lines have been drawn in the US, however, with an anti-ESG campaign coming from the political right opposing consideration of climate action, DEI, and social issues in investment decisions.[83]

The Dow Jones Sustainability Indices were first launched in 1999, creating a family of indices evaluating the sustainability performance of thousands of companies traded publicly. Since then, several other commercial and nonprofit ESG ratings providers have emerged, including MSCI, Sustainalytics, Moody's, ISS, and S&P Global. Such ESG ratings have become essential data for investment firms in screening companies for their various sustainability-oriented funds. Indeed, by 2020, there were nearly five hundred actively managed funds in the US alone that included ESG criteria in their prospectuses.[84] Efforts are also under way by the International Sustainability Standards Board and others to consolidate these various ratings into a single global standard.[85]

Despite recent opposition, ESG investing has experienced exponential growth, with fully one-third of assets under management now invested using some form of ESG screen. This is clearly a positive trend. Yet ESG investing is really more about impression management than it is driving positive impacts in the real world: ESG ratings do not generally measure whether a highly rated company is an actual leader in reducing negative impacts or taking steps to build a more just and sustainable world through their business. What the ESG ratings do reflect is a company's exposure to industry-specific material ESG *risks* and how well a company is positioned to manage those risks. In other words, ESG ratings are designed to protect investors from risk in the current business, not redefine the meaning of value to encourage eco-innovation or social inclusion.[86]

The removal of Tesla from the S&P 500 ESG Index in May 2022 is a case in point. S&P claimed that Tesla had "fallen behind its peers," attributing its removal to risks associated with recent claims of racial discrimination and poor working conditions at the company's Fremont, California, factory, among other factors. Yet, as GreenBiz's Joel Makower observed, the removal came just two weeks after Tesla released its annual *impact* report. That report revealed that the company was making huge strides in its efforts to help accelerate the world's shift to renewable and sustainable energy through both its vehicle and solar-and-storage businesses. The report also detailed the company's diversity efforts (62 percent of the US workforce belonged to underrepresented groups). Needless to say, Elon Musk did not take kindly to the S&P's decision, tweeting that "ESG is the devil incarnate."[87]

To make matters worse, ESG investing also depends heavily on computer algorithms—automated "data scrapping" from the web—to populate the ESG ratings used to select stocks. Such an approach has enabled the asset class to scale quickly but calls into question both the validity and reliability of the resulting portfolios, let alone their presumed ability to produce "alpha"—above average returns—for investors. Some researchers have even concluded that ESG investing is little more than a ruse to build reputation for listed firms and assuage guilt for investors.[88]

Debate also rages on about whether it is feasible—or even desirable—to translate societal impacts (such as social equity, carbon neutrality, biodiversity) into a *single* measure of impact represented in dollars and cents through "impact-weighted accounting."[89] Advocates argue such new accounting practices are key to redefining value and evaluating total impact as the new "bottom line."[90] Skeptics argue that proposals for monetizing corporate sustainability impacts are alluring, but impractical and potentially perilous, given that we turn the evaluation of impacts over to a relatively small group of experts and analysts.[91] Furthermore, given the variety of assumptions that often feed into such efforts and the uncertainties surrounding them, there is a real danger that such an approach would cause users to "luxuriate in false precision," thereby obliterating the nuanced understanding about impacts desired.[92]

Setting aside the question of whether all impacts can be meaningfully translated into dollar terms, most would agree that we can and must pay attention to a *broader* set of performance metrics and indicators. Rather than fixating on purely financial metrics such as earnings growth, earnings per share, or return on equity, we can and must begin to value public companies based on metrics such as the following:

- *Future Cash Flows.* Shareholder capitalism's preoccupation with quarterly earnings is actually a poor indicator of company performance since earnings per share (EPS) can be manipulated by short-term actions that create no real value (such as stock buybacks). McKinsey finds that 70–90 percent of a given company's value is related to cash flows expected three or more years out. If the vast majority of firms' value depends on results more than three years in the future, then management preoccupation with what's reportable three months from now is downright counterproductive. Finance theory has long preached the importance of future cash flows as a key basis for valuing companies. Perhaps it is time to go back to the future?[93]

- *Reinvestment.* Share repurchase to boost short-term EPS has become a trademark of shareholder capitalism. On average, stock buybacks and dividends together account for more than 90 percent of the profits of public corporations, with some companies spending virtually all of their profits (and more) on share repurchase for the purpose of driving up the share price in the short term. Looking forward, share repurchase done purely to boost short-term stock price should carry a financial penalty—or be prohibited altogether.[94] Instead, we should value what percentage of a company's profits are *reinvested* in building new sustainable capabilities as drivers of long-term value creation.[95]

- *Innovation.* A key focus for reinvestment as a driver of long-term value is R&D and new product development. Tools such as Real Options can help incorporate learning in making a series of decisions regarding investments for the future. Looking forward, we should measure and track the percentage of profits reinvested in R&D and the percentage of sales from new products as two key indicators—and drivers—of long-term value creation.[96]

- *Pay Equity.* Shareholder capitalism has driven executive compensation to astronomical levels while leaving the rank-and-file employees in the dust, with hourly wages often insufficient for basic life support. Never before has the difference between CEO and front-line worker compensation been so great—in excess of 350:1. The first step in achieving pay equity is to tie executive compensation to long-run societal and financial goals rather than to short-term stock price. The second step is to upgrade the pay of *everyone* in the company such that the lowest-paid worker still receives a *living* wage, as defined by the cost of basic necessities in the region where they live plus some margin for disposable income and savings.[97]

- *Company Footprint.* Companies have increasingly taken responsibility for the environmental impacts of their own facilities and operations. In the years ahead, however, it will become essential to measure, track, and improve *all impacts* associated with the company's activities, from deep in the supply chain to the end of life of the company's products. The aim should not be to just reduce the scale of the negative impact; instead, the goal should be to become "net positive"—solving bigger societal problems than any new problems and unintended consequences they create.[98]

- *System Change.* Companies should demonstrate a real commitment— through dedicated investment and effort—to the building of partnership ecosystems needed to bring about system-level change and redesign in areas of direct material relevance to the firm's future. This means becoming actively engaged in the sort of "positive advocacy" that can actually reorient systems—business education, financial systems, tax policy, subsidy regimes—such that they encourage and enable the sustainable and inclusive economy of the future.[99]

- *Payment of Income Taxes.* Tax avoidance costs governments an estimated $500–600 billion per year and undermines both the capacity of the public sector and the quality of key public services and infrastructure. Paying taxes is thus one of the most important ways in which corporations contribute to society; paying their fair share of taxes should therefore be a stated policy—and operating reality—for companies, for which they are held accountable in financial markets.[100]

Big asset management firms like BlackRock are increasingly using their sizable holdings to force public companies to address societal issues including climate change, circularity, diversity, equity, and inclusion. Still, business leaders are faced with the challenge of demonstrating that societal contribution and environmental sustainability do not damage short-term profitability, limiting their initiatives to those capable of passing the "win-win" test.

The question therefore remains: How do we change the game for aspiring IPOs and large corporations already in the public market? How can public corporations be incentivized to become the societal *institutions* they really need to be? How can companies be recognized and rewarded financially for creating long-term societal value rather than being kept on the short leash of shareholder primacy? For that, we need a completely new public equity market with a fundamentally different philosophy and objective function. The time has come to finally blow up the dam. Enter the Long-Term Stock Exchange.

Tomorrow's Markets: The Long-Term Stock Exchange

Eric Ries became a Silicon Valley icon a decade ago after integrating the lessons he learned as an entrepreneur into a systematic approach for launching new ventures—the Lean Startup method.[101] As Ries became a star on the entrepreneurship circuit, he met thousands of businesspeople, from early stage startup entrepreneurs to managers in companies poised to go public. One theme seemed to unite them all: innovators dreaded going public because it meant losing control of the company to short-term-focused shareholders and activist investors, thereby compromising the company's mission and purpose. This fear is actually reflected empirically in the fact that the number of American companies listed on public stock markets actually dropped by *half* between the mid-1990s and the early 2010s, paralleling the rise of shareholder primacy.[102]

Increasingly, entrepreneurs were choosing to delay going the IPO route—or shunning it altogether—so as to avoid being punished for investing in anything other than actions to drive short-term performance. Ries began calling these short-term expectations "vanity metrics"—accounting measurements that can be easily manipulated to convey short-term performance but have no bearing on the long-term health or profitability of the enterprise. The vanity metrics he most often cited? Earnings per share and return on equity.[103]

While Ries was just starting to connect the dots on the negative effects of short-termism on innovation and entrepreneurship, some companies had been trying to avoid the pressure of public equity markets for years.[104] In the tech space, for example, Facebook, Google, and Amazon all went public by issuing dual-classes of stock, with the founders owning the class of stock with the majority of the voting rights to retain control. Other more established corporations, like Unilever, with a commitment to long-term sustainability, declared that they were no longer going to issue quarterly earnings guidance, creating a stir in investment circles. Of course, neither of these approaches has been entirely effective: the tech companies have been assailed as private dictatorships with little if any public accountability, and Unilever and other sustainability-focused corporations have received even *greater* scrutiny from activists the moment their stock has failed to outperform on conventional short-term metrics.

When Ries was drafting the epilogue for his book, he introduced the idea of creating a new public equity market to overcome these shortcomings:

> Part of the reason established companies struggle to invest consistently in innovation is intense pressure from public markets to hit short-term profitability and growth targets. Mostly, this is a consequence of accounting methods we have developed for evaluating managers which focus on the kinds of gross "vanity" metrics [discussed earlier]. What is needed is a new kind of stock exchange, designed to trade in the stocks of companies that are organized to sustain long-term thinking. I propose that we create a Long-Term Stock Exchange.[105]

When Ries was finalizing his draft manuscript, colleagues and editors advised him to "kill that crazy part about the Long-Term Stock Exchange" because in their view, the idea was so radical that it would ruin the credibility of the rest of the book. The book was published nonetheless with the section about the exchange intact. And after four years of no action by others, Ries decided to tackle this challenge himself.[106]

LAUNCHING THE NEW EXCHANGE

The Long-Term Stock Exchange (LTSE) was founded as a for-profit company in 2015 with the mission of creating a new US stock exchange to reshape the incentives for a new generation of public companies focused on societal contribution and the long term. The aim was to challenge and (eventually) dislodge incumbents like the New York Stock Exchange by reshaping incentives to change how corporations think about the long term and the conduct of capitalism itself.[107]

With an initial round of $3 million from "friends and family" and another capital raise of $15 million, Ries assembled a team of more than twenty finance executives, software engineers, and attorneys to build the organization—and the new exchange. Ries initially envisioned operating the new exchange in a way that followed all the usual SEC rules but with several new features unique to the LTSE, such as the following:

- Tenured shareholder voting power; shareholders' votes would be proportionally weighted by the length of time the shares had been held to discourage speculation, short-termism, and day-trading

- Mandated ties between executive pay and long-term performance to counter the prevailing practice of tying executive compensation to short-term stock price

- Disclosing what long-term investments companies make and the identities of long-term shareholders or investors so as to encourage a better match between the motivations of companies and investors[108]

As Chief Communication Officer Steven Goldstein quipped, there would be "no bull" and "no opening bell." Designing and building such a trading system out of whole cloth was no small task: the exchange would need to execute trades seamlessly, but also enable the tracking of how long an investor had owned the stock, show whether executive pay was staying within prescribed bounds, and see what investments in innovation were being made by the company.[109]

The LTSE took a major step forward in March 2016 with the release of a free, fully featured management tool called *Captable.io*, which provides a snapshot of who holds what securities of a company at a given time. Companies use cap tables to determine how much equity to award to employees, how much equity to sell to investors, and which investors are needed to approve major company actions. Cap tables help startups and early stage businesses manage and plan equity in preparation for IPOs. Cap tables can also be used, however, by established public companies interested in differentiating long-term investors from speculators, short-sellers, and activist raiders.[110]

The LTSE thus enables both company founders or executives and investors focused on the long term to become better aligned with one another. Investors in LTSE-listed companies are asked to commit to the long term so companies know that enough of their stock is owned by investors willing to stick by them through ups and downs. In return, founders and executives are held accountable to the commitments they make by both the board and the long-term investors.[111]

The LTSE filed with the Securities and Exchange Commission for registration as a national securities exchange in November 2018 and was approved in May 2019, to the surprise of some: the "incumbents" in the industry are massive—the NYSE has twenty-eight hundred companies listed with a market value of $28 trillion, for example, and could have offered stiff resistance. Indeed, the existing major players—NYSE, NASDAQ, and high-frequency trading firms—had previously opposed the creation of the Investors Exchange, which was designed to combat predatory high-speed trading.[112]

Nonetheless, the LTSE was formally launched in September 2020.[113] Companies that list their shares on the exchange are required to publish a series of policies that focus on long-term value creation and are designed to provide shareholders with insight into the ways that companies operationalize their commitment to the long term. Specifically, companies must publish policies regarding the following five LTSE principles:

1. *Long-Term Stakeholder Policy.* Companies must explain how they operate their business to consider all the stakeholders critical to long-term success, including employees, communities, and the environment.

2. *Long-Term Strategy Policy.* Companies must explain how they prioritize long-term strategic decision making and long-term success, including a discussion of what time horizon the company considers long term, metrics used to measure long-term success, and how the long-term strategy is implemented throughout the organization.

3. *Long-Term Compensation Policy.* Companies must explain how they align executive compensation and board compensation with their long-term strategy and success metrics.

4. *Long-Term Board Policy.* Companies must explain how they engage the board of directors in their long-term focus, including whether they have

explicit oversight of and responsibility for long-term strategy and success metrics.

5. *Long-Term Investor Policy.* Companies must explain how the company engages with long-term investors.[114]

Initially, two companies were listed on the LTSE—Asana and Twillo— effective early 2021. The exchange is in conversation with other companies in the IPO pipeline, but it is quite possible that few will want to take the risk of being the first to agree to these new requirements as part of their IPO process. The problem is akin to the age-old chicken-and-egg conundrum: everyone would love such an exchange but no one wants to go first.

CREATIVELY DESTROYING THE PUBLIC EQUITY MARKET

The challenge thus becomes how the LTSE reaches the "tipping point"—the critical mass of listed companies needed for a functioning market of buyers and sellers to emerge, all focused on long-term performance and a sustainable future. It would seem that the LTSE is the natural platform upon which to take the burgeoning number of B Corps public. Indeed, most successful B Corps resist going public for all the same reasons that Eric Ries cited for creating the LTSE in the first place.

To take the pressure off the need for rapid generation of listed companies, the LTSE has instead adopted a "dual listing" strategy, meaning that initially LTSE companies must *already* be listed on one of the established stock exchanges— NYSE or NASDAQ, for example. Thus, in addition to focusing on IPOs for smaller, purpose-driven B Corps, the LTSE also has the opportunity to become the exchange of choice for those large, public corporations that have committed to long-term sustainability but have thus far paid the price when it comes to activist investors and take-over pressures on the established, shareholder-primacy-driven stock exchanges.

Indeed, a few early mover corporations in the sustainability space— Unilever and Danone, for example—have been exploring the possibility of becoming certified as B Corps and changing their legal status to benefit corporations. But since the B Corp process was originally designed for smaller, privately held companies, the complexity has held back the rapid conversion of large, global companies to B Corp status.[115] The LTSE therefore provides a viable alternative for large public companies—both to "signal" their intentions regarding sustainability and to institutionalize and celebrate such strategies by listing on an exchange that literally *requires* it.

Listing large, public corporations committed to sustainability and the long term would also help the LTSE deal with one of its other major challenges—getting institutional investors to decide the new exchange is worth their attention. Ries says they have already signed up a number of institutions as part of its investor coalition—a signup list of supporters. The key is to convert moral support into actual commitments to trade on the new exchange and participate in IPOs.[116]

The LTSE's Captable.io service also helps large public companies committed to sustainability realize one of their most critical objectives when it comes to corporate governance—transforming the portfolio of investors from those focused on short-term returns to those committed to serving all the stakeholders and generating long-term value. By taking B Corps public and enabling the world's existing large public corporations to accelerate their transformations to long-term sustainability, the LTSE could then establish sufficient critical mass to justify converting to a *sole listing* exchange while also rejuvenating the IPO market—and reorienting it to one focused on societal value. Ultimately, the dream would be for the LTSE to *creatively destroy* the current public equities market, meaning that the large incumbents—NYSE, NASDAQ—either change or die.

In many ways, the challenge—and opportunity—faced by the LTSE is similar to that of the Sustainable Innovation MBA program discussed in the previous chapter: starting over with a "clean sheet" enables transformational sustainability to be incorporated into the core DNA of the exchange. Yet, just as incumbent business schools and MBA programs have adopted "saddlebags" of sustainability as their means for dealing with the existential world challenges we face (without changing their core curricula), so too has the financial sector promoted ESG investing as its means for coping without changing the underlying logic of short-termism and shareholder primacy in equity and capital markets. As Clayton Christensen has shown us, truly disruptive innovators almost always start small and gradually work their way from the fringes to the core of incumbent markets. The Long-Term Stock Exchange could prove to be such a bellwether for the coming transformation to sustainable capitalism—the "David" that ultimately slays the Goliath of shareholder primacy.

Getting to the Root of the Matter

If we are to redefine the meaning of value, business leaders will have to muster the courage to raise their voices in support of the kind of government and institutions we need to realize the next capitalist reformation. Indeed, sustainable capitalism will require the right policies and institutions as well as a supportive culture if capitalists are to co-create a sustainable future. This means reinvigorating the classical sense of *virtue* propounded by Adam Smith and the American Founders. As they taught us, pursuing one's self-interest is not the same thing as behaving selfishly. Selfishness is narrow and may pay off in the short term. Behaving with virtue, however, is more encompassing and pays much bigger dividends in the longer term—by promoting meaning and enabling a shared prosperity that makes everyone better off. It is high time that business self-interest once again serves to promote the common good—the creation of long-term, inclusive, and sustainable value.[117]

Business virtue means advocating for political candidates who stand not only for democracy but also for the crucial role that business can and must play in driving the sustainability transformation. Political advocacy need not mean pouring more money into campaign contributions. In fact, Adam Smith and the Founders would be appalled by the massive corporate campaign spending that has come to pervade politics over the past forty years: they would have considered it the essence of corruption. True virtue on the part of sustainable capitalists will instead mean advocating strongly for campaign finance *reform*—getting money out of politics—and political candidates who stand for the same![118]

Business leaders must also reconcile their companies' lobbying efforts with their sustainability agendas. No longer can we tolerate corporate duplicity, when one part of the company works hard to promote aggressive sustainability goals and strategies while another part of the same company lobbies to defeat the very public policies and regulations that would accelerate these stated goals and strategies. Companies must become champions for the *policy* reforms and innovations needed to drive system change and usher in a new objective function for capitalism. Business leaders must ensure that their companies speak with one unified voice that is unambiguously focused on the promotion of sustainable capitalism—what the University of Michigan's Thomas Lyon calls "corporate political responsibility."[119]

Given the fraught nature of political and legislative advocacy, however, growing numbers of companies are banding together with civil society to build partnership ecosystems to confront directly a range of sustainability *issues and problems*. The issues selected are usually determined by what is material for a given company or industry—deforestation, climate change, regenerative agriculture, species loss, water scarcity, gender bias, racism, human rights, and inequality, to name a few. Unlike policy advocacy, such issue-based collaborations can be organized voluntarily, across political jurisdictions—particularly important when problems are transboundary or global in scope.

To achieve the truly deep change required, however, the *root causes* of our current crisis must be confronted—the *institutional infrastructure* underpinning shareholder primacy and market fundamentalism. As we have seen, such institutions include the business schools that have embedded shareholder primacy in the minds of a generation of graduates and the stock exchanges that have embraced short-termism as the driving force for value creation.

It is useful to visualize these three strategies for system change (issue management, policy advocacy, and institutional change) as being akin to the three parts of a tree—crown, trunk, and roots (Exhibit 8.2). The *crown* of the tree is composed of an ever-changing flourish of branches, flowers, and fruits—like the myriad issues and problems related to democracy and sustainability that proliferate in today's world. For companies, trying to manage these issues is bit like playing "whack-a-mole:" Just when you think you have one under control, another one pops up somewhere else forcing your attention to be redirected to it. Issue

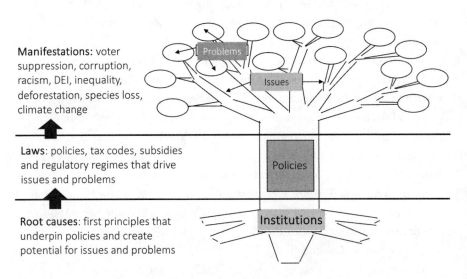

Manifestations: voter suppression, corruption, racism, DEI, inequality, deforestation, species loss, climate change

Laws: policies, tax codes, subsidies and regulatory regimes that drive issues and problems

Root causes: first principles that underpin policies and create potential for issues and problems

Exhibit 8.2. **Leverage Points for Fundamental System Change**

management treats symptoms rather than underlying causes; they are manifestations of the institutional misalignments and policy blunders that create them.

More than fifty years ago, Anthony Downs wrote a classic piece on the perils of issue management titled "Up and Down with Ecology: The Issue-Attention Cycle."[120] Downs noted that issues and problems have the unfortunate tendency to suddenly leap into prominence, remain there for a short time, and then—though still largely unresolved—fade from public attention. Issue management is therefore an inherently *reactive* game, making it difficult for companies to establish a consistent and principled set of positions and commitments. Companies that ride the wave of the issue-attention cycle—taking stands on controversial issues at the vanguard of social activism as they emerge—have increasingly experienced backlash and even retaliation from certain political officials who have labeled them as "woke." The retaliation against Disney by the governor of Florida for their public stance against the so-called "Don't Say Gay" law provides a particularly vivid example of this phenomenon.[121]

A focus on policy allows companies to be more purposeful when it comes to system change. Like the *trunk* of the tree, it is more solid and enduring—and requires a long-term commitment by companies to realize actual change. Policies and laws that govern the conduct of capitalism include such things as corporation law, property rights, antitrust, bankruptcy, tax codes, labor laws, safety nets, subsidies, and regulatory regimes. Policies are supposed to function as the "guardrails"—the basic rules upon which the legitimacy of capitalism depends. Unfortunately, outmoded or retrograde policies are also important *drivers* of issues and problems in society—from pollution and climate change to inequality and racial bias.

Policy advocacy on the part of business will be important when it comes to realizing the next capitalist reformation. There can be little doubt, for example, that a price on carbon, elimination of perverse subsidies, and changes in corporation law to require broader accountability would fundamentally change the game, enabling sustainable and long-term strategies by companies to become the norm.[122] Elizabeth Warren's proposed Accountable Capitalism Act, for example, could be one such catalytic force. The Act includes the following provisions:

- Large American corporations (with more than $1 billion in annual revenues) must obtain a federal charter as a "United States Corporation," which obligates company directors to consider the interests of all corporate stakeholders.

- The boards of such US corporations must include employee participation, with no fewer than 40 percent of its directors selected by the corporation's employees.

- Directors and officers of such US corporations are prohibited from selling their company shares within five years of receiving them or within three years of a company stock buyback.

- US corporations must obtain shareholder and board approval for all political expenditures.

- A US corporation that engages in repeated and egregious illegal conduct may have its charter revoked.[123]

Unfortunately, the ideologically charged and partisan nature of today's politics, along with continued lobbying by many industry incumbents to block such policies, makes their passage unlikely in the immediate future. It is for this reason that a focus on institutional change—the root causes of our predicament—is so important. Like the *roots* of a tree, the institutions that underpin capitalism determine how it grows, from the education of future business leaders to the objective function of the game defined by the financial infrastructure and equity markets.

For business leaders, then, it is important to decide how to allocate time, attention, and resources when it comes to the crown, trunk, and roots of the system change tree. We must locate the leverage points that will most effectively drive larger system transformation and double down on them. Donella Meadows wrote what is now widely recognized as the classic piece on leverage points—where to intervene in a system for maximal effectiveness. Her top two leverage points: (1) The *mindset or paradigm* out of which the system arises, and (2) The *goals* of the system.[124]

Neoliberals and advocates for market fundamentalism focused on education and thought leadership (law and economics, think tanks) and investment logic (agency theory and efficient markets) to drive the shareholder capitalism revolution—the mindset and paradigm and the goals of the system. Advocates for sustainable capitalism must now focus on a similar set of leverage points to drive deeper system transformation. I believe the key leverage points are *business education* (mindset and paradigm) and *equity markets* (goals of the system). We must concentrate our energy on creatively destroying the America-style, finance-driven MBA that has swept the world in the last forty years, with devastating consequences. We must also concentrate on creatively destroying the capital market infrastructure—particularly the public equity markets—to focus on and reward sustainable and long-term performance. Disruptive innovations like the Sustainable Innovation MBA program and the Long-Term Stock Exchange represent models for such transformation, models that must be scaled and spread in the years ahead if we are to avoid calamity.

Putting the Horse Back in Front of the Cart

For the past forty years, shareholder capitalism has demanded that before incumbent business leaders can seek to "change the world," they must *first* satisfy investors: "At the end of the day, it's about quarterly earnings and the stock price if you are a public company," as the saying goes. The time has now come to flip this script: to generate above-market returns, business leaders must henceforth *first* make clear how they change the world for the better—through credible and demonstrably positive contributions to society through their businesses.

From now on, *all* public companies will need to be "benefit" corporations, just like they were during the eras of market and welfare capitalism in the nineteenth and twentieth centuries. It is high time to put the proverbial horse back in front of the cart. To make this happen, we must overthrow shareholder primacy and redefine value to mean profit in service of societal purpose. Yet individual companies can only push this capitalist reformation so far on their own. *Systemic* unsustainability can only be redressed by transforming the *infrastructure*—the policies and institutions—that underpin and enable capitalism itself.[125]

The time is now to assemble the resources and persuasive power of business to accelerate innovation around two key leverage points—to make sustainable business education and long-term investing the institutional norms rather than the exceptions—and to do so within the next decade. Achieving such dramatic change will require unprecedented focus, resource commitment, and dedication by a set of change agents, just as we saw with capitalists including Olin, Scaife, Volker, Coors, Bradley, and the Koch brothers when it came to market fundamentalism. We must build a new "coalition of the willing" composed of businesspeople, financiers, entrepreneurs, civil society leaders, deans and higher education leaders, public figures, media representatives, and thought leaders dedicated to ushering in the new operating system for sustainable capitalism. We call on sustainable capitalists everywhere to step up to help drive the transformation around these two key leverage points so that the third capitalist reformation becomes reality before it is too late.[126]

How will we know when we have succeeded in ushering in the new age of sustainable capitalism? The answer: when we have redefined the meaning of value such that business schools promote and the financial infrastructure rewards companies that serve all stakeholders and demonstrate a commitment to sustainability and the long term. How will we know when we have changed the objective function of capitalism? When politicians are no longer able to curry favor with voters by short-term stock market stimulation through regulatory rollbacks and tax cuts for the rich. They, like corporate leaders, will have to deliver truly long-term, sustainable value in order to be recognized by the voters (and equity markets) of the future. When that day comes, we will have rediscovered what Louis Brandeis knew over a century ago—that a "good" market economy is one that is truly purpose-driven.

DENOUEMENT

What Does It All Mean?

"People can't just give up a story . . . you have to have another story to
be in. . . . Not just stopping things. Not just less of things. People need
something positive to work for. . . . They need more than a vision of
doom. They need a vision of the world and of themselves that inspires
them."

DANIEL QUINN, *ISHMAEL*

When the first edition of my earlier book, *Capitalism at the Crossroads,* appeared in 2005, some readers commented that the title of the book seemed a
bit "over the top." I don't hear those comments anymore. I still use the book in
my teaching with nary a whiff of concern that it is now nearly twenty years old.
However, the fact that a book about sustainable business written in the early
2000s is still relevant today is frankly terrifying. Our lack of transformational
change in the ensuing years means we have now pushed well past planetary
boundaries, almost certainly making the earth less hospitable for human habi-
tation in the decades ahead. We passed the proverbial *crossroads* a while ago and
are now at a point where we must dramatically *change course.* Nothing short of
transformation will suffice.[1]

While I have stressed the usefulness of learning from history in this book,
the reality is we live in a time unlike any other in human history. In fact, there
is growing scientific consensus that we have literally entered a new geological
age—the Anthropocene—a time when human activities, rather than natural events, have become the main drivers of earth system changes. The International Commission on Stratigraphy's Anthropocene Working Group has

actually voted to formally designate the Anthropocene as an official chrono-stratigraphic unit.[2]

While there is debate about the exact starting date of the Anthropocene, there is little disagreement that the last half century—the age of shareholder capitalism—has been a time of accelerating disruption, contributing signifi-cantly to the breaching of planetary boundaries and widening of inequality. Some have even suggested renaming the new epoch the *Capitalocene*, to high-light the responsibility of capitalism, rather than humanity in general, for pre-cipitating our current predicament.[3] Assigning blame and forecasting doom, however, do us little good. As I've argued in this book, what we need now more than anything else is a new *story*—a new "myth" to live and work by, one that offers the possibility of a sustainable future. And given the outsized role of shareholder capitalism in creating the problem over the past four decades, the new myth must necessarily be accompanied by a new *operating system* for busi-ness.

The New Mythmakers

In his deeply reflective book *The Purpose of Capital*, sustainable finance pioneer Jed Emerson offered much-needed historical context for our current quandary. He observed that business and finance have become obsessed in recent years with the *how*—the quantifiable elements of strategy, execution, and metrics—while losing sight of the *why*—the positive contributions business might seek to make in the world. He concluded that if we are to get past our current financial-ized myopia, we must "rediscover the *mythology* of impact." I could not agree more.[4]

I have spoken frequently throughout this book about the need for a new myth. It is likely, however, that most people today probably first think of "myth" according to its second definition: "a widely held but false belief or idea." It is indeed a sign of the times that myth today connotes something false, phony, or fantastical. My reference to myth in this book, however, relates to its *primary* definition: "a traditional story, especially one concerning the early history of a people or explaining some natural or social phenomenon, and typically in-volving supernatural beings or events."[5] Yuval Harari referred to such myths as *narratives*—the legends and ideologies that enable humans to bond and cooper-ate in relationship-rich groups. Capitalism desperately needs a new myth in this sense—a compelling new story, one that brings out our "better angels" rather than encouraging only our "animal spirits."[6]

Humans have always been mythmakers. As historian Karen Armstrong so convincingly argued in her book *A Short History of Myth*, we are meaning-seeking creatures. Humans, unlike other sentient creatures, are aware both of their own mortality and the plight of their brethren and have always sought a story—a myth—to help them come to terms with both. Humans also possess imagination, the faculty that inspires the development of both myth and religion. There has always been an important element of "spiritual make-believe" when it comes to myth: What if there were more to life than what meets the eye? Myths help us cope with the human condition and are "true" only insofar as they are *effective* in giving us hope and enabling us to live more fully. As Armstrong puts it, myth enables people to "get beyond the chaotic flux of random events, and glimpse the core of reality."[7]

Early hunter-gatherer myths affirmed that people belonged to the earth in the same way as the animals, rocks, rivers, and trees. Agricultural myths continued to venerate the earth, but also taught that Mother Earth was not a gentle, forgiving goddess. In the book of Genesis, for example, the loss of the primordial paradise was experienced as a "falling" into agriculture, forcing man to wrest a living from the soil by the "sweat of his brow." The advent of urban settlement brought even more insecurities. The myth of the Great Flood, for example, reflected a growing concern about civilization's fragility and impermanence.[8]

Humans began to see themselves as independent agents, separate from the gods and creation. Such separation resulted in a growing spiritual vacuum and sense of disillusion. By the eighth century BC, such malaise was becoming widespread, stimulating the emergence of prophets and sages, and the beginning of "religion" as we now know it: Confucianism and Taoism in China, Buddhism and Hinduism in India, and monotheism in the Middle East (Judaism and later, Christianity and Islam).[9]

In premodern societies mythology was indispensable in helping people make sense of the world. Myth was core to their societies' story and cosmology; it was truly "embedded." The Renaissance was sparked by the translation of ancient Greek and Arabic works into Latin beginning in the thirteenth century, accelerated by the invention of the printing press in 1440. With its focus on philosophy and art, however, the Renaissance did not constitute a radical departure from the premodern ways of myth. Indeed, the natural world was still viewed as exhibiting a "World Soul," or *anima mundi*.[10]

Beginning with the Enlightenment in the seventeenth century, however, the world embarked on the creation of a new kind of civilization built upon reason and hard fact. In the early days of the Enlightenment, science was still steeped in religion, framed as "natural philosophy" with the presumption of "final causes"—the belief that nature and the universe were divine creations and therefore sacred. Francis Bacon's seventeenth-century vision for a "New Atlantis," for example, was really a systematic scientific plan for discovering nature's hidden secrets (as designed by God), with the intent of improving the human condition. Remember also that Adam Smith was a professor of moral philosophy; the discipline of economics would only come into being a century later after science had been fully secularized.[11]

The Enlightenment was a time of great upheaval, with plagues and famines happening alongside the rise of Protestantism, rationalism, and empiricism. As the Industrial Revolution gathered steam, philosophers including Goethe and Kant began to cast doubt on the idea of final causes, in favor of secondary or "material" causes. Immanuel Kant stated it clearly in his 1790 treatise *Critique of Teleological Judgment*: "The freedom of man's causality enables him to adapt physical things to the purposes he has in view." The eighteenth century thus ushered in the modern age of rational secularism and simultaneously introduced the enveloping sense of *darkness* that came to characterize modernity. Natural philosophy gave way to the thoroughly secularized methodology of *positivism*, effectively stripping the cosmos of all inherent purpose.[12]

In the nineteenth century, philosopher Friedrich Nietzsche proclaimed that God was "dead." In many ways he was right: without myth, ritual, or cosmology, the sense of the sacred dies. As Mircea Eliade elaborated in *The Sacred and the Profane*:

> For non-religious men of the modern age, the cosmos has become opaque, inert, mute; it transmits no message, it holds no cipher. . . . Their religious experience is no longer open to the cosmos. In the last analysis, it is a strictly private experience.[13]

As science became secularized then, it created an intellectual environment increasingly *hostile* to myth. Instead of dependence on the gods—and the vicissitudes of nature—like premodern civilizations, modern (capitalist) societies were now premised on science, the drive for "improvement," and technological progress.[14] Mythical thinking fell into disrepute, dismissed as useless and outmoded. Intuitive modes of thought were denigrated in favor of the pragmatic and logical spirit of scientific rationality. Unfortunately, we soon discovered that rationality and reason do not quench the human thirst for meaning: *logos* is no substitute for *mythos*.[15]

Anomie, despair, and alienation came to pervade modern capitalist societies. The Age of Reason and rationality began witnessing the eruption of unreason and irrationality. The witch craze of the sixteenth and seventeenth centuries, for example, showed that scientific rationalism could not hold the dark forces of the mind at bay. As Karen Armstrong observed, the witch craze was really a "collective demonic fantasy"—one that led to the torture and execution of thousands of men and women.[16]

The twentieth century only multiplied such demonic fantasies and accelerated irrationality and nihilism—Hitler's death camps, Hiroshima and Nagasaki, Bosnia, and September 11, not to mention the storming of the US Capitol on January 6, 2021. It seems all too clear that rationality and reason do not quench the human thirst for meaning. Without a powerful mythology to elevate people's hopes and explain their unconscious fears, they tend to rationalize their fears into "facts," and they end up "looking for purpose in all the wrong places."[17]

Since the Enlightenment and the advent of capitalism, we have thus experienced a sort of "great reversal" (Exhibit D.1). For premodern societies *myth* was the primary organizing principal for the people: ritual, legend, cosmology, and gods were sacred and truly "embedded" in everyday life. Myth helped people cope with their own mortality and showed them how to live and behave. Economic activities (*trading*) such as bartering and exchange with other communities were more transactional—"profane" activities that were not seen as central to the society's identity or well-being.

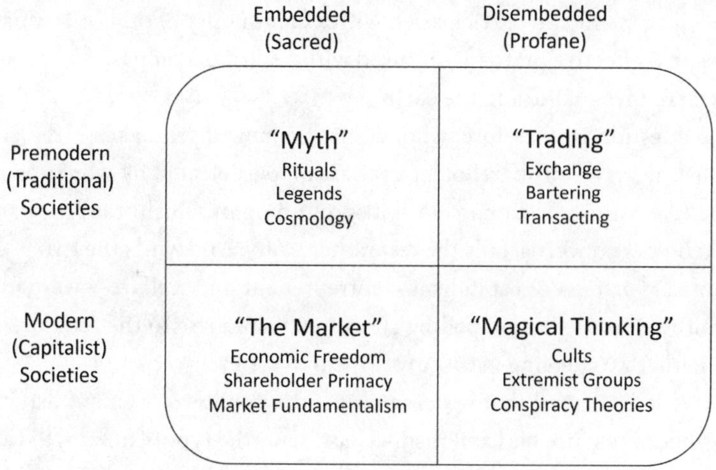

	Embedded (Sacred)	Disembedded (Profane)
Premodern (Traditional) Societies	"Myth" Rituals Legends Cosmology	"Trading" Exchange Bartering Transacting
Modern (Capitalist) Societies	"The Market" Economic Freedom Shareholder Primacy Market Fundamentalism	"Magical Thinking" Cults Extremist Groups Conspiracy Theories

Exhibit D.1. The Great Reversal

In contrast, modern (capitalist) societies flipped the script by making economic activities—the *market*—the primary organizing principal, elevating it in some cases to mythical, even sacred, status. The "invisible hand" and the "magic of the market" became like providential deities; the market possessed a wisdom that individuals, companies, and governments did not.[18] Indeed, during the era of shareholder capitalism, such market fundamentalism was elevated to quasi-religious status by some true believers. Unfortunately, the mythology of the market has not served the psychic needs of the vast majority of the people. As organized religion has continued its long-term decline, many peoples' thirst for myth and meaning has turned to the less-than-sacred domains of online affinity groups or worse—cults, extremist groups, and conspiracy theories. Rather than something sacred, *magical thinking* has now become a derogatory term used to describe those who believe in patently unhinged narratives and "alternative facts." We now lack a compelling story that can provide the sense of meaning and purpose that people desperately seek.

In short, we need a new myth that helps people to face up to the realities of our unprecedented historical situation. As Karen Armstrong noted, we have to "find ways of doing what religion—at its best—has done for centuries: build a sense of global community, cultivate a sense of reverence and 'equanimity' for all, and take responsibility for the suffering we see in the world. We are all, religious or secularist alike, responsible for the current predicament of the world."[19] Some try to enter the dimension of myth through art, literature, music, or even drugs, in pursuit of "flow" or transcendence. Yet, effective myth must be more than mere personal experience or contemplation; it must lead to active engagement and participation with a community of others. History also teaches that effective myths are infused with a spirit of compassion and a belief in the sacredness of life and the earth.[20]

The question is, therefore, who will be the new mythmakers? The current capitalist narrative of shareholder capitalism, perpetrated by would-be mythmakers like Milton Friedman, with its grounding in selfishness and dismissal of stakeholder concerns, fails the test rather badly. And while the two previous "reformed" versions of capitalism—entrepreneur and welfare—were important, neither included a compelling story that would rise to the level of "myth" since neither was dealing with truly *existential* crises.

I have long argued that *sustainability*—the countermovement driving the emergence of sustainable capitalism—represents the type of new myth we need for the twenty-first century.[21] Sustainability provides the ethics through which science can once again be applied appropriately to technology, including a reverence for the earth and life in all its guises. Sustainability represents a sort of new religion of scientific self-restraint based upon ecological awareness, systems thinking, and social inclusion; it captures the essence of the classical idea of "virtue" discussed in the first three chapters; it provides the basis for redefining the "objective function" for business; it provides the "North Star" for transforming the infrastructure of capitalism—the systems and institutions that support the enterprise system itself; it even provides the moral clarity needed to answer the question posed by Louis Brandeis over a century ago: what is the *purpose* of the economy?

The fundamental difference between this new myth and myths of old is that humankind itself now disposes of the powers of life or death over other species, whereas in earlier schemes, only the god(s) could withdraw the license to live. While that is an awesome responsibility, to say the least, it is one that we can ill-afford to ignore. As Herman Daly made clear nearly a half-century ago, capitalism has *never* been truly sustainable—it has always been premised on *quantitative* growth through the exploitation of physical and/or human resources. We must now transform the underlying logic of capitalism—toward a focus on *qualitative* growth and social inclusion.[22]

My University of Vermont colleague Jon Erickson makes this distinction crystal clear in *The Progress Illusion*.[23] He contrasts the conventional logic of *environmental* economics with that of the emerging field of *ecological* economics. The former adheres to neoclassical traditions by seeking to place an economic value on "natural capital" and measure the marginal societal costs and benefits of projects, thereby framing environment as an element of the larger economy. In contrast, ecological economics begins with the understanding that all economic activity is embedded in the environment—that the economy is a *wholly-owned subsidiary* of nature—not the other way around. The next decade or two thus represent a crucial time in human history—our species will either innovate and make the transformation to a truly sustainable way of working and living, or nature will have its way—which could get ugly.

Advocates for social equity and racial justice have also long recognized the importance of addressing deeper systemic and structural issues—including capitalism and the values that underpin it—in the quest for a more just society. Indeed, the modern civil rights movement had its origins in Black advocacy before the Civil War, calling for a fundamental reordering of American society. Martin Luther King Jr. focused increasingly on these broader issues in his later years.[24]

In fact, in his last presidential address to the Southern Christian Leadership

Conference in 1967, King called upon his followers to honestly face the fact that the civil rights movement must address itself to the question of restructuring the whole of American Society:

> There are 40 million poor people here. And one day we must ask the question, why are there 40 million poor people in America? When you ask that question, you begin to question the capitalistic economy. . . . We are called upon to help the discouraged beggars in life's marketplace. But the day must come to see that an edifice which produces beggars needs restructuring.[25]

Sustainable capitalism, with its focus on environmental regeneration and social equity, might thus represent the myth—the "new story," as Ed Freeman calls it—that people so desperately need.[26] Sustainable business can fill people with a sense of purpose and meaning, enabling employees to become deeply engaged with something that is bigger than themselves. The larger capitalist reformation can bring with it a quest worthy of peoples' full professional and emotional commitment: lifting the poor and serving the needs of everyone while simultaneously regenerating the natural capital that supports all life on Earth . . . and making money to accelerate the pace!

In Chapter 3, I noted the importance of having both an *intellectual catalyst*—the source of conceptualization for transformation—and a *motive force* for bringing about larger capitalist reformations. I believe the big idea of "sustainability"—environmental regeneration and social inclusion—provides the intellectual catalyst for dealing with our current predicament. The question is where the motive force will come from. In past capitalist reformations, government has played a critical role in redefining the rules of the game in favor of greater participation, equity, and social responsibility. For this to happen again, given the polarized state of our politics, business leaders will have to rise to the challenge—by becoming champions not only of corporate transformation, but also of government reinvention and system redesign.

Given the fact that business is currently the most powerful institution on the planet, with its outsized role in driving the existential crises we now face, it represents the key *leverage point* for changing the conversation—not only about the economy, but also with the wider set of cultural, political, educational, and social institutions that perpetuate the current economic era of shareholder capitalism. Business leaders must thus step up to the plate to serve as the catalysts for the wider societal transformation needed to make sustainable capitalism the reality before it is too late.

Thirty years from now, people may look back and realize that those who stepped up to lead the transformation to sustainable capitalism in our time became the new mythmakers for the twenty-first century—latter-day versions of Adam Smith or Louis Brandeis. To make this new story truly "stick," however, we also need a new *operating system*—a playbook business leaders can use to make the myth come to life. In the following, I pull together the learnings and lessons from the foregoing chapters and distill them into a set of principles and an integrative framework for business action. My hope is that this synthesis provides the basis for such a new capitalist operating system—one that helps accelerate, and eventually realize, the next capitalist reformation.

A New Operating System for Sustainable Capitalism

Part I of the book distilled four lessons from the history of capitalism that provide important principles and a philosophical foundation for the new capitalist operating system:

1. *Self-interest is not the same thing as selfishness.* Adam Smith's original concept of self-interest in a market economy was grounded in virtue and ethical behavior. As he wrote in his 1759 work *The Theory of Moral Sentiments*, "The wise and virtuous man is at all times willing that his own private interest be sacrificed to the public interest."

   BOTTOM LINE: Think how to create wins for all the stakeholders, not just yourself.

2. *Managerial stewardship trumps the "principal-agent" problem.* Rather than subscribing to the caricature of managers as shirking opportunists requiring control by principals (as advocated by agency theory), it is possible to lead companies in such a way that agents' interests actually *align* with those of the principal, as well as other key stakeholders, in the pursuit of a larger purpose.

   BOTTOM LINE: Aim to fulfill employees' need for purpose by engaging them in a company quest worthy of their commitment.

3. *Monopolies are disabling to markets.* The societal benefits of market economies are largely nullified when capitalists are allowed to concentrate in-

dustries and wealth. Preserving competition in markets is thus crucial to the economy of a good society.

BOTTOM LINE: Temper the urge for market power with the desire to see the business continually challenged and rejuvenated with new ideas and innovations.

4. *Reinvestment is key to a sustainable capitalism.* Just as competition is a prerequisite for a market economy to function properly, so too is reinvestment of profits by successful businesses. Extraction of profits by executives and shareholders is anathema to the very idea of capitalism and leads to inequality, inertia, regulatory capture, and minority rule.

BOTTOM LINE: Place the long-term interests of the company's core operational stakeholders—customers, suppliers, and employees—ahead of short-term financial payoffs for shareholders.

As important as these lessons are, Chapter 4 also made clear that neither of the previous two capitalist reformations dealt with the scale and scope of the challenges we now face—never before has capitalism actually threatened the life support system of the planet. The fact that we have now crossed the Rubicon into the Anthropocene means we are in uncharted territory and are literally in a race against time.

Twenty-five years ago, I developed a strategy tool called the "Sustainable Value Framework."[27] The framework linked the societal challenges of global sustainability directly to the creation of shareholder value by the firm. It was designed to help identify "win-win" strategies that contribute to a more sustainable world while simultaneously driving financial performance. It helped business leaders make the *business case* for sustainability. It was a valiant effort to reconcile the challenges of sustainability with the financial demands of shareholder capitalism.

As important as this framework has been, the Great Race demands that we now move beyond shopworn notions like proving the "business case" for sustainability. The business case has really been nothing more than a subtle requirement that anything "sustainable" not violate the Milton Friedman Doctrine of short-term profit maximization, forced upon us by the dictates of shareholder primacy. We must shed the tyranny of the business case and realize that looking forward, sustainability *is* the business. We must redefine value to mean profit *in service* of societal purpose. Positive impact thus becomes the *objective function* (rather than the side benefit) of sustainable capitalism.

To hasten such transformation, Parts 2 and 3 of this book emphasized that business leaders must dedicate themselves to change both within their own companies *and* at the larger system level. No longer will the articulation of sustainability goals, adoption of "best practices," and third-party certification suffice. Articulation of an authentic societal purpose operationalized through transformational investment in innovation and serious Business Aspirations will become the watchword. Companies will also be challenged to articulate a larger Corporate Quest aimed at challenging—and changing—the systems and institutions that threaten or constrain their ability to truly transform.

The "Sustainable Capitalism Framework" (Exhibit D.2) distills the prescriptions from these chapters into a single unified framework for companies committed to putting positive impact first. It provides a tool for firms and business leaders to move beyond sustainability hyperbole and "greenwish" through corporate transformation and larger system redesign. The exhibit integrates the development of Aspirations and Quests discussed in Chapter 5 with the necessity of fully engaging and aligning the entire organization found in Chapter 6. The exhibit also emphasizes that the firm must commit to transforming not only its own "House," but also the larger system in which it operates, especially the institutions that define the capitalist game itself, as discussed in Chapters 7 and 8. Through the development of one or more Corporate Quests, the firm chooses which leverage points in the larger system it commits to help redesign.

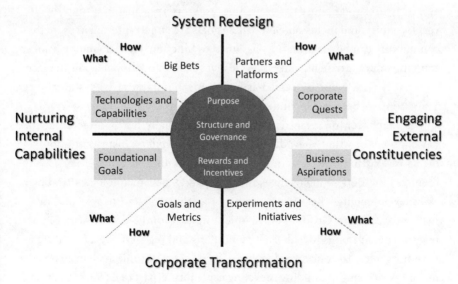

Exhibit D.2. The Sustainable Capitalism Framework

The vertical axis in Exhibit D.2 reflects the firm's need to undertake simultaneous action at the two levels mentioned above—corporate transformation and system redesign. Gone are the days when companies could focus only on themselves and their value chains. System redesign is essential if the objective function of capitalism and the corporation is to be successfully redefined. The horizontal axis then reflects the firm's need to nurture and build internal organization skills, technologies, and capabilities while simultaneously infusing the firm with new perspectives and capacities by engaging with outside stakeholders, constituencies, and partners.

Juxtaposing these two dimensions produces a matrix with four distinct yet interrelated quadrants, which taken together enable the larger transformation process. Each quadrant is divided into two components: the "what" (strategic elements) and the "how" (actions and initiatives). The items in the center represent the "glue" that holds the four quadrants together: a compelling societal *Purpose* provides the "North Star" that aligns the four elements with a *Governance Board*, which includes the necessary expertise in sustainability guiding the way, along with a system of *Rewards and Incentives* that seek to engage everyone in the organization.

The lower-left quadrant is composed of those elements internal to the firm that are prerequisite for any larger corporate transformation effort to be credible. *Foundational Goals* underpin everything the firm seeks to achieve when it comes to sustainability and societal impact, and include goals for such things as energy use, greenhouse gas emissions, water use, raw material sourcing, diversity, equity, and inclusion. Since these goals are largely internal in scope, accountability can be meaningfully assigned to functional leaders in operations, sourcing or procurement, and HR. Without such Foundational Goals in place, a company risks being perceived as hypocritical, if its external sustainability aspirations are betrayed by underperformance in its own facilities.

The upper-left quadrant is also focused internally but is directed at the development of wholly new *Technologies and Capabilities* instead of improvements to existing ones. Building entirely new skills and capabilities usually requires "Big Bets"—major investments in R&D, new technologies, and new skill development—that enable the firm to deliver on its Purpose and drive real system change. Griffith Foods, for example, committed to making Big Bet investments in things like alternative proteins and regenerative agriculture as part of its quest to transform the larger food system. Similarly, Novelis made major investments in building recycling capability as part of its quest to drive a closed-loop aluminum system.

The lower-right quadrant, in contrast, extends the focus externally, to the firm's entire value chain. Societally oriented *Business Aspirations* seek to lead customers, suppliers, and other key value chain stakeholders toward a future vision of true sustainability and inclusion. Business Aspirations enable the firm's purpose to come to life in the world, and they can *only* be realized through new business experiments and initiatives—new products, strategies, and business models—with business leadership held accountable. We saw such audacious Business Aspirations developed at firms including Interface, Dow, Seventh Generation, and Unilever, and explored the process for setting such Aspirations with our in-depth examination of Griffith Foods.

Finally, the upper-right quadrant widens the aperture beyond the firm's value chain to the larger system level. *Corporate Quests* are bigger than any single company. They seek to fundamentally transform an industry, policy, or institutional landscape through partnerships and collective action. Deciding where the best leverage points for system change reside is an important strategic decision for each firm. Some companies choose to focus on specific policy reforms (for example, subsidy regimes) while others concentrate on issues of salience such as climate change, deforestation, or inequality. As we saw in Part III, however, truly high-leverage Quests that address the root causes of our predicament include such things as the reinvention of business education and the redefinition of value in equity markets. Building the Partnerships and Platforms to drive these larger system redesigns represents one of the most important—and challenging—aspects of the next capitalist reformation.

Think of these four quadrants together as a portfolio. The challenge for company leaders is to decide which elements, actions, and initiatives to prioritize and how best to fund and manage them. To use this framework as a tool, assess the level of your company's capability for each of the four quadrants as (1) nonexistent, (2) emerging, (3) established, or (4) institutionalized. Unbalanced portfolios spell missed opportunity and vulnerability. A bottom-heavy portfolio indicates a strong corporate commitment to sustainability but insufficient attention to building the vision and partnership ecosystems necessary for broader system change. A top-heavy portfolio suggests an overemphasis on tomorrow's technology and systemic change to the detriment of functional excellence and business transformation. A portfolio skewed to the left side of the chart indicates an overly inward focus that could lead to myopia and ignore important external developments, perspectives, and prospective partners. Finally, a portfolio skewed to the right side, while highly transparent and externally engaged, runs the risk of being labeled "greenwish" because the underlying company operations and core technologies do not match the professed sustainability Aspirations and Quests.

With such a new operating system, we can redefine what it means to be a capitalist in the twenty-first century. The world faces existential challenges in the years ahead, calling for a new generation of enlightened businesspeople and corporations to step forward. Do we have what it takes to reinvent capitalism and the corporation once again?

Déjà vu All Over Again?

I began this book by noting that the current movement to "reimagine" capitalism is not the first time the economic system has undergone significant transformation. Indeed, capitalism has undergone *three* major cycles of transformation in its evolution, beginning with the fall of feudalism and the rise of mercantilism in the seventeenth century. Through it all, there has been a certain sense of déjà vu—that which goes around comes around again. Many of the challenges capitalism faces today—concentration of wealth at the top, monopoly power, environmental degradation, and toxic levels of inequality—have indeed been confronted before. So, while the scale and scope of the challenges we face today are unprecedented, I have sought to learn from history so that, as the saying goes, we are not doomed to repeat it. Remember that the Jungian principle of Enantiodromia teaches us that extreme one-sidedness builds up a tension, and the more extreme the position, the more easily it can shift to its opposite.

In October 1973, for example, the Organization of Petroleum Exporting Countries (OPEC) proclaimed an oil embargo against the US and other nations perceived as supporting Israel during the Yom Kippur War. The embargo sent shockwaves through the global economy, sending gas prices sky high. I was in college at the time and still have vivid memories of sitting in gas lines more than a block long. When the embargo ended in March 1974, the price of oil had risen nearly 400 percent—a "rhyme" of the 2022–23 spike in gas prices that resulted from pandemic-related supply chain disruptions and the Russian invasion of Ukraine. For an economy already suffering from prolonged slow growth *and* inflation ("stagflation"), however, the OPEC oil embargo was a devastating blow to America and contributed significantly to what came to be known as the "lost decade" of the 1970s.[28]

Enter Milton Friedman. On the heels of his famous 1970 article in *New York Times Magazine*, "The Social Responsibility of Business Is to Increase Profits," Friedman saw the OPEC oil embargo as an opportunity. Noted Friedman,

"Only a crisis, actual or perceived, produces change. When that crisis actually occurs, the actions taken depend on the ideas that are already lying around."[29] The Mont Pèlerin Society, which Friedman then chaired, had gained considerable momentum since its inception in 1947. It now boasted a well-funded group of think tanks, corporate donor support, and a program of policy prescriptions consistent with its neoliberal philosophy. The oil crisis and ensuing stagflation provided the opening for the neoliberals to assert themselves. And with the ascent to power of Ronald Reagan and Margaret Thatcher in the late 1970s, neoliberalism finally had the political champions it needed. And so, the era of market fundamentalism and shareholder primacy was born.

The countermovement to shareholder capitalism has now been gathering momentum for more than thirty years. While it is not as well-organized as the Mont Pèlerin Society, the concepts, values, frameworks, tools, and methods are now well developed under such banners as sustainable enterprise, regenerative capitalism, circularity, inclusive business, conscious capitalism, just transition, social entrepreneurship, impact investing, ESG, and economic democracy. More and more companies and business schools are rising to the challenge. To use Friedman's language, there are plenty of ideas already "lying around."

We live once again in a time defined by crisis. We have been shaken to the core by the coronavirus pandemic; experienced a precipitous economic meltdown; witnessed mass protests over racial injustice; watched entire regions burn while others were washed away by climate-change-driven fires and floods; endured an attempted coup d'état fueled by disinformation and magical thinking; witnessed a former president be criminally indicted; and the authoritarian coup de grâce—saw the Russian invasion of Ukraine in February 2022, bringing with it the specter of World War III.

So, the questions for our time are: Will *this* constellation of crises serve as the opening—the inflection point—to bring about the next capitalist reformation? Will today's crises be like the OPEC oil embargo and stagflation curse were for the rise of market fundamentalism? Will a new generation of sustainable capitalists—in concert with political, cultural, civil society, and educational leaders—seize the moment to usher in the age of sustainable capitalism? Will 2020 prove to have been an *Annus Mirabilis*?

My fervent hope is that this book helps stimulate those in positions of leadership to act—to become what racial justice champion Layla Saad calls "good ancestors."[30] Because only people like my granddaughters Mallison and Hazel will live to bear witness to the real denouement, yet to be written.

NOTES

Preface

1. Academic articles include Stuart Hart, "A Natural Resource-Based View of the Firm," *Academy of Management Review* 20 (1995): 986–1014; Stuart Hart and Gautam Ahuja, "Does It Pay to Be Green? An Empirical Examination of the Relationship Between Emission Reduction and Firm Performance," *Business Strategy and the Environment* 5 (1996): 30–37; Glen Dowell, Stuart Hart, and Bernie Yeung, "Do Corporate Global Environmental Standards Create or Destroy Market Value?" *Management Science* 46, no. 8 (2000): 1059–1074; and Ted London and Stuart Hart, "Reinventing Strategies for Emerging Markets: Beyond the Transnational Model," *Journal of International Business Studies* 35 (2004): 350–370. Practitioner articles include Stuart Hart, "Beyond Greening: Strategies for a Sustainable World," *Harvard Business Review*, January-February 1997, 66–76; C. K. Prahalad and Stuart Hart, "The Fortune at the Bottom of the Pyramid," *Strategy+Business* 26 (2002): 54–67; and Stuart Hart and Mark Milstein, "Creating Sustainable Value," *Academy of Management Executive* 17, no. 2 (2003): 56–69.

2. Stuart Hart, *Capitalism at the Crossroads* (Upper Saddle River, NJ: Wharton School Publishing, 2005). Other books include Ted London and Stuart Hart, eds., *Next-Generation Business Strategies for the Base of the Pyramid: New Approaches for Building Mutual Value* (Upper Saddle River, NJ: Financial Times Press, 2011); and Fernando Casado and Stuart Hart, eds., *The Green Leap to an Inclusive Economy* (Oxford, UK: Routledge, 2019).

3. http://www.e4sw.org; http://www.bopglobalnetwork.net/.

4. University of Michigan's Erb Institute Dual Master's Program, University of North Carolina Kenan-Flagler Business School's Center for Sustainable Enterprise, Cornell University Johnson School of Management's Center for Sustainable Global Enterprise, and, most recently, the University of Vermont Grossman School of Business's Sustainable Innovation MBA Program.

5. The University of Vermont's Sustainable Innovation MBA Program is the excep-

tion. It is one of the few clean-sheet redesigns of the MBA currently in existence. Much more about this in Chapter 7.

6. Sanjay Sharma and Stuart Hart, "Beyond 'Saddle Bag' Sustainability for Business Education," *Organization & Environment* 27, no. 1 (2014): 10–15.

7. Duncan Austin, "The Towering Problem of Externality-Denying Capitalism, 2022, https://bothbrainsrequired.com/wp-content/uploads/2022/10/2022-10-Towering-Problem-Essay-Final.pdf.

8. World Bank, *State and Trends of Carbon Pricing 2022* (Washington, DC: World Bank, 2022).

9. https://www.forcegood.org/frontend/img/2021_report/pdf/final_report_2021.

10. Austin, The Towering Problem, 3.

11. Some of those exceptions, such as Novelis and Griffith Foods, are discussed in depth in this book.

Acknowledgments

1. Jed Emerson, *The Purpose of Capital* (San Francisco: Blended Value Press, 2018), 273.

2. D. A. Schön, *The Reflective Practitioner: How Professionals Think in Action* (Oxford, UK: Routledge, 2017).

Prologue

1. Gale Christianson, *Isaac Newton* (Cambridge, UK: Cambridge University Press, 2005).

2. William Federer, "Great Plague of London and Sir Isaac Newton," *The Patriot Post*, 2020, https://patriotpost.us/.

3. No, I am not comparing myself to Sir Isaac Newton here. Read on!

4. Willis Harmon, *Global Mind Change* (San Francisco: Berrett-Koehler, 1998).

5. Marjorie Kelly, *The Divine Right of Capital* (San Francisco: Berrett-Koehler, 2003).

6. Carl Jung, "Symbols of Transformation," in: *Collected Works*, 5, 2nd ed. (Princeton, NJ: Princeton University Press, 1956).

7. My thanks to Jed Emerson, and his book *The Purpose of Capital* (San Francisco: Blended Value Press, 2018) for this wonderful metaphor.

8. Business Roundtable Statement on the Purpose of the Corporation, 2019, https://www.businessroundtable.org/business-roundtable-redefines-the-purpose-of-a-corporation-to-promote-an-economy-that-serves-all-americans; Davos Manifesto, 2019, https://www.weforum.org/agenda/2019/12/why-we-need-the-davos-manifesto-for-better-kind-of-capitalism/

9. See Vivek Ramaswamy, *Woke, Inc.: Inside Corporate America's Social Justice Scam* (New York: Center Street, 2021).

10. John Maynard Keynes, *The General Theory of Employment, Interest and Money* (London: MacMillan, 1936).

11. Abraham Lincoln, First Inaugural Address, Washington, DC, March 4, 1861.

12. Ed Chambliss, *A One-Legged Stool: How Shareholder Primacy Has Broken Business* (New York: Best Friend Brands, 2022).

13. R. Edward Freeman, Kirsten Martin, and Bidham Parmar, *The Power of AND: Re-*

sponsible Business Without Trade-Offs (New York: Columbia Business School Publishing, 2020).

14. Joseph Bower, Herman Leonard, and Lynn Payne, *Capitalism at Risk: How Business Can Lead* (Boston: Harvard Business Review Press, 2020).

15. David Kotz, *The Rise and Fall of Neoliberal Capitalism* (Cambridge, MA: Harvard University Press, 2017).

Chapter 1: Capitalism's Heritage

1. Bernie Sanders, *It's OK to Be Angry About Capitalism* (New York: Crown, 2023); Ramaswamy, *Woke, Inc.*

2. William Steffens, et al., "Planetary Boundaries: Guiding Human Development on a Changing Planet," *Science* 15 (January 2015); Duncan Austin, "Win-Win in the Time of Net Zero: A Tale of Two Sustainabilities," 2021, https://bothbrainsrequired.com/wp-content/uploads/2021/05/2021-05-17-Win-Win-in-the-Time-of-Net-Zero-Final-16pp.pdf.

3. John Elkington, *Green Swans* (New York: Fast Company Press, 2020); Rebecca Henderson, *Reimagining Capitalism in a World on Fire* (New York: Hachette Group, 2020); Paul Polman and Andrew Winston, *Net Positive* (Boston: Harvard Business Review Press, 2021); Philip Kotler, *Confronting Capitalism* (New York: American Management Association, 2015); Andrew Winston, *The Big Pivot* (Boston: Harvard Business Review Press, 2014); James O'Toole, *The Enlightened Capitalists* (New York: HarperCollins Publishers, 2019); Dominic Barton, Dezso Horvath, and Matthias Kipping, eds., *Re-Imagining Capitalism* (Oxford, UK: Oxford University Press, 2016), David Grayson, Chris Coulter, and Mark Lee, *All In: The Future of Business Leadership* (London: Greenleaf,2018).

4. John McMillan, *Reinventing the Bazaar: A Natural History of Markets.* (New York: W.W. Norton, 2002).

5. Jeffrey Sachs, *The End of Poverty: Economic Possibilities for Our Time* (New York: Penguin, 2006).

6. Daron Acemoglu and James Robinson, *Why Nations Fail: The Origins of Power, Prosperity, and Poverty* (New York: Currency, 2012), 183–184.

7. Peter Frankopan, *The Silk Roads: A New History of the World* (New York: Vintage Books, 2015).

8. Jurgen Kocka, *Capitalism: A Short History* (Princeton, NJ: Princeton University Press, 2016).

9. Ibid.

10. Patrick Wyman, *The Verge: Reformation, Renaissance, and Forty Years That Shook the World* (New York: Hachette Book Group, 2021).

11. Ibid.

12. Ibid, 26.

13. Acemoglu and Robinson, *Why Nations Fail.*

14. Wyman, *The Verge.*

15. Nell Irvin Painter, *The History of White People* (New York: W.W. Norton, 2010).

16. Jay Coen Gilbert, "Larry Fink, Tucker Carlson, David Brooks and the Call for a

Capitalist Reformation," 2019, https://www.forbes.com/sites/jaycoengilbert/2019/01/24/larry-fink-tucker-carlson-david-brooks-and-the-call-for-a-capitalist-reformation/.

17. Fernand Braudel, *The Wheels of Commerce*. (Berkeley, CA: University of California Press, 1992).

18. Kocka, *Capitalism*.

19. Ellen Meiksins Wood, *The Origins of Capitalism* (New York: Verso Books, 2017).

20. Ibid.

21. Sven Beckert, *Empire of Cotton: A Global History* (New York: Vintage Books, 2014).

22. Of course, the educated had long known that the earth was round. The Greek mathematician Eratosthenes actually measured its circumference in 240 BC.

23. Francis Bacon, *Novum Organum* (London: Clarendon Press, 1878).

24. As quoted in Thomas McCraw, ed., *Creating Modern Capitalism* (Cambridge, MA: Harvard University Press, 1997), 3.

25. Ibid.

26. Edward Chancellor, *The Price of Time: The Real Story of Interest* (New York: Atlantic Monthly Press, 2022), 27.

27. Stuart Hart, "The Environmental Movement: Fulfillment of the Renaissance Prophesy," *Natural Resources Journal* 20, no. 3 (1980): 501–522.

28. McCraw, *Creating Modern Capitalism*.

29. Joseph Schumpeter, *Capitalism, Socialism and Democracy*, 3rd ed. (New York: Harper, 1950), 209.

30. Now, of course, we are awash in capital and nature has become scarce, so the original logic no longer applies. See, for example, Paul Hawken, Amory Lovins, and Hunter Lovins, *Natural Capitalism* (Boston: Little, Brown, 1999); Peter Barnes, *Capitalism 3.0* (San Francisco: Berrett-Koehler, 2006).

31. Walter Prescott Webb, *The Great Frontier* (Austin: University of Texas Press, 1964).

32. Elkington, *Green Swans*.

33. Kenneth Pomerantz, *The Great Divergence: China, Europe, and the Making of the Modern World Economy* (Princeton, NJ: Princeton University Press, 2000).

34. Bhu Srinivasan, *Americana: A 400-Year History of American Capitalism* (New York: Penguin, 2017).

35. Ibid.

36. Nick Robbins, *The Corporation That Changed the World* (London: Pluto Press, 2006).

37. Ibid.

38. Yuval Noah Harari (2015) *Sapiens: A Brief History of Humankind* (New York: HarperCollins, 2015).

39. Srinivasan, *Americana*.

40. Beckert, *Empire of Cotton*.

41. Robbins, *Corporation That Changed the World*, 22.

42. Ibid.

43. John Keay, *The Honorable Company* (London: HarperCollins, 1993).

44. Ramkrishna Mukherjee, *The Rise and Fall of the East India Company* (New York: Monthly Review Press, 1974).

45. Acemoglu and Robinson, *Why Nations Fail*.

46. Mukherjee, *Rise and Fall of the East India Company*.

47. Mike Davis, *Late Victorian Holocausts* (London: Verso, 2002), 294.

48. P. J. Marshall, *East India Fortunes: The British in Bengal in the Eighteenth Century* (Oxford, UK: Clarendon Press, 1976), 33.

49. Beckert, *Empire of Cotton*.

50. Jon Wilson, *India Conquered: Britain's Raj and the Chaos Empire* (London: Simon & Schuster, 2016).

51. Beckert, *Empire of Cotton*.

52. Robbins, *Corporation That Changed the World*.

53. Sushil Chaudhuri, *From Prosperity to Decline: 18th Century Bengal* (New Delhi: Manohar, 1999).

54. Much more about this problem below.

55. Robbins, *Corporation That Changed the World*, 83–84.

56. Jesse Norman, *Edmund Burke: The First Conservative* (New York: Basic Books, 2013).

57. Robbins, *Corporation That Changed the World*.

58. Jawaharial Nehru, *The Discovery of India* (London: Meridian Books, 1946), 248.

59. Robbins, *Corporation That Changed the World*.

60. Iqbal Quadir, "Bangladesh: The Booster Rocket," *Innovations* 24 (January 2022).

61. Beckert, *Empire of Cotton*.

62. Ibid, xv–xvi.

63. Robbins, *Corporation That Changed the World*, 61.

64. Colin Woodard, *American Nations: A History of the Eleven Rival Regional Cultures of North America* (New York: Penguin Books, 2022).

65. Robbins, *Corporation That Changed the World*.

66. Ibid.

67. Ted Nace, *The Gangs of America: The Rise of Corporate Power and the Disabling of Democracy* (San Francisco: Berrett-Koehler, 2005).

68. Robbins, *Corporation That Changed the World*.

69. Adam Smith, *An Inquiry into the Wealth of Nations* (New York: Modern Library, [1776]; 2000), Book 1, Chapter XI, 287.

70. Benjamin Friedman, *Religion and the Rise of Capitalism* (New York: Alfred Knopf, 2021).

71. Ultimately, however, it was recognized that virtue *alone* was insufficient. As a result, the Constitution included "checks and balances" to curb the emerging influence of what the Founders called "factions" and today we would call partisanship. See Thomas Ricks, *First Principles: What America's Founders Learned from the Greeks and Romans and How That Shaped Our Country* (New York: HarperCollins, 2020).

72. For an insightful discussion of how Adam Smith's two very different works actually mesh around the idea of reciprocal exchange and relationships, see Russ Roberts, *How Adam Smith Can Change Your Life* (New York: Penguin, 2014); Paul Collier, *The Future of Capitalism* (New York: HarperCollins, 2018).

73. Matthew Stewart, *Nature's God: The Heretical Origins of the American Republic* (New York: W.W. Norton, 2014); John Locke, *Second Treatise on Civil Government* (1689).

74. David Korten, *The Post-Corporate World: Life After Capitalism* (San Francisco: Berrett-Koehler, 1999).

75. Douglas Rushkoff, *Life Inc.: How the World Became a Corporation and How to Take It Back* (New York: Random House, 2009).

76. Adolph Berle and Gardiner Means, *The Modern Corporation and Private Property* (New York: Harcourt Brace, 1932).

77. Ricks, *First Principles*, 277.

78. Ibid.

79. Nace, *Gangs of America*, 74.

80. Beckert, *Empire of Cotton*, 81.

81. Ibid.

82. McCraw, *Creating Modern Capitalism*, Chapter 9, "American Capitalism."

83. Alfred Chandler, *The Visible Hand: The Managerial Revolution in American Business* (Boston: Harvard Belknap, 1977).

84. Woodard, *American Nations*.

85. Srinivasan, *Americana*, Chapter 4.

86. Beckert, *Empire of Cotton*.

87. Ibid.

88. Sven Beckert and Seth Rockman, *Slavery Capitalism: A New History of American Economic Development* (Philadelphia: University of Pennsylvania Press, 2016).

89. Ibid.

90. Srinivasan, *Americana*.

91. Stephen Cohen and J. Bradford Delong, *Concrete Economics: The Hamilton Approach to Economic Growth and Policy* (Boston: Harvard Business School Press, 2016).

92. Ibid.

93. Jon Erickson, *The Progress Illusion: Reclaiming our Future from the Fairytale of Economics* (Washington, DC: Island Press, 2022), 42.

94. Henry George, *Progress and Poverty: An Inquiry into the Cause of Industrial Depressions and the Increase of Want with Increase of Wealth, the Remedy* (London: K. Paul, Trench and Company, 1879).

95. Erickson, *The Progress Illusion*.

96. Ibid.

97. Andreas Malm, *Fossil Capital: The Rise of Steam Power and the Roots of Global Warming* (London: Verso, 2016).

98. Ibid.

99. Nell Irvin Painter, *Standing at Armageddon* (New York: W.W. Norton, 1987); Alan Trachtenberg, *The Incorporation of America* (New York: Farrar, Straus and Giroux, 2007).

100. Mark Twain and Charles Warner, *The Gilded Age: A Tale of Today* (New York: American Publishing Company, 1873).

101. As quoted in David Korten, *When Corporations Rule the World* (San Francisco: Berrett-Koehler, 1995), 58.

102. As quoted in Nace, *Gangs of America*, 118.

103. Trachtenberg, *Incorporation of America*.

104. Nace, *Gangs of America*.

105. Ibid.

106. Korten, *When Corporations Rule the World*, 58.

107. Painter, *Standing at Armageddon*.

108. Ibid, 44.

109. Srinivasan, *Americana*.

110. Ibid, 218.

111. Painter, *Standing at Armageddon*.

112. Trachtenberg, *Incorporation of America*.

113. McCraw, *Creating Modern Capitalism*, Chapter 9, "American Capitalism."

114. Charles Morris, *The Tycoons* (New York: Owl Books, 2005).

115. Thom Hartmann, *The Hidden History of Monopolies* (Oakland, CA: Berrett-Koehler, 2020).

116. Rushkoff, *Life Inc.*.

117. Ibid.

118. See Morris, *The Tycoons*.

119. Matt Stoller, *Goliath: The 100-Year War Between Monopoly Power and Democracy* (New York: Simon & Schuster, 2019).

120. As cited in Amy Klobuchar, *Antitrust: Taking on Monopoly Power from the Gilded Age to the Digital Age* (New York: Alfred Knopf, 2021), 180–181.

121. Webb, *The Great Frontier*.

122. Klobuchar, *Antitrust*.

123. Karl Polanyi, *The Great Transformation* (New York: Beacon Press, 1944); John Kenneth Galbraith, *American Capitalism: The Concept of Countervailing Power* (Boston: Houghton Mifflin, 1952).

124. The sixteenth amendment, establishing a national income tax, was approved by Congress in 1909 and ratified by all the states in 1913.

125. Tim Wu, *The Curse of Bigness: Antitrust in the New Gilded Age* (New York: Columbia Global Reports, 2018).

126. Stoller, *Goliath*.

127. Ibid.

128. Melvin Urofsky, *Louis D. Brandeis: A Life* (New York: Penguin, 2009).

129. As quoted in Wu, *Curse of Bigness*, 39–40, 77.

130. Painter, *Standing at Armageddon*.

131. Stoller, *Goliath*.

132. Berle and Means, *Modern Corporation and Private Property*.

133. Ibid.

134. Mark Roe, *Strong Managers, Weak Owners* (Princeton, NJ: Princeton University Press, 1994).

135. Joseph Stiglitz, *People, Power and Profits* (New York: W.W. Norton, 2019).

136. Berle and Means, *Modern Corporation and Private Property*, 312–313.

137. Ibid, 355.

138. Justin Fox, *The Myth of the Rational Market* (New York: Harper Business, 2009).

139. Kim Phillips-Fein, *Invisible Hands: A Businessmen's Crusade Against the New Deal* (New York: W.W. Norton, 2009).

140. Klaus Schwab, *Stakeholder Capitalism* (Hoboken, NJ: Wiley, 2021).

141. Tragically, the adoption of this crude measure as the panacea set the stage for a

cascading set of unintended consequences—what came to be known by economists as negative "externalities"—pollution, waste, resource exploitation, ill-health, and inequity.

142. Stoller, *Goliath*.

143. McCraw, *Creating Modern Capitalism*.

144. Gerald Davis, *The Vanishing American Corporation* (San Francisco: Berrett-Koehler, 2016).

145. Alfred Chandler, *The Visible Hand*; Berle and Means, *Modern Corporation and Private Property*.

146. Mariana Mazzucato, *The Entrepreneurial State* (New York: Hachette Book Group, 2015); Cohen and Delong, *Concrete Economics*.

147. https://www.history.com/news/gi-bill-black-wwii-veterans-benefits .

148. Roland Marchand, *Creating the Corporate Soul* (Berkeley, CA: University of California Press, 1998).

149. https://www.forbes.com/sites/gautammukunda/2020/06/05/whats-good-for-gm-is-good-for-americawhat-should-you-do-during-a-national-crisis/?sh=7fcfc45f6d3b.

150. Gerald Davis, *Managed by the Markets: How Finance Reshaped America* (Oxford, UK: Oxford University Press, 2009).

Chapter 2: The Next Capitalist Reformation

1. Kotz, *Rise and Fall of Neoliberal Capitalism*.

2. Luigi Zingales, *A Capitalism for the People* (New York: Basic Books, 2012).

3. Gary Gerstle, *The Rise and Fall of the Neoliberal Order* (New York: Oxford University Press, 2022).

4. Paulo Gerbaudo, *The Great Recoil: Politics After Populism and Pandemic* (London: Verso, 2021).

5. https://www.weforum.org/great-reset.

6. Kotz, *Rise and Fall of Neoliberal Capitalism*.

7. Jeffrey Sachs, "A Brief History of Global Capitalism," *Oxford Review of Economic Policy* 14, no. 4 (1999): 90–101.

8. McCraw, *Creating Modern Capitalism*.

9. Ibid., Chapter 5, "German Capitalism."

10. Michel Albert, *Capitalism vs. Capitalism* (New York: Four Walls Eight Windows, 1993).

11. McCraw, *Creating Modern Capitalism*, Chapter 12, "Japanese Capitalism."

12. https://fpif.org/capitalism-with-chinese-characteristics.

13. Peter Hall and David Soskice, eds., *Varieties of Capitalism: The Institutional Foundations of Comparative Advantage* (Oxford, UK: Oxford University Press, 2001).

14. Barton, Horvath, and Kipping, *Re-Imagining Capitalism*.

15. Joseph Stiglitz, *Globalization and Its Discontents* (New York: W.W. Norton, 2002).

16. Ibid.

17. Ha Joon Chang, *Bad Samaritans: The Myth of Free Trade and the Secret History of Capitalism* (New York: Bloomsbury Press, 2008).

18. Milton Friedman, "The Social Responsibility of Business Is to Increase Profits," *New York Times Magazine*, September 13, 1970.

19. Frederich Hayek, *The Road to Serfdom* (Chicago: University of Chicago Press, 1944).

20. Milton Friedman, *Capitalism and Freedom* (Chicago: University of Chicago Press, 1962); Angus Bergin, *The Great Persuasion: Reinventing Free Markets Since the Great Depression* (Cambridge, MA: Harvard University Press, 2012); Philip Mirowski and Dieter Plehwe, *The Road from Mount Pelerin: The Making of the Neoliberal Thought Collective* (Cambridge, MA: Harvard University Press, 2015); Phillips-Fein, *Invisible Hands.*

21. Phillips-Fein, *Invisible Hands.*

22. Gerstle, *Rise and Fall of the Neoliberal Order*, 2–3.

23. See William Whyte's classic *Organization Man* (New York: Doubleday Anchor, 1956).

24. Pete Seeger made this song, written by Malvina Reynolds, a hit in 1963.

25. Rachel Carson, *Silent Spring* (Greenwich, CT: Fawcett Crest, 1962).

26. For details, see https://scholarlycommons.law.wlu.edu/powellmemo/.

27. Kurt Anderson, *Evil Geniuses: The Unmaking of America* (New York: Random House, 2020), 80.

28. Davis, *Vanishing American Corporation.*

29. Rumelt, "Diversification Strategy and Profitability," *Strategic Management Journal* 3, no. 4 (1982): 359–369.

30. Jennifer Burns, *Goddess of the Market: Ayn Rand and the American Right* (New York: Oxford University Press, 2009).

31. Anderson, *Evil Geniuses.*

32. Jonathan Levy, *Ages of American Capitalism* (New York: Random House, 2021).

33. Ibid, 589.

34. Davis, *Vanishing American Corporation.*

35. David Gelles, *The Man Who Broke Capitalism* (New York: Simon & Schuster, 2022).

36. Ibid.

37. Ibid.

38. See Davis, *Managed by the Markets*; Nancy MacLean, *Democracy in Chains* (New York: Penguin Books, 2017).

39. Davis, *Vanishing American Corporation.*

40. Michael Porter, *Competitive Strategy* (New York: Free Press, 1980).

41. Davis, *Vanishing American Corporation.*

42. Levy, *Ages of American Capitalism*, 590.

43. Joseph Stiglitz, "Foreword," in Karl Polanyi, *The Great Transformation* (New York: Beacon Press, 2001).

44. Cohen and Delong, *Concrete Economics.*

45. Steven Pearlstein, *Can American Capitalism Survive?* (New York: St. Martin's Press, 2018).

46. Eugene Fama, "Efficient Capital Markets: A Review of Theory and Empirical Work," *Journal of Finance* 25 no. 2 (1970): 383–417.

47. Fox, *Myth of the Rational Market.*

48. Note that this same problem of separation of ownership from control was noted by Adam Smith when it came to the unrestrained and speculative behavior of the Trading Companies.

49. Michael Jensen and William Meckling, "Theory of the Firm: Managerial Behavior, Agency Costs and Ownership Structure," *Journal of Financial Economics* 3, no. 4 (1976): 305–360.

50. Fox, *Myth of the Rational Market*.

51. https://www.wsj.com/articles/ceo-pay-heads-for-record-as-pandemic-recedes-11649008102.

52. Ibid.

53. Gelles, *Man Who Broke Capitalism*.

54. Chambliss, *One-Legged Stool*.

55. Ibid.

56. Stoller, *Goliath*, 230.

57. Ibid.

58. Robert Bork and Ward Bowman, "The Crisis in Antitrust," *Columbia Law Review* 65, no. 3 (1965): 363–376.

59. Anderson, *Evil Geniuses*.

60. Ibid.

61. Jonathan Tepper, *The Myth of Capitalism: Monopolies and the Death of Competition* (Hoboken, NJ: John Wiley and Sons, 2019); Gretchen Morgenson, *These Are the Plunderers: How Private Equity Runs—and Wrecks—America* (New York: Simon & Schuster, 2023).

62. Klobuchar, *Antitrust*.

63. Geoffrey Parker, Marshall Van Alstyne, and Sangeet Paul Choudary, *Platform Revolution* (New York: W. W. Norton, 2016).

64. Ibid.

65. Stiglitz, *People, Power and Profits*.

66. For a full exposition of this phenomenon, see Anderson, *Evil Geniuses*.

67. Monique Leroux, "Cooperatives: Stakeholder-Oriented by Design, Long-Term Focused by Necessity," in *Re-Imagining Capitalism*, ed. Dominic Barton, Dezso Horvath, and Matthias Kipping (Oxford, UK: Oxford University Press, 2016).

68. Davis, *Vanishing American Corporation*.

69. Gelles, *Man Who Broke Capitalism*.

70. Davis, *Vanishing American Corporation*.

71. Ed Freeman, *Strategic Management: A Stakeholder Approach* (Boston: Pittman, 1983).

72. Stephan Schmidheiny, *Changing Course* (Cambridge, MA: MIT Press, 1992).

73. Paul Hawken, *The Ecology of Commerce: A Declaration of Sustainability* (New York: HarperCollins, 1993); John Elkington, *Cannibals with Forks: Triple Bottom Line for the 21st Century* (London: Wiley, 1997); Hart, "Beyond Greening," 66–76.

74. Charles Holliday, Stephan Schmidheiny, and Philip Watts, *Walking the Talk* (San Francisco: Berrett-Koehler, 2002).

75. Daniel Kahneman and Amos Tversky, "Judgment Under Uncertainty: Heuristics and Biases," *Science* 185, no. 4157 (1974): 1124–1131.

76. Robert Shiller, *Irrational Exuberance* (New York: Crown Business, 2006).

77. George Soros, *The Alchemy of Finance* (New York: Wiley, 1987).

78. Ibid, 201.

79. George Akerlof and Rachel Kranton, *Identity Economics* (Princeton, NJ: Princeton University Press, 2010).

80. Michael Jensen, "Putting Integrity into Finance Theory and Practice: A Positive Approach," 2006, http://ssrn.com/abstract=876312.

81. Fox, *Myth of the Rational Market.*

82. Stuart Hart, *Capitalism at the Crossroads*, 3rd ed. (Upper Saddle River NJ: Wharton School Publishing, 2010).

83. Marianna Mazzucato, *Mission Economy: A Moonshot Guide to Changing Capitalism* (New York: Hachette Group, 2021).

84. For example, Korten, *When Corporations Rule the World*; Michael Shuman, *Going Local* (New York: Routledge, 1998); Gar Alperovitz, *America Beyond Capitalism* (Boston: Democracy Collaborative Press, 2011).

85. Christopher Marquis, *Better Business: How the B Corp Movement Is Remaking Capitalism* (New Haven, CT: Yale University Press, 2020).

86. Kelly, *Divine Right of Capital.*

87. Davis, *Managed by the Markets.*

88. https://smartasset.com/investing/what-is-the-average-stock-holding-period.

89. John Bogle, *The Battle for the Soul of Capitalism* (New Haven, CT: Yale University Press, 2005).

90. Klobuchar, *Antitrust.*

91. Lynn Stout, *The Shareholder Value Myth* (San Francisco: Berrett-Koehler, 2012).

92. George Serafeim, *Purpose + Profit: How Business Can Lift Up the World* (New York: HarperCollins Leadership, 2022).

93. Gelles, *Man Who Broke Capitalism.*

94. Francis Fukuyama, *The End of History and the Last Man* (New York: Free Press, 1992).

95. For more on this, see Gerstle, *Rise and Fall of the Neoliberal Order.*

96. Gerbaudo, *The Great Recoil.*

97. Antonio Gramsci, *Selections from the Prison Notebooks of Antonio Gramsci* (New York: International Publishers, 1971).

98. https://www.macrotrends.net/stocks/charts/XOM/exxon/gross-profit.

99. https://www.cbsnews.com/news/retail-price-gouging-lowes-amazon-target-accountable-us/.

Chapter 3: History Rhymes

1. John Kenneth Galbraith, *American Capitalism: The Concept of Countervailing Power* (Boston: Houghton Mifflin, 1952).

2. Carlota Perez, *Technological Revolutions and Financial Capital* (Cheltenham, UK: Edward Elgar, 2002).

3. For an in-depth exploration of these alternative futures, see Gerbaudo, *The Great Recoil*; Kotz, *Rise and Fall of Neoliberal Capitalism.*

4. Roberts, *How Adam Smith Can Change Your Life.*

5. Friedman, *Religion and the Rise of Capitalism.*

6. Ibid.

7. Stewart, *Nature's God.*

8. Robert Reich, *The Common Good* (New York: Alfred Knopf, 2018).

9. The work of Epicurus had been lost to history until a single copy of his work—a Latin translation by Lucretius—was discovered in the fifteenth century.

10. It is also true, however, that the younger Founders—Hamilton and Madison in particular—concluded that "virtue" in the classical sense was insufficient when it came to governing. They observed that "factions" and "interests" would inevitably arise, requiring specific mechanisms in government to harness these differences for the public good. It is for this reason that the US Constitution explicitly includes three branches of government as "checks and balances." See Ricks, *First Principles.*

11. Stewart, *Nature's God.*

12. Ibid.

13. Harari, *Sapiens.*

14. Nace, *Gangs of America.*

15. Collier, *Future of Capitalism,* 26–27.

16. Roberts, *How Adam Smith Can Change Your Life.*

17. Beinhocker, *The Origin of Wealth: Evolution, Complexity and the Radical Remaking of Economics* (Boston: Harvard Business School Press, 2006).

18. Mariana Mazzucato, *The Value of Everything: Making and Taking in the Global Economy* (New York: Penguin, 2018).

19. Ibid.

20. Collier, *Future of Capitalism.*

21. Mark Carney, *Value(s): Building a Better World for All* (New York: PublicAffairs, 2021).

22. Friedman, *Religion and the Rise of Capitalism.*

23. Mazzucato, *The Value of Everything.*

24. Beinhocker, *Origin of Wealth.*

25. Ibid.

26. Milton Friedman, "The Methodology of Positive Economics," in *Essays in Positive Economics* (Chicago: University of Chicago Press, 1953).

27. Herbert Simon, "Problems of Methodology—Discussion," *American Economic Review* 53 (1963): 229–231.

28. Daniel Kahneman, Paul Slovic, and Amos Tversky, *Judgment Under Uncertainty: Heuristics and Biases* (Cambridge, UK: Cambridge University Press, 1982).

29. Richard Thaler, *Quasi Rational Economics* (New York: Russell Sage Foundation, 1991).

30. Kahneman, Slovic, and Tversky, *Judgment Under Uncertainty.*

31. Beinhocker, *Origin of Wealth,* 70.

32. Schumpeter, *Capitalism, Socialism and Democracy.*

33. Ibid.

34. Ramaswamy, *Woke, Inc.*

35. Freeman, Martin, and Parmar, *The Power of AND.*

36. Jay Barney and William Ouchi, *Organizational Economics* (San Francisco: Jossey-Bass, 1986).

37. Michael Jensen and William Meckling, "Theory of the Firm: Managerial Behavior,

Agency Costs and Ownership Structure," *Journal of Financial Economics* 3, no. 4 (1976): 305–360.

38. Oliver Williamson, *Markets and Hierarchies: Analysis and Antitrust Implications* (New York: Free Press, 1975).

39. Sumantra Ghoshal, "Bad Management Theories Are Destroying Good Management Practices," *Academy of Management Review* 4, no. 1 (2005): 75–91.

40. Douglas McGregor, "Theory X and Theory Y," *Organization Theory* 358, no. 1 (1960): 374.

41. Lex Donaldson, "The Ethereal Hand: Organizational Economics and Management Theory," *Academy of Management Review* 15, no. 3 (1990): 369–381.

42. Robert Quinn and Anjan Thakor, *The Economics of Higher Purpose* (Oakland, CA: Berrett-Koehler, 2019).

43. Harari, *Sapiens*.

44. Berle and Means, *Modern Corporation and Private Property*.

45. Managerial primacy can be taken to an extreme. For example, post-1990s Japan lapsed into an extended period of decline because Japanese managers, still firmly in control at most Japanese corporations, became complacent and were slow to exit underperforming businesses or explore new opportunities. This situation was aided and abetted by a compliant corporate governance structure that provided little in the way of critical oversight. For more on the downsides of managerial primacy, see Henderson, *Reimagining Capitalism*.

46. Peter Wright, Ananda Mukherji, and Mark Kroll, "A Reexamination of Agency Theory Assumptions: Extensions and Extrapolations," *Journal of Socio-Economics* 30 (2001): 413–429.

47. Charles Perrow, *Complex Organizations* (New York: Random House, 1986).

48. Stout, *Shareholder Value Myth*.

49. Carney, *Value(s)*.

50. The one exception to this rule is the so-called "exit" problem, when there is legal precedent for requiring that boards secure the highest selling price for a company when it is being sold—through either acquisition or IPO. Companies enter the "Revlon mode" when they have multiple offers, this in reference to the Delaware Supreme Court opinion in *Revlon v. MacAndrews & Forbes Holdings*, which stated that firms with multiple offers were obligated to sell to the highest bidder. The exit problem is especially significant for purpose-driven and benefit corporations that seek to sell but fear "selling out" to companies that do not share their purpose or values. For further discussion of this issue, see Marquis, *Better Business*.

51. Amartya Sen, *Development as Freedom* (New York: Anchor Books, 2000).

52. Kathleen Conner and C. K. Prahalad, "A Resource-Based Theory of the Firm: Knowledge Versus Opportunism," *Organizational Science* 7, no. 5 (1996): 477–501.

53. Marquis, *Better Business*.

54. Yasemin Saltuk Lamy, Christina Leijonhufvud, and Nick O'Donohoe, "The Next 10 Years of Impact Investment," *Stanford Social Innovation Review*, 16 (March 2021); https://thegiin.org/research/publication/impinv-market-size.

55. https://www.pionline.com/article/20170425/INTERACTIVE/170429926/80-of-equity-market-cap-held-by-institutions.

56. Bogle, *Battle for the Soul of Capitalism*.

57. https://www.theguardian.com/business/2017/feb/20/how-unilever-foiled-kraft -heinzs-115m-takeover-bid-warren-buffett.

58. This assertion is based on a conversation with Mike Lamach, CEO of Trane Technologies, and Scott Tew, Chief Sustainability Officer at Trane, where ESG and "sympathetic" long-term investors now hold a majority of the company's stock, effectively insulating it from old-school activist investors and hedge funds.

59. Steven Mufson, "ExxonMobil Rebel Shareholders Win Board Seats," *Washington Post*, May 26, 2021.

60. Joel Makower, "The Week Everything Changed," *GreenBuzz*, May 24, 2021.

61. https://www.marketwatch.com/story/esg-investing-now-accounts-for-one-third -of-total-u-s-assets-under-management-11605626611.

62. Smith, *Inquiry into the Wealth of Nations*.

63. Wu, *Curse of Bigness*.

64. Ibid.

65. John Campbell and John Hall, *What Capitalism Needs: Forgotten Lessons of Great Economists* (Cambridge, UK: Cambridge University Press, 2021).

66. Wu, *Curse of Bigness*.

67. Stoller, *Goliath*.

68. Klobuchar, *Antitrust*.

69. Wu, *Curse of Bigness*, 106.

70. As quoted in Ibid., 109.

71. Anderson, *Evil Geniuses*.

72. Thom Hartmann, *The Hidden History of Monopolies* (Oakland, CA: Berrett-Koehler, 2020).

73. Gerald Davis, *Corporate Power in the 21st Century* (Cambridge, UK: Cambridge University Press, 2022).

74. Ibid.

75. Ibid.

76. Joseph Stiglitz, *The Price of Inequality* (New York: W.W. Norton, 2013).

77. Luigi Zingales, *A Capitalism for the People* (New York: Basic Books, 2012).

78. Henderson, *Reimagining Capitalism*.

79. Harari, *Sapiens*, 311–12.

80. Mazzucato, *The Value of Everything*, 38.

81. McCraw, *Creating Modern Capitalism*, 3.

82. Robbins, *Corporation that Changed the World*.

83. Malm, *Fossil Capital*; Polanyi, *The Great Transformation*.

84. Reich, *The Common Good*.

85. Stiglitz, *People, Power and Profits*, 54.

86. Ibid, 113.

87. Tepper, *The Myth of Capitalism*.

88. Robert Reich, *Saving Capitalism: For the Many Not the Few* (New York: Vintage Books, 2015).

89. Ibid.

90. Gilbert, "Larry Fink, Tucker Carlson, David Brooks," 11.

91. Freeman, Martin, and Parmar, *The Power of AND*.

Chapter 4: The Great Race

1. Bill McKibben, *Falter: Has the Human Game Begun to Play Itself Out?* (New York: Henry Holt, 2019).

2. Polanyi, *Great Transformation*, 40.

3. Ibid.

4. Campbell and Hall, *What Capitalism Needs*.

5. Robert Neuwirth, *Shadow Cities: A Billion Squatters, a New Urban World* (New York: Routledge, 2005).

6. The World Commission on Environment and Development, *Our Common Future* (Oxford, UK: Oxford University Press, 1987).

7. William Steffens, et al., "Planetary Boundaries: Guiding Human Development on a Changing Planet," *Science*, January 15, 2015.

8. https://sdgs.un.org/goals.

9. https://clintonwhitehouse4.archives.gov/WH/New/other/sotu.html.

10. Hart, "Natural Resource-Based View of the Firm."

11. See, for example, Hart, "Beyond Greening," 66–76.

12. Prahalad and Hart, "Fortune at the Bottom of the Pyramid," 54–67.

13. Millennium Development Goals, http://www.un.org/millenniumgoals/bkgd.shtml.

14. The income definition of extreme poverty has since been revised to $1.90 per day per capita by the UN.

15. "China Lifts 740 Rural Poor Out of Poverty Since 1978," *Xinjua*, (2018), http://www.xinjuanet.com/english/2018-19/03/c_137441670.htm.

16. H. Kharas, "The Unprecedented Expansion of the Global Middle Class," *Brookings Report*, 2017.

17. $10 per day per capita was chosen as the cut-off point for middle class given the growing evidence that income above this level enables a family to endure a setback (e.g., an illness, death, or event) without returning to the ranks of extreme poverty.

18. https://www.worldbank.org/en/news/press-release/2020/10/07/covid-19-to-add-as-many-as-150-million-extreme-poor-by-2021#.

19. https://www.ndtv.com/world-news/united-nations-study-says-covid-19-could-push-over-200-million-more-people-into-extreme-poverty-by-2030-2334817.

20. It should be pointed out that extreme poverty is now and will continue to be concentrated in Africa, where additional resources to address it will continue to be needed.

21. Damien Cave, Emma Bubola, and Choo Sang-Hoo, "Long Slide Looms for World Population, with Sweeping Ramifications," *New York Times*, May 22, 2021.

22. https://www.wsj.com/articles/chinas-population-declined-in-2022-for-first-time-in-decades-11673921036.

23. Cave, Bubola, and Sang-Hoo, "Long Slide Looms"; see also Donella Meadows et al., *Limits to Growth* (New York: Universe Books, 1972).

24. Mauro F. Guillén, *2030: How Today's Biggest Trends Will Collide and Reshape the Future of Everything* (New York: St. Martin's Press, 2020).

25. Christoph Lakner and Branko Milanovic, "World Panel Income Distribution Data," 2013, 198802008, www.worldbank.org/en/research/brief/World-Panel-Income -Distribution.

26. Campbell and Hall, *What Capitalism Needs*.

27. Global Resources Outlook, 2019, http://www.resourcepanel.org/reports/global -resources-outlook.

28. "22 of World's 30 Most Polluted Cities are in India, Greenpeace Says," *The Guardian*, March 2019.

29. "Extinctions Increasing at Unprecedented Pace, UN Study Warns," *Financial Times*, May 6, 2019.

30. https://www.theenergymix.com/2022/02/15/great-climate-backslide-takes-shape -as-banks-pour-trillions-into-fossils/.

31. McKibben, *Falter*.

32. https://www.ipcc.ch/assessment-report/ar6/.

33. For a compelling discussion of this issue, see Duncan Austin, "Greenwish: The Wishful Thinking Undermining the Ambition of Sustainable Business," https:// preventablesurprises.com/wp-content/uploads/2019/07/2019-07-19-Greenwish-Essay. pdf.

34. D. Roberts, "Good Environmental Intentions Are Swamped by the Effects of Money," *Vox.com*, December 1, 2017.

35. Guillén, *2030*.

36. See http://www.footprintnetwork.org.

37. https://www.brookings.edu/research/the-climate-crisis-migration-and-refugees/.

38. Z. Qureshi, "Trends in Income Inequality: Global, Intercountry, and Within Countries," *Brookings Report*, 2017. There is, however, recent evidence that the nearly $2 trillion Covid Relief Package introduced in 2021 in the US has had a salutary impact on household incomes and wages. In addition, more and more people are quitting their low-paying jobs in the hopes of securing work that pays more in what has been termed the "Great Resignation."

39. Klaus Schwab, *The Fourth Industrial Revolution* (Geneva: World Economic Forum, 2016).

40. https://migrationdataportal.org/themes/urbanisation-et-migration.

41. Megumi Muto, "The Impacts of Mobile Phones and Personal Networks on Rural-to-Urban Migration: Evidence from Uganda," *Journal of African Economies* 21, no. 5 (2012): 787–807.

42. https://www.habitatforhumanity.org.uk/blog/2017/12/the-worlds-largest-slums -dharavi-kibera-khayelitsha-neza/.

43. Personal conversation, Simon Winter, Executive Director, Syngenta Foundation for Sustainable Agriculture, January 2022.

44. Kate Raworth, *Doughnut Economics* (White River Junction, VT: Chelsea Green Publishing, 2017).

45. https://www.nytimes.com/2020/07/14/world/americas/global-population -trends.html.

46. Abhijit Banerjee and Esther Duflo, *Poor Economics: Rethinking Poverty and the*

Ways to End it (Noida, India: Random House, 2011); Jeffrey Sachs, *Common Wealth: Economics for a Crowded Planet* (New York: Random House, 2008).

47. Leon Festinger, "A Theory of Social Comparison Processes," *Human Relations* 7, no. 2 (1954): 117–140; Richard Wilkinson and Kate Pickett, *The Spirit Level: Why Greater Equality Makes Societies Stronger* (New York: Bloomsbury Press, 2011).

48. www.fao.org/fileadmin/templates/nr/sustainability_pathways/docs/Factsheet _SMALLHOLDERS.pdf.

49. https://www.ideglobal.org/what-we-do.

50. https://www.banquapp.com.

51. http://www.ekutirsb.com/ekutir-global.html.

52. https://www.worldbenchmarkingalliance.org/food-and-agriculture-benchmark/.

53. https://www.mars.com/global/our-news/our-stories/smallholder-farms-research.

54. https://sustainablefoodlab.org/how-we-work/pre-competitive-collaborations/.

55. https://www.wbcsd.org/Programs/Food-and-Nature/Food-Land-Use/Scaling -Positive-Agriculture/Farm-of-the-Future.

56. Mujib Mashal, Emily Schmall, and Russell Goldman, "Why Are Farmers Protesting in India?," *New York Times*, January 27, 2021.

57. Rohini Kurup, "Why Are Farmers Protesting in India?," *Lawfare*, February 18, 2021.

58. Ibid.

59. See, for example, London and Hart, *Next-Generation Business Strategies*.

60. Robert Chambers, *Rural Development: Putting the Last First* (New York: Longman, 1983).

61. Parts of this section are adapted from Priya Dasgupta and Stuart L. Hart, "Creating an Innovation Ecosystem for Inclusive and Sustainable Business," in *Base of the Pyramid 3.0: Sustainable Development Through Innovation and Entrepreneurship*, ed. Fernando Casado and Stuart Hart (Sheffield, UK: Greenleaf Publishing, 2015).

62. http://www.novozymes.com/en/news/news-archive/Pages/NewFire-Africa -files-for-voluntary-liquidation.aspx.

63. https://www.kfw.de/stories/economy/companies/koko-networks/.

64. http://www.drishtee.com/.

65. Andrew Yang, *The War on Normal People* (New York: Hachette Books, 2018).

66. Ibid.

67. https://www.greenbuildermedia.com/blog/capitalism-conundrum.

68. Anderson, *Evil Geniuses*.

69. The assertion of minority rights is the central message of James Buchanan's "Public Choice Theory," which has served as the primary intellectual justification for the neoliberals' extreme agenda of tax cuts and deregulation over the past forty years. For an excellent account of this tale, see MacLean, *Democracy in Chains*.

70. For a wonderful description of how capitalists become separated and isolated from the masses to their own detriment, as if living in a "bell jar," see Hernando de Soto, *The Mystery of Capital* (New York: Basic Books, 2000).

71. Klaus Schwab, the founder of the World Economic Forum, has provided an excellent account of how shareholder primacy's focus on a single stakeholder results in poor

outcomes for society—and the business itself in the long term. See Schwab, *Stakeholder Capitalism*.

72. See my work on the Sustainable Value Framework: Stuart Hart and Mark Milstein, "Creating Sustainable Value," *Academy of Management Executive* 17, no. 2 (2003): 56–69.

73. Isabel Wilkerson, *Caste: The Origins of Our Discontents* (New York: Random House, 2020).

74. Heather McGhee, *The Sum of Us: What Racism Costs Everyone and How We Can Prosper Together* (New York: One World, 2021).

75. Schwab, *Fourth Industrial Revolution*.

76. Peter Diamondis and Steven Kotler, *Abundance: The Future Is Better Than You Think* (New York: Free Press, 2012).

77. https://www.nytimes.com/2022/01/11/technology/income-inequality-technology.html.

78. For an in-depth discussion of ITC's impact on employment, see Davis, *Corporate Power in the 21st Century*.

79. https://www.nrel.gov/docs/fy17osti/68214.pdf.

80. https://greenmountainpower.com/gmps-energy-storage-programs-deliver-3-million-in-savings/.

81. Kingsmill Bond, Amory Lovins, Oleksiy Tatarenko, Jules Kortenhorst, and Sam Butler-Sloss, "From Deep Crisis, Profound Change," Rocky Mountain Institute, 2022, https://rmi.org/insight/from-deep-crisis-profound-change/.

82. Ibid.

83. See, for example, Casado and Hart, *Green Leap to an Inclusive Economy*.

84. Guillén, *2030*, Chapter 5.

85. https://www.prnewswire.com/news-releases/the-indoor-farming-technology-market-is-projected-to-reach-usd-40-25-billion-by-2022-from-usd-25-40-billion-in-2017-at-a-cagr-of-9-65-300645387.html.

86. https://www.iconbuild.com/new-story.

87. https://naacp.org/issues/environmental-justice/.

88. https://www.brookings.edu/blog/up-front/2020/02/27/examining-the-black-white-wealth-gap/.

89. Ibram X. Kendi, *How to Be an Antiracist* (New York: Penguin Random House, 2019).

90. Laysha Ward, "What an Anti-Racist Business Strategy Looks Like," *Harvard Business Review*, November 30, 2020.

91. https://www.jpmorganchase.com/news-stories/jpMc-investment-in-detroit.

92. https://www.citigroup.com/citi/about/esg/citi-impact-fund.html.

93. https://www.goldmansachs.com/our-commitments/sustainability/one-million-black-women/index.html.

94. https://bthechange.com/meaningful-careers-for-ex-convicts-and-welfare-recipients-3007ee84209f.

95. Portions of this section describing the Ben & Jerry's initiative are excerpted from their Practicum Project description for the Sustainable Innovation Program at the University of Vermont (2020).

96. https://www.benjerry.com/about-us/media-center/reparations-statement.

97. See, especially, Erik Simanis, Stuart Hart, et al., "Strategic Initiatives at the Base of the Pyramid: A Protocol for Mutual Value Creation," Cornell University: Center for Sustainable Global Enterprise, 2005, www.bop-protocol.org; and London and Hart, *Next-Generation Business Strategies*.

98. Casado and Hart, *Green Leap to an Inclusive Economy*; Casado and Hart, *Base of the Pyramid 3.0*.

99. Layla Saad, *Me and White Supremacy: Combat Racism, Change the World, and Become a Good Ancestor* (Naperville, IL: Sourcebooks, 2020).

100. https://justforall.com/en-us/stories/mission.

101. https://www.bloomberg.com/news/articles/2021-09-20/eat-just-raises-97-million-more-to-fund-cultured-meat-production.

102. I. Dechow and R. Selove, *ByFusion Practicum Final Report* (Burlington, VT: University of Vermont, 2018).

103. Hart. "Beyond Greening."

104. Duncan Austin, "From Win-Win to Net Zero: Would the Real Sustainability Please Stand Up?" https://www.responsible-investor.com/articles/from-win-win-to-net-zero-would-the-real-sustainability-please-stand-up.

105. Polman and Winston, *Net Positive*.

106. Casado and Hart, *Base of the Pyramid 3.0*.

Chapter 5: Re-Embedding Purpose

1. Force for Good, *Capital as a Force for Good: Capitalism for a Secure and Sustainable Future*, 2021, https://www.forcegood.org/frontend/img/2021_report/pdf/final_report_2021_Capital_as_a_Force_for_Good_Report_v_F2.pdf.

2. Ronald Coase, "The Nature of the Firm," *Economica* 4 (1937): 386–405.

3. Transaction cost economics theory was extensively developed by Oliver Williamson. See Oliver Williamson, "The Economics of Organization: The Transaction Cost Approach," *American Journal of Sociology* 87, no. 3 (1981): 548–577.

4. The digital transformation of business has proven some of Coase's propositions correct: lowering transaction costs through digitization has enabled firms to outsource many key functions—manufacturing and distribution or fulfillment, for example—enabling companies to piece together business models largely online. App-based gig workers have also enabled firms to shed legions of formerly full-time employees. Nonetheless, digital transformation has still not obviated the need for a core of people to work together in devising and implementing company strategy. For more on how digitization has changed the dynamics of corporate organization and power, see Davis, *Corporate Power in the 21st Century*.

5. Andrew Campbell and Laura Nash, *A Sense of Mission* (New York: Addison-Wesley, 1992).

6. Hart, *Capitalism at the Crossroads*, 3rd ed.

7. The Sustainable Development Goals, https://sdgs.un.org/goals; The World Business Council for Sustainable Development, "The SDG compass," 2015, https://sdgcompass.org/.

8. Louise Scott and Alan McGill, *From Promise to Reality: Does Business Really Care About the SDGs?* PwC UK, 2018.

9. https://prod.ucwe.capgemini.com/wp-content/uploads/2022/11/CRI_Sustaina bility-Transformation_Infographic.pdf.

10. Becky Williams, "The Evolution of Purpose Wash and How to Avoid It," https:// www.ceotodaymagazine.com/2020/12/the-evolution-of-purpose-wash-and-how-to -avoid-it/.

11. https://www.vice.com/en/article/7kvgad/Mcdonalds-cannot-get-to-net-zero -feeding-the-world-hamburgers-experts-say.

12. James Edney, " 'Greenwashing Is Dangerous': Lessons for Purpose-Driven Brands from Innocent's Recent Lashing," https://sustainablebrands.com/read/marketing-and -comms/greenwashing-is-dangerous-lessons-for-purpose-driven-brands-from-innocent -s-recent-lashing.

13. https://www.thedrum.com/news/2019/06/19/unilever-chief-alan-jope-keith -weed-s-successor-working-with-networks-and-the-need.

14. Kenneth Pucker, "Overselling Sustainability Reporting," *Harvard Business Review*, May-June, 2021.

15. Leon Kaye, "One Year After the Business Roundtable Statement, Purpose Is Still a Work in Progress," *Triple Pundit*, September 1, 2020.

16. Anand Giridharadas, *Winners Take All: The Elite Charade of Changing the World* (New York: Alfred A. Knopf, 2018), 9.

17. Ramaswamy, *Woke, Inc.*, 6.

18. https://rmi.org/insight/from-deep-crisis-profound-change/.

19. Austin, "Greenwish."

20. https://www.triplepundit.com/story/2009/circumspect-firms-may-fall-victim -greenhush/101216.

21. Henderson, *Reimagining Capitalism*.

22. Hart, *Capitalism at the Crossroads*.

23. Ibid.

24. Pivot Goals is a project of Winston Eco-Strategies in partnership with Sustain-serv, Inc. (see www.pivotgoals.com).

25. Andrew Winston, "The Rise of Corporate Sustainability Goals: Some Hard Data," https://sustainablebrands.com/read/marketing-and-comms/the-rise-of-corporate -sustainability-goals-some-hard-data; Andrew Winston, *The Big Pivot* (Boston: Harvard Business School Press, 2014).

26. Elkington, *Green Swans*.

27. Hart, *Capitalism at the Crossroads*.

28. Neil Hawkins, former Chief Sustainability Officer at Dow, personal communica-tion.

29. Jeff Gowdy and Jessica Forrest, "Transformational Goals in Corporate Strategy: A Review of the ESG Goals of 50 Global Companies, 2020, https://sustainablebrands.com /read/new-metrics/transformational-goals-in-corporate-strategy-a-review-of-the-esg -goals-of-50-global-companies.

30. Leon Kaye, "Corporate Net-Zero Pledges Add Up to Little More Than Zero," *Triple Pundit*, 2022, https://www.triplepundit.com/story/2022/net-zero-pledges-zero/ 759111.

31. Joel Makower, "The Coming Net-Zero Backlash," *GreenBuzz*, March1, 2021.

32. Jonathan Foley, "Carbon Offsets Should Make You Nervous," 2021, https://global ecoguy.org/carbon-offsets-should-make-you-nervous-9995a00dbod6

33. Joel Makower, "The Profession of Sustainability Is Doing Just Fine," *GreenBuzz Weekly*, April 11, 2022.

34. Robert Eccles and Alison Taylor, "The Evolving Role of the Chief Sustainability Officers," *Harvard Business Review*, July-August 2023.

35. Christopher Bartlett, "Uniliver's New Global Strategy: Competing Through Sustainability," *Harvard Business School*, 2016, Case #9-916-414; David Grayson, Chris Coulter, and Mark Lee, *All In: The Future of Business Leadership* (New York: Routledge, 2018).

36. https://www.unilever.com/news/news-search/2020/the-unilever-compass-our -next-game-changer-for-business/.

37. https://www.thedrum.com/news/2019/06/19/unilever-chief-alan-jope-keith -weed-s-successor-working-with-networks-and-the-need.

38. https://www.reuters.com/business/retail-consumer/unilever-ceo-alan-jope-re tire-end-2023-2022-09-26/.

39. Amy Brown, "US Companies Are Lagging on Stakeholder Capitalism," *Triple Pundit*, August 6, 2020).

40. Marquis, *Better Business*.

41. Henderson, *Reimagining Capitalism*.

42. Porter Novelli, *Purpose Perception: An Implicit Association Study*, 2021, https:// www.porternovelli.com/findings/ .

43. Thanks to Martin Wolf, Chief Authenticity Officer at Seventh Generation, for his insights in how the company has evolved since its inception in developing its company Aspirations.

44. Personal communication with Martin Wolf, Seventh Generation, September, 2018.

45. Thanks to Erin Meezan, Interface's Chief Sustainability Officer, for her insights into how the company's mission and sustainability goals have evolved over the years.

46. Given that stock price in the age of shareholder capitalism is premised on short-term profits which are artificially enhanced by negative externalities dumped on the environment and the poor, Interface's stock price drop should not come as a great surprise. As we make the transition to a truly sustainable form of capitalism, which will sometimes mean companies taking transformational actions that are not "win-win" in the short term, perhaps public companies need to prepare themselves for such periods of financial adjustment. More about the need to redefine the meaning of value in the Denouement.

47. Benoit Leleux and Jan Van Der Kaaij, *Winning Sustainability Strategies: Finding Purpose, Driving Innovation and Executing Change* (Cham, Switzerland: Palgrave Mac-Millan, 2019).

48. Rosabeth Moss Kanter, "Taking Leadership to a New Place: Outside-the-Building Thinking to Improve the World, in: *The Business of Building a Better World*, ed. David Cooperrider and Audrey Selian (Oakland, CA: Berrett-Koehler, 2022).

49. Andrew Hoffman, "The Next Phase of Business Sustainability," *Stanford Social Innovation Review*, 16, no. 2 (2018): 34–39.

50. https://www.nbs.net/articles/how-to-handle-complexity-advice-from-john-ster man-and-jason-jay.

51. Polman and Winston, *Net Positive*.

52. Ibid.

53. Marc Benioff, *Trailblazer: The Power of Business as the Greatest Platform for Change* (New York: Currency, 2019).

54. Ben Kellard, *Leading with a Sustainable Purpose* (Cambridge, UK: University of Cambridge: Institute for Sustainability Leadership, 2020).

55. Parts of this section are excerpted from Stuart Hart, "Griffith Foods: Nourishing the World," in *Pioneering Family Firms' Sustainable Development Strategies*, ed. P. Sharma and S. Sharma (New York: Edward Elgar, 2021).

56. As an aside: Brian's son Colin, who was a student at Colorado College at the time, majoring in environmental science, aided and abetted this process of learning. "He was giving me books and articles to read," said Brian, "by authors like Bill McDonough, Paul Hawken, Michael Pollan, and Stuart Hart."

57. Dave Stangis and Katherine Valvoda Smith, *21st Century Corporate Citizenship* (Bingley, UK: Emerald, 2017).

58. Upton Sinclair and Lee Earl, *The Jungle: The Uncensored Original Edition* (Tuscon, AZ: Sharp Press, 2003).

59. Sausage production, for example, once a hit-or-miss proposition, became more dependable and efficient thanks to Griffith's liquid seasonings. Griffith's adoption of artery pumping, once an overlooked process, cured hams in as little as twelve days instead of three months, leading to a reduction in spoilage rates of pork products. Prague Powder, a mixture of sodium nitrate and sodium nitrite acquired from Europe, radically improved the curing process for meats. By writing a curing handbook and teaching customers how to properly use the powder, along with its other food science innovations, the Griffiths did nothing less than *revolutionize* the American meat industry.

60. Michael Pollan, *The Omnivore's Dilemma* (New York: Penguin Books, 2006).

61. Vaclav Smil, *Enriching the Earth: Fritz Haber, Carl Bosch, and the Transformation of World Food Production* (Cambridge, MA: MIT Press, 2001).

62. Pollan, *Omnivore's Dilemma*.

63. Smil, *Enriching the Earth*. Industrial agriculture also has a large environmental and climate footprint, accounting for about 10 percent of greenhouse gas emissions. Indeed, ammonia production alone (synthetic nitrogen fertilizer) accounts for nearly 2 percent of global carbon emissions.

64. https://www.pnas.org/content/109/31/12302.

65. There are also growing numbers of large, organic producers as well as a cottage industry of "farm to table" small producers close to wealthy urban consumers willing to pay premium prices. However, these account for a small proportion of total production. For details, see https://sustainablefoodlab.org/.

66. https://www.ers.usda.gov/amber-waves/2012/december/rising-concentration-in -agricultural-input-industries-influences-new-technologies.

67. https://www.iatp.org/sites/default/files/2020-04/03_CBD_Corporate%20Con centration_web_0.pdf.

68. Pollan, *Omnivore's Dilemma*.

69. https://www.globenewswire.com/news-release/2021/08/18/2282854/0/en/

Quick-Service-Restaurants-QSR-Market-Worth-USD-577-71-Billion-by-2028-at-3-65
-CAGR-Report-by-Market-Research-Future-MRFR.html.

70. https://www.hsph.harvard.edu/nutritionsource/processed-foods/.

71. https://ourworldindata.org/hunger-and-undernourishment.

72. https://www.worldbank.org/en/topic/water-in-agriculture#1.

73. https://www.scientificamerican.com/article/only-60-years-of-farming-left-if-soil
-degradation-continues/.

74. Jeremy Rifkin, *Beyond Beef* (New York: Dutton, 1992).

75. Griffith stock value is based upon a combination of sales and profit growth and peer group financial performance, benchmarked against the S&P 500. Thanks to Jim Thorne, Chief Strategy Officer at Griffith, for this information regarding competition.

76. I'd like to acknowledge again here the work of my ESW colleagues Priya Dasgupta and Kate Napolitan with regard to this SDG assessment at Griffith.

77. The companies studied were Unilever, Interface, Dow, DuPont, DSM, Essilor, Ingersoll Rand/Trane Technologies, Mars, Cemex, SC Johnson, Ben & Jerry's, Seventh Generation, Novozymes, and Novelis. The overall results are summarized in Stuart Hart, Kate Napolitan, and Priya Dasgupta, *Transformational Sustainability Benchmarking* (Ann Arbor, MI: Enterprise for a Sustainable World, 2018). Available upon request from the authors.

78. See www.ecovadis.com; www.cdp.net.

79. Members of the sustainability advisory council included Don Seville (Sustainable Food Lab), Matt Arnold (JPMorgan Chase), Simon Winter (Syngenta Foundation), Jane Nelson (Harvard Kennedy School), Melanne Verveer (Georgetown University), and me.

80. https://griffithfoods.b-cdn.net/wp-content/uploads/2021/09/Griffith-Foods
-2020-Sustainability-Report-September-2021.pdf.

81. See P. J. DiMaggio and W. Powell, eds., *The New Institutionalism and Organizational Analysis* (Chicago: University of Chicago Press, 1991), 1–38.

82. Benioff, *Trailblazer*, 211.

Chapter 6: Redesigning the Corporate Architecture

1. Recent research by McKinsey indicates that when a minimum of 7 percent of employees are meaningfully engaged in a transformation effort, the likelihood of success doubles. See Laura London, Stephanie Madner, and Dominic Skeritt, "How Many People Are Really Needed in a Transformation?," *McKinsey & Company Transformation*, September 23, 2021.

2. Again, the companies studied were Unilever, Interface, Dow, DuPont, DSM, Essilor, Ingersoll Rand/Trane Technologies, Mars, Cemex, SC Johnson, Ben & Jerry's, Seventh Generation, Novozymes, and Novelis. The overall results are summarized in Hart, Napolitan, and Dasgupta, *Transformational Sustainability Benchmarking*.

3. Our thanks once again to Griffith Foods for the metaphor of the "House" in describing our model of purpose-driven corporate transformation.

4. The idea of a new corporate architecture and the "House" metaphor discussed in this chapter are related to but different in scope from the idea of "architectural innovation" developed by Rebecca Henderson and presented most recently in her book *Reimag-*

ining Capitalism in a World on Fire. Architectural innovation is a form of *product* or *technological* innovation that has implications for the entire *business model* of delivery (e.g., digital versus conventional photography). The idea of the new "corporate architecture" presented here, however, is focused on the wholesale *corporate* transformation needed to deliver on a new societal purpose based upon sustainability.

5. Alfred Chandler, *Strategy and Structure* (Cambridge, MA: MIT Press, 1962).

6. Kenneth Andrews, *The Concept of Corporate Strategy* (Homewood, IL: Richard D. Irwin, 1971).

7. Jay Galbraith and Robert Kazanjian, *Strategy Implementation: Structure, Systems and Process* (St. Paul, MN: West, 1986).

8. Jay Galbraith, *Designing Dynamic Organizations* (San Francisco: Jossey-Bass, 2002).

9. Stangis and Valvoda Smith, *21st Century Corporate Citizenship.*

10. The classic works reinforcing this bias are Charles Hofer and Dan Schendel, *Strategy Formulation: Analytical Concepts* (St. Paul, MN: West, 1978); and Galbraith and Kazanjian, *Strategy Implementation.*

11. Henry Mintzberg and James Waters, "Of Strategies, Deliberate and Emergent," *Strategic Management Journal* 6, no. 3 (1985): 257–272.

12. McKinsey 7-S Framework, March 2008, https://www.Mckinsey.com/business-functions/strategy-and-corporate-finance/our-insights/enduring-ideas-the-7-s-framework#.

13. Stuart Hart, "An Integrative Framework for Strategy-Making Processes," *Academy of Management Review* 17 (1992): 327–351; Stuart Hart and Kate Banbury, "How Strategy-Making Processes Can Make a Difference," *Strategic Management Journal* 15 (1994): 235–246.

14. Hart, "An Integrative Framework.

15. Hart and Banbury, "How Strategy-Making Processes Can Make a Difference."

16. Hart, Napolitan, and Dasgupta, *Transformational Sustainability Benchmarking.*

17. Griffith Foods was also one of the sponsors of this study, along with the University of Vermont's Grossman School of Business. We thank them both for their support.

18. https://www.scjohnson.com/en/about-us/this-we-believe.

19. Chester Barnard, *The Functions of the Executive* (Cambridge, MA: Harvard University Press, 1938).

20. Philip Selznick, *Leadership in Administration* (New York: Harper and Row, 1957).

21. Trane Technologies is focused on climate control, cooling, and refrigeration, with the core brands being Trane and Thermo King. The other company created by the demerger retained the name Ingersoll Rand and is focused on the industrial market—tools, industrial pumps, and compressors—complemented by the acquisition of Gardner Denver Holdings, Inc.

22. https://www.tranetechnologies.com/en/index/sustainability/our-2030-commitments.html.

23. Our thinking on this element benefitted greatly from an article by Roger L. Martin: https://hbr.org/2010/05/the-five-questions-of-strategy.

24. Ante Glavas, "Corporate Social Responsibility and Organizational Psychology: An Integrative Review," *Frontiers in Psychology* (2016).

25. C. S. Rigby and R. Ryan, "Self-Determination Theory in Human Resource Devel-

opment: New Directions and Practical Considerations," *Advances in Developing Human Resources* 20, no. 2 (2018): 133–147.

26. Quinn and Thakor, *Economics of Higher Purpose*, 39.

27. Ibid.

28. https://www.paulpolman.com/wp-content/uploads/2023/02/Mc_Paul-Polman_Net-Positive-Employee-Barometer_Final_web.pdf.

29. Thanks to Erin Meezan, Interface's Chief Sustainability Officer, for her insights into how the company has sought to harness the hearts and minds of its employees around its new mission and goals.

30. Rigby and Ryan, "Self-Determination Theory."

31. Parts of this section are excerpted from the first case in a series written on Novelis by Stuart Hart, Priya Dasgupta, and Andrea Shpak; "Novelis Case A: Can Novelis Turn the World of Aluminum Upside Down?" Ann Arbor, MI: Enterprise for a Sustainable World, 2014.

32. A second downstream spin-off company, Constellium, was also formed a little later to avoid antitrust issues.

33. See "Novelis Case B: Creating the Global Aluminum Vacuum Cleaner."

34. See "Novelis Case C: evercan™: The Next Generation Green Beverage Can"; and "Novelis Case D: The All-Aluminum Automobile."

35. See "Novelis Case E: Building a Sustainable Organization and Culture."

36. See "Novelis Case F: The Aditya Birla Paradox."

37. Jim Collins and Jerry Porras, *Built to Last* (New York: HarperCollins, 1994).

38. The description that follows is excerpted from Peter Diamandis and Stephen Kotler, *Abundance: The Future Is Better Than You Think* (New York: Free Press, 2012).

39. Not unlike the challenge with "fixing" nitrogen discussed in the previous chapter.

40. For details on industry structure and evolution, see Carmine Nappi, *The Global Aluminum Industry: 40 Years from 1972*, 2013, www.world-aluminum.org. This section about the aluminum industry draws heavily from this source.

41. Subodh Das, "Climate Change and the Global Aluminum Industry—the Role of China," AICircle Blog, October 29, 2013, http://blog.alcircle.com/?p=415.

42. $2,000 per ton for primary aluminum verus $1,500–1,600 per ton for scrap aluminum.

43. Moving beyond the simple collection of used beverage cans meant developing a global "take-back" infrastructure from the ground up, beginning with the existing scrapers and street collectors but quickly moving beyond these immediate sources to access the entire waste stream of aluminum in cars, electronics, buildings, and perhaps even landfills. See "Novelis Case B: Creating the Global Aluminum Vacuum Cleaner."

44. See "Novelis Case D: The All-Aluminum Automobile."

45. See "Novelis Case C: evercan™: The Next Generation Green Beverage Can."

46. The council included Matt Arnold, Head of Environmental Affairs, JP Morgan Chase; Stuart Hart, SC Johnson Professor in Sustainable Global Enterprise, Cornell University; Jeffrey Keefer, Former Executive VP, DuPont; Miguel Milano, Board Member Instituto LIFE, Funcacao O Boticario de Protecao a Natureza, Brazil; and Jonathon Porritt, founder, Forum for the Future.

47. Hart, Napolitan, and Dasgupta, *Transformational Sustainability Benchmarking*.

48. Novelis Partnering with Purpose Report, 2016, https://www.novelis.com/wp-con tent/uploads/2020/04/2016-Novelis-full-report.pdf.

49. Hart, Napolitan, and Dasgupta, *Transformational Sustainability Benchmarking.*

50. It is interesting and somewhat ironic to note that the 60 percent number is where the discussion began with Phil Martens and his team in 2011.

51. Novelis Purpose Report, 2020, https://www.novelis.com/wp-content/uploads/ 2020/11/2020-Purpose-Report-ENG-Page.pdf.

52. https://www.recyclingtoday.com/article/novelis-sees-record-highs-in-financial -report/#:~:text=For%20its%20full%20fiscal%20year,with%20%2412.3%20billion%20in %202021.

53. See C. Rey and M. Bastons, "Three Dimensions of Effective Mission Implementa- tion," *Long Range Planning* 51 (2018): 580–585.

54. Quinn and Thakor, *Economics of Higher Purpose.*

55. One training program that I have been involved with that has been used effectively to build an internal coalition of change agents in companies is "Leading the Sustainabil- ity Transformation," https://www.wholeworks-lst.com/.

56. Such an approach of unleashing positive energizers is described in detail in Quinn and Thakor, *Economics of Higher Purpose.*

57. This was the approach used by Interface, described earlier in this chapter.

58. Quinn and Thakor, *Economics of Higher Purpose*, describes how this approach was effectively used at KPMG through an initiative called the "10,000 Stories Challenge."

59. G. Slemp, et al., "Leader Autonomy Support in the Workplace: A Meta-Analytic Review," *Motivation and Emotion*, 2018, https://doi.org/10.1007/s11031-018-9698-y.

60. This approach was key to the success of Seventh Generation in realizing their sus- tainability aspirations and goals.

Chapter 7: Reinventing Business Education

1. MacLean, *Democracy in Chains*, 117.

2. Ibid., 119.

3. Anderson, *Evil Geniuses.*

4. Rakesh Khurana, *From Higher Aims to Hired Hands: The Social Transformation of American Business Schools and the Unfulfilled Promise of Management as a Profession* (Princeton, NJ: Princeton University Press, 2007).

5. Professor Sydney Finkelstein at the Tuck School has recently referred to today's business schools and MBA programs as little more than elite "social clubs" for network- ing and job search. See Riley Webster, "Superstar Prof Asks: Are B-Schools a Scam?" *Poets & Quants*, February 19, 2022.

6. Donald Hambrick, "What If the Academy Actually Mattered?" *Academy of Manage- ment Review* 19, no. 1 (1994): 11–16.

7. My thanks to my colleague Chuck Schnitzlein for this astute observation.

8. As described in Webster, "Superstar Prof."

9. Caroline Flammer, "Inside the Battle for the Hearts and Minds of Tomorrow's Busi- ness Leaders," *Time Magazine*, October 21, 2021, 5.

10. Srikant Datar, David Garvin, and Patrick Cullen, *Rethinking the MBA: Business Education at the Crossroads* (Boston: Harvard Business Press, 2010).

11. https://www.quora.com/How-many-business-graduate-students-are-there-in-the-United-States-each-year.

12. Flammer, "Inside the Battle."

13. https://poetsandquants.com/2020/10/18/covid-19-puts-b-schools-mba-app-plunge-firmly-in-the-past/?pq-ab-wall=b.

14. John Byrne, "It's Official: The MBA Degree Is in Crisis," *Forbes*, 2019, https://www.forbes.com/sites/poetsandquants/2019/08/20/its-official-the-mba-degree-is-in-crisis/?sh=68e77d7952df.

15. Jasmin Godemann, Christian Herzig, Jeremy Moon, and Annie Powell, "Integrating Sustainability into Business Schools—Analysis of 100 PRME Sharing Information on Progress (SIP) Reports," Nottingham University Business School, *ICCSR Research Paper Series*, 2011, ISSN 1479–5124; Chris Laszlo, Robert Stroufe, and Sandra Waddock, "Torn Between Two Paradigms: A Struggle for the Soul of Business Schools," *AI Practitioner* 19, no. 2 (2017).

16. Some of the text in this section is abstracted from Sharma and Hart, "Beyond 'Saddle Bag' Sustainability," 10–15.

17. Sarah Murray, "Business Schools Urged to Integrate ESG Topics in Core Courses," *Financial Times*, 2021, https://www.ft.com/content/64211d86-ef52-4cf5-ba38-0fe64e18b58f.

18. This argument is made in convincing fashion in Concepción Galdón et al., "Business Schools Must Do More to Address Climate Change," *Harvard Business Review*, February 1, 2022.

19. See, for example, James Stoner, "Business School Leadership for a Sustainable, Flourishing, and Regenerated World," *Journal of Management for Global Sustainability* 7, no. 2 (2019): 1–10.

20. For an excellent exposition of this theme, see Andrew Hoffman, *Management as a Calling* (Stanford, CA: Stanford Business Books, 2021).

21. Robert Stroufe, Stuart Hart, and Hunter Lovins, "Transforming Business Education: 21st Century Sustainable MBA Programs," *Journal of Management for Global Sustainability* 9, no. 1 (2021): 15–41.

22. As of this writing, two business schools have launched new MBA programs based at least in part on our SI-MBA experience: the MBA in "Sustainable Innovation" at the University of Victoria and the "Impact" MBA at Colorado State University.

23. See Martin Parker, *Shut Down the Business School* (London: Pluto Press, 2018).

24. Steven Sass, *The Pragmatic Imagination: A History of the Wharton School, 1881–1981* (Philadelphia: University of Pennsylvania Press, 1982).

25. Alfred Chandler, *The Visible Hand: The Managerial Revolution in American Business* (Boston: Harvard Belknap, 1977).

26. Khurana, *From Higher Aims to Hired Hands*, 3.

27. Srinivasan, *Americana*; C. Wootton and C. Roszkowski, "Legal Aspects of Corporate Governance in Early American Railroads," *Business and Economic History: Journal of the Business History Conference* 28 (1999): 325–336.

28. Daniel Wren and David Van Fleet, "History in Schools of Business," *Business and Economic History Journal* 12 (1983): 29–35.

29. Erickson, *The Progress Illusion*.

30. Fredrick Taylor, *The Principles of Scientific Management* (New York: Harper & Brothers, 1919).

31. Berle and Means, *Modern Corporation and Private Property*.

32. John Byrne,. *The Whiz Kids: The Founding Fathers of American Business—and the Legacy They Left Us* (New York: Doubleday, 1993).

33. For example, James Howell, "The Ford Foundation and the Revolution in Business Education," Ford Foundation Archives, No. 006353, 1966.

34. Khurana, *From Higher Aims to Hired Hands*.

35. Robert Gordon and James Howell, *Higher Education for Business* (New York: Columbia University Press, 1959); Thomas Carroll, "A Foundation Expresses Its Interest in Higher Education for Business Management," *Academy of Management Journal* 2, no. 3 (1959): 155–166.

36. Khurana, *From Higher Aims to Hired Hands*.

37. Erickson, *The Progress Illusion*.

38. Davis, *The Vanishing American Corporation*.

39. Khurana, *From Higher Aims to Hired Hands*.

40. Hart, "Natural Resource-Based View of the Firm,"986–1014; Hart, "Beyond Greening," 66–76.

41. William Whyte, *The Organization Man* (New York: Simon & Schuster, 1956).

42. J. Doh and P. Tashman, "Half a World Away: The Integration and Assimilation of Corporate Social Responsibility, Sustainability, and Sustainable Development in Business School Curricula," *Corporate Social Responsibility and Environmental Management* (2012): D.O.I. 10.1002/csr 1315.

43. Sharma and Hart, "Beyond 'Saddle Bag' Sustainability."

44. Stephan Schmidheiny, *Changing Course* (Cambridge, MA: MIT Press, 1992).

45. Anderson, *Evil Geniuses*.

46. Selin Arac and Canan Madran, "Business School as an Initiator of the Transformation to Sustainability: A Content Analysis for Business Schools in PRME," *Social Business* 4, no. 2 (2014): 137–152.

47. Recently, the *Financial Times* and *Bloomberg Businessweek* have announced their intention to rank business schools on the basis of measures of societal impact.

48. Sanjay Sharma, "Pathways of Influence for Sustainability in Business Schools: A Dean's Eye View," *Organization and Environment* 26, no. 2 (2013): 230–236; Godemann, Herzig, Moon, and Powell, "Integrating Sustainability into Business Schools."

49. Sharma and Hart, "Beyond 'Saddle Bag' Sustainability."

50. Parts of this section have been adapted from Jon Reidel, "Going All In, *BizEd*, September-October 2015; and Alexandra Skinner, "Creating Change Makers, *CEO-mag. com*, Spring-Summer 2018. Portions were also published as part of Stroufe, Hart, and Lovins, "Transforming Business Education."

51. After I penned a blog about moving "beyond saddlebag sustainability in business education" in 2012, Sanjay Sharma and I went on to write an entire article with this title: Sharma and Hart, "Beyond 'Saddle Bag' Sustainability."

52. Datar, Garvin, and Cullen, *Rethinking the MBA*.

53. Descriptions of the dozens of practicum projects we have conducted over the past nine years can be found at https://www.uvm.edu/business/simba_practicum_projects.

54. John Della Volpe, *Fight: How Gen Z Is Channeling Their Fear and Passion to Save America* (New York: St. Martin's Press, 2021).

55. Ibid. See page 5.

56. For a thorough, historical account of the neoliberalist long game in transforming education, I highly recommend Anderson, *Evil Geniuses*.

Chapter 8: Redefining the Meaning of Value

1. Urofsky, *Louis D. Brandeis.*

2. Ibid., 39.

3. Mazzucato, *Mission Economy.*

4. Joseph Bower, Herman Leonard, and Lynn Paine, *Capitalism at Risk: How Business Can Lead* (Boston: Harvard Business Review Press, 2020), xix.

5. Ibid., vii.

6. Naomi Oreskes and Erik Conway, *The Big Myth: How Business Taught Us to Loathe the Government and Love the Free Market* (New York: Bloomsbury, 2023).

7. Acemoglu and Robinson, *Why Nations Fail.*

8. Mazzucato, *The Entrepreneurial State.*

9. Cohen and DeLong, *Concrete Economics.*

10. Ibid.

11. Reich, *Saving Capitalism*, 4.

12. Carney, *Value(s).*

13. Ibid., 82.

14. Ibid.

15. Andrew King and Kenneth Pucker, "The Dangerous Allure of Win-Win Strategies," *Stanford Social Innovation Review*, Winter 2021, 35–39; Austin, "From Win-Win to Net Zero"; Ramaswamy, *Woke, Inc.*

16. Henderson, *Reimagining Capitalism.*

17. Schwab, *Fourth Industrial Revolution.*

18. Joel Makower, "Why Lobbyists Are Winning," *GreenBuzz Weekly*, April 18, 2022.

19. Some of the earliest thinking about the need for radical government reinvention can be found in Korten, *When Corporations Rule the World*; more recently, see Volans, "Reinventing Capitalism: Vision 2050 Issue Brief," London, Volans, 2020.

20. Mazzucato, *Mission Economy*, 173.

21. For a thoughtful and thorough examination of the role of finance and financial markets in the world, see Carney, *Value(s).*

22. Michael Hirsh, "Capital Offense: How Washington's Wise Men Turned America's Future Over to Wall Street," *The New York Times*, February 8, 2010.

23. Cohen and DeLong, *Concrete Economics.*

24. Edward Chancellor, *The Price of Time: The Real Story of Interest* (New York: Atlantic Monthly Press, 2022).

25. *The Economist*, "Islamic Finance: Big Interest, No Interest," *The Economist Newspaper Limited*, September 13, 2014.

26. Niall Ferguson, *The Ascent of Money* (New York: Penguin, 2008). Queen Elizabeth finally legalized lending for interest in 1571, opening the door to the investor-driven Age of Mercantile Capitalism.

27. Ferguson, *Ascent of Money*.

28. Ibid, 342.

29. Carney, *Value(s)*.

30. Jacob Soll, *The Reckoning: Financial Accountability and the Making and Breaking of Nations* (New York: Penguin, 2014).

31. Ibid.

32. Robbins, *Corporation that Changed the World*.

33. Malm, *Fossil Capital*.

34. Cohen and DeLong, *Concrete Economics*.

35. Berle and Means, *Modern Corporation and Private Property*.

36. John Maynard Keynes, *A General Theory of Employment, Interest and Money* (London: Macmillan, 1936).

37. Cohen and Delong, *Concrete Economics*.

38. Davis, *Managed by the Markets*.

39. Henry Manne, "Mergers and the Market for Corporate Control," *Journal of Political Economy* 73 (1965): 110–120.

40. Stiglitz, *People, Power and Profits*.

41. Davis, *Managed by the Markets*.

42. Henderson, *Reimagining Capitalism*.

43. Bogle, *Battle for the Soul of Capitalism*.

44. Robin Wigglesworth, "The Power of Twelve," *Financial Times*, June 17, 2022, https://www.ft.com/content/cb818afb-4ac3-430b-8e17-2de9129f5ac7.

45. Hirsh, "Capital Offense."

46. Stiglitz, *People, Power and Profits*.

47. Ibid.

48. Stiglitz, *The Price of Inequality*.

49. Thomas Philippon and Ariell Reshef, "An International Look at the Growth of Modern Finance," *Journal of Economic Perspectives* 27, no. 2 (2013): 73–96.

50. Kelly, *Divine Right of Capital*.

51. Stiglitz, *People, Power and Profits*.

52. https://www.usatoday.com/story/money/business/2014/04/01/ozy-nifty-50-stocks/7156447/.

53. London and Hart, *Next-Generation Business Strategies*.

54. https://thegiin.org/imm/.

55. Casado and Hart, *Base of the Pyramid 3.0*.

56. https://banqu.co/.

57. Hirsh, "Capital Offense."

58. Carney, *Value(s)*, 124.

59. Anderson, *Evil Geniuses*.

60. Austin, "Greenwish."

61. Saijel Kishan and Noah Buhayar, "Al Gore's Struggles with ESG Show the Messiness of Green Investing," 2023, https://www.bloomberg.com/news/articles/2023-02-15/al-gore-esg-fund-generation-shows-messiness-of-green-investing.

62. Carney, *Value(s)*.

63. Spencer Israel, "The Number of Companies Publicly Traded in the US Is Shrink-

ing—Or Is It?" *Marketwatch.com*, October 30, 2020, https://www.marketwatch.com/story/the-number-of-companies-publicly-traded-in-the-us-is-shrinkingor-is-it-2020-10-30.

64. Knowledge at Wharton Staff, "Why SPACs Are Booming," *Knowledge at Wharton*, May 4, 2021, https://knowledge.wharton.upenn.edu/article/why-spacs-are-booming/.

65. Hannah Zhang, "BlackRock Identifies Factors Fueling the Growth in Private Equity," *Institutional Investor*, January 5, 2022, https://www.institutionalinvestor.com/article/b1w69bngfm3j8g/BlackRock-Identifies-Factors-Fueling-the-Growth-of-Private-Equity#.

66. Robert Eccles, Vinay Shandal, David Young, and Benedicte Montgomery, "Private Equity Should Take the Lead in Sustainability," *Harvard Business Review*, July-August 2022.

67. Hugh MacArthur, Rebecca Burack, Christophe De Vusser, and Kiki Yang, "The Private Equity Market in 2021: The Allure of Growth," *Bain & Company*, March 7, 2022, https://www.bain.com/insights/private-equity-market-in-2021-global-private-equity-report-2022/.

68. https://markets.businessinsider.com/news/stocks/spac-prices-deflates-10-worst-performing-ipo-mergers-blank-check-2021-8.

69. The section about WeWork is adapted from Charles Duhigg, "How Venture Capitalists Are Deforming Capitalism," *Newyorker.com*, November 23, 2020.

70. Ibid.

71. Ibid.

72. Hirsh, "Capital Offense."

73. https://fourweekmba.com/wework-scandal/.

74. Duhigg, "How Venture Capitalists Are Deforming Capitalism," 13–14.

75. https://www.nytimes.com/2022/11/13/business/ftx-effective-altruism.html.

76. https://www.nasdaq.com/articles/a-record-year-for-ipos-in-2021.

77. Fox, *Myth of the Rational Market*.

78. Laura Asiala and Neil Hawkins, "System Change Is Harder Than It Looks: Systems Shift May Be the Answer," *Cutter*, April 26, 2022, https://www.cutter.com/article/systems-change-harder-it-looks-systems-shift-may-be-answer.

79. https://www.morningstar.com/features/esg-investing-history.

80. https://www.globalreporting.org/.

81. https://www.sasb.org/.

82. Carney, *Value(s)*.

83. Corporate Eco Forum, "Who's Behind the Right's Anti-ESG Campaign?" *CEF Spotlight*, October 23, 2022.

84. Joel Makower, "The Secret Life of ESG Ratings," GreenBiz.com, May 9, 2022, https://www.greenbiz.com/article/secret-life-esg-ratings#:~:text=The%20basics,their%20various%20funds%20and%20portfolios.

85. Ronald Cohen, *Impact: Reshaping Capitalism to Drive Real Change* (New York: Random House, 2020).

86. Cam Simpson, Akshat Rathi, and Saijel Kishan, "The ESG Mirage," *Bloomberg Businessweek*, December 21, 2021.

87. Joel Makower, "Can Elon Musk Save ESG?" *GreenBuzz Weekly*, 2022, https://esginvesting.london/2022/05/23/can-elon-musk-save-esg-greenbiz-greenbiz/.

88. Andrew King and Kenneth Pucker, "ESG and Alpha: Sales or Substance," *Institutional Investor,* February 25, 2022.

89. George Serafeim, *Purpose + Profit: How Business Can Lift Up the World* (New York: HarperCollins Leadership, 2022).

90. See, for example, Cohen, *Impact.*

91. Andrew King and Kenneth Pucker, "Heroic Accounting," *Stanford Social Innovation Review,* 2021, https://ssir.org/articles/entry/heroic_accounting.

92. Carney, *Value(s),* 447.

93. Dominic Barton, "Capitalism for the Long-Term," *Harvard Business Review,* March 2011, 84–91.

94. Some share buybacks are done appropriately to reduce the dilution associated with Employee Stock Ownership Plans (ESOPs).

95. Kelly, *Divine Right of Capital.*

96. Michael Lennox and Aaron Chatterji, *Can Business Save the Earth?: Innovating our Way to Sustainability* (Stanford, CA: Stanford Business Books, 2018).

97. Marquis, *Better Business.* See also the discussion about PayPal's adoption of the metric of Net Disposable Income (NDI) in Gelles, *The Man Who Broke Capitalism.*

98. Polman and Winston, *Net Positive.*

99. Ibid.

100. Schwab, *Stakeholder Capitalism.*

101. Eric Ries, *The Lean Startup* (New York: Crown, 2011).

102. Davis, *The Vanishing American Corporation.*

103. Andrew Hoffman, *Ending the Woes of Short-Termism: The Long-Term Stock Exchange* (Ann Arbor, MI: WDI Publishing, 2017), case W05C04.

104. Ibid.

105. Ries, *Lean Startup,* 282.

106. Interview with Steve Goldstein, Chief Communications Officer, Long-Term Stock Exchange, November 10, 2021.

107. Theodore Schleifer, "America's Newest Stock Exchange Wants to Fix One of Capitalism's Fundamental Challenges," *Vox.com,* May 22, 2019.

108. Hoffman, *Ending the Woes of Short-Termism.*

109. Interview with Steven Goldstein.

110. https://ltse.com/software/knowledge-base/capitalization-table-startup/.

111. Schleifer, "America's Newest Stock Exchange."

112. Hoffman, *Ending the Woes of Short-Termism.*

113. https://ltse.com/companies.

114. Interview with Steven Goldstein.

115. Marquis, *Better Business.*

116. Schleifer, "America's Newest Stock Exchange."

117. Cameron, "Business as an Agent of World Benefit: The Role of Virtuousness," in *The Business of Building a Better World,* ed. David Cooperrider and Audrey Selian (Oakland, CA: Berrett-Koehler, 2022).

118. For an excellent discussion of this point, see Thomas Ricks, *First Principles: What America's Founders Learned from the Greeks and Romans and How That Shaped Our Country* (New York: HarperCollins, 2020).

119. Andrew Winston, Elizabeth Doty, and Thomas Lyon, "The Importance of Corporate Political Responsibility," *Sloan Management Review,* October 24, 2022, https://sloanreview.mit.edu/article/the-importance-of-corporate-political-responsibility/.

120. Anthony Downs, "Up and Down with Ecology—The Issue-Attention Cycle," *Public Interest* 28 (Summer 1972).

121. https://www.politico.com/news/2022/04/22/desantis-disney-special-status-dont-say-gay-00027302.

122. John Elkington, *Reinventing Capitalism: Vision 2050 Issue Brief* (London: Volans, 2020).

123. https://www.warren.senate.gov/imo/media/doc/Accountable%20Capitalism%20Act%20One-Pager.pdf.

124. https://donellameadows.org/archives/leverage-points-places-to-intervene-in-a-system/.

125. World Business Council for Sustainable Development, *Time to Transform: How Business Can Lead the Transformations the World Needs* (Geneva, Switzerland: WBCSD, 2021).

126. We are organizing a Sustainable Innovation Conclave to build a movement to pursue exactly these two aims. If you are interested in getting engaged, please contact me at stuart.hart@e4sw.org.

Denouement: What Does It All Mean?

1. William Steffen, Katherine Richardson, Johan Rockström, Sarah E. Cornell, Ingo Fetzer, Elena M. Bennett, and Reinette Biggs, "Planetary Boundaries: Guiding Human Development on a Changing Planet," *Science* 347, no. 6223 (2015): 1259855.

2. Anthropocene Working Group, "Working Group on the 'Anthropocene'." *Subcommission on Quaternary Stratigraphy,* 2022, http://quaternary.stratigraphy.org/working-groups/anthropocene/.

3. J. Moore, "The Capitalocene, Part 1: On the Nature and Origins of Our Ecological Crisis," *The Journal of Peasant Studies* 44, no. 3 (2017): 594–630.

4. Jed Emerson, *The Purpose of Capital* (San Francisco: Blended Value Press, 2018).

5. https://languages.oup.com/google-dictionary-en/.

6. Harari, *Sapiens.*

7. Karen Armstrong, *A Short History of Myth* (New York: Canongate, 2005), 7.

8. Ibid.

9. Emerson, *Purpose of Capital.*

10. Giles Hutchins, *The Illusion of Separation: Exploring the Cause of Our Current Crisis* (New York: Floris Books, 2014).

11. William Leiss, *The Domination of Nature* (Montreal: McGill-Queens Press, 1972).

12. As noted in Hart, "The Environmental Movement," 501–522.

13. Mircea Eliade, *The Sacred and the Profane* (New York: Houghton Mifflin, 1959).

14. Ellen Meiksins Wood, *The Origin of Capitalism* (London: Verso Books, 2017).

15. Armstrong, *Short History of Myth.*

16. Ibid.

17. To borrow (and adapt) a line from the theme song for the movie *Urban Cowboy*— "Lookin' for Love" by Johnny Lee.

18. Fox, *Myth of the Rational Market.*

19. Karen Armstrong, *Fields of Blood: Religion and the History of Violence* (New York: Anchor Books, 2014).

20. Armstrong, *Short History of Myth.*

21. This is the core of my argument in Hart, "The Environmental Movement."

22. Herman Daly, *The Steady-State Economy* (Washington, DC: Island Press, 1977).

23. Erickson, *The Progress Illusion.*

24. James Gustave Speth and J. Phillip Thompson III, "A Radical Alliance of Black and Green Could Save the World, 2016, https://www.thenation.com/article/archive/a-radical-alliance-of-black-and-green-could-save-the-world.

25. As cited in ibid, p. 5.

26. Freeman, Martin, and Parmar, *The Power of AND.*

27. Hart, "Beyond Greening," 66–77.

28. Daniel Yergin, *The Prize: The Epic Quest for Oil, Money and Power* (New York: Simon & Schuster, 2012).

29. Milton Friedman, *Capitalism and Freedom* (Chicago: University of Chicago Press, 1962).

30. Saad, *Me and White Supremacy.*

INDEX